Contemporary European Foreign Policy

edited by

Walter Carlsnaes

Helene Sjursen

and Brian White

SAGE Publishers

London • Thousand Oaks • New Delhi

Editorial Arrangement © Walter Carlsnaes, Helene Sjursen and Brian White 2004

Introduction © Walter Carlsnaes 2004
Chapter 1 © Brian White 2004
Chapter 2 © Knud Erik Jørgensen 2004
Chapter 3 © Helene Sjursen 2004
Chapter 4 © Michael Smith 2004
Chapter 5 © Brian Hocking 2004
Chapter 6 © Bengt Sundelius and Magnus Ekengren 2004

Chapter 7 © Ulrich Sedelmeier 2004
Chapter 8 © Janne Haaland Matlary 2004
Chapter 9 © Bertrand Badie 2004
Chapter 10 © Annika Hansen 2004
Chapter 11 © Ricardo Gomez and George Christou 2004
Chapter 12 © Alasdair Blair 2004
Chapter 13 © Magnus Ekengren 2004
Chapter 14 © Michelle Pace 2004
Chapter 15 © Agustín José Menéndez 2004
Chapter 16 © Frédéric Charillon 2004

First Published 2004

SAGE Publications Ltd
1 Oliver's Yard
55 City Road
London EC1Y 1SP

SAGE Publications Inc.
2455 Teller Road
Thousand Oaks, California 91320

SAGE Publications India Pvt Ltd
B-42, Panchsheel Enclave
Post Box 4109
New Delhi 100 017

British Library Cataloguing in Publication data

A catalogue record for this book is available from the British Library

ISBN 0-7619-4499-0
ISBN 0-4129-0001-8 (pbk)
MSE:14129 00018

Library of Congress Control Number available

Typeset by C&M Digitals (P) Ltd., Chennai, India
Printed in Great Britain by Athenaeum Press, Gateshead

Contemporary European Foreign Policy

Contents

List of Contributors

Bertrand Badie is Professor at the Institut d'Etudes Politiques in Paris. He is the author of several books, articles and chapters on international relations, comparative political science and on Islam, including *The Imported State: The Westernization of the Political Order* (2000); and *La Diplomatie des Droits de L'Homme* (2002).

Alasdair Blair is Jean Monnet Reader in International Relations at Coventry University. His publications include *Saving the Pound? Britain's Road to Monetary Union* (2002) and (with Anthony Forster) *The Making of Britain's European Foreign Policy* (2002). He is currently completing a book titled *The European Union since 1945*, to be published as part of the Longman Seminar Studies Series in History.

Walter Carlsnaes is Professor of Government at Uppsala University, as well as Adjunct Professor at the Norwegian Institute of International Affairs. He has published six books, including three co-edited volumes, the most recent of which is the *Handbook of International Relations* (2002). He was also the founding editor of the *European Journal of International Relations*. His research interests are in foreign policy analysis, IR theory and the philosophy of social science, EU external relations, and Swedish foreign and security policy.

Frédéric Charillon is Professor of International Relations at the Institut d'Etudes Politiques de Paris and at the University of Clermont I. He is the head of the foreign policy section of the French Political Studies Association, and currently also a researcher at CERSA (Research Centre for Administrative Science – Paris II – Assas). He has published several books and articles on foreign policy, including *Politique Etrangère: Nouveaux Regards* (2002).

George Christou is a Research Associate working on an ESRC funded project on European Regulation of Internet Commerce, co-ordinated at the Department of Information and Communications, Manchester Metropolitan University. His research interests include the European Union and conflict resolution/prevention, European Union external relations as governance, European Union regulation of e-commerce and the internet. He is currently completing a monograph on the *European Union and Enlargement: The Case of Cyprus*, to be published by Palgrave in 2004.

Magnus Ekengren is Senior Lecturer at the Swedish National Defence College and was previously with the Policy Planning Unit of the Swedish Ministry for Foreign Affairs. His main research interests are in the fields of European foreign and security policy and the Europeanisation of the nation-state. Recent publications include *The Time of European Governance* (2002).

Ricardo Gomez is a Lecturer in European Policy Studies in the School for Policy Studies at the University of Bristol. He has previously published work on EU foreign policy and is currently researching UK devolution and European Union policy making.

Annika S. Hansen is currently the acting Chief Political Adviser to the European Union Police Mission in Bosnia and Herzegovina (EUPM). She is on leave from her position as Senior Scientist at the Norwegian Defence Research Establishment (FFI), where she works on peacekeeping issues, including public security and military-police co-operation in peace operations. A former Fulbright scholar and Research Associate at the International Institute for Strategic Studies (IISS), she is the author of the Adelphi Paper *From Congo to Kosovo: Civilian Police in Peace Operations,* as well as numerous other publications.

Brian Hocking is Professor of International Relations at Coventry University. He has taught and held visiting fellowships at universities in Australia, the USA and Europe. In terms of research interests, he is particularly concerned with the interaction between domestic and international forces in the conduct of foreign and foreign economic policy and the impact of globalisation on the nature and organisation of diplomacy. Publications include: *Localizing Foreign Policy: Non-Central Governments and Multilayered Diplomacy* (1993); *Beyond Foreign Economic Policy: the United States and the Single European Market* (with M.H. Smith, 1997); *Foreign Ministries: Change and Adaptation* (contributor and editor, 1999); *Trade Politics: Domestic, International and Regional Perspectives* (co-editor, with S.M. McGuire, 1999); and *Foreign Ministries in the European Union: Integrating Diplomats* (co-editor, with D. Spence, 2002).

Knud Erik Jørgensen is Associate Professor in the Department of Political Science at the University of Aarhus. He has published widely on issues related to European foreign policy and is currently preparing a book on the topic.

Janne Haaland Matlary is Professor of International Politics at the University of Oslo. Her most recent publication is *Intervention for Human Rights* (2002), while her current research is on norms of intervention and the empirical power of norms in foreign policy. Her major research fields are EU/European foreign policy and international security policy. During 1997–2000 she was Norwegian Deputy Minister of Foreign Affairs.

Agustín José Menéndez is Ramón y Cajal Researcher at the Universidad de León (Spain) and CIDEL fellow at ARENA, University of Oslo. He has published a monograph on tax justice (*Justifying Taxes*, 2001) and co-edited two volumes on European constitutional law, together with Erik O. Eriksen and John E. Fossum (*The Chartering of Europe*, 2003 and *Developing a Constitution for Europe*, 2004).

Michelle Pace is a Research Fellow on an EU funded Fifth Framework programme project called the 'European Union and Border Conflicts: The Impact of Integration and Association' co-ordinated at the Department of Political Science and International Studies (POLSIS), University of Birmingham. She is also a Research Associate at the Europe in the World Centre, University of Liverpool, and book reviews editor for the journal *Mediterranean Politics*. Her monograph on *The Politics of Regional Identity: Meddling with the Mediterranean* will be published in 2004. Her research interests include the European Union and border conflicts, the politics of identity in the Euro-Mediterranean area, discourse analysis, European-Mediterranean relations and the Euro-Mediterranean Partnership.

Ulrich Sedelmeier is an Assistant Professor of International Relations and European Studies at the Central European University in Budapest. His work has been published in the *Journal of Common Market Studies*, *Journal of European Public Policy*, *Politique Européenne*, *West European Politics*, and in edited volumes. He is co-editor (with Frank Schimmelfennig) of a special issue of the *Journal of European Public Policy* ('European Union Enlargement: Theoretical and Comparative Approaches', Vol. 9, No. 4, August 2002).

Helene Sjursen is a Senior Researcher at ARENA at the University of Oslo. Recent publications include *The United States, Western Europe and the Policy Crisis: International Relations in the Second Cold War* (2003); 'Why Expand? The Question of Legitimacy and Justification in the EU's Enlargement Policy', in the *Journal of Common Market Studies* (3, 2002); and (co-edited with John Peterson) *A Common Foreign Policy for Europe? Competing Visions of the CFSP* (1998).

Michael Smith is Professor of European Politics and Jean Monnet Chair in the Department of Politics, International Relations and European Studies at Loughborough University. His principal areas of research are transatlantic relations, relations between the EU, the US and Japan, the making of EU external policies and the role of the EU in post-Cold War Europe, as well as more general issues of international political economy. Among his books are *The United States and the European Community in a Transformed World* (1993, with Stephen Woolcock); *Beyond Foreign Economic Policy: the United States, the Single European Market and the Changing World Economy* (1997, with Brian Hocking); *Europe's Experimental Union: Rethinking Integration* (2000, with Brigid Laffan and Rory O'Donnell); *The State of the European Union, Volume 5:*

Risks, Reforms, Resistance and Revival (2000, edited with Maria Green Cowles); and *Foreign Policy in a Transformed World* (2002, with Mark Webber).

Bengt Sundelius is Professor of Government at Uppsala University and at the Swedish National Defence College. He has been a professor of political science and Director of the International Graduate School at the University of Stockholm and Director of Security Policy Research at the Swedish National Defence Research Establishment. He has published fifteen books and numerous scholarly articles on European security and foreign policy issues. He has extensive experience in training high level public officials in decision-making under pressure and has contributed to various government commissions in the area of security and defence policy.

Brian White is Professor of International Relations at Warwick University and Staffordshire University, and also an Associate Professor at the Institut d'Etudes Politiques, Toulouse University. His publications include *British Foreign Policy: Tradition, Change and Transformation* (1988, with Steve Smith and Michael Smith); *Understanding Foreign Policy* (1989, with Michael Clarke); *Britain, Detente and East-West Relations* (1992); 'The European Challenge to Foreign Policy Analysis', *European Journal of International Relations* (Vol. 5, No. 1, 1999); *Issues in World Politics* (second edition, 2001, with Richard Little and Michael Smith); *Understanding European Foreign Policy* (2001); and 'Expliquer la Défense Européenne: un défi pour les analyses théoriques', *Revue International et Stratégique* (48, Winter, 2002).

Introduction

Walter Carlsnaes

During the past few years scholars of both International Relations (IR) and European Union (EU) studies have paid increasing attention to foreign policy developments in Europe, in particular the emergence of what is often referred to as a distinctly European foreign policy system, based not on traditional state boundaries but on a progressively robust form of transnational governance. The growth of this complex and multilayered European foreign policy system represents not only a novelty but – as a direct consequence of this – also poses a challenge to conventional foreign policy analysis. This challenge is both analytical and substantive, in so far as it questions the applicability of the traditional tools and analytical foci of Foreign Policy Analysis (FPA) to the new empirical domain of European foreign policy, claiming that this sphere is *sui generis* and hence in need of a radically new reconceptualisation of its subject-matter. More specifically, what is at issue is the question of how to penetrate analytically a European constellation of states characterised by three types of 'foreign' interactions cutting across both member state and EU boundaries (see White, 2001: 40–1).

The first of these is traditional *national* foreign policy, constituted by the separate and distinguishable foreign policy activities of the members states, which have arguably not decreased during the past decade despite a substantial increase in the scope of the other two types of relations. The second form of activity is EU foreign policy, referring to EU co-ordination of its *political* relations with the outside world, commonly referred to in terms of a commitment to establish a Common Foreign and Security Policy (CFSP) as specified in the Treaty on European Union (TEU) and figuratively expressed as Pillar II in the EU firmament. More recently the European Security and Defence Policy (ESDP) was launched to augment the CSFP, mainly in response to European powerlessness in the face of the blood-drenched dissolution of the former Yugoslavia. Finally, we also have EC foreign policy, which incorporates the more long-standing foreign *economic* policy aspects of European foreign policy.

It is in order to penetrate these complex and interrelated European developments within foreign policy broadly conceived that the chapters of this volume have been commissioned as part of an international research project that has roots in research conducted at the Norwegian Institute of International Affairs (NUPI) – which has functioned as its institutional base – and the ARENA programme at the University of Oslo.[1] The project as a whole has been financed by grants from the Norwegian Research Council. The aim has been to present a series of analyses on how the end of the Cold War and subsequent developments have changed the very nature of foreign policy in Europe, both with respect to the conduct of foreign policy by single member states as well as by the EU itself. What we have aimed for are individual contributions – standing on their own feet, but certainly not written in isolation of one another – on three dimensions of European Foreign Policy (EFP) as a new analytic focus of analysis: a first (and rather short) part on *theories and concepts* defining the general nature of this emerging field; a second examining a number of central *analytical dimensions* or *issue areas* characterising some of the most important empirical activities of European foreign policy-making; and a final section containing *empirical case studies* written in close conjunction with the respective analytical chapters in Part II. The intention has been for the analytical chapters to address their foci in general terms (incorporating both national-level and Union-level foreign policy, as well as the interaction between the two), reserving the chapters in the third part for more in depth analyses of particular empirical instances of each respective analytic dimension. Hence, although each of the chapters in this volume is self-contained and thus can be read by itself, there is an underlying logic sustaining the structure of the volume, especially in the way that the chapters in the second and third parts of the volume are interconnected in a pair-wise manner (this is also signalled in their respective chapter headings).

Some additional caveats and commentary may be in order here. The first is that the co-editors have purposely avoided constructing and imposing a general or comparative framework of analysis in this volume. This does not mean that we have not been aware of, or uninterested in, the metatheoretical, theoretical and/or conceptual aspects of foreign policy analysis, or that we have felt that such concerns are misplaced in a volume such as this or with respect to the kind of topics it addresses.[2] On the contrary: at least two of the co-editors have in the past dedicated considerable analytical energy to issues of this kind, and will undoubtedly continue to do so (see, for example, Carlsnaes, 2002; 2003, 2004; and White, 1999, 2001, 2004). However, in this particular volume we decided to leave generous space for the consideration of such questions to the two theoretically and conceptually oriented chapters in Part I, and then to allow individual or joint authors in the subsequent chapters to decide for themselves how to structure their contributions. It is in any case no easy task to apply a comparative approach to a subject-matter that not only encompasses the foreign policy activities of *individual* states, but also those of a *single* European actor constituted by the same *member* states. In other words, the very notion of multilevel governance with overlapping jurisdictions and partially pooled sovereignty complicates – perhaps even effectively undermines – the feasibility of the comparative analysis of foreign policy as conventionally conceived.

The second is that despite the obvious fact that Europe – and the world at large – has experienced extra-ordinary turbulence in the very recent past, little of this will be reflected in the pages to follow. A major reason for this is that although joint European foreign policy interaction was notoriously passive during the Cold War period – pursued mainly within the rather quiescent ambit of European Political Co-operation (EPC) for a long time – this is no longer the case, and hence it has become difficult in a project such as this to keep track of what has become a very fast-moving target. There will, therefore, be very little discussion here of such highly topical and relevant issues as European divisions regarding the war on Iraq or of the current state of European–American relations. Instead, our specific aim has been to penetrate in some depths the more enduring developments that have characterised the conduct of foreign policy in Europe during the past decade or so.

Third, there are other substantive lacunae in this volume as well, as we are the first to recognise. A major shortcoming is its very strong focus on Europe itself, to the detriment of European relations with states, international actors and developments beyond its immediate borders. Themes that spring to mind here, and which deserve extensive analysis in their own right in a context of this kind, are not only development assistance, humanitarian aid and democracy promotion in general – all strong European commitments for years – but also active peace-building and other diplomatic attempts in such disparate areas as Central America, the Middle East and the Korean Peninsula (see, for example, Bretherton and Vogler, 1999; and Smith, 1995, 2002). However, the past decade has been very much a period dominated by European issues and developments, from the collapse of the Berlin Wall to the civil and ethnic wars in the Balkans, in all of which Europe – and especially the EU – has played an important (albeit often a dismally impotent) role. This dominance of European issues and problems during this period should, of course, not make us forget that the EU in fact plays a powerful global role despite its often indecisive and ineffective stance in European affairs. However, in this volume we have consciously chosen to concentrate on the former, since it is these that over the past decade or so have brought EFP to the fore as an exceedingly intriguing area of analysis.

Finally, during the time period that this project has been underway at least two political processes – both highly relevant to the development of European foreign policy – have dominated European politics: the imminent enlargement of the EU and the constitutional reforms which will emerge in response to the recommendations of the Constitutional Convention on the Future of Europe, established at the Laeken Summit in 2001. While enlargement is discussed in some of the chapters of this volume, this does not pertain to the work of the Convention.[3] In view of this, I would like to conclude this short introduction by expanding very briefly and provisionally on the latter and on how its recommendations may potentially affect the foreign policy decision-making processes of both the EU and its member states.

Looking Towards the Future

The Convention was not simply faced with the task of coming to grips with problems of size and effective decision-making procedures within the context of enlargement, but was also given a broad mandate to show the way toward a clear and open, as well as an effective and democratically controlled Community approach.[4] In short, underlying its creation lay not only a concern with the future problem-solving effectiveness of EU institutions, even though these are clearly of an overriding nature. Of equal importance was the normative appropriateness of EU institutions and processes, especially in the light of the increased demand within Europe for a greater clarity of competencies, a greater transparency of decision processes, and a greater democratic accountability of decision-makers (Scharpf, 2002: 2).[5] The crucial question has been how the Constitutional Convention would be able to contribute to both aims without compromising either. In the past successful institutional reforms – such as those adopted in the Single European Act (SEA) or at Maastricht – were focused almost exclusively on substantive policy issues or goals on which prior agreement had been reached, whereas present concerns seem less preoccupied with questions of policy effectiveness and more with criteria pertaining to institutional appropriateness and democratic legitimacy.

Although the tension between these two aims will affect the future of the EU as a whole, particularly in view of the challenge posed by the upcoming integration of the new accession states, it also complicates the ambition of making the CFSP more effective. This increased concern with foreign policy and security issues was already evident prior to the events of 11 September 2001 (particularly in connection with the launch of the ESDP in 1998), and has become even more pronounced subsequently as the US has expanded – mainly in a unilateralist and militarist mode – its all-out campaign against international terrorism and various so-called rogue regimes. Hence, although the Convention was initially set up in response to a general unease with the functioning of the EU, it perhaps came as no surprise that it also quickly came to embrace foreign policy aspects and attempts at reforming Pillar II structures as well, even though CFSP/ESDP issues were scarcely mentioned either in the Treaty of Nice or in the Laeken Declaration (see Hill, 2002). It is in this light that we should view the proposal to create a new and single position as EU 'foreign secretary', in addition to that of a new and presumably stronger presidency of the Council to replace the rotating national presidencies. However, before focusing more specifically on these EFP aspects, let us first briefly consider more generally the institutional ramifications of the current functioning of the EU and how these relate to the overarching concerns of the Constitutional Convention.

At present, as Fritz Scharpf has argued, EU policy-making is conducted in terms of three different modes of governance differing substantially with respect to the criteria of effectiveness and legitimacy (Scharpf, 2002). The first and most fundamental is that of *intergovernmental negotiation*, based essentially on the principle of unanimity. Its polar opposite is *supranational centralisation*, requiring – as, for example, with the European Central Bank – no agreement whatsoever on the part of national governments. However, the most frequently employed mode is what Scharpf has called *joint decision-making*, in Brussels often referred to as 'the Community method'. It has a number of procedural variants (one of the tasks of the Convention has, in fact, been to simplify these), but the dominant mode is that policy proposals must originate in the Commission, and in order to become effectuated, they need to be approved by a qualified majority vote in the Council of Ministers and by an absolute majority of the members of the European Parliament (EP).

As Scharpf has also argued, all three modes differ on how they balance the dual desiderata of effectiveness and legitimacy. Based on the power (both positive and negative) of the veto, the first scores high on legitimacy but considerably less on its problem-solving effectiveness. The second, not dependent on national agreement or preferences, is potentially very effective, but achieves legitimacy only within the narrow boundaries of its specific mandate, premised on earlier joint and essentially irrevocable commitments. The third mode produces considerably better effectiveness than intergovernmentalism, and – given its beholdenness to support from both national governments and the European Parliament – has a broader foundation underwriting its legitimacy than the supranational model.

Why, given the availability of these three types of governance, and especially the advantages of the joint-decision mode, is there nevertheless a perceived need to reform the institutional framework for making EU foreign policy decisions? If these have worked in the past, why has the Convention come to feel that reform is now necessary? The answer is clearly anything but straightforward, but the following factors hint at the dilemma involved.

Given the establishment and rapid development of the ESDP as an integral part of the CFSP, including the Rapid Reaction Force (RRF), intended to consist of national armed forces ready for swift deployment to high risk conflict areas, any decisions made in its name will of necessity achieve high political salience within member states. As a result it will be well nigh impossible for their governments to be bound by *majority decisions* involving the sending of national contingents of RRF troops to combat zones. As Wolfgang Wessels has laconically noted, 'only national authorities are legitimated to send out soldiers with the risk to be killed' (Wessels, 2002: 5). At the same time it will be very difficult – for all kinds of historical, ideological and other reasons – to attain *unanimity* on European missions of this nature. Instead, any attempts to do so will undoubtedly provoke both divisive national debates and sticky negotiations on the European level, none of which is conducive to constructive diplomatic behaviour in crisis situations or, if the need arises, the kind of fleet-footed capability envisaged by the architects of RRF.

In the light of this dilemma and the need for high levels of consensus on foreign policy issues, essentially two options are available within the Community framework. The first is to downgrade the influence of member governments in favour of upgrading the role of the Commission and the European Parliament. However, as Scharpf has argued, proposals along these lines are 'based on an inadequate understanding of the normative preconditions of legitimate majority rule' (Scharpf, 2002: 11). There is in any case little reason to expect the upcoming Intergovernmental Conference (IGC) to move in this direction, and any attempts by the Convention to propel European institutions towards a more majoritarian system could very well backfire by provoking current European debate and opinion to go against such change.

The second option, advocated by Scharpf, is to accept the legitimacy of divergent national interests and preferences, and hence also the continued functionality of the current three modes of governing within the Union. The crucial issue then becomes how to cope with legitimate diversity in the pursuit of European foreign and security policy. If the Union is not to become wholly impotent in its foreign and security policy-making, this means that its members have to be willing to compromise on the requirement of uniformity.

The magic words here are 'differentiated integration', opportunities for which already exist within the framework of the Treaties. In theory this means that it would be 'possible for some governments to pool their military resources and to integrate their foreign policy even if such initiatives were not supported by all members states ... In short, differentiated integration could facilitate European solutions in policy areas where unilateral national solutions are no longer effective while uniform European solutions could not be agreed upon' (Scharpf, 2002: 14). However, this solution has one major drawback: while 'in theory' possible, this type of proposal is highly circumscribed by the Amsterdam Treaty, and policies promulgated in its name cannot challenge the existing body of European law. Also, it has never been tried.

The underlying scepticism – even hostility – towards differentiated integration emanates from a deep-rooted ideological commitment to uniform law as a precondition for full integration. Scharpf's conclusion, and one which I find persuasive, is not only that a distinction should be made in the ongoing constitutional debate in Europe between legitimate and illegitimate diversity, but also that the upcoming IGC should take upon itself the task of trying to override this negative frame of mind and, instead, base its deliberations on an acceptance of the reality of a multi-level European polity. If this task is taken seriously, we can perhaps also look forward to European foreign and security policy in due course becoming both more effective and more legitimate.

Notes

1   ARENA is an acronym for Advanced Research on the Europeanisation of the Nation-State, a research programme and centre established 10 years ago and located at the University of Oslo.

2 For a recent example of a comparative approach attempting to structure an entire edited volume on the foreign policy actions of the EU member states, see Manners and Whitman (2000). It should be added here, however, that White does argue for a comparative analytical framework for EFP in Chapter 1, based on a systems model approach used extensively in Ginsberg (2001) and White (2001).

3 On enlargement issues, see in particular the chapters by Sedelmeier, Menéndez and Charillon.

4 This final section is extensively based on Carlsnaes (2003). I would also like to add – and this is evident from the text itself – that my thinking here has been strongly influenced by a recent contribution to this topic by Fritz Scharpf (2002).

5 I would like to add here that normative considerations of this kind, including the central issue of legitimacy, constitute one of the central themes of this volume. See, e.g., the chapters by Sedelmeier, Matlary, Menéndez and Sjursen.

References

Bretherton, C., and Vogler, J. (1999) *The European Union as a Global Actor*. London: Routledge.

Carlsnaes, W. (2002) 'Foreign policy', in W. Carlsnaes, T. Risse and B. Simmons (eds), *Handbook of International Relations*. London: Sage. pp. 331–49.

Carlsnaes, W. (2003) 'An effective and legitimate CFSP: challenges faced by the constitutional convention and the next IGC', *EUSA Review*, 16 (1): 7–8.

Carlsnaes, W. (2004) 'Comparative foreign policy analysis in a historical and contemporary context', in M.G. Hermann and B. Sundelius (eds), *Comparative Foreign Policy Analysis: Theories and Methods*. Englewood Cliffs, NJ: Prentice-Hall.

Ginsberg, R.H. (2001) *The European Union in International Politics: Baptism by Fire*. Lanham: Rowman and Littlefield.

Hill, C. (2002) 'EU foreign policy since 11 September 2001: renationalising or regrouping?'. Lecture given at the University of Liverpool, 24 October 2002.

Manners, I. and Whitman, R.G. (eds) (2000) *The Foreign Policies of European Union Member States*. Manchester: Manchester University Press.

Scharpf, F. (2002) 'What a European constitution could and could not achieve'. Lecture given at the Tessin Palace, Stockholm, 3 October 2002.

Smith, H. (1995) *European Union Foreign Policy and Central America*. New York, NY: St. Martin's Press.

Smith, H. (2002) *European Union Foreign Policy: What It Is and What It Does*. London: Pluto.

Wessels, W. (2002) 'Security and defence of the European Union: the institutional evolution: trends and perspectives'. Paper given at the 6th ECSA-World Conference, Brussels, 5–6 December 2002.

White, B. (1999) 'The European challenge to foreign policy analysis', *European Journal of International Relations*, 5 (1): 37–66.

White, B. (2001) *Understanding European Foreign Policy*. Basingstoke: Palgrave.

White, B. (2004) 'The European union as a foreign policy actor', in M. Hermann and B. Sundelius (eds), *Comparative Foreign Policy Analysis: Theories and Methods*. Englewood Cliffs, NJ: Prentice-Hall.

Part I
Theories and Concepts

1 Foreign Policy Analysis and the New Europe

Brian White

As noted in a recent overview of the field, there is a 'relatively stable consensus' about the subject matter of foreign policy analysis (Carlsnaes, 2002: 335). A conventional definition of foreign policy that would be accepted by scholars working within this field refers to actions (broadly defined) taken by governments which are directed at the environment external to their state with the objective of sustaining or changing that environment in some way. This formulation captures the centrality of states and of governmental actors, the boundary-crossing deployment of policy instruments, and the purposive nature of the resulting actions. But there is no consensus, it is also noted in this overview, with respect to methods of explaining or understanding foreign policy nor on broader theoretical and metatheoretical perspectives. Indeed, much of the development of foreign policy analysis since it was first delineated as a significant field of International Relations (IR) in the 1950s has been preoccupied with theoretical issues.

There are two important challenges to the foreign policy analyst posed by an empirical domain of foreign policy associated with the 'new Europe'. First, it is bound to cause controversy to the extent that it erodes the existing consensus about subject matter. Whatever 'European foreign policy' might mean, it cannot easily be contained within a state-centric analysis with relatively clear boundaries between internal and external policy environments. The absence of consensus on the nature of this new foreign policy domain, itself contested, must also add a distinctive new dimension to existing debates about the appropriate theoretical perspective(s) from which to make sense of foreign policy. Therefore, the second challenge to foreign policy analysts posed by the notion of a European foreign policy is to conceive and apply appropriate methods of analysis to a very different subject from that dealt with by foreign policy analysts in the past. It is apparent that European foreign policy must be the 'object' as well as the 'subject' of the analysis in a qualitatively different way from national foreign policies. Can a traditionally state-centred foreign policy analysis be adapted to deal with this phenomenon? What are the implications of doing this, both for that which is being explained and also for the field itself?

The purpose of this first chapter is to provide the reader with a 'route map' that might serve as an initial guide through conceptual, analytical and empirical issues that are dealt with more fully in the chapters that follow. It begins with an initial clearing of some of the conceptual undergrowth. The central ontological question posed here is what is meant by European foreign policy. Some 'deconstruction' of this term is necessary if we are to proceed further with analysis. The next section identifies and critiques the two major theoretical approaches to analysing Europe's international role that have been developed in the existing literature. The objective here is not only to use them as a springboard to develop a theoretical context for this project but also to underline at an early stage in the book how our conceptions of European foreign policy cannot be detached from different theoretical perspectives which 'frame' our understanding of European foreign policy in various ways. This section is followed by the establishment of a 'pre-theoretical' approach derived from foreign policy analysis and constructed around the idea of European foreign policy as a system of action. The chapter concludes with a review of two recent applications of this framework (White, 2001; Ginsberg, 2001). These studies will be used to illustrate the potential of a foreign policy analysis approach to this field of study.

European Foreign Policy and the New Europe

Following the publication of a volume edited by Walter Carlsnaes and Steve Smith a decade ago (1994), the label 'European foreign policy' (EFP), or close variants such as 'Europe's foreign policy' (Hill, 1996), have appeared increasingly in book titles over the last few years (examples include Zielonka, 1998; Nuttall, 2000; Hill and Smith, 2000) without necessarily an accompanying clarification with respect to its precise meaning or the connotations associated with it. Even books that begin with more complex formulations in their titles usually resort to referring to European foreign policy in the body of the text – for example, in Manners and Whitman's rather awkwardly titled *The Foreign Policies of European Union Member States* (2000). This suggests a label that appears to serve minimally as a useful shorthand expression for something else. But is European foreign policy merely a shorthand expression for the foreign policies of European Union (EU) member states, in some collective form perhaps, or is it a synonym for EU foreign policy, since 1993 labelled the Common Foreign and Security Policy (CFSP), or possibly for the external relations of the European Community (EC)?

While further conceptual reflections on this theme are offered in the next chapter, this section offers some preliminary linguistic-conceptual analysis. What are the merits of 'European' as the qualifying adjective in this context rather than the still more popular 'European Union' or 'EU' foreign policy? One important argument is that foreign policy activity in Europe is not coterminous with the territorial and institutional boundaries of the EU. As

Christopher Hill has argued, foreign policy in Europe features what he calls a 'mixity of organisations and actors' that extend beyond the EU family of players (Hill, 1998b: 45). Even within the EU 'family', we might add, to the extent that member states continue to pursue their own foreign policies as well as contributing to the EU's Common Foreign and Security Policy the label 'EU foreign policy' is too restrictive. A broader location within 'European foreign policy' enables studies of members states' foreign policy to be undertaken without assuming or implying that national foreign policies can now be entirely subsumed within CFSP.

A second related argument is that the boundaries of the EU are scarcely fixed markers denoting a clear territorial and analytical boundary between internal and external policy environments. The almost continuous expansion of the EC/EU since the 1970s means that, at any point in time, there is a grey area in terms of relations between existing members and other European candidates for membership. This links to the idea that 'Europe' rather than the 'EU' is a more appropriate label to enable us to capture more accurately relevant developments in Europe as a whole since the end of the Cold War. Prior to the 1990s, of course, the process of integration in Europe was limited by ideological East–West divisions to western Europe. The end of the Cold War has opened up the prospect of including the states of former Eastern Europe in the process of integration. Given that that process has an external dimension (even if we have to keep updating the external boundary!), this makes the possibility of a Europe-wide foreign policy at least a theoretical possibility that should not be ruled out by unnecessarily restrictive language.

A third argument for opting for the adjective 'European' rather than 'EU' in a foreign policy context is that it facilitates a discussion of the idea of the 'new Europe' (rather than simply the 'new EU') which has been designated as the analytical focus of this book. Whether or not this idea is useful in denoting significant foreign policy-related change is a key research question to be pursued later but, clearly, it is important to offer some elucidation of the term at the outset. What is meant by the 'new Europe'? What is the relationship between the 'new Europe' and 'European foreign policy'? One important dimension of 'newness' has already been touched upon, the idea that the end of the Cold War has changed the nature of Europe as an international actor in significant ways.

Minimally, the context in which Europe operates internationally has been dramatically changed. The removal of the Soviet threat, the end of the bipolar divide, a unified Germany at the heart of Europe, the expansion of the EU to the East, a new, more problematic relationship with the US – all powerfully suggest a transformed political, economic and security context. If the external context has been transformed, the internal context has also been radically changed by progress in the process of integration producing a single European market, the establishment of the European Union, a single currency in most member states, and further expansion in membership.

This transformed, interacting external and internal context in turn has generated expectations from within and without that 'Europe', however defined, will use its enhanced capabilities to play a more influential role in international relations. These expectations focused initially on the space created by a post-Cold War world for 'civilian power' Europe to play to its strengths by deploying non-military instruments (in providing aid to Central and East European countries, for example). More recently, the debate has focused on the role that might be played by a distinctive European defence capability 'separate but not separable from' the North Atlantic Treaty Organisation (NATO). From a broader political economy perspective, Europe conceived as a regional actor fits neatly into post-Cold War analyses of regionalisation and globalisation (for a useful review of this literature, see M. Smith, 2001).

The discussion so far has focused on the merits of analysing 'European' rather than 'EU' foreign policy. But it remains the case that many analysts still prefer to stay with the latter designation. There are various reasons for this. The European Union in this context may be regarded simply as a more focused and more manageable subject for analysis than the much vaguer 'Europe'. The EU may be regarded as a more accurate focus, allowing analysts to chart the progress but also the limits of foreign policy co-operation (as opposed to other areas of 'external relations') within an EU context. The most serious objection to the term 'European foreign policy', and hence the strongest preference for a different label, however, is likely to be theoretical and/or ideological. It starts from the state-centric (realist) premise that foreign policy is, or at least should be, the preserve of states and governments. If EU member states wish to retain national foreign policies they cannot also be a party to something called European foreign policy. The latter is a contradiction in terms at best and a myth at worst. David Allen, for example, has argued that 'the determination to preserve national foreign policies is ultimately at odds with the ambition to create a European foreign policy' (Allen, 1998: 42). Quite simply, the EU is not a state – it may well never become one – and therefore it does not qualify as a foreign policy actor. Indeed, from this perspective, the very concept of 'European foreign policy' is an intrinsic part of an ideological, federalist vision of Europe.

This perspective offers a clear view about what European foreign policy is and what it is not. It also serves as a useful reminder that we are not simply dealing here with an issue that excites academic interest. We need to recognise that the notion of a *European* foreign policy is a controversial idea subject both to sharp intellectual debate and to the same passions and emotions that the whole process of European integration evokes (Hill, 1992: 109–10). Any discussion of European foreign policy, in short, is part of a wider debate about European integration and, as such, is a very live political issue. A recent spat between European Commission President Romano Prodi and British Prime Minister Tony Blair reminds us that even key European policy-makers themselves are not immune to emotional outbursts on the subject of European foreign policy. Prodi accused the Blair government of overvaluing its relationship with the US and refusing to throw its full weight behind a European foreign policy (*Economist*, 4 May 2002).

Moving on from the qualifying adjective 'European' to the *foreign policy* substance of our central concept of European foreign policy, we again need to ask what it means. Let us begin with a broad definition that provides a useful focus and also underlines the uniqueness of this actor and its associated foreign policy domain. 'EFP [European foreign policy] activity', Roy Ginsberg suggests, 'refers to the universe of concrete civilian actions, policies, positions, relations, commitments and choices of the EC (and EU) in international politics.' He goes on to note that 'EFP activities – broadly defined to include the competence or purview of the EC, the EU, CFSP, or a mixture thereof – have expanded to cover nearly all areas and issues of international politics' (Ginsberg, 2001: 3). Pausing only to observe that the sheer scope of this activity now equals or exceeds that of any single national foreign policy, including the US, it is clear that we are dealing here with a complex and unique policy domain in at least two senses: context and types of activity.

First, EFP emerges from and is contextualised by a unique experiment in political integration in Europe. The outcome of this process is an actor, the European Union, which is quite unlike any other international actor. While it may be possible to characterise the EU by reference to possible analogies, most obviously to states and/or international organisations, the EU is sufficiently distinct from both extant types of institution to be labelled a unique type of international actor or *sui generis*. Analysing any aspect of this new polity is problematic, but its external behaviour is particularly challenging to the theorist. Second, it is clear from Ginsberg's definition that EFP does not emerge from a single, authoritative source but comes in at least three forms or types of activity. These types can be characterised by different sets of actors and appear to be driven by different sorts of policy-making processes.

The first form can be identified as the foreign policy or 'external relations' of the European Community that emerged as a direct consequence of the establishment of the original European Communities in 1957. These powers established by the Treaties of Rome codify the external consequences of the Common Commercial Policy and cover principally trade, aid and development relations with third parties. Despite the continuing preference in Brussels for the label 'external relations' to maintain the fiction that these areas of activity are not 'real' foreign policy which might threaten the sovereign prerogatives of member states (see Smith, 2002), this type of policy can be regarded as constituting the foreign *economic* policy dimension of European foreign policy.

If EC foreign policy is constituted by economic issues, the more overtly *political* dimension of European foreign policy can be differentiated from it not only by issue area but also by its location in the 'pillar' structure established by the Maastricht Treaty in 1993. EC foreign policy was located in the first pillar of the European Union, where policies are made by the supranational Community method of decision-making, while the CFSP, replacing the process known as European Political Co-operation (EPC), was located in a separate second pillar to underline the intention that policy making in this area would be an intergovernmental process wholly controlled by member states. To make this distinction clear, CFSP might be labelled generically as EU foreign policy.

There is also a third type of EFP implied at least by Ginsberg's separate references to CFSP *and* activities which come under the purview of the EU – namely the foreign policies of the *member states* themselves. Though some studies of EFP implicitly or explicitly exclude national foreign policies, analysis of European foreign policy should include, in Hill's words, 'the sum of what the EU *and* its member states do in international relations' (Hill, 1998a: 18, my italics). Agency is clearly fragmented at the European level and the variety of forms of action should be reflected in analysis. What is important here from a policy analysis perspective is to understand the two-way relationship between national foreign policies and EC/EU policy. The key analytical questions here are to what extent is European foreign policy shaped by national policies and to what extent have national foreign policies themselves been transformed or 'Europeanised' by operating over many years within an EC/EU institutional context? As we shall see later, the idea of the 'Europeanisation' of member states' foreign policies is a very fertile area for investigation.

Having identified important economic, political and national dimensions of European foreign policy, it is appropriate to ask what other significant types of activity might be omitted from this typology. The most obvious omissions include activities associated with the relatively newer issue areas related to security, defence (since 1999 the European Security and Defence Policy, or ESDP), humanitarian issues pertaining both to human rights and humanitarian intervention, and important issues associated with ideology and identity. All of these issue areas are addressed in later chapters of this book to provide a comprehensive analysis of the contemporary scope and status of European foreign policy. Given both the complexity of this policy agenda as well as the uniqueness of this policy domain, however, we need to ask some general questions about how we might proceed in developing analysis. How can we explain European foreign policy? What theories or approaches to analysis might we adopt? More ambitiously, can we develop a theory of European foreign policy? These important questions are discussed in the next section.

Approaches to Analysis

There are two different approaches in the literature that dominate existing analyses of the EU's international role and which might inform our analysis of European foreign policy. In epistemological terms, one is essentially actor-based, the other more broadly structure-based.

The European Union as actor

The first, the 'EU-as-actor' approach, concentrates on the impact of Europe on world politics. Working backwards, as it were, from impact, scholars have tried to identify what sort of an 'actor' Europe is that has enabled it to be such an influential global player. Implicitly or explicitly, the working model has been the state, but increasingly scholars have moved beyond a statist model to identify a distinctive non-state but nevertheless collective entity, with the EC and latterly the EU providing the 'actor' focus of the analysis. This approach has made a major contribution to our understanding of the EU's global role in both empirical and conceptual terms.

First, it has generated a wealth of useful empirical data about the capabilities that the EU can and does deploy on a global stage (see, for example, Smith, 2002; Bretherton and Vogler, 1999; Whitman, 1998). But analysts have not simply gathered data. The evidently patchy record of the EC/EU in converting capabilities into usable power and influence – impressive in some areas of activity, much less so in others – has generated debates since the 1970s about how best to characterise this new international actor. One continuing debate has been on whether the EC/EU is best described as a 'civilian power' (Duchêne, 1972; Bull, 1983; Hill, 1990; Smith, 1998), denoting its strengths in the economic sphere and weaknesses in the military sphere; or, in less restricted terms, as a genuine 'superpower in the making' (Galtung, 1973; Buchan, 1993). The limits of that debate located within a realist framework led in the 1990s to different, less action-orientated ways of conceptualising 'actorness', with the EC/EU characterised as an international 'presence' (Allen and Smith, 1990) or as an 'international identity' (Whitman, 1998). More recently, Charlotte Bretherton and John Vogler have offered a different perspective again, seeing the various external roles of the EU as constructed from the 'interaction of external expectations and internal capability' (Bretherton and Vogler, 1999: 13). This important book can clearly be located within the 'EU-as-actor' school, but its explicit social constructivist approach enables it to make a significant connection to structuralist approaches (discussed below). Significantly, it tries to analyse the dialectical relationship between agent and structure rather than privileging either the one or the other.

Important though this body of work as a whole has been in developing our understanding of Europe's global role, as a guide to analysing European foreign policy the 'EU-as-actor' approach is limited in two particular respects. First, the focus is on outcomes rather than process. As Bretherton and Vogler admit, they are essentially concerned to assess 'the overall impact of the EC/EU' on world politics. They are much less concerned with analysing the processes through which the external policy of the EU is formulated. Indeed, they explicitly reject the relevance of a policy analysis approach to understanding EU external policy (Bretherton and Vogler, 1999: 2–3, 20). A different view is taken here and a more policy-orientated approach is offered later in this chapter. The foreign policy analyst is arguably less concerned with explaining and evaluating policy outcomes and more concerned to understand the policy process itself – how policy emerges, from whom and why (Clarke and White, 1989). To the extent that 'actorness' or 'presence' characterises the EU in world politics, the assumption here is that it is related to and emerges from other elements of a policy system in action, such as the context in which policy is made, the nature of the policy process, the issue in question and so on.

A second problem area with this approach is the persistent assumption that the EU can be appropriately analysed and evaluated as a single actor. The position taken here is that to conceive of the EU as *an* actor, *a* presence or *an* 'international identity' – in short, to adopt an approach to analysis which focuses on 'singleness' or 'unitariness' – is to misrepresent what Knud Eric Jorgensen calls the 'multiple realities' that constitute the EU and by implication European foreign policy (Jorgensen, 1997: 12). Hence the assumption here is that the EU/Europe is more appropriately analysed in foreign policy terms as a non-unitary or disaggregated entity in world politics.

Structuralist approaches

The other popular approach in the literature is very different from the first in terms of the perspective from which the EU/Europe is analysed. This approach can be located within institutionalist theory which, rather than focusing on actor-generated behaviour, attempts to provide an explanation of actor behaviour as a function of the international institutions or other structures within which actors are located. Institutionalism is a very broad school which contains some approaches that are more actor-centred (for a useful survey, see Rosamond, 2000: 113–22), but the essential focus of liberal institutionalism is on structures rather than actors, hence variants of this approach have also been referred to as 'structuralist' approaches (Hill, 1996: 6). Liberal institutionalism initially emerged in the 1970s as a reaction to the dominance of realist thinking in International Relations (IR) theory. By the 1990s, however, the sharp differences between realists and liberal institutionalists had become blurred. New versions of both theories brought them closer together (see Baldwin, 1993; Kegley, 1995). In particular, both now accept the anarchic nature of the international system and both regard states rather than other actors (highlighted in earlier institutionalist accounts) as the key actors within that system. While these theories remain divided by their concern to explain two very different international outcomes – conflict and co-operation – they are united by a common structuralist approach to explaining actor behaviour.

Though not initially developed in a European context, the relevance of institutionalist thinking to the increasingly institutionalised process of European co-operation and integration is evident. Indeed, institutionalist ideas stimulated the integration process in Europe, and the EU is an important test case of institutionalist expectations about regional and international co-operation. The foreign policy of the EU has not been a major preoccupation for institutionalists, but here too they have made a significant contribution to our understanding of Europe's global role. First, they have been fascinated by the growth of EC/EU institutions and the extent to which decision-making has become institutionalised. They have analysed the ways in which institutions like the European Commission have constructed their own agenda and developed their own capabilities. Second, institutionalists have become increasingly interested in analysing member state behaviour, identifying ways in which states have adapted their behaviour as a result of operating within an EU institutional context. They have noted that the broadening agenda of European integration has tended to strengthen institutional and weaken governmental control. Third, institutionalists have been well placed to observe that the EU is not simply an intergovernmental system of states (as realists maintain) but is characterised by a wider range of policy processes including transnational, transgovernmental and supranational processes.

As a guide to analysing European foreign policy, however, structuralist approaches of either a neorealist or neoliberal variety have their limitations, stemming largely from the level at which they analyse the behaviour of states and other actors. What might be called the 'actor problem' is the first in a set of interrelated problems. The assumption that structural imperatives determine the behaviour of the actors within the system leaves little room to explain those occasions when the state, or some other actor, does not behave in accordance with the dictates of the system. Clearly, for those occasions at least, some other more actor-centred perspective is required which investigates the particularity of the actors. An analytical focus on states themselves (or on other actors) is also required to make sense of what may be called a predisposition to defect or 'free ride'. This is a major problem for structuralists.

If structuralists are weak on agency, it follows that their conception of the foreign policy process within states and their understanding of the role of domestic factors in that process will be underdeveloped or understated at best. Certainly a focus on structural imperatives leads to a simplified view of policy processes. If the behaviour of states (or of other actors) is essentially determined by international (or other) structures, the assumed reaction of those actors will be limited to recognising what they are required to do by the system and adapting their behaviour more or less effectively. Clearly, there is a problem relating the imperatives of structuralist approaches to an understanding of European foreign policy, and there is arguably a need to complement the 'macro' approach of structuralism with some form or forms of 'micro', actor-centred analysis but one which, unlike the EU-as-actor approach, does not make inappropriate assumptions about single actorness. A key question is whether a foreign policy analysis approach can be adapted to fill this role. Before answering that question, however, it is important to discuss two other related theoretical developments that might offer an alternative way forward.

Connecting levels of analysis: 'Europeanisation'

The brief commentary above on the two dominant approaches to analysing Europe's international role suggests that they are not necessarily the best guides to developing theory in the context of European foreign policy. Some further contextualisation of them in related epistemelogical and methodological debates about levels of analysis and the agent-structure relationship reveals that these approaches offer the putative European foreign policy analyst some stark and limited choices. In term of levels of analysis, we are offered a choice between 'macro' and 'micro', system and unit. Structuralist approaches clearly privilege the former, the 'EU as actor' generally the latter with the additional limitation that the unit – the EU – is conceived in unitary terms. With reference to the relationship between agents and structures, these are also in effect polarised by our two approaches. With the noted exception of Bretherton and Vogler's work, the 'EU-as-actor' approach favours an agent-based explanation while structuralist approaches, of course, privilege a structuralist explanation. Additionally, the dominant theoretical orientation is rationalist. To use Martin Hollis and Steve Smith's now famous distinction between 'two stories' to be told, explanation from the 'outside' rather than understanding from the 'inside' is the dominant epistemological perspective here, even with respect to the 'EU-as-actor' school (Hollis and Smith, 1990).

If we reflect upon our conceptualisation of European foreign policy in the last section, the limitations of these approaches become apparent. EFP clearly operates at different levels of analysis, most obviously at both the European and state levels. We need, therefore, an analytical perspective that enables us to explore the linkages between them. Given also what Ginsberg calls the 'partially constructed' nature of agency within EFP (Ginsberg, 2001: 9) and its interaction with a constantly evolving institutional structure, it would be unwise either to separate agent and structure for explanatory purposes or to privilege a particular epistemological position with respect to them. Indeed, as we shall see, analysing EFP from an 'inside' perspective may be particularly productive. Connecting levels of analysis is explored here through the concept of Europeanisation. Connecting agents and structures is explored in the next part of this section by reviewing the potential contribution of social constructivist approaches.

Ginsberg argues that Europeanisation is an important 'partial explanation' of European foreign policy. Drawing upon the work of Michael E. Smith on *European Political Co-operation* (1996), Europeanisation is characterised as 'the process by which CFSP, and EPC before it, moved closer to EC norms, policies and habits without EPC/CFSP becoming supranationalised ... as EPC habits and procedures of political co-operation became institutionalised into a corporate body of European values and norms, they eventually caused member states to change their attitudes and preferences ... [EPC] changed the ways individual states determined and pursued their interests' (Ginsberg, 2001: 37–8). The impact of European processes on member state policy-making is clearly important and has become a growing focus of research (for example, Soetendorp and Hanf, 1998; Tonra, 2001).

But, it might be argued, Europeanisation should also mean that the European political system is the unit of analysis rather than either the European level or national systems. Thus, as Jorgensen notes (2002: 228), both levels of policy-making need to be taken into account: the flow of influence from member states to European policy-making (Hill, 1996; Manners and Whitman, 2000) as well as the impact of EC/EU processes on national systems. One interesting attempt to capture the linkages between actors and institutions operating at both levels is the concept of the 'Brusselisation' of European foreign policy-making which, it is argued, is facilitated by the 'steady enhancement of Brussels-based decision-making bodies' such as the Political Committee of the Council of Ministers (Allen, 1998: 56–8).

The concept of Europeanisation as a means of bridging levels of analysis, however, has its critics. It is said to be a vague concept applied indiscriminately to a wide range of phenomena and under-researched in terms of determining which outcomes are a function of Europeanisation. Significantly for our purposes here, it can be argued that Europeanisation is a descriptive rather than an explanatory concept. It describes a process of interaction rather than explaining how or why it occurs (Richards and Smith, 2002: 157). Certainly, the Europeanisation debate with respect to European foreign policy has tended to be located within the limited rationalist discourse noted above in terms of whether these processes of change favour states or Community institutions. Michael E. Smith, for example, having developed a theoretically challenging analysis of EPC , is content to locate EPC in a 'variable position between the ideal types of intergovernmentalism and supranationalism' (Ginsberg, 2001: 38). The next section explores the potential contribution of social constructivism to locating these important changes in a different theoretical framework.

Connecting agents and structures: social constructivism

As noted above, the concept of Europeanisation may not necessarily lead to a critique of rationalist approaches to European foreign policy, but its focus on describing processes of interaction and change has led several analysts to locate this descriptive concept within a social constructivist approach to theory. As Helene Sjursen comments, 'in order to identify a process of Europeanization the effects of ideas, values and identities that are often set aside in the rationalist analytic tradition, have to be taken into consideration' (Sjursen, 2001: 199–200). To explore this further, a brief review of the potential of constructivist theory here will identify its critique of rationalist approaches, its distinctive position in the agent-structure debate, and its 'take' on state-centred approaches to explaining European foreign policy – its critique of intergovernmentalism in particular.

Strictly speaking, constructivism is not a theory, nor is it a single approach. Indeed, it might more accurately be portrayed as a metatheoretical standpoint in political analysis as a whole (Hay, 2002). Nevertheless, two common starting points for constructivists are first, the assumption that the important structures of world politics are social rather than material, and that the behaviour of actors is not simply determined by environmental factors: through their social interaction, the actors themselves help to construct their own environment. The second premise is that social interaction is not random but is governed by rules, norms, ideas and patterns of behaviour which are agreed and practised. These 'intersubjective' practices in turn are assumed to play a major role in shaping the identities and the interests of actors. Thus, it follows that structures are neither fixed and external to state interaction, nor are the identities and interests of actors formed exogenously but rather are endogenous to and constructed by social interaction. This immediately brings constructivists into conflict with rationalist approaches, which hold that the most important structures in world politics are material and external to actor behaviour, and that the identities and interests of actors derive essentially from their material position.

It also follows from these key assumptions that constructivists take up a distinctive 'structurationist' position on the agent-structure debate (see Giddens, 1984), a position which rejects an 'either/or' approach as too simple. From this perspective, as Ben Rosamond puts it, 'neither structural determinism nor intentionalism are viable theoretical starting points. Agents are bound by structures, but they are also capable through action of altering the structural environment in which they operate, albeit in ways that may be structurally contained' (Rosamond, 2000: 172). For Bretherton and Vogler, adopting a structurationist position means that actors genuinely have agency and are conceived as 'rule makers as well as rule takers', and structures do not determine behaviour but rather provide 'action settings' or 'distinct patterns of opportunity and constraint within which agency is displayed' (Bretherton and Vogler, 1999: 28–9). Thus constructivists see structure and agency as mutually constitutive and only 'theoretically separable' (Hay, 1995: 200).

An approach that reflects upon the socially constructed nature of European foreign policy has considerable potential. Most obviously, EFP, like the EU itself, is in the process of construction and an approach that focuses specifically upon the dynamics of that process from the perspective of the actors themselves, has evident promise. Bretherton and Vogler's view of the EU as reflecting the dynamic interaction between innovative actors and changing structures can also be applied to EFP to illustrate the utility of the concept of structuration – defined by them as 'a cyclical process of social construction and reconstruction' (Bretherton and Vogler, 1999: 29; see also Carlsnaes, 1992). Work on EFP from a broadly constructivist perspective has concentrated to date on the interface between CFSP and national foreign policies (see, for example, Tonra, 2001; Larsen, 1997, 2001; Jorgensen, 1997; Glarbo, 1999), but there is no reason in principle why this approach cannot be applied to and across other forms of European foreign policy as well.

One useful and challenging set of insights has come from a constructivist analysis of ostensibly intergovernmental bargaining in CFSP. Exploring the C(ommon) in CFSP, Jorgensen has argued that intergovernmentalism may capture the formal institutional reality, but it ignores the 'written and unwritten rules and norms [that] constitute a common framework for appropriate behaviour … states might formally be in control of decision-making, but processes of socialisation and institutional dynamics are responsible for a number of significant outcomes'. Significantly, he concludes that national and European levels of formal and informal decision-making constitute a 'whole' which he calls 'European governance in the field of foreign policy' (Jorgensen, 1997: 168). In a later work with Christiansen (Christiansen and Jorgensen, 1999: 3), intergovernmentalism is also criticised as a flawed actor-centred approach which, in Rosamond's commentary, 'has the twin failing of losing sight of the structural environment in which bargains take place and aggregating and unifying actors into implausible collectivities such as the "state"' (Rosamond, 2000: 174). This underlines the importance of the dialectic between agency and structure and, reinforcing a point made earlier in the context of the 'EU-as-actor' approach, of avoiding inappropriate unitary conceptions of the actors in European foreign policy.

Beyond specific insights, potentially the most radical contribution of a constructivist approach to understanding EFP is to change the research agenda by asking different sorts of questions about foreign policy. In this sense, 'rationalism and constructivism are ontologically opposed' (Rosamond, 2000: 173). Rationalists are concerned to ask why particular decisions are made and actions taken; in short, to explain choices and behaviour. Constructivists, on the other hand, are concerned to ask 'how such decisions are possible – what are the bases (in dominant belief systems, conceptions of identity, symbols, myths and perceptions) upon which such choices are made' (Tonra, 2001: 29). It is already apparent that a constructivist approach enables us to make sense of CFSP as a collective process that goes beyond strict intergovernmental boundaries and to understand the relationship between CFSP and national foreign policies that remain salient elements of a European foreign policy.

Foreign Policy Analysis and European Foreign Policy

However, what we do not have is an agreed theory of European foreign policy that might integrate in some way the various approaches we have reviewed in the last section. But this may not necessarily be a problem. Ginsberg makes a point of eschewing any single theory of EFP for some important reasons. These include 'the complexity and multidimensionality of EFP which does not lend itself to a single theory; the moving nature and unfinished construction of the CFSP and ESDP; the still elementary level of theoretical analysis of EFP; the still limited scope of empirical research; and the remaining differences among scholars over concepts most suitable to explaining the role of the EU in world politics' (Ginsberg, 2001: 21). For many of the same reasons, it might be argued that an eclectic approach to theory-building is positively desirable. Some EFP issues might best be explained by rationalistic methods, while others might be more amenable to an interpretative approach. The important point to be derived from the last section is the need for analysts to practise theoretical reflexivity, to be theoretically aware and conscious of the assumptions that underpin different approaches

(Rosamond, 2000: 173). But in the absence of consensus, desirable or not, how do we proceed with the process of theory building and, given the analytical focus of this book, what might a foreign policy analysis (FPA) approach contribute to our understanding of European foreign policy?

The applicability of a 'transformed' FPA

Given its state-centred focus and its traditional location within a classical realist perspective, it might be thought that the contribution of FPA would be restricted to analysing the nature and substance of member state foreign policy, albeit in a distinctive EU context. Indeed, several comparative country studies have been done which have not always been constrained by a conventional realist approach (see, for example, Hill, 1983, 1996; Stavridis and Hill, 1996; Soetendorp and Hanf, 1998; Manners and Whitman, 2000). But the key question is whether FPA can be adapted to provide a framework for analysing the more complex phenomenon of European foreign policy. We have already established that EFP is constituted by a range of significant actors beyond states/governments and that a state-centred approach in the form of intergovernmentalism is problematic as a dominant explanation of the policy process. Clearly, without implying that states are not key actors in EFP, if FPA remains tied to 'state-centric realism', its value in this context is limited.

The argument here – also developed elsewhere (White, 2001: 32–6) – is that FPA is not wedded to traditional state-centric realism. Indeed, the development of FPA as a field of study since the 1950s can be characterised as a continuing adaptive response to the challenges to traditional assumptions emerging from a transforming world politics. With respect to state-centricity, there is no obvious reason why the perspective of and the analytical techniques associated with FPA cannot be transferred from the state to other international actors, or indeed to mixed actor systems. FPA happened to emerge at a time when the state was evidently the principal actor in IR, but arguably it was always the actor perspective rather than a specific actor that was important to the foreign policy analyst.

What of the associated FPA focus on governments and governmental power? Clearly, the emergence of what Stephen Krasner has called 'authority structures that are not coterminus with geographical borders' (Krasner, 1995/96: 116) has created problems for political analysis in general. One solution has been to substitute 'government' with 'governance' to facilitate the study of government-like activities. As with replacing 'state' by 'actor', it does not obviously damage the essence of an FPA approach to follow suit (see, for example, the use of the term 'governance' by Jorgensen above). Indeed, if governance is taken to 'contain' government, it can provide a framework for analysing policy-making and policy outputs that emerge from a political system such as the EU, which is constituted by interactions between traditional 'authority structures' (that is, states/governments) and newer forms of non-state authority (see Rosenau, 1992: 3–6). The focus on policy at the international level is arguably what is important to the foreign policy analyst rather than whether the actor is a conventional government or not.

Finally, there is no necessary connection between FPA and classical realism, or for that matter, between FPA and structuralist approaches based upon a rationalist epistemology. Manners and Whitman develop a useful distinction between 'traditional' FPA and a 'transformational' FPA. The latter is characterised by a focus on a wider range of policy actors than states, a grappling with a 'foreign policy' that is far more interconnected with other areas of policy-making and hence a far less distinct domain of activity, and dealing with a much broader agenda of issue areas than the traditional (military) security politics agenda. But, most importantly perhaps, analysing the 'transformed' foreign policies of EU member states, in their view, necessitates challenging the dominance of traditional approaches to FPA (Manners and Whitman, 2000: 12).

Ginsberg goes beyond national foreign policies to characterise European foreign policy as an integrated system of foreign policy-making. From this perspective, a foreign policy system approach to analysis which links variables such as actors, processes and outputs has the distinct advantage of offering 'a useful and neutral characterization of EFP'. This approach also, in his view, 'breaks free of debates about whether or not the EU can have a foreign policy and over whether or not liberalism [neofunctionalism and/or supranationalism] or realism [intergovernmentalism] is the theory of choice' (Ginsberg 2001: 32). In the absence of a consensus on theory, we might add, the attraction of a foreign policy system approach is twofold: it neither privileges a particular theoretical position, nor does it rule out alternative theoretical perspectives. In this sense, a 'transformed' FPA focused essentially upon actor-directed policy with outputs and outcomes at the international level, offers an eclectic 'pre-theoretical' approach to the European foreign policy analyst.

Applications of an FPA approach

In order to illustrate the potential of this approach, the final part of this section reviews two recent applications which take the form of policy system models (White, 2001; Ginsberg, 2001). Both studies start from the assumption that EFP can be conceived as an interacting system of action. Brian White's study has three objectives. First, it tries to understand Europe's relations with the rest of the world as illustrative of a relatively new area of foreign policy activity – European foreign policy. The second objective is to analyse whether a common European foreign policy is emerging or has emerged. The third objective is explicitly to test out in a relatively simple format the utility of an adapted FPA approach to analysing EFP. The three types of European foreign policy introduced in the first section of this chapter – Community foreign policy, Union foreign policy and national (member state) foreign policy – are developed as 'sub-systems' of a European foreign policy system that constitute and possibly dominate it.

The core chapters of this book are devoted to applying an FPA framework to these three sub-systems of EFP, identifying differences between them but, more significantly, charting over time the growing overlaps between them with a view to drawing conclusions about the current nature and status of European foreign policy as a whole. Each chapter has the same structure and the analysis is framed by the key elements of the framework. The comparative framework is constituted by the *context* within which policy is made, the *actors* involved and the *process* that characterises policy-making, the *instruments* used to achieve policy objectives, and the *outputs* that emerge from the policy process. Each chapter concludes with a detailed case study of a particular type of EFP in action (White, 2001: 23–5).

Ginsberg, on the other hand, has developed a much more complex system model (Ginsberg, 2001: 23). Inspired by Easton's classic input–output model of governmental decision-making (Easton, 1965), Ginsberg's model consists of contexts, inputs, the EFP system itself, outputs and feedback loops. The central foci of Ginsberg's study are the outcomes of the EFP process, the point at which outputs generate what he calls 'external political impact'. Where this analysis differs from earlier 'EU-as-actor' work, however, is the explicit linkage that Ginsberg makes between policy outcomes and the policy process through the feedback mechanism. As he explains, the 'book is the first of its kind to provide a comprehensive theoretical framework for the study of EFP that depicts, explains and contextualises the relationship among EFP outputs (decisions/actions that flow from the EFP decision-making system), outcomes (effects or political impact on nonmembers' interests and on issues in international politics) and new sources of (or inputs into) EFP decision-making' (Ginsberg, 2001: 274). Having established the model and the focus of the analysis, Ginsberg then develops three comparative cases studies to test empirically the external political impact of EFP: on the conflict in the former Yugoslavia; on Israel, the Palestinians and the Middle East peace process; and, finally, the impact on the US.

FPA Applications Reviewed

What do we learn about European foreign policy from these applications? The final section of this chapter discusses the contribution of this work to developing our understanding of EFP. Two sets of insights are discussed here, one pertaining to the empirical domain of EFP, the other relating to theorising about EFP. The last part of this section concludes by returning briefly to the important question posed at the beginning of this chapter: what are the implications of studying European foreign policy for foreign policy analysis itself?

The scope and impact of European foreign policy

One important result of focusing on the outputs and outcomes of the EFP system is that we are beginning to get a clear sense of both the scope and the impact of European foreign policy. Ginsberg concentrates on the Balkans, the Middle East and the US in his analysis but, as he notes, 'EFP activity also extends to Central and Eastern Europe, the former Soviet Union, Central and Latin America, the Caribbean, Africa and Asia' (Ginsberg, 2001: 278). The genuinely global scope of this activity is confirmed by the findings of a more recent empirical study by Hazel Smith that adopts an issue area approach to policy analysis (Smith, 2002).

Smith argues persuasively that the range of issues dealt with in EFP (which she continues to refer to as 'EU foreign policy') cross the now hopelessly breached divide between 'high' and 'low' politics and extend well beyond the 'classic issues of high politics and military security'. In her view, the five most important issue areas that substantiate EFP at the beginning of the 21st century are security and defence, external trade, development aid, interregional co-operation and enlargement. The scope of EFP is further underlined by her 'unpacking' of the concept of security to include issues like transnational crime, drugs, migration, and environmental protection (see also the discussion of the relationship between security and defence in White, 2001: Ch. 7). She also maintains that other key issues associated with the 'new', post-Cold War Europe – ensuring political stability and promoting economic growth – lie at the core of the current agenda (Smith, 2002: 17–18, 224).

Detailed empirical studies not only establish the scope of EFP, but also its impact. Ginsberg's study is particularly useful here because it establishes criteria for evaluating impact without making unhelpful judgements about 'success' and 'failure'. Several writers (for example, Sjursen, 2001: 190) have argued that EFP activity addresses more or less effectively the particular issues and problems of a post-Cold War world. Thus not only is EFP activity highly germane, but arguably Europe can and does play an agenda-setting role, on some issues at least (international environmental policy and human rights, for example). Clearly, the world has changed radically again in the aftermath of the horrific events of 11 September 2001, and a European approach that highlights the virtues of multilateralism, 'soft' power, peacebuilding and economic and political reconstruction looks if anything even more relevant today, especially when contrasted with the more overtly traditional approach of the US to the 'war on terrorism'. The more general point here is that the nature of foreign policy activity itself appears to be changing and there are already indications that Europe and EFP are in the vanguard of those changes.

A major problem, of course, is that recognition of the scope and impact of European foreign policy on contemporary international relations is hampered by either a poor press or, more typically perhaps, by no media attention at all. Like some policy-makers (and some theorists), the media continues to inhabit a largely state-centric, 'high politics' world where recognition of the changes indicated above scarcely penetrates. Thus, the headlines continue to feature issue areas, crises in particular, where the performance of the EFP is measured against inappropriate statist criteria. The characteristically 'civilian power' activities of EFP simply do not translate into significant actions as evaluated by the press and popular opinion. Poor marketing of its foreign policy achievements by the EU itself, Ginsberg adds, has not helped to challenge popular perceptions of the EU as an 'economic superpower' but a 'political dwarf' in world politics (Ginsberg, 2001: 276).

Theorising about European foreign policy

How do FPA applications contribute to our ability to theorise about European foreign policy? The first important point in the context of this book is that conceptually 'European foreign policy' is established as the focus of description and analysis. EFP is not simply a convenient shorthand for the collective foreign policies of member states. Nor is it simply EU or EC foreign policy. EFP provides a term that encompasses them but goes beyond a narrow focus on any one of them. Second, FPA frameworks that highlight the relationship between policy processes and policy outputs effectively highlight the evolutionary trends at work in EFP. The two frameworks we have selected here are both heuristic and productive. They are also complementary in the sense that they pick up and highlight different aspects of the actor-process-output/outcome relationship. White's focus on actors and processes enables him to track the growing interrelationships between different 'sub-systems' of activity particularly at the operational end of activities. He notes the 'ratcheting up' of co-operation and a capacity to act which is improving incrementally over time (White, 2001: 167). Ginsberg's focus on processes and outcomes shows the growing impact of EFP on non-member states and on a range of issue areas and in a number of regions.

These applications not only highlight the continuing importance of member states in EFP, but also raise major questions about whether these states act as the classic interest-maximising 'rational actors' of realist theory. Member states' foreign policy is certainly unrecognisable as traditional foreign policy. White's case study of UK foreign policy illustrates radical changes in terms of context, process and instruments, though there is an incomplete transformation in ideational terms (see White, 2001: Ch. 6). But it is important to remember that Europeanisation is not a one-way process. Ginsberg stresses the input of 'national actors rooted in domestic politics and political cultures' (Ginsberg, 2001: 277). White comments upon continuing national discourses on foreign policy as evidenced by Henrik Larsen's work (White, 2001: 175–7). The link between member states and European policy is clearly a two-way process – a 'reciprocal relationship' that needs further research (Tonra, 2001: 279).

European foreign policy and foreign policy analysis

Both our studies underline the adaptability of FPA and also the utility of this general approach in the context of EFP. But it is also apparent that studying European foreign policy poses wider theoretical challenges to the foreign policy analyst, with implications that go beyond the European focus. To return to the issue raised right at the beginning of this chapter, studying EFP does indeed challenge the *explanandum* – that which FPA seeks to explain or understand – as well as the *explanans* – the theoretical approach adopted. Four related theoretical challenges to traditional FPA can be identified here.

First, making sense of EFP offers a fundamental challenge to 'state-centric realism' as the organising focus of this field. Foreign policy analysts must be prepared to 're-tool' in order to study the international policy outputs of a wider range of actors and policy processes. Second, EFP powerfully illustrates a different actor focus for analysing policy at the international level. The assumption that this actor is unique poses particular problems for foreign policy analysts who have been traditionally wedded to a comparative cross-country methodology. The contested nature of statehood in Europe highlights the problem of making comparative generalisations about state behaviour. Nevertheless, both White and Ginsberg illustrate that different types of comparative methodology can still be important and useful. Third, the contested nature of statehood in Europe also means that foreign policy analysts can no longer avoid trying to develop an explicit theory of the state, an evident lacuna in traditional analysis (see White, 2001: 172–4). As Chris Brown has noted, there is a problem trying to understand foreign policy if we have no 'clear sense of what it is that states are motivated by, what their function is, how they work' (Brown, 1997: 69).

Finally, mirroring wider debates in IR, studies of EFP illustrate the limitations of traditional approaches and the potential of newer theoretical ones that have an applicability in FPA beyond the European case. But again it is the contested nature of statehood in Europe together with the partially formed nature of EFP that open up important questions at best underplayed by traditional analysis – about the role of ideas, identity, social beliefs, discourse and socialisation. Already the range of possible theoretical approaches of both a positivist and a post-positivist orientation is more clearly delineated. We have focused specifically in this chapter on the potential of the Europeanisation concept and constructivist approaches, but there is also interesting work emerging from more mainstream public policy perspectives that are now being applied to EFP, on transnational policy networks, multilevel governance and policy entrepreneurs (see, for example, Krahmann, 2002; Bicchi, 2002).

References

Allen, D. (1998) ' "Who speaks for Europe?": the search for an effective and coherent external policy', in J. Peterson and H. Sjursen (eds), *A Common Foreign Policy for Europe?* London: Routledge.

Allen, D. and Smith, M. (1990) 'Western Europe's presence in the contemporary international arena', *Review of International Studies*, 16 (3): 19–38.

Baldwin, D. (1993) *Neorealism and Neoliberalism: the Contemporary Debate.* New York, NY: Columbia University Press.

Bicchi, F. (2002) 'Actors and factors in European foreign policy making: insights from the Mediterranean case'. Paper presented to the International Studies Association Conference, New Orleans, March 2002.

Bretherton, C. and Vogler, J. (1999) *The European Union as a Global Actor*. London: Routledge.

Brown, C. (1997) *Understanding International Relations*. Basingstoke: Macmillan.

Buchan, D. (1993) *Europe: The Strange Superpower*. Aldershot: Dartmouth.

Bull, H. (1983) 'Civilian power Europe: a contradiction in terms?', in L. Tsoukalis (ed.), *The European Community: Past, Present, Future*. Oxford: Blackwell.

Carlsnaes, W. (1992) 'The agency-structure problem in foreign policy analysis', *International Studies Quarterly*, 36 (3): 245–70.

Carlsnaes, W. (2002) 'Foreign policy', in W. Carlsnaes, T. Risse and B.A. Simmons (eds), *Handbook of International Relations*. London: Sage.

Carlsnaes, W. and Smith, S. (eds) (1994) *European Foreign Policy*. London: Sage.

Christiansen, T. and Jorgensen, K.E. (1999) 'The Amsterdam process: a structurationist perspective on EU treaty reform', *European Integration On-Line Papers*, 3 (1), http://eiop.or.at/eiop/texts/1999-001a.htm.

Clarke, M. and White, B. (eds) (1989) *Understanding Foreign Policy: The Foreign Policy Systems Approach*. Aldershot: Elgar.

Duchêne, F. (1972) 'Europe's role in world peace', in R. Mayne (ed.), *Europe Tomorrow: Sixteen Europeans Look Ahead*. London: Fontana.

Easton, D. (1965) *A Systems Analysis of Political Life*. New York, NY: Wiley.

Economist 'The EU's Romano Prodi Annoys Britain' 4 May 2002: 42.

Galtung, J. (1973) *The European Community: A Superpower in the Making?* London: Allen and Unwin.

Giddens, A. (1984) *The Constitution of Society: Outline of the Theory of Structuration*. Basingstoke: Macmillan.

Ginsberg, R. (2001) *The European Union in World Politics*. Boulder, CO: Rowman and Littlefield.

Glarbo, K. (1999) 'Wide-awake diplomacy: reconstructing the common foreign and security policy of the European Union', in T. Christiansen, K.E. Jorgensen and A. Wiener (guest eds), 'The social construction of Europe', *European Journal of Public Policy*, 6 (4): 634–51.

Hay, C. (1995) 'Structure and agency', in D. Marsh and G. Stoker (eds), *Theory and Method in Political Science*. Basingstoke: Macmillan.

Hay, C. (2002) *Political Analysis*. Basingstoke: Palgrave.

Hill, C. (ed.) (1983) *National Foreign Policies and European Political Co-operation*. London: Allen and Unwin.

Hill, C. (1990) 'European foreign policy: power bloc, civilian model – or flop?', in R. Rummel (ed.), *The Evolution of an International Actor*. Boulder, CO: Westview.

Hill, C. (1992) 'The foreign policy of the European Community: dream or reality?', in R. Macridis (ed.), *Foreign Policy in World Politics* (8th edn). Englewood Cliffs, NJ: Prentice Hall.

Hill, C. (ed.) (1996) *The Actors in Europe's Foreign Policy*. London: Routledge.

Hill, C. (1998a) 'Closing the capability-expectations gap', in J. Peterson and H. Sjursen (eds), *A Common Foreign Policy for Europe?* London: Routledge.

Hill, C. (1998b) 'Convergence, divergence and dialectics: national foreign policies and the CFSP', in J. Zielonka (ed.), *Paradoxes of European Foreign Policy*. The Hague: Kluwer Law International.

Hill, C. and Smith, K. (eds) (2000) *European Foreign Policy: Key Documents*. London: Routledge.

Hollis, M. and Smith, S. (1990) *Explaining and Understanding International Relations*. Oxford: Clarendon.

Jorgensen, K.E. (1997) 'Poco: the diplomatic republic of Europe', in K.E. Jorgensen (ed.), *Reflective Approaches to European Governance*. Basingstoke: Macmillan.

Jorgensen, K.E. (2002) 'Making the CFSP work', in J. Peterson and M. Shackleton (eds), *The Institutions of the European Union*. Oxford: Oxford University Press.

Kegley, C. (ed.) (1995) *Controversies in International Relations Theory: Realism and the Neoliberal Challenge*. New York, NY: St Martins.

Krahmann, E. (2002) *Multilevel Networks in European Foreign Policy*. Aldershot: Ashgate.

Krasner, S. (1995/96) 'Compromising Westphalia', *International Security*, 20 (3), 115–51.

Larsen, H. (1997) *Foreign Policy Discourse Analysis: Britain, France and Europe*. London: Routledge.

Larsen, H. (2001) 'Still a national foreign policy? Danish foreign policy in an EU context', Paper presented to the British International Studies Association Conference, Edinburgh, December 2001.

Manners, I. and Whitman, R. (2000) *The Foreign Policies of the European Union Member States*. Manchester: Manchester University Press.

Nuttall, S. (2000) *European Foreign Policy*. Oxford: Oxford University Press.

Richards, D. and Smith, M.J. (2002) *Governance and Public Policy in the UK*. Oxford: Oxford University Press.

Rosamond, B. (2000) *Theories of European Integration*. London: Palgrave.

Rosenau, J.N. (1992) 'Governance, order and change in world politics', in J.N. Rosenau and E.O. Czempial (eds), *Governance Without Government: Order and Change in World Politics*. Cambridge: Cambridge University Press.

Sjursen, H. (2001) 'The common foreign and security policy', in S. Andersen and K. Eliassen (eds), *Making Policy in Europe* (2nd edn). London: Sage.

Smith H. (2002) *European Union Foreign Policy*. London: Pluto.

Smith, K. (1998) 'The instruments of European foreign policy', in J. Zielonka (ed.), *Paradoxes of European Foreign Policy*. The Hague: Kluwer Law International.

Smith, M. (2001) 'Regions and regionalism', in B. White, R. Little and M. Smith (eds), *Issues in World Politics* (2nd edn). London: Palgrave.

Smith, M.E. (1996) *The Europeanization of European Political Co-operation*. Berkely, CA: Center for German and European Studies.

Soetendorp, B. and Hanf, K. (1998) *Adapting to European Integration: Small States and the European Union*. London: Longman.

Stavridis, S. and Hill, C. (eds) (1996) *Domestic Sources of Foreign Policy: West European Reactions to the Falklands Conflict*. Oxford: Berg.

Tonra, B. (2001) *The Europeanisation of National Foreign Policy*. Aldershot: Ashgate.

White, B. (2001) *Understanding European Foreign Policy*. London: Palgrave.

Whitman, R. (1998) *From Civilian Power to Superpower?* Basingstoke: Macmillan.

Zielonka, J. (ed.) (1998) *Paradoxes of European Foreign Policy*. The Hague: Kluwer Law International.

2 European Foreign Policy: Conceptualising the Domain

Knud Erik Jørgensen[1]

The complexity of European foreign policy (EFP) continues to puzzle observers, perhaps more so than ever.[2] The simple fact that the number of European states has been growing logically implies that the number of policies and bilateral relationships has been significantly extended. The development of a European Union (EU) foreign policy only adds to this complexity, as does the increasing number and diversity of issues dealt with under the heading 'foreign policy'. The introduction of information and communication technologies has changed the temporal dimension of policy-making and public demands for transparency have increased (Coles, 2000; see also Ekengren, Ch. 13 in this volume). Given this background, any research focusing on the relationship between national and EU foreign policies constitutes a genuine analytical challenge.

The rationale of the present volume is to examine EFP change, and specifically to address the following question: how the end of the Cold War and the developments within the EU since then have changed the nature of foreign policy in Europe, both with respect to the conduct of foreign policy by individual European states and by the EU itself. In what follows, I will therefore consider conceptual implications of addressing this question, involving three key notions – 'foreign', 'policy' and 'nature'. The concept 'foreign' is key because it designates a boundary between 'inside' and 'outside', the latter considered to be the domain of 'foreign' affairs.[3] In other words, when we analyse the 'foreign' policies of European states, we are also analysing the identity of the political (imagined) communities and the boundaries between them. Or, rather, following Anthony P. Cohen, we focus on the meanings people give to it, and thus on 'the symbolic aspect of community boundary. In so far as we aspire to understand the importance of the community in people's experience, it is the most crucial' (1998: 11–12; see also Anderson, 1983). The notion 'policy' is no less a key concept, because what is mutually acknowledged as policy can vary considerably. While many politicians, diplomats and observers often have no problem with assigning

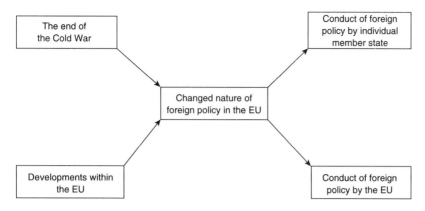

Figure 2.1 *Device for approaching, mapping and conceptualising European foreign policy*

key features of policy to the foreign policies of EU member states, they often demonstrate considerable reluctance to do so when it comes to EU foreign policy-making. This reluctance has not necessarily much to do with the nature of the policy in question. Finally, 'nature' is a key notion because it suggests much more than mere adjustments arising from the trivial fact that foreign affairs vary from time to time. Instead, it signifies change of the 'soul' of policy. Furthermore, the question involves two independent variables ('the end of the Cold War' and 'developments within the EU'), and one dependent variable (the conduct of foreign policy by individual states and by the EU, respectively). Figure 2.1 shows how the parts of the project are connected.

Keeping the overall aim of the volume in mind, the purpose of this chapter is to discuss how a conceptual 'raster' can be created, capable of examining the bold claim about a presumed change in the nature of foreign policy in Europe. Figure 2.2 (p. 34) summarises aspects that will be examined here, showing three different relationships and two different dimensions of output in the form of 'foreign policy'. The Figure also points to two distinct features. First, it puts aspects of EFP into perspective, that is, connecting these aspects to one another, indicating that to exclude some will result in pre-determined and biased analysis. In my view, operating with three levels and two dimensions of output strikes an appropriate balance between being parsimonious and being too inclusive, aiming at realism in the sense that this term is understood in literature or art.

In the first section of this chapter, I *approach* the general theme by presenting four axioms concerning: (i) the EU's foreign policy; (ii) our task; (iii) the importance of the topic; and (iv) the relationship between object and observer. This approach is, first of all, designed to help conceptualisation in order to understand better contemporary foreign policy practices in the EU. Second, Figure 2.2 will be used to *map* theoretical or analytical approaches. Hence, in the second part of the chapter, I trace connections between leading theories and substantive issues, pointing out where leading theories prefer

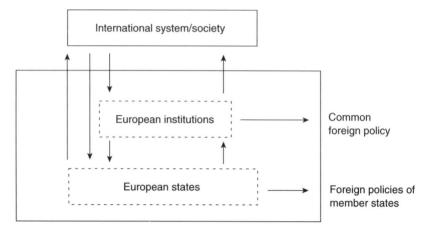

Figure 2.2 *Changed nature of foreign policy in Europe*

to operate or are capable of operating and where their weak spots are located. Additionally, the task of mapping comprises a *conceptualisation* of the domain. In this way, the Figure functions as a guide for reflection on issues deemed fruitful for analysts. In the third part of this chapter I summarise my findings and point to perspectives for further research.

Approaching EFP Axiomatically

The first axiom is that a *common* EFP actually does exist, and that it has existed for a considerable amount of time – in some issue areas for more than three decades.[4] Furthermore, almost since it was launched in the early 1970s, it has had a security policy component (involvement in the Conference on Security and Co-operation in Europe (CSCE) process, among other things), and since the mid-1980s also a defence policy component (for which the Western European Union (WEU) has been responsible). The components in the field of security and defence may have been of little importance in the past. Yet they have nevertheless existed and their degree of importance remains an empirical question. Something similar can be said about the umbrella, that is, the common foreign policy. For periods of time and in some issue areas this common policy was nothing more than declaratory in character. It has occasionally been an ineffective policy, often lacking coherence, vision or clout. Yet, despite having been a *policy without qualities*, it has nevertheless existed and, furthermore, important dimensions of the common foreign policy have from the very beginning been *communautarian*, that is, conducted with the European Commission (EC) at the centre of policy-making. In summary, the first axiom contradicts the rather common view that a common EFP has either failed to take form, or that it suffers from a perpetual existential crisis.

The second axiom is derived from the first, claiming that the existence of a common EFP makes the analysis of EFP theoretically and conceptually more challenging than many analysts are ready to accept. The question is quite simply how we can know whether or not the nature of foreign policy has changed in Europe. The assumption here is that the emergence of a European (multilateral) foreign policy implies that our analysis should be based on conceptualisations that *differ* from those applied in the analysis of traditional foreign policy of states. We should thus carefully consider whether or not we can or should continue to conduct the analysis of foreign policy in conventional terms. I argue that the emergence of a multi-level system of policy-making severely undermines the usefulness of some of the conceptual lenses to be found in traditional studies of national foreign policy, even when these lenses occasionally have been developed into highly sophisticated analytical tools. In turn, this means that we either have to con-ceptualise *da novo* or re-conceptualise and, eventually, to build new theory. Otherwise we could end up by providing answers to yesterday's questions. Needless to say, this diagnosis may be wrong, and I am perfectly aware that a number of theoretical perspectives assume that it is still quite feasible – and perhaps even desirable – to continue as if nothing has changed.

Even if we accept that a common EFP exists, and even if this new creature has theoretical consequences, does the policy really matter? The third axiom holds that it does. The end of the Cold War has made EFP markedly more interesting and more relevant to the foreign policy analyst. While policy-making during the Cold War primarily had been reactive and significantly constrained by bipolar superpower dynamics, the room for manoeuvre has now significantly increased, meaning that EU member states are able to make a difference – if they so decide. Some of the key dilemmas during the first post-Cold War decade have been whether this increased room for manoeuvre should be used; and if yes, then how, where and why? Should foreign policy be conducted unilaterally, multilaterally or in some sort of *ad hoc* grouping? EFP after the Cold War not only has become more interesting and relevant to study, it has also, in a sense, become easier to study – the simple reason being that whereas in the early 1990s many factors and issues were floating and many policy-makers somewhat confused, a number of key decisions have since then been taken, certain issues have been settled, and certain patterns have been established.

The fourth axiom holds that the conceptual lenses which observers apply have an impact on what can be observed and how it is observed.[5] In John Ruggie's concise wording, 'How we think about transformation fundamen-tally shapes what we look for; what we look for obviously has an effect on what we find' (1989: 32). When dealing with a domain such as EFP, we are dealing with a set of social realities, meaning that observers may have an impact on that which is observed. Consequently, for better or worse, we should note that among the most important distinctions in this domain is the distinction between practice and theory, and between concepts *of* practice (concepts in political or administrative discourse) and concepts *in* theory (analytical or theoretical concepts, usually to be found in academic discourse).[6] Certainly, some overlap does exist and one should be aware of such dual usage.[7] Furthermore, observers can be of two kinds. Many players in the game, whether politicians or diplomats, probably reflect upon their own practice, that is, engage in self-observation. Yet some also present their reflections in writing, that is, make them directly accessible to outsiders.[8] However the literature written by insiders plays, or could play, an important role for those of us who – on the outside – try to understand and describe what, from our perspective, seems to be happening. Why an important role? Because conceptualising the domain in another way risks being a rather sterile exercise that has little to do with the social reality of EFP.[9] It is, however, even more complicated than that. Foreign policy analysts have difficulty in avoiding being part of public political discourse on EFP. Some 'go native', with the predictable result that they become *part of the game*. Concepts being used sometimes become conceptual blinders – perhaps because these concepts very accurately describe situations, developments or features of past practices rather than the present. Hence, analysts employing them are hindered in reaching accurate images of the present. Scholars employing them may even be aware of this situation yet live happily in their conceptual prisons. In such situations, concepts do not just contribute to constructing (social) reality, but also do so in a biased fashion.

These four axioms are far from theoretically neutral. Rather, they constitute part of a theoretical stance. As an illustrative example, let us consider neorealism in this context. From a neorealist perspective, the first axiom is questionable if not nonsensical. Neorealists argue that European institutions function merely as arenas on which great powers pursue power politics (Mearsheimer, 1995). Furthermore, if a common foreign policy can be detected, it can and should be explained as national foreign policy disguised in multilateral clothes, that is, as being national foreign policy writ large, or as the outcome of the traditional dynamics of alliance formations. From a neorealist perspective, the second axiom looks even more dubious, primarily because a minor reconfiguration in world politics, such as a degree of co-operation between a number of European states does not really disturb a deductive structural theory such as neorealism. On the other hand, the third axiom makes much more sense to neorealists. It comes close to arguing that a major change in the distribution of power, that is, the international system moving from a bipolar to a unipolar configuration, determines state behaviour. The fourth axiom runs counter to the behaviouralist underpinnings of neorealism, which are based on the assumption that realism can 'tap' reality directly.

Mapping and Conceptualising the Domain

Having discussed general issues on how EFP can be approached, the task of mapping and conceptualising EFP can now be taken up in a more direct mode. The first issue to consider here is whether the end of the Cold War has changed the nature of foreign policy in Europe. This is a perfectly feasible and timely issue to raise, and it may even result in very valuable findings. Yet it is likely to lead only to an analysis of a 'thinly' changed foreign policy, for example, by demonstrating that contemporary EFP is addressing new issues or providing new answers to old problems. In short, we would find out to which degree policies after the Cold War are different from policies during the Cold War and, potentially, how a balance between member states' and the EU's conduct of foreign policy has been established (cf. Keohane et al., 1993; Hill, 1996). However, to specify what is likely does not exclude what is possible. In other words, it could turn out that the end of the Cold War has produced dramatic changes in the nature of EFP, for instance, resulting in new principles, doctrines or means of conducting foreign policy.

The second issue to consider is whether developments in the EU are responsible for changes in the nature of foreign policy in Europe. In contrast to the first issue, this one is likely to have more far-reaching ramifications, in particular because it opens up for investigation whether such changes have occurred in a 'thick' sense. In other words, it potentially goes beyond questions triggered by the 'end of the Cold War' factor. Instead, it implies changes in the ontological nature of foreign policy, suggesting that intersubjective understandings of what counts as foreign policy have either changed or at least have become contentious.

The third issue to consider is the consequences of the changed nature of foreign policy on the conduct of foreign policy by both individual European states and by the EU itself. The 'thin' version merely suggests that member states conduct foreign policies differently from the days of the Cold War; or, that they use the EU as a complementary carrier for conducting (part of) their foreign policies. The 'thick' version implies considerably more, touching upon issues such as shared representation in foreign affairs or pooled competencies. The 'thick' version can be illuminated by means of historical comparison: what happened to the 'foreign services' of political entities merging into nation-states in the late 19th century (Germany or Italy); or what happened to predominant mindsets about foreign affairs during fundamental reconfigurations of polities (for example, the US after the Civil War)? Or are we perhaps not yet there but rather in some kind of interregnum where member states no longer conduct traditional foreign policy and the EU is not yet ready to conduct foreign policy in a new (upgraded) key? Does the changed conduct of foreign policy only apply to intra-EU relations (consider, for example, the widespread uncertainty in member states as to whether the EU is 'foreign' or 'domestic' policy); or does it also apply to the EU's conduct of foreign policy vis-à-vis the non-EU world?

In the following, I will use Figure 2.2 (see p. 34) to map the major 'axes' on which different theoretical conceptions of EFP have their 'heartland'. Furthermore, I will use Figure 2.2 to consider which concepts seem capable of helping us to examine the claim about a presumed changed nature of EFP.

EU member states and the international system/society

Relations between the international system/society and the conduct of foreign policy by the EU and its member states, respectively, have not attracted much interest among foreign policy analysts. It is, therefore, worthwhile to mine two theoretical orientations here: neorealism and the English School.

The causal relationship between systemic structure and state behaviour constitutes the preferred hunting ground for neorealists. In this view, systemic structural impulses, transmitted via balance of power dynamics, determine state behaviour. In other words, we have a flow of influence from the system, via states, to their behaviour in the form of foreign policy. This perspective is not at all irrelevant for our analysis of EFP. First of all, because a neorealist perspective provides at least to some degree the *rationale* for this study as a whole, it is not an insignificant part of this enterprise. It is the end of bipolarity and the emergence of a new polarity that makes us analyse the presumed changed nature of EFP. Furthermore, the perspective directs our attention to those European states that realists consider to be great powers and therefore worthy of attention.[10] Hence, the perspective forces us to address the distribution of capabilities and balance of power issues, that is, issues which largely have been ignored by most foreign policy analysts. Neorealists would also be quick to point out that deadlocks in developing the Common Foreign and Security Policy (CFSP) and Common European Security and Defence Policy (CESDP) are easily explained by bringing NATO into the equation and thereby the presence of the US in Europe. Additionally, it seems as if the institutional design of the EFP decision-making system has largely been outlined by precisely the West European great powers. Thus, the CESDP was launched in a successful manner as soon as a shared understanding was created between the UK, France and Germany. It also seems that in the event of severe crisis situations, the multilateral EU common foreign policy system is short-circuited and replaced by, once again, the major European players.[11] Finally, the notion *multiple bilateralism* seems relevant because it suggests the existence of underwood institutions based on exclusion and informal hierarchy. Proposals concerning *directoires* are different precisely because they suggest codification of *de facto* informal institutions. In summary, the realist conceptual repertoire seems eminently suited to improve our understanding of contemporary behaviour by European states.

However, there are three major problems with this approach. First, neorealists have not produced comprehensive theory-informed empirical studies in this area. Second, if there is an unexploited potential in neorealist theory, there are also numerous problems in addressing issues like transformation, change and relations between the EU and its member states. Third, in contrast to the neorealist image, some diplomats and analysts argue that within the EU it is not brute force but in fact argumentative power that matters.[12]

Turning to the English school, we have a theoretical orientation that on the face of it should have something important to contribute to our subject matter. Indeed, much can potentially be analysed by using the school's conceptual repertoire, ranging from the very conception of international society, via the notion of fundamental institutions (including their relations to so-called pseudo-institutions such as the UN, NATO or the EU), to perspectives on classic ethical issues. Originally, international society consisted of the European states system, and hence European states can be said to have created international society. The Concert of Europe, many rules of conduct in diplomacy, diplomatic discourse, international law and so on – all have originated on the European historical arena. During the 20th century, international society has expanded to cover the entire globe. In other words, international society has become global and the European states system has become but a part of international society. However, what in the present context is important is that as originators of international society, and as powerful members of it, European states continue to be very influential actors in international society. Norms and rules that help constitute international society are to a considerable degree the result of the very existence of this society. However, once rules and norms have been institutionalised in international society, the dynamics of the game have tended to go in the opposite direction. Intervention policies provide an illustrative example. UN authorisation is, as a rule, considered a precondition for European states to engage in interventions or peace support operations. It is increasingly a norm that such operations are conducted in a collective fashion in order to avoid action based on excessive national self-interest. There have been exceptions to the rule, but not to the norm. For example, the Kosovo campaign in 1999 was to some degree an exception to the rule, yet basic principles for interventionist policies were never endangered. What is worthwhile noting, both from a political and an analytical perspective, is that among European states this rule is not uncontested. Some EU member states claim UN authorisation as a precondition for any military intervention, while other member states find this to be preferable but not mandatory. As a result, we currently seem to be witnessing a reconfiguration of attitudes to the rule calling for UN authorisation.

However, the English school has less to offer than one would expect. One reason is that the school, like realism, is a general International Relations (IR) theory, having little interest in or awareness of 'specificities' in any particular part of the world. A second and related reason is that early members of the school seemed to have lost analytical interest in contemporary European affairs, focusing instead on historical systems of states, or on contemporary global politics. The result is that the school has little to say about the European state system (and its constituent entities) *after* it became part of global international society and *after* European states launched and cultivated the process of European integration. The possibility that the EU should develop into a significant international actor and conduct foreign policy is at best dealt with in a fashion quite similar to how it is handled within neorealism, that is, as a hypothetical but unlikely outcome.[13] We are thus forced to conclude – once more – that although possessing a seemingly valuable set of concepts, members of this school have not found it worth their while to address the problematic features of it as an approach to the analysis of EFP.

European states and EU institutions

While the relationship between states and system has been analysed by means of a limited number of approaches, a whole cluster of theories, pre-theories and approaches has focused on relations between member states and EU institutions. In the following, three key perspectives will be examined with a view to conceptualisation. The first perspective concerns 'bottom-up' approaches, privileging flows of influence from states to institutions. Approaches like intergovernmentalism, liberal intergovernmentalism and classical realism belong to this category of 'second image' approaches. By contrast, the second perspective includes 'top-down' approaches, privileging impact flowing from the external environment to states, that is, what Gourevitch (1978) calls 'second image reversed' approaches. Such approaches comprise Europeanisation, multi-level governance, supranationalism and others. The third perspective concerns constitutive relationships between states and EU institutions.

Second image approaches   Processes of common identity and interest formation have obviously not 'destroyed' state actors. Stretching our historical imagination, it is even possible to imagine European states *without* EU institutions. Historically, European institutions were created by their founding 'father' states, not vice versa. This genealogy is the ultimate refuge of realists, principal-agent and intergovernmentalist theorists, always eager to point out the constructedness of European institutions but seldom the constructedness of European states (Grieco, 1997; Pollack, 1999; Moravcsik, 1998). Each of these approaches has something to offer. Liberal intergovernmentalism offers a sequential theoretical triad, consisting of mid-range theories of interest formation, bargaining and institutional design. The package also includes a sophisticated methodology and novel ideas concerning thorough theory testing. Unfortunately none of these approaches have been systematically applied in studies of EFP. Leaving that task for another occasion, I turn instead to the terms 'k-group' and 'minilateralism'. Having been used to squaring the circle between influential states and multilateral institutions, the terms exist in the grey zone between realism and liberalism, suggesting that in formulating or implementing specific policies, some states are more 'key' than others. They make up a k-group. The outcome is called minilateralism because on the surface it looks like multilateralism but has its origin in a k-group within a multilateral grouping (Kahler, 1992).

An illustrative example of European minilateralism could be seen during the early 1990s in European policy-making on Bosnia. France and the UK constituted a k-group that got its policy multilaterally accepted and legitimised, first within the EU and then, with EU backing, in the UN Security Council. A second prominent example of a k-group – the Franco-German axis – has been very active in the area of institutional design. The Anglo-Italian connection sometimes plays the role as balancing k-group, whereas Nordic member states have been largely inactive in this field (Jørgensen, 1999). Multilateral outcomes emerging due to k-group action may have a peculiar genesis, but they are nevertheless highly relevant to an adequate understanding of the dynamics between member states and European institutions. Relevant, both because the outcomes in question may have a significant political role and because successful minilateralism requires persuasive reasons for (k-group) action and provides legitimacy to multilateral outcomes. Thus, the creation of the Contact Group was from some corners publicly criticised for undermining the role of EU institutions (which indeed was the case), yet among most member states it was a shared understanding that launching the Contact Group was a necessary step in order to provide increased effectiveness (Jakobsen, 2000).

In general, second image approaches highlight flows of influence from states to institutions. They contribute well-developed analytical frameworks and focus on important features of the EU system. Their weaknesses are therefore not to be found in what they cover, but in their omissions. Privileging flows of influence from states to institutions, the opposite flow is either regarded as so insignificant that it requires no attention whatsoever, or it constitutes one of the recognised or unrecognised blind spots of this approach.

Second image reversed approaches These approaches all turn the second image upside-down. In the words of Gourevitch, 'In using domestic structure as a variable in explaining foreign policy, we must explore the extent to which that structure itself derives from the exigencies of the international system' (Gourevitch, 1978: 882).[14] While systemic impact has been dealt with above, it is possible to transfer the logic to a lower level of analysis, for instance, the European sub-system. Turning independent variables into dependent variables opens up a huge research agenda; yet transforming the general argument into an operational research agenda on European foreign policy requires careful thinking. Some important work has nevertheless been done here. Part of the literature on Europeanisation explores the impact on domestic structures and institutions (Radaelli, 2000; Cowles et al., 2000; Bulmer and Lequesne, 2002). Furthermore, according to Magnus Ekengren (1997, 2002), the timing of policy-making in member states has been brought into Brussels mode, that is, synchronised with reference to ministerial meeting sequences. Similarly, Ben Tonra (1997) has shown how even intergovernmental co-operation in the field of foreign policy has an impact on national policies and institutions, while Hocking and Spence (2002) demonstrate how several foreign ministries have been thoroughly reorganised due to processes of European integration. According to a very comprehensive study (Güssgen, 2002), the French Ministry of Foreign Affairs constitutes the real hard case concerning reorganisation of ministries. Many attempts at reforming the ministry have been made, yet none with much success. For better or worse, it seems that the Quay d'Orsay has been entirely immune to reform or outside influence. Nevertheless, *socialisation* is one of these terms that continues to pop up in studies of EFP. Compared to Europeanisation, we are here dealing with the properties of agents at the micro level, that is, with politicians, diplomats and officials active in the EFP system.[15] It thus refers to properties of individuals.

Finally, the distinction between 'hardware' and 'software' dimensions of European foreign policy seems highly relevant, particularly in the context of a possibly changed nature of foreign policy.[16] Among 'hardware' dimensions of foreign policy, organisations play a key role. They embody, so to speak, software dimensions. When something is institutionalised it is taken for granted that an element of inertia has been introduced to a domain that used to be more in flux before institutionalisation. Furthermore, people working in organisations tend to develop ideas and interests of their own. Sometimes an organisation is even being tasked to provide some degree of guidance to a process as, for example, in the original role of the European Commission (though not its role in CFSP policy-making). If we aim at reaching a comprehensive understanding of EFP, it would be necessary but insufficient to look at just European institutions (organisations) and their inter-relationship.[17] It would be necessary, additionally, to include traditional sites of policy-making, such as foreign ministries, defence ministries and embassies (Hocking and Spence, 2002; Ekengren, 2002), but not as timeless, never-changing organisational structures. Instead, keeping an eye on both levels of policy-making, the contemporary system can be regarded as a multi-level system of governance, represented as the dotted area in Figure 2.2 (p. 34). The foreign ministries of member states constitute a crucial part of such a system. Thus, instead of having formal legal competencies and decision-making power transferred to Brussels, we have an almost virtual European 'centre' of policy-making, which, in turn, has significant effects on policy-making in the capitals of the EU.

All these studies suggest that a comprehensive, systematic research programme on 'second image reversed' logics would be able to improve significantly our understanding of the contemporary multi-level system of EFP-making.

Constitutive approaches   Having now accounted for two very different perspectives on the making of EFP, the time has come to explore the possibility of somehow merging the two perspectives. In the present context, I am only interested in the kind of merger that allows us to explore constitutive approaches to the study of EFP. This aim implies that we have to leave causal explanation and the search for truly independent and dependent variables behind. Constitutive explanation belongs to a different kind of analytical game.

According to Alexander Wendt, a social structure *constitutes* an agent 'when the properties of those agents are made possible by, and would not exist in the absence of, the structure by which they are "constituted"'

(Wendt, 1995: 72, 1998: 105), pointing out that 'social structures also constitute actors with certain identities and interests' (1999: 78). Wendt refines his conceptual framework by making a distinction between internal and social structure, that is, between the structure of an actor as such (a rogue state is rogue because it rejects the norms of international society) and 'the set of relationships with other actors that define a social kind as such' (Israel is not considered a rogue state because great power discourse avoids this possibility) (Wendt, 1998: 113). Furthermore, constitutive explanation goes to the heart of the purpose of this chapter – to conceptualise the domain. Why? Because this kind of explanation is done by means of classifying observations and claiming they can be unified as parts of a coherent whole. In short, 'subsuming observations under a *concept*' (Wendt, 1998: 110). Finally, Wendt points out, conceptualisation is often more than simple labelling. It can be explanatory because conceptualising the properties of things is also to point to dispositions, that is, 'propensities to behave in certain ways under certain conditions' (1998: 111). What does this imply for our study of EFP?

Wendt (1998) provides a few hints. Thus, one of his examples is the 'what-question': 'What kind of political system is the EU?' Answering this question involves conceptualisation – classifying numerous observations and unifying the parts under a concept, for instance, a 'quasi-federation', in turn pointing to certain dispositions of this kind of federation. Similarly, what-questions like 'What is a civilian power?', 'What is an international actor?' or 'What is a "common" foreign policy?' require constitutive explanation. Various answers to such questions have been suggested. The EU is not 'rogue' because the EU does not reject norms of international society. Rather, the EU has often acted as a norm entrepreneur or a defender of international norms. Furthermore, ever since the concept 'civilian power' was coined, it has been highly contested. To Bull (1982) it is best characterised as 'a contradiction in terms', whereas Johan Galtung (1973) summarised his conclusion with the term 'a superpower in the making'. Finally, foreign policy analysts are, generally, not used to analysing 'common' policies and hard thinking has been required to study the making of such policies. Turning to the distinction between internal and social structure, we see that several intriguing issues pop up. Thus the EU has a very 'rich' internal structure, a structure that, combined, makes a whole class of preconditions for being a foreign policy actor of a certain kind. In order to examine the interconnectedness of (state) agents and (institutional) structures, we can ask how it is possible for member states to reproduce social structures present in the EU system? At the same time, a class of external preconditions also exists. Thus, do other actors *recognise* the EU as an international actor? How is membership of several UN organisations possible for a non-state like the EU? In sum, constitutive approaches invite us to study how social structures, whether internal or external, constitute an actor like the EU with certain identities and interests. In turn, we can ask how such processes of constitution have consequences for the identities and interests of member states. We can analyse 'national interests', perhaps contending that member states do pursue perceived national interests, but these interests have been derived from processes of identity formation, whether collective or individual. If social interaction indeed does have an impact on processes of identity and interest-formation, something claimed by a broad range of constructivist approaches, then it is time to put these approaches to work on the European case (Wendt, 1994; Katzenstein, 1996; Jørgensen, 1997; Glarbo, 2001; Christiansen et al., 2001).

Constitutive approaches make up a huge and important research agenda. Such approaches make it possible to go beyond reification – if we deem it appropriate to do so – for instance, by critically analysing 'natural' things like borders, currencies or states, or 'artificial' things like a common foreign policy, the euro or the EU polity.

The Conduct of EFP

The purpose of this section is to understand better the interplay between the conduct of national and EU foreign policy-making. First, ontological conceptual issues will be addressed. Does a common policy exist? Do national policies? Second, the concept of 'policy' will be examined. What does it take to be a policy? Finally, I turn to processes of Europeanisation, focusing on three different meanings.

Ontological issues

Many EU foreign policy analysts take a narrow perspective, focusing exclusively on the common policy, as if member states or their foreign ministries did not exist or matter. When reading the CFSP literature, it is easy to get the impression that member states and their foreign policies have disappeared. Vis-à-vis CFSP analysts, it is therefore necessary to state the obvious fact that the foreign policies of member states have not withered away. However, not only CFSP analysts tend to commit the sin of omission. It is equally necessary, and even more so, to state a few obvious points vis-à-vis conventional analysts of national foreign policy.

Reaching an adequate understanding of contemporary EFP is hindered by the unfortunate fact that many remain doubtful about the very existence or importance of a common EFP. Most analysts of national foreign policy avoid the European dimension and analyse the conduct of foreign policy by individual European states as if the EU does not exist.[18] Perhaps the nature of national foreign policies is no longer quite what it used to be.[19] At the very least, traditional foreign policy analysts should seriously consider this idea (cf. Figure 2.3, p. 45). They could also consider the fact that national embassies in Europe used to play a significant role in the past but no longer do so, thus contributing to a crucial difference between the traditional European states system and the contemporary system. Finally, EFPs used to be directed at *other* European states, thus constituting European international relations, the paradigm case for our, *grosso-modo*, Euro-centric

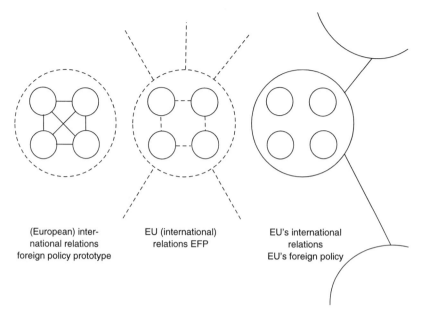

Figure 2.3 *Changing nature of foreign policy in the EU*

discipline, IR. Against this background the common foreign policy can be conceptualised in two very different ways. First, it can be conceptualised as, basically, having a function vis-à-vis what used to be European international relations. That is, the prime function of the common policy is to address the well-known enemy Western European states have faced in the past, namely themselves. From this perspective we are dealing with an EU *internal* function, and conceptualisation should reflect this. Of course, the second – and more intuitive – perspective is that the common policy either is elevated from the national to the EU level, or viewed as co-existing with national policy-making. These reflections trigger two intriguing questions: Could it be that the existence or importance of national foreign policies amounts to less than a trivial fact? If yes, where should we expect to find the origins of a common policy?

Some analysts claim the existence of a Danish policy on the Middle East (Haagerup and Thune, 1983). Yet it remains questionable to suggest a Danish 'policy' on the Middle East on the same level as US – and perhaps UK, Russian, French or EU – policies on the Middle East. Several (critical) studies indicate that Italian foreign policy has been a low-key affair well into the 1980s. Thus Joseph LaPalombara (1989) writes about *immobilismo* in Italian foreign policy, while Edward Luttwak (1993), in his usual blunt fashion, characterises Italian foreign policy under Gianni DeMichelis as a somewhat farce-like affair. Ben Tonra (2001) describes Irish foreign policy as being very limited in substantive scope and spatial reach. Germany has only been Germany since its unification in 1990, and Western Germany was widely considered merely a semi-sovereign state, hardly the best foundation for the conduct of a 'genuine' national foreign policy. Ben Soetendorp (1996) has described a moment of truth in the Dutch foreign policy establishment, when it realised that The Netherlands had less leverage on Indonesia than it was used to in the past. Certainly, all EU member states continue to have foreign ministries (however small), diplomats (however few) and a foreign policy process (however insignificant for all but the involved). But only a small minority of member states has had great power status. The shadow of this asymmetrical configuration is likely to have a significant impact on the sources of EU foreign policy.

Finally, conditions during the Cold War strengthen the general argument. Four decades of superpower overlay are likely to have dissolved significant previously existing national foreign policy traditions, defined in terms of national interests or images of the national 'self'. Unless, that is, analysts believe in a 'frozen' primordial foreign policy behaviour, only waiting to be reinstantiated with the lifting of the 'overlay'. More likely, the 1990s has been a decade of thorough (re-)considerations concerning the 'self' and all 'others'. Obviously, more examples could be presented, but these should suffice to illustrate my point. Yet, despite all these striking limitations, each EU member state has no doubt been cultivating processes called 'foreign policy making' by politicians, diplomats and analysts alike. It is a perfect example of an efficient speech act in practice, and foreign policy analysts have been very active participants in such acts.

As noted above, the foreign policy traditions of most EU member states have, one way or another, been undermined in the past decades, meaning that their spatial reach, substantive volume and instruments for conducting foreign policy have been significantly reduced. A range of traditional foreign policy instruments has been 'removed' from the toolbox of EU member states, to be used instead in the foreign policy conducted by the EU. Indeed, if the same criteria are applied to the determination of national policies as criteria of the EU foreign policy to the EU, how many national foreign policies would in fact survive a critical analysis? Finally, although it is trivially true that member states continue to pursue their perceived national interests, it is worthwhile to consider the hypothesis that these interests have been redefined due to a changed institutional setting. Constructivist arguments, as put forward by Wendt and others, lead us to predict that interaction at both the European and international levels have effects on processes of identity and interest formation among European states. This hypothesis has not yet been thoroughly tested. What we do have are merely hints, for instance, when Nicole Gnesotto comes to the following conclusion: 'That all countries of the Union ... now subscribe to the political and operational aims set out at Cologne and Helsinki, is certainly a major political revolution' (Gnesotto, 2000).

The problematic nature of 'policy'

Of all the concepts being employed in the analysis of foreign policy, the concept 'policy' is probably the most over-stretched, devalued and least precisely defined. It would make sense to be more restrictive, to ask what is and what is not a policy. For example, it is widely believed that during the Cold War, France actually had a policy towards Eastern Europe. However, it appears not to be as simple as that. Pierre Hassner has issued a well-taken warning against a casual employment of the term, concluding that 'from de Gaulle to François Mitterrand French leaders were cast more than ever as specialists in vision rather than policy, in words rather than deeds' (1987: 189). Hassner's provocative view may trigger contending views. Some will probably argue that it is a very inaccurate perception of French foreign policy. Others will argue that Hassner characterises well features of the Cold War period, but not policy-making in the post-Cold War era. No matter which attitude is chosen to Hassner's criticism, the aim has been to illustrate the point about the necessity of some minimum standards for qualifying or not qualifying for the concept of 'policy'.

A second problem with the term policy is that it is a very egalitarian term, suggesting that all policies belong to the same league, have comparable features and share fundamental qualities. In the past we have tended to assume, uncritically, that a policy is a policy is a policy, which is a powerful device in any process of (self)-presentation – sometimes self-aggrandisation – but hardly an assumption that automatically has relevance for the analysis of European states during the Cold War. The interesting question is whether the assumption has become more adequate for states in the contemporary system. Though all policies can be said to have areas of concentration, being formulated through policy-making processes and conducted by politicians or diplomats, does it follow that they are in the same league, belonging to the same category? Are there not good reasons to establish a hierarchy according to which some qualify and others do not? Is it really impossible to create meaningful limits, for instance, in terms of volume, portfolio, reach or clout? In any case, research on this subject matter should at least cast some doubt on the actual justification for speaking about national foreign policy traditions and thus, in turn, raise serious questions about some of the standard explanations for the difficulties in developing a common EFP.

A third problem has to do with the noun 'common', an often employed term of Euro-speak. Proponents of analytical individualism prefer to arrive at something 'common' by aggregating individual intentions, actions or policies. However, intentionality does not need to be individual, which means that the term 'collective intentionality' seems particularly relevant for studies of common EU policies.[20] Collective intentionality is fully agnostic concerning progress or regress in integrative dynamics. It can function both as a pre-condition for integration and as a brake. The 'successful' non-function of the WEU during the decade 1973–83 is a prominent example of 'negative' collective intentionality. The presence of a strong inter-subjective understanding among members of the organisation meant that the WEU was a no-go organisation. No meetings at ministerial level were organised, no political declarations were issued, no statements were made. Brussels treaty provisions were dead letters. In short, members acted as if the organisation did not exist, despite the fact that the WEU had a postal address; it was based on a comprehensive treaty, officials were paid salaries and a parliamentary assembly held sessions. Similarly, the absence during the Cold War of a European defence policy and a European army has often been explained by a lack of political will. In a certain sense, there was a very conscious political will to *avoid* such political initiatives, because they could 'rock the bipolar boat' and risk a severe de-stabilisation of international relations. Remnants of this strong (negative) political will are probably responsible for the opaque wording of the Maastricht Treaty on defence issues. The two examples show that the concept of collective intentionality is far from being 'married' to a notion of progressive institutional dynamics.

Finally, a distinction between four different roles of foreign policy demonstrates how further specification could be achieved. The first role is the inside-out function, meaning that foreign policy is regarded as an extended image of the (national or European) self, that is, related to issues of national, state or EU identity. The second role is a projection image of foreign policy, implying the projection of ideas, values, institutions, models – or just brute power. The third role is a protection image of foreign policy, for instance, protecting interests or values of a given state. The fourth role includes the symbolic representation of foreign policy, showing its value when national decision-makers realise that their international influence is limited, yet pretend the opposite in front of their constituency – and are believed. The de-constructive part of the story, then, is to acknowledge that sometimes it is analytically helpful to step three steps backwards and ask which role of foreign policy we observe in action. In summary, a given policy may play a significant role in celebrating the self of an imagined community, yet hardly be detectable across the boundaries of the very same community. It has been claimed that the opposite characterised Italian foreign policy during the Cold War. International events were for consumption in Italian domestic politics.

Processes of Europeanisation

Policy-makers and analysts widely share the view that the term 'Europeanisation' is both relevant and helpful in describing one of the key processes in contemporary European foreign policy. However, the term has been employed in a variety of ways, sometimes even in a casual fashion. Radaelli (2000) is therefore right in pointing out that the term is currently in danger of being over-stretched, at least as an analytical concept. In the context of EFP, Europeanisation has at least three different meanings.

Adaptation The term 'Europeanisation' has been employed in order to describe how interaction at the European level has certain effects on national foreign policy. A cluster of concepts deals with more or less the same process: how national foreign policies have been changed, transformed or adapted as a result of European integration. Some analysts employ the term 'adaptation' here (see Hanf and Soetendorp, 1998). David Allen (1998), on the other hand, argues that European foreign policies have been 'Brusselised', that is, not transformed into a communautarian mode but nevertheless moulded into a Brussels-focused mode. Mike Smith (1998), writing about elements of foreign policy within Pillar 1, employs the term 'communitarised'. These observations lead to the proposition that the foreign policies of EU member states have become 'something' they would not have been had the process of European integration not happened in the first place.

Obviously, the proposition forces us to engage in counterfactual reasoning, which is not always easy. However, whether easy or not, such reasoning appears to be highly relevant to accomplish our mission and is, in any case, difficult to avoid. Furthermore, much hinges on the features of the 'something', on which methods we can employ in order to detect the 'something' and, eventually, on how we can describe the 'something'. Intuitively one could expect the distinction between larger and smaller member states to be highly relevant for refining the proposition. That is, does Europeanisation only apply to minor and medium member states? What about the larger member states, for instance the (two) hard cases? According to Brian White (2001: 118–41), UK foreign policy too has been Europeanised. Furthermore, UK officials claim that the CFSP department in the British Foreign Office has become increasingly popular among the young, smart and career minded during the 1990s. John Coles is more sceptical, arguing, however, that the CFSP has become 'an important dimension of British foreign policy' (2000: 150). The French case is less well described, yet seems to be similar to the UK case (Hill, 1996; Manners and Whitman, 2001).

Elevating policy-making   The second meaning of Europeanisation has to do with aspects of foreign policy being 'taken out' of the exclusively national conduct of foreign policy and elevated to EU policy-making. As such it concerns the balance between member states' and the EU's conduct of foreign policy, leading to the proposition that, in the EU, foreign policy is increasingly conducted by the EU.

Examples that come to mind include foreign economic policy, that is, decision-making on tariffs and other trade issues. Volker Rittberger and Frank Schimmelfennig point out that:

> Germany's foreign trade policy cannot be observed directly in the GATT [General Agreement on Tarifs and Trade] negotiations of the Uruguay Round. The EEC [European Economic Community] treaty stipulates that member states must co-ordinate their foreign trade policy with the EC/EU. As a result, the EC/EU Commission has been charged with conducting the negotiations in the GATT. Consequently, Germany's foreign trade policy toward the GATT can be examined only at the European level, i.e. by looking at the processes of co-ordination from which the European position within the GATT negotiations results. (1997)

A few examples, however, do not suffice to 'close the case'. To be persuasive, analysts must present findings pointing out that *more and more* 'modules' of policy are being elevated to the EU and, consequently, that national foreign policies are being significantly 'diluted', perhaps leading to a domain that is increasingly populated by symbolic politics.

Empowerment The third meaning refers to how processes of Europeanisation are connected to processes of empowerment. Only two member states, France and the UK, have been traditional great powers, while Germany for a long time has followed a different trajectory. Italy has always been considered the least of the European great powers and has thus also followed its own path. What about the rest – what about Spain, Finland, Greece, Portugal, The Netherlands, Sweden, Belgium, Luxembourg, Ireland, Denmark and Austria? What has the multi-layered system of foreign policy-making to offer these states and their bureaucracies? Adaptation of policy and administrative culture? Certainly. Europeanisation of policy and international horizon? Probably. Socialisation of representatives? Most likely. But, research findings suggest, also empowerment in the sense of having increased information at their disposal, access to major decision-makers (Tonra, 1997) and participation in the making of EU foreign policy. In other words, processes of Europeanisation imply an empowerment of most member states of the EU, meaning that they can now, finally, participate in conducting a foreign policy that matters beyond their own borders.

Europeanisation also implies reduced fears of being entrapped in traditional European great power politics and reduced fears of being 'targeted' by major non-EU actors, such as the US, Russia or China, in response to foreign policy initiatives that are regarded as unfriendly by the latter. Interestingly, realism has the term 'voice opportunity' to offer for this kind of dynamics. Drawing on Hans Morgenthau and Paul Schroeder, Joseph Grieco points out that states attempt to achieve the dual purpose of balancing against adversaries and constrain 'and modulate the behaviour of partners' (Grieco, 1997: 200). In other words, Grieco claims that 'relatively weaker states may choose to cooperate through an institution in order both to pursue balancing against an external challenger and to mitigate their domination by the stronger partner in the balancing coalition by ensuring that the institution is composed of rules and practices that provide the weaker partners effective "voice opportunities"' (Grieco, 1997: 185).

Conclusion

Between the Scylla of theoretical orthodoxy and the Charybdis of detailed description, conceptualisation provides a means for keeping a steady innovative analytical course. Furthermore, conceptualisation is a precondition for theory building, in turn a precondition for theory-guided empirical research. In this chapter, I first (re-)visited some of the general conceptual issues, including so-called 'strategic' conceptions that carry a whole toolbox of more directly applicable concepts. Using Figure 2.2 (p. 34) as a guide through key *problématiques* believed to be particularly relevant for the study of EFP, I conclude that in order to improve our understanding of EFP we need to refine further our conceptual framework of analysis. When doing this we should keep in mind that contemporary EFP is conducted at several levels, implying that mutually constitutive features should be privileged. Furthermore, EFP is conducted by a number of different sets of collective actors, applying several methods of decision-making, and making policies that are more or less efficient in terms of reaching stated goals.

When addressing these issues, five dilemmas emerge on the horizon. First, are we content with detailed description of the conduct of foreign policy or do we want some kind of theory-informed analysis? Second, do we want to develop a *European* approach to the study of foreign policy, or do we agree with scholars who argue that, quite simply, there is no such thing as a 'regional' approach to research on foreign policy? Third, do EFP analysts want to focus on foreign policy *tous azimut* or just focus on European foreign policies? Fourth, in continuation of the focus issue and provided theory-building is part of our research practice, do we aim at universal applicability or at limited, confined applicability? Fifth, do we want to aim for grand theory or for mid-range theory?

Ian Manners (2000) observes two predominant trends in contemporary foreign policy analysis, pointing out that (increasingly) different approaches are being cultivated in the US and Europe, respectively. His analysis suggests that most scholars in the US continue to opt for seemingly general theories, presumably applicable everywhere. By contrast, European scholars increasingly opt for theorising with limited applicability. If we combine these trends with the fact that most Europeans focus on European foreign policies, it is easy to predict that we will end up with theory synthesising European experiences, but not very much beyond that. In other words, if we continue down the road, keeping the present goal in mind, we will potentially become knowing specialists on EFP, but not necessarily on foreign policy as such. Whether or not this is regarded as a satisfactory state of things remains an issue for prudent consideration.

Notes

1 I am grateful to Thomas Christiansen, Hans-Henrik Holm and Sonia Lucarelli for commenting on earlier versions of this chapter. Having presented drafts of the chapter at two workshops in Oslo, I also thank the participants for their valuable comments and suggestions.
2 We should, however, not underestimate previous instances of complexity, for instance, after the First World War when several of Europe's traditional empires disappeared and the ideology of Communism appeared, or the post-Second World War period, characterised by processes of de-colonisation, the emergence of nuclear weapons and the creation of numerous multilateral institutions.

3   In principle, foreign policy could be considered a public policy, being like all other public policies. Yet, because foreign policy deals with relations between a polity and its environment, it has traditionally been assigned a special status, reflected in provisions in constitutions and, in the scholarly community, in cultivating the study of foreign policy as a sub-branch of the field of International Relations. On this issue, see Carlsnaes (2002) and Kleistra and Mayer (2001).

4   In a sense, the *European Foreign Policy Bulletin online* (EFPB) documents the existence of a common policy. While this is particularly valid concerning the policy conducted within the framework of the CFSP, the *Bulletin on the European Union* documents the *communautarian* parts of the common policy. Both the EFPB and the Bulletin are therefore ideal points of departure for research on the common European foreign policy. This axiom is not based on wishful thinking but on the conclusions of comprehensive research; see for instance Piening (1997), Jørgensen (1997), Cameron (1999), Ginsberg (2001), Bretherton and Vogler (2001) and White (2001).

5   Admittedly, this is an old hat axiom (see Kaiser, 1966; Allison, 1971; Keohane and Nye, 1977), but even old hats have their use, and it is highly relevant to explore what the axiom means in the context of conceptualising and analysing contemporary European foreign policy.

6   Concepts of practice can be found in speeches, declarations, statements or Council Presidency conclusions. They are political or diplomatic discourse. By contrast, observers reflecting on developments in the field of foreign policy by describing, conceptualising, re-conceptualising or theorising tend to employ concepts of theory.

7   On this problematic, see Hellmann's (1994) very informative analysis on German foreign policy analysts and their conceptions of German foreign policy.

8   Among those who have contributed to the literature on European foreign policy, we find David Owen, Philippe de Schoutheete de Tervarent, Simon Nuttall, David Spence, Horst Günter Krenzler, Graham Messervy-Whyting, Henry Wynaendts, Peter Brückner, etc.

9   For an extended argument, see Andersen (1998), Glarbo (2001) and Jørgensen (1997).

10 Having identified the 'great powers', we also automatically have the out-group which, in a neorealist perspective, we can forget about, i.e., most members of the European Union.

11 Cf. for example the case of the Contact Group, which was established as an attempt to handle the Balkan crisis more swiftly and efficiently than was possible by the EU, or European military responses to the 11 September 2001 terrorist attack.

12 The former Secretary-General of the Council Secretariat, Niels Ersbøll, argues along such lines. Among analysts, see Müller (2001) and Lose (2001). See also Risse (2000).

13 Compare Waltz (1979) to Wight (1977) and Bull (1977). For the pros and cons of the English School analysing European integration, see Buzan (2001), Little (1999), Diez and Whitman (2002), Jørgensen (2000) and Manners (2000).

14 These approaches can draw on a long research tradition. Gourevitch points to Otto Hintze, Perry Anderson, Stein Rokkan and Theda Skocpol, among others. Interestingly, a realist like Grieco (1997: 182–3) draws on the same literature. Peter Katzenstein, in explaining the emergence of corporativism in Nordic states, puts forward a similar type of argument.

15 This in contrast to Waltz's (1979) conception of socialisation, i.e., the view that states in a competitive anarchic environment, through processes of socialisation, become 'like units' (or perish!). Socialisation in this sense refers to macro-phenomena, specifically states.

16 'Hardware' includes phenomena like organisational infrastructure, personnel, military gear, industrial base etc. 'Software' includes phenomena like ways of thinking, visions, aspirations, world views, key concepts of practice, principles, norms in both the sociological and legal meaning, beliefs etc.

17 We should thus abstain from regarding the European institutions as the only site of importance for the common European foreign policy, discussing relations between the Commission, the Council and the Parliament, including their various sub-departments (the Commission DGs, the working groups within the CFSP, the CFSP Secretariat and the High Representative etc.). This is the focus privileged by CFSP analysts.

18 Comparison of the websites of foreign ministries in EU member states shows considerable variation concerning whether or not to include links to EU 'partner' foreign ministries. There are reasons for analysts to be doubtful about a high degree of common policy.

19 Cf. Coles' (2000) telling chapter title 'Not What It Was: The Nature of Foreign Policy Today', reflecting experiences from a long career in the British Foreign Office.

20 For a thorough philosophical explication of the term, see John Searle (1995).

References

Allen, D. (1998) 'Who speaks for Europe? The search for effective and coherent external policy', in J. Peterson and H. Sjursen (eds), *A Common Foreign Policy for Europe?* London: Routledge. pp. 41–58.

Allison, G.T. (1971) *Essence of Decision: Explaining the Cuban Missile Crisis*. London: Harper Collins.

Andersen, K.G. (1998) *The (Re)Construction of a Common Foreign and Security Policy for the European Union*. Aarhus: Department of Political Science.

Anderson, B. (1983) *Imagined Communities: Reflections on the Origin and Spread of Nationalism*. London: Verso.

Bretherton, C. and Vogler, J. (1999) *The European Union as a Global Actor*. London: Routledge.

Bretherton, C. and Vogler, J. (2001) *The European Union and International Environmental Politics*. Paper presented at ISA Conference in Hong Kong, July.

Bull, H. (1977) *The Anarchical Society. A Study of Order in World Politics*. London: Macmillan.

Bull, H. (1982) 'Civilian Power Europe: A Contradiction in Terms', *Journal of Common Market Studies*, 21 (1–2): 149–64.

Bulmer, S. and Lequesne, C. (2002) 'New perspectives on EU-member state relationships', *Question de recherches/Research in question*, No 4. Paris: Institut des Sciences Politiques.

Buzan, B. (2001) 'The English school: an unexploited resource in IR', *Review of International Studies*, 27 (3): 471–88.

Cameron, F. (1999) *Foreign and Security Policy of the European Union*. Sheffield: Sheffield Academic Press.

Carlsnaes, W. (2002) 'Foreign policy', in W. Carlsnaes, T. Risse and B. Simmons (eds), *Handbook on International Relations*. London: Sage. pp. 331–49.

Christiansen, T., Jørgensen, K.E. and Wiener, A. (eds) (2001) *The Social Construction of Europe*. London: Sage.

Cohen, A. (1998) *The Symbolic Construction of Community*. London: Routledge.

Coles, J. (2000) *Making Foreign Policy. A Certain Idea of Britain*. London: John Murray.

Cowles, M.G., Caporaso, J.A. and Risse, T. (2000) *Europeanization and Domestic Change*. Cambridge: Cambridge University Press.

Diez, T. and Whitman, R. (2002) 'Analysing European integration: reflecting on the English school', *Journal of Common Market Studies*, 40 (1): 43–67.

Ekengren, M. (1997) 'The Temporality of European Governance', in K.E. Jørgensen (ed.), *Reflective Approaches to European Governance*. Basingstoke: Macmillan.

Ekengren, M. (2002) *The Time of European Governance*. Manchester: Manchester University Press.

European Foreign Policy Bulletin online <http://www.iue.it/EFPB/Welcome.html>

Galtung, J. (1973) *The European Community: A Superpower in the Making*. London: Allen and Unwin.

Ginsberg, R.H. (2001) *The European Union in World Politics: Baptism by Fire*. Lanham, MD: Rowman and Littlefield.

Glarbo, K. (2001) 'Wide-awake diplomacy: reconstructing the common foreign and security policy of the European Union', in T. Christiansen, K.E. Jørgensen and A. Wiener (eds), *The Social Construction of Europe*. London: Sage.

Gnesotto (2000) *Western European Union Institute for Securing Studies*, Newsletter, March.

Gourevitch, P. (1978) 'The second image reversed: the international sources of domestic politics', *International Organization*, 32: 881–912.

Grieco, J.M. (1997) 'Realist international theory and the study of world politics', in M.W. Doyle and G.J. Ikenberry (eds), *New Thinking in International Relations Theory*. Boulder, CO: Westview.

Güssgen, F. (2002) '*Resources for Europe? The Transformation of Foreign Service Organization(s) in France and Germany in the light of a European Diplomatic Capability* (1970–2001). PhD dissertation, European University Institute, Florence.

Haagerup, N.J. and Thune, C. (1983) 'Denmark: a European pragmatist', in C. Hill (ed.), *National Foreign Policies and European Political Cooperation*. London: Allen and Unwin.

Hanf, K. and Soetendorp, B. (eds) (1998) *Adapting to European Integration: Small States and the European Union*. London: Longman.

Hassner, P. (1987) 'The view from Paris', in L. Gordon (ed.), *The Eroding Empire: Western Relations with Eastern Europe*. Washington, DC: Brookings Institution.

Hellmann, G. (1996) 'Goodbye to Bismarck?', 40 (1): 1–39 *Mershon Review of International Studies*.

Hill, C. (ed.) (1996) *The Actors in Europe's Foreign Policy*. London: Routledge.

Hocking, B. and Spence, D. (eds) (2002) *Foreign Ministries: Change and Adaptation*. Basingstoke: Macmillan.

Jakobsen, P.V. (2000) 'Kontaktgruppen i Kosovo: Koncert trods mislyde', *Politica*, 32 (2): 157–71.

Jørgensen, K.E. (1997) 'PoCo: The diplomatic republic of Europe', in K.E. Jørgensen (ed.), *Reflective Approaches to European Governance.* Basingstoke: Macmillan.

Jørgensen, K.E. (1999) 'Possibilities of a "Nordic" influence on the development of the CFSP', in M. Jopp and H. Ojanen (eds), *European Security Integration: Implications for Non-Alignment and Alliances.* Helsinki: ulkopoliittinen instituutti.

Jørgensen, K.E. (2000) 'Blind dating: the English school meets European integration'. Paper presented at the British International Studies Association Conference, Bradford.

Kahler, M. (1992) 'Multilateralism with small and large numbers', *International Organization,* 46 (3): 681–708.

Kaiser, K. (1966) '*L'Europe des Savants.* European integration and the social sciences', *Journal of Common Market Studies,* 41 (1): 36–46.

Katzenstein, P.J. (ed.) (1996) *The Culture of National Security: Norms and Identity in World Politics.* New York, NY: Columbia University Press.

Keohane, R.O. and Nye, J.S. (1977) *Power and Interdependence: World Politics in Transition.* Boston: Little Brown.

Keohane, R.O., Nye J.S. and Hoffmann, S. (eds) (1993) *After the Cold War: International Institutions and State Strategies in Europe, 1989–1991.* Cambridge, MA: Harvard University Press.

Kleistra, Y. and Mayer, I. (2001) 'Stability and flux in foreign affairs: modelling policy and organisation change', *Cooperation and Conflict,* 36 (4): 381–414.

LaPalombara, J. (1989) 'Italian Foreign Policy–Declining Immobility', *Relazioni Internazionali,* Settembre: 95–105.

Little, R. (1999) 'The English school's contribution to international relations', *European Journal of International Relations,* 6: 395–422.

Lose, L.G. (2001) 'Communicative action and diplomacy', in K. Fierke and K.E. Jørgensen (eds), (2001) *Constructing International Relations: The Next Generation.* New York, NY: M.E. Sharpe.

Luttwak, E. (1993) 'Italy's Ancien Regime', *Society,* 31 (1): 70–7.

Manners, I. (2000) 'The study of the foreign policies of European member states'. Paper presented at the European Consortium for Political Research Joint Session of Workshops, Copenhagen, April.

Manners, I. and Whitman, R. (eds) *The Foreign Policies of the European Union Member States.* London: Pinter/Cassell.

Mearsheimer, J. (1995) 'The false promise of international institutions', *International Security,* 19 (3): 5–49.

Moravcsik, A. (1998) *The Choice for Europe: Social Purpose and State Power from Messina to Maastricht.* London: UCL Press.

Müller, H. (2001) 'International relations as communicative action: a critique of utilitarian theories of action', in K. Fierke and K.E. Jørgensen (eds), *Constructing International Relations: The Next Generation.* New York, NY: M.E. Sharpe.

Piening, C. (1997) *Global Europe: the European Union in World Affairs.* Boulder, CO: Lynne Rienner.

Pollack, M. (1999) 'Delegation, agency and agenda setting in the Treaty of Amsterdam', *European Integration online Papers.*

Radaelli, C.M. (2000) 'Whither Europeanization? Concept stretching and substantive change', *European Integration online Papers.*

Risse, T. (2000) 'Let's argue!' *International Organization*, 54 (1): 1–39.

Rittberger, V. and Schimmelfennig, F. (1997) *German Foreign Policy After Unification. On the Applicability of Theoretical Models of Foreign Policy.* Center for German and European Studies Working Paper. Washington, DC: Edmund A. Walsh School of Foreign Service, Georgetown University.

Ruggie, J.G. (1989) 'International structure and international transformation: space, time, and method' in E.-O. Czempiel and J.N. Rosenau (eds), *Global Changes and Theoretical Challenges: Approaches to World Politics for the 1990s.* Lexington, Massachusetts: Lexington Books.

Searle, J.R. (1995) *The Construction of Social Reality.* New York, NY: The Free Press.

Smith, M. (1998) 'Does the flag follow trade?: politicisation and the emergence of a European foreign policy', in J. Peterson and H. Sjursen (eds), *A Common Foreign Policy for Europe?* London and New York: Routledge.

Soetendorp, B. (1996) 'The Netherlands: the weakening pull of Atlanticism', in C. Hill (ed.), *The Actors in Europe's Foreign Policy.* London: Routledge.

Tonra, B. (1997) 'The impact of political cooperation' in K.E. Jørgensen (ed.), *Reflective Approaches to European Governance.* Basingstoke: Macmillan.

Tonra, B. (2001) *The Europeanisation of National Foreign Policy.* Aldershot: Ashgate.

Waltz, K. (1979) *Theory of International Politics.* New York: McGraw-Hill.

Wendt, A. (1994) 'Collective identity formation and the international state', *American Political Science Review'*, 88 (2): 384–96.

Wendt, A. (1995) 'Constructing international politics: a response to Mearsheimer', *International Security*, 20 (1): 71–81.

Wendt, A. (1998) 'Constitution and causation in IR', *Review of International Studies*, 24 (Special Issue): 101–17.

Wendt, A. (1999) *Social Theory of International Relations.* Cambridge: Cambridge University Press.

White, B. (2001) *Understanding European Foreign Policy.* Basingstoke: Palgrave.

Wight, M. (1977) *Systems of States.* Leicester: Leicester University Press.

Part II

Analytical Dimensions of European Foreign Policy

3 Security and Defence

Helene Sjursen[1]

Studies of the integration process in the European Union (EU) increasingly suggest that analyses might benefit from the insights provided by the theory of communicative action developed by Jürgen Habermas (1981). The starting point for such analyses is often a suspicion that European integration cannot be understood exclusively as the result of bargains that reflect the relative power of actors with fixed preferences (Moravscik, 1998). More specifically, it is suggested that so-called rationalist theories of co-operation should take into consideration that processes of communication that are more than mere exchanges of threats and promises may have an impact on collective decision-making in the EU. Such proposals have been presented most systematically in the literature on comitology in the EU, where it is argued that the so-called comitology committees transform governance from intergovernmental bargaining to supranational deliberation (Joerges and Neyer, 1997a, 1997b). However, this perspective is increasingly applied also to broader issues in the European integration process (Risse-Kappen, 1996; Eriksen and Fossum, 2000; Sjursen, 2002; Eriksen, 2003a; Neyer, 2003; Jacobsson and Vifell, 2003; Gehring, 2003) and in some cases also to other international organisations (Lose, 2001; Müller, 2001; Risse, 2000).

In the study of European security and defence, however, the role of communicative processes and the possibility that actors co-ordinate their action through arguments and deliberation is rarely considered. This is not so surprising: security policy has traditionally been considered to be about the use of military force. Thus, one would not expect much room for communicative processes. Nevertheless, in recent years alternative understandings of security in international relations have gained ground – it is increasingly argued and accepted that security is something other than, or something in addition to, military force. Building on the idea that the security concept should be 'enlarged', concepts such as 'comprehensive security', 'human security', 'desecuritisation', 'soft power' and 'soft security' flourish in the study of both European and international security. Against this backdrop it might make sense to talk about deliberation and actors seeking agreement through arguments.

With regard to the EU, the above concepts are among those used both to discuss the EU's relations with third states and to discuss security within the

EU itself. The EU today is at an advanced stage of its unification process. Relations between member states are no longer organised solely in accordance with the set of norms and rules embodied in the Westphalian system of states (Held, 1993). Increasingly, they are linked together in a network of 'domesticated' relations. A growing number of policy fields are co-ordinated at the central level in Brussels. Even though there is no clear centre of authority above the member states, it is evident that the EU represents a radical (peaceful) challenge to our traditional understanding of international relations. Consequently, one should expect that European integration also has affected the conditions under which security policy is made, as well as the *meaning* of security in Europe. It is, amongst other things, in order to capture this that the concepts of comprehensive security, soft security, human security, securitisation, desecuritisation and so forth have been introduced. However, are these concepts satisfactory in order to capture central features of European security?

This chapter suggests that the concept of communicative action might be a useful additional tool. It is common knowledge that the conceptual strategies we use allow us to see some things very clearly, whereas others are, if not excluded, then at least underplayed. Hence, an alternative conceptual strategy might help to highlight those dimensions. The particular dimensions that are 'lost' with existing tools may in the end turn out not to be particularly important in empirical terms. However, the theoretical possibility that they are important must at least be worked out in order for us to investigate this. There are two main reasons why the approach suggested here might be helpful.

First, the concept of communicative action might contribute to establish alternative and more precise micro-foundations to those of the rational choice perspective. Such micro-foundations seem to be lacking in much of the 'widening' literature on security. A growing body of literature argues that state-centric rationalist approaches do not tell the whole story of European security and that 'norms' and 'ideational forces' are important for understanding the European security context (Farrell, 2002; Adler and Barnett, 1998; Buzan et al., 1998; Gärtner and Hyde-Price, 2001). However, this literature rarely specifies the underlying mechanisms that might help us understand why and how norms or ideational forces actually are important.

Second, the concept of communicative action might help us by providing a critical standard that enables us to handle the normative ambiguity in security studies more directly. As Steve Smith has argued, traditional realist approaches to security studies are highly problematic from a normative perspective. This is because an exclusive focus on military security contributes to a legitimisation of such policies, even if this is not the intention (Smith, 2000: 73). The problem, however, is that the 'new' approaches to security do not necessarily fare much better. In particular, the empirical and normative dimensions to several of the new conceptions are not disentangled. Although to some, the enlarged security concept is useful simply because it does a better job in capturing the empirical reality, to others it also implies that an enlarged security concept is better from a normative standpoint. However, the critical standard that allows analysts to make such claims is rarely clarified – we are somehow expected to trust that the analyst actually knows what is right. An explicit critical standard is important in order to assess the validity of such normative claims. Concepts like 'soft power', 'human security' or 'comprehensive security' are no doubt seductive – but do they unequivocally entail the right security policy from a normative perspective?

The first part of this chapter discusses ways in which the concept of communicative action might complement more recent approaches that emphasise the enlarged security concept. Particular attention is paid here to the so-called Copenhagen school because it represents one of the most comprehensive and systematic attempt at providing an alternative analytical framework to state-centric realism. The second part of this chapter highlights some features of security relations in Europe and in Europe's relations with third states that indicate a need for such a theoretical endeavour. It has not been possible in this chapter to 'test' the utility of the concept of communicative action to European security in any systematic way. Rather, the aim of this part of the chapter is to point to some trends that are difficult to understand without these theoretical tools.

Analysing Security

According to Buzan et al.'s (1998) new framework for security studies, two views of security are available in the literature: the 'old' military and state-centred view and the 'new' view that questions the primacy of the military and the state in conceptualisations of security. A central point for them, in line with the 'new' view, is to indicate how we should conceptualise threats and vulnerabilities as they arise in numerous areas, both military and non-military. They suggest that security must be studied as a discourse in which certain issues are 'securitised' (in other words, become security issues) or 'desecuritised'. They define security as '… the move that takes politics beyond the established rules of the game and frames the issue either as a special kind of politics or above politics. Securitization can thus be seen as a more extreme version of politization. In theory, any public issue can be located on the spectrum ranging from nonpoliticized … through politicized … to securitized (meaning the issue is presented as an existential threat requiring emergency measures and justifying actions outside the bounds of political procedure)' (Buzan et al., 1998: 23–4).

They suggest a multisectoral approach to the study of security. Five sectors are identified: the military sector, the environmental sector, the economic sector, the societal sector and the political sector. Each of these may be 'securitised', yet they are likely to display distinctive patterns of interaction in this process. In each sector, the referent object of security is also different. Whereas in the military and political sectors, existential threats are usually defined in terms of the state, or its constituting principle (sovereignty), in the societal sector, for example, the referent object is identity, or 'more specifically, it is about the sustainability, within acceptable conditions for evolution, of traditional patterns of language, culture, association, and religious and national identity and custom' (Wæver et al., 1993: 23). In this case, clearly it is no longer only the security of states that is in focus but also the security of *particular* societies with *particular* life forms. Societal insecurity is thus considered to exist when 'communities of whatever kind define a development or potentiality as a threat to their survival as a community' (Buzan et al., 1998: 119).

In terms of re-conceptualising security, this approach is useful. This is so in particular because it not only sets out to 'widen' the security agenda, but also highlights that the distinction between what is inside the (domestic) state territory and what is outside it (in the international sphere) is not always vitally important if we want to understand security policy. The study of security is relieved of the ties that by definition bind it to the state as a referent object of security as well as to state sovereignty as the value to be protected. It is possible with this framework to show that the referent object is re-articulated to focus on other actors and other values. The relevance of such an approach is underlined in particular with respect to European security in the post-Cold War period and has led to several interesting studies of security and the relationship between security and identity in the European integration process (Wæver, 1996; 1998). As Buzan and Wæver argue, European security '… is difficult to grasp if seen simply as a constellation of nation states. Much more of the dynamics can be brought out by a constellation made up of at least three kinds of (non-like) units: states, nations and the EU. Here, societal identity can become a referent object for security action' (1997: 249).

This concept of 'societal security' has provoked debate (McSweeney, 1996, 1998; Buzan and Wæver, 1997). More important here, however: the potential existence of and respect for rules and norms that define the purpose and legitimacy of security policy, is left unexplored and unexplained in the overall framework (Buzan et al., 1998). The concepts of securitisation and desecuritisation and the emphasis on studying security as a discourse allow us to escape state-centric realism, but this framework is at the same time unable to account for a possible change in normative standards for conflict resolution and the strengthening of legally binding agreements. In other words, the possibility that security policy is, or can be, transformed into an instrument to uphold a global or regional legal order, rather than being an instrument with which the interest of the most powerful is protected, is not investigated. In order to bring such a possibility back into the analysis, we need a theory that can capture the existence and binding character of rules, norms and principles. We need a theory that can identify the mechanisms that lead to an accumulation of norms as well as help us understand why these norms are accepted and upheld. Hence, we need a theory that allows us to capture actors' potential normative competence. In the 'Copenhagen approach' there seems to be few alternatives between actors that are instrumentally rational or that are emotional in the sense that they react instinctively on the basis of a particular identity. Hence, security policy will either be governed by the most powerful, or it will be taken into the hands of particular groups in response to perceived threats to their survival.

Part of the reason might be that although the Copenhagen school challenges much of the conventional wisdom in 'security studies'; it does at the same time maintain core realist assumptions and starts from a 'conflict' model of politics (Wæver, 2000). Although they emphasise the importance of the so-called 'linguistic turn' in philosophy and social theory and explicitly start from the insight that intersubjective meaning is constituted by language, their description of the role of language seems too restricted. Discourses seem (implicitly) to be considered only as instruments of power: a particular representation of reality is produced through discourse, which allows for securitisation. The 'linguistic turn' needs to be taken a step further. We need a theory that shows that there is an alternative to the conception of discourse as power. Even though the social world is intrinsically linked to language (Kratochwil, 1989: 6), and language therefore provides us with a point of departure for inquiry into security policy, the power of arguments can be understood quite differently from the way it is understood by the Copenhagen school. In fact, arguments can be challenged; hence they are highly unreliable as instruments of power in democratic societies. If we accept this point, we must consider that attempts at securitising an issue will not succeed, in the sense that they will not be considered legitimate, unless they can be backed by convincing arguments as well as following the proper legal procedures. Although agents can be manipulated through the strategic use of arguments, this is not the only possible scenario in democratic societies. There are mechanisms that permit 'illegitimate' attempts at securitisation to be exposed.

A second weakness with this approach is linked to the ambiguity about whether or not there is a normative claim involved in it. Some claims seem to indicate that there are some implicit assumptions of what security policy ought to be about. Hence, the Copenhagen school argues, with reference to the treatment of Kurds in Turkey, 'If one wants to take this minority seriously and say societal security is about *their* security, one has to open up to a more complex landscape of multiple referent points for security' (Buzan and Wæver, 1997: 248). In a different context, Wæver poses the question:

> Should developments be securitised (and if so, in what terms)? Often our reply will be to aim for de-securitisation and then politics meet metapolitics; but occasionally the underlying pessimism regarding the prospects for orderliness and compatibility among human aspirations will point to scenarios sufficiently worrisome that responsibility will entail securitisation in order to block the worst. (Wæver, 2000: 285)

For a similar argument for desecuritisation, see Neumann and Ulriksen, 1995. However, in order to make such claims it would be useful to have categories for distinguishing 'real' threats and risks that legitimately call for action from those that are simply 'constructed' for other purposes. The above arguments would suggest that some processes of 'securitisation' are considered more legitimate than others. However, the normative standards used for such considerations are not made explicit.

Communicative rationality

In order to imagine the possibility that security policy can be transformed into an instrument to uphold a global legal order rather than merely be an instrument that is manipulated at the will of the most powerful, a conception of actors as communicatively competent is helpful (Eriksen and Weigård, 2003). The concept of communicative action '… operates with dialogical actors who co-ordinate their plans through argumentation aimed at reaching mutual agreements' (Eriksen and Weigård, 1997: 221). Such a model of politics relies on a conception of rationality where actors are seen as rational when they are able to justify and explain their actions, and not only when they seek to maximise their own interests. It follows from this that they are capable of assessing the validity of different arguments. These arguments could refer to material gain, but they could also be formulated with reference to an actor's sense of identity or understanding of the 'good life'. Actors could also justify and explain their actions with reference to a sense of what is right or fair, in other words, without reference to a particular identity, but with regard to what is just when everybody's interest and values are taken into consideration. Thus, there is an alternative both to the rational-instrumentalist and the 'emotional' actor.

Based on this conception of actors as communicatively competent, it is possible to understand how norms can be established and upheld. In this way, it might be possible to theorise about a change away from the Westphalian logic in European security policy. From this perspective, norms are not only practical arrangements, held together through '… mutual agreement about their advantageousness or through the use of coercive power' (Eriksen and Weigård, 1997: 224–5). Nor are they only common understandings of the 'good life'. It is not necessarily the thickness of the social environment that would explain the emergence of dependable expectations of peace and commitment to common norms. Rather, social norms and institutions are also upheld because actors consider them valid. Without actors that have the competence to follow and assess the validity of norms, they will not be produced in the first place. Neither will they be produced and reproduced in concrete situations.

It is possible that an accurate empirical description of European security is dependent upon a certain idea of security being imposed from above. It is also possible that the changed conceptions of security entail abuses of power that are unacceptable. In other words, the perspective outlined above may very well not fit with the empirical landscape. However, the possibility of providing a different account has at least to be worked out theoretically. And to discard the potential utility of an alternative account by simply arguing that 'To assume that general "opening" and democratisation lead to people resisting the bad and choosing the good would be a surprising Enlightenment optimistic audacity' (Wæver, 2000: 284) would only reveal or reflect a particular world view. It is true that we need something more than the goodwill of actors to ensure fairness and stability. One important part of this 'more' is the strengthening of rights through legal procedures, which ensures that justice does not depend on altruism. The theory of communicative rationality may provide the micro-foundations that allow us to understand how such a different version or interpretation of European security might be possible. The next question, then, is to investigate to what extent this interpretation fits with political realities in Europe. While it is not possible here to test this systematically, the aim of the next section of this chapter is to highlight some trends in European security that might indicate a need for this kind of theoretical framework.

Changes to European Security

Three main trends may be identified. First, we have witnessed a significant change in the understanding of what constitute central threats to European security. After the end of the Cold War there has been a move away from the almost exclusive focus on military threats from territorial states and towards a focus on a number of highly diverse issues. These range from social and economic inequalities to terrorism, the spread of weapons of mass destruction, ethnic conflict, international crime or even migration. Such issues are now often defined as security issues of equal importance to military issues.

The changes to the understanding of what constitute central threats to security are not exclusive to Europe. They represent a general trend in the international system, although the emphasis on the different types of threat varies. With regard to Europe, this changed understanding of what constitute central threats is well illustrated by the following quote from a speech by Danish foreign minister Niels Helveg Pedersen: '... preoccupation with the so-called soft security issues are increasingly the centre of attention: political and economic instability, ethnic conflict, minority problems, border conflicts, refugees, transitional environmental issues and organised crime' (Helveg Pedersen, 1996). The Petersberg declaration (1992) of the West European Union (WEU), later incorporated in the EU's definition of its responsibilities in security and defence, is a further example of how the 'new' security agenda is reflected in the formulation of security policy in Europe. The declaration points to 'soft security' as an important security task in addition to military matters. 'Soft security' is defined in terms of social and economic inequality, environmental risks and crime. These are identified as the 'new' security issues that the EU and its member states face in the post-Cold War world (WEU, 1992).

Assertions of change in the European security agenda are echoed in the academic literature by authors coming from very different theoretical perspectives. Whalen argues that 'While Europe today faces less of a direct threat to its military security than at any time in its history, a diffuse multitude of risks has taken its place' (1999: 257). According to Gärtner and Hyde-Price, 'Human rights, environmental degradation, political stability and democracy, social issues, cultural and religious identity, and immigration are issues that are becoming ever more important for security and conflict prevention' (2001: 4). And Buzan et al. argue that 'Our solution comes down on the side of the wideners in terms of keeping the security agenda open to many different types of threats. We argue against the view that the core of security studies is war and force ...' (1998: 4).

The second trend that indicates a need for an additional theoretical approach is related to the conception of how to handle security threats and challenges. Here there has been a move away from military alliances and the search for balances of military force and towards institutionalisation and legally-binding agreements. European security is increasingly sought through multilateral institutions. We can observe an increasing institutionalisation of relations between European states, and a European order is no longer guaranteed (if it ever was) by a balance of power between military forces. Increasingly, European states are bound together by legal agreements that constrain and condition policy choices. This is also the case across the old East–West dividing line in Europe. We see this, for example, in the neutrals' – Sweden, Austria and Finland – membership in the EU (including the second pillar) since 1995 and later the eastward enlargements of both NATO and the EU. The establishment of NATO's Partnership For Peace, which includes almost all of the Central and East European states as well as the former republics of the Soviet Union, and the NATO partnership with Russia, can also be mentioned in this context.

Inside the EU this trend is even stronger, as member states have long since moved from a balance of power to 'co-operative security' with regard to problems arising. The EU has successfully domesticated security within the Union in the sense that it is extremely unlikely that member states would use military force to resolve disputes with fellow members. What characterises the European situation is the high degree of institutionalisation at the supranational level. Here states have moved further than most states elsewhere in terms of establishing international institutions that are based on a commitment to common rules and norms. What is more, within its field of competence, community law is supreme.

Arguably, the EU is exporting this approach to the rest of Europe through enlargement. This at least is the image that the EU itself seeks to project. Hence Javier Solana, High Representative for the EU's Common Foreign and Security Policy (CFSP), argues that 'European integration has worked as a strong catalyst for political stability and economic prosperity in Western Europe. We are now extending the benign effect of integration to the rest of the continent. ... An enlarged Union means strengthening the stability of the continent' (Solana, 2001). We will return to this in the next section of the chapter.

As an implication of the first two trends, a third trend would be a change in the standards for conflict resolution. By this is meant that the position of the individual as a right holder within international law has been strengthened, and there is no longer an exclusive focus on the sovereign state. Traditionally, international law was not seen as an instrument that should protect individuals from abuses of power, but as an instrument that would guarantee the sovereign control of the state over a specific territory.

As a result, *inter alia*, of the EU's Charter of Fundamental Rights and the European Convention on Human Rights, there are now agents outside the nation state that can sanction illegitimate abuses of power and to whom citizens can appeal if national decisions seem unacceptable (Menéndez, 2002). Hence human rights are not merely moral categories, but are also becoming positive legal rights with the capacity to be reinforced in Europe. European states today are expected to respect human rights and basic civil and political rights (Zürn, 2000). In other words, when we ask 'security for whom', the answer is no longer self-evidently the state. What is developing in Europe is something 'more' or qualitatively different from a situation of interdependence as described in much of the literature on international relations. Increasingly, it is also argued that this implies that the EU will be, and is, faithful to these norms in its external action (Manners, 2002; Rosencrance, 1998).

Manipulating the security agenda?

It might be argued that some of these trends, particularly the first, are not really new. Social and economic inequalities were obviously a problem also during the Cold War. Several states experienced acts of terrorism before 1989 and ethnic conflict is not a creation of the post-Cold War world. Thus, in one sense, the change with regard to the so-called 'new' security issues is only a change in emphasis, as these issues have emerged on top of the agenda of security politics. Most importantly, the ideas about a new security context could simply be the result of efforts to 'redefine the policy agendas of nation states' (Baldwin, 1997: 5) and the outcome of a struggle between different actors where the most powerful have successfully defined the policy agenda in accordance with their own interests. The increased focus of the US on the threat of terrorism, for example, might fall in this category. Such an interpretation would be supported by Amnesty International's annual report of 2002 that concludes that with respect to the security of the individual citizen, states still pose more important threats than terrorists. However, the resistance to the exclusive focus on terrorism as a security threat, as well as to the US's view on how to handle such a threat, suggest that there are also other forces and processes at play in the international system.

Thus, as already noted, the argument here is that if we do not work out an alternative theoretical approach we have few ways of distinguishing between different kinds of political processes. This means that we risk losing important dimensions of the current transformations in European security.

We must at least consider the possibility that some of these trends, consciously or unconsciously, reflect broader challenges to traditional perspectives on security and international relations. In fact, many scholars argue that if we look closer at Europe's security relations with the rest of the world, this can be confirmed.

Civilian Power Europe?

A growing literature makes a strong case that the EU not only has an impact on the international system, but that it has a *particular* impact due to the nature of the EU as an organisation (Rosencrance, 1998; Manners, 2002; Aggestam, 2000). An explicit example of this argument is found in Ian Manners' (2002) study of the EU's international pursuit of the abolition of the death penalty. Manners argues that the EU represents a normative power in world politics. He suggests that the EU's work for the abolition of the death penalty cannot be understood on the basis of material incentives and instrumental bargaining because there are few rewards for promoting this issue in terms of domestic political support and because this policy creates difficulties for the EU in its relations with close allies such as the US. He thus concludes that the EU can be conceptualised as a changer of norms in the international system. Rosencrance (1998: 22) also defines the EU's attainment in international politics as 'normative rather than empirical'. Furthermore, he observes that it is paradoxical that with their history as imperial powers that ruled the world with the help of physical force, the European states now set normative standards for the world.

These conceptions of the EU as representing something different from states in the international system seem to some extent to be reflected in the way member states describe the EU. In France, for example, there is '... an emphasis on Europe as an ethical and responsible power' (Aggestam, 2000). Thus, there are some signs that suggest the emphasis on the need to maximise interests, if not abandoned altogether, seems to have at least been modified by an emphasis on universal principles and the rights of individuals under a collective security regime. This is further illustrated by the following quote from Jacques Chirac: 'So a Europe which is more ethical, which places at the heart of everything it does respect for a number of principles which, in the case of France, underpins a republican code of ethics, and, as far as the whole of Europe is concerned, constitute a shared code of ethics' (Aggestam, 2000: 75).

This literature follows the tradition of defining Europe as a 'civilian power'.[2] First launched by François Duchêne in 1972, the idea of civilian power Europe consists of arguing that the EU (then EC) is a special international actor whose strength lies in its ability to promote and encourage stability through economic and political means. Hence, this is an image of the EU that would be contrary both to the realist understanding and to the account that might be provided by the Copenhagen school. However, this literature has been less preoccupied with working out theoretically how this is possible. The importance of such an endeavour becomes particularly evident if one considers the argument that it is only because the EU does not have the means to be anything else that it chooses to be a civilian power (Kagan, 2003). From a realist perspective, this is the only possible interpretation. However, with the concept of communicative action as a starting point it might be possible to work out theoretically and investigate empirically whether an alternative understanding of the EU's role as normative power is plausible. It is possible that the EU acts this way because it thinks it ought to do so. Furthermore, this perspective might help us to discover how it is possible that instruments other than military power, such as arguments and public deliberation, can also make a difference to international security. Abstaining from the use of military power, in other words, does not necessarily have to be a sign of weakness, as Kagan (2003) seems to assume.

Limitations to civilian power Europe

At the same time, there are serious limitations to the ability of the EU to act as a 'normative power'. These limitations do not only have to do with the lack of coherence in the CFSP or with the lack of 'hard' instruments to back up policy declarations. The limitations are also linked to the far more limited role of international law in the international system outside the EU. This perspective emphasises the need for rights to be legally binding in order to ensure that justice does not depend on altruism. Unless the principles of human rights become positive legal rights that can be enforced, it is difficult to avoid the argument that the most powerful only use a 'moral' foreign policy for their own interest and that when they don't, they are still suspected of doing so (Eriksen, 2003b; Sjursen, 2003). In turn this leads to arbitrariness, as human rights are not universal principles applied equally to all. Moreover, as Karen Smith shows, the EU's commitment to 'civilian' principles, and in particular to human rights, is inconsistent (Smith, 2001).

In order to overcome this problem, all international relations would have to be subordinated to a common judicial order that would transform the parameters of power politics. As Habermas puts it:

> Things look different when human rights not only come into play as a moral orientation for one's own political activity, but as rights which have to be implemented in a legal sense. Human rights possess the structural attributes of subjective rights which, irrespective of their purely moral content, by nature are dependent on attaining positive validity within a system of compulsory law. (1999: 270)

With the strengthening of the United Nations (UN), the principles of human rights have gained more force in international politics. Thus one might see a gradual change in the content of norms at the international level away from an exclusive emphasis on state sovereignty and a strengthening of the principles of human rights. However, the international system is still one in which legal procedures for protecting human rights are weak and where their enforcement is therefore dependent on the willpower of the great powers.

This is where the contrast between European security and international security becomes evident. In Europe, there are now several legal sources that create a link between the EU and the promotion of human rights and democracy. Some sources date back a long way, such as the affirmation by the European Assembly in 1961 that respect for fundamental rights and democratic principles was a condition for membership in the EC, although the founding treaties of the EU made little reference to human rights. And, as Menéndez argues elsewhere in this volume, the legal competence of the Union to promote human rights has been strengthened as a result of the proclamation of the Charter of Fundamental Rights. Furthermore, the charter is likely to become a central benchmark in assessing compliance with fundamental rights by third countries. Such developments in the Treaties have led EU foreign affairs commissioner Chris Patten to state that 'we have a legal framework for human rights in our external policy' (Patten, 2000). Nevertheless, as long as such rights are not legally binding in the international system at large, there is an obvious risk of arbitrariness.

Hence, the concept of communicative rationality might be helpful in providing analytical building blocks that allow us to capture a larger part of the empirical landscape and at the same time highlighting the limitations to a security policy that relies on moral principles in a context where these are not enshrined in legal procedures that are equally binding for all. Actors' strategic or communicative behaviour depends to a large extent on the specific context in which they find themselves. Within the EU, the incentives to act communicatively are stronger than in the international system.

Conclusion

This chapter has sought to make a contribution to the discussion about how to study European security and defence. It has highlighted the concept of communicative rationality and deliberation as supplementary analytical tools not only to the realist or rational choice approaches, but most importantly also to the 'widening' literature on security. These additional analytical tools should be helpful by providing a more systematic theoretical account of how it is possible that normative considerations and the respect for rules and regulations also play a part in European – and international – security. Furthermore, they should help by providing an explicit critical standard for evaluating current security and defence policies. The latter is particularly important in a context where arguments about national security and the threat of terrorism dominate the agenda of world politics and thus risk undermining the concerns about human rights and respect for international law.

It has not been possible in this chapter systematically to investigate the utility of this approach. And it is possible that when this is done, the realist account will appear the most convincing. Yet it is difficult to check if this is so without having the alternative analytical categories that would allow us to hypothesise and 'test' a different scenario. Then again, a systematic investigation might reveal traces or elements in European security that confirm the need for an additional theoretical framework. Finding and making sense of such traces would be important and valuable because this would provide us with a more nuanced understanding of European security than we would otherwise have.

These analytical tools, in turn, might also allow us to look at the history of European security through different lenses. The idea that security and defence issues should be dealt with through common institutions was certainly present before the end of the Cold War and found expression in concepts such as 'common security' and processes such as the Conference for Security and Co-operation in Europe (now OSCE). Furthermore, the emphasis, then, on the link between human rights and security is similar to arguments presented in post-Cold War Europe. Hence, the analytical tools highlighted in this chapter might also allow us to investigate more systematically such historical developments in European international relations.

Notes

1 This chapter is a contribution to the CIDEL project co-ordinated by ARENA and financed by the Fifth Framework Programme of the European Commission. It was also supported by a grant from the Norweigiana Ministry of Defence. Many thanks to Erik Oddvar Eriksen, John Erik Fossum, Agustín Menéndez, Morten Kelstrup and Brian White for comments on previous drafts of this chapter.
2 For the original debate, see Duchêne (1972) and Bull (1982).

References

Adler, E. and Barnett, M. (eds) (1998) *Security Communities*. Cambridge: Cambridge University Press.

Aggestam, L. (2000) 'Europe puissance: French influence and European independence', in H. Sjursen (ed.), *Redefining Security? The Role of the European Union in European Security Structures*. ARENA Report, 7: 67–82.

Amnesty International. Report 2002. Available on http://web.amnesty.org/web/ar2002.nsf/home/home?/OpenDocument.

Baldwin, D.A. (1997) 'The concept of security', *Rewiew of International Studies*, 23 (1): 5–26.

Bull, H. (1982) 'Civilian power Europe: a contradiction in terms?', *Journal of Common Market Studies*, 21 (2): 149–64.

Buzan, B. and Wæver, O. (1997) 'Slippery? contradictory? sociologically untenable? The Copenhagen school replies', *Review of International Studies*, 23 (2): 241–50.

Buzan, B., Wæver, O. and de Wilde, J. (1998) *Security: A New Framework of Analysis.* Boulder, CO: Lynne Rienner.

Duchêne, F. (1972) 'Europe's role in world peace', in R. Mayne (ed.), *Europe Tomorrow: Sixteen Europeans Look Ahead.* London: Fontana. pp. 32–47.

Eriksen, E.O. (2003a) 'Integration and the quest for consensus. On the microfoundation of supranationalism', in *European Governance, Deliberation and the Quest of Democratisation.* Oslo: ARENA – EUI Report, 02/03: 159–225.

Eriksen, E.O. (2003b) 'Why a Constitutional Bill of Rights?' in E.O. Eriksen, J.E. Fossum and A. Menéndez (eds), *The Chartering of Europe. The European Charter of Fundamental Rights and its Constitutional Implications.* Baden-Baden, Nomos: 48–70.

Eriksen, E.O. and Fossum, J.E. (eds) (2000) *Democracy in the European Union: Integration Through Deliberation?* London: Routledge.

Eriksen, E.O. and Weigård, J. (1997) 'Conceptualising politics: strategic or communicative action?', *Scandinavian Political Studies*, 20 (3): 219–41.

Eriksen, E.O. and Weigård, J. (2003) *Understanding Habermas. Communicative Action and Deliberate Democracy.* London and New York: Continuum.

Farrell, T. (2002) 'Constructivist security studies: portrait of a research program', *International Studies Review*, 4 (1): 49–72.

Gehring, T. (2003) 'Communicative Rationality in European Governance? Interests and Communicative Action in Functionally Differentiated Single Market Regulation', in *European Governance, Deliberation and the Quest of Democratisation.* Oslo: ARENA – EUI Report, 02/03: 57–140.

Gärtner, H. and Hyde-Price, A. (2001) 'Introduction', in H. Gärtner, A. Hyde-Price and E. Reiter (eds), *Europe's New Security Challenges.* London: Lynne Rienner pp. 1–23.

Habermas, J. (1981) *Theorie des kommunikativen Handelns.* Frankfurt am Main: Surhkamp.

Habermas, J. (1999) 'Bestiality and humanity: a war on the border between legality and morality', *Constellations*, 6 (3): 263–73.

Held, D. (1993) 'Democracy: from city-states to a cosmopolitan order?', in D. Held (ed.), *Prospects for Democracy: North, South, East, West.* Oxford: Polity.

Helveg Pedersen, N. (1996) 'Danmark, NATO og Østersjøen', *Det sikkerhetspolitiske bibliotek.* Nr. 10. Oslo: Den Norske Atlanterhavskomite.

Jacobsson, K. and Vifell, Å. (2003) 'Integration by Deliberation? On the Role of Committees in the Open Method of Coordination', in *European Governance, Deliberation and the Quest of Democratisation.* Oslo: ARENA – EUI Report, 02/03: 411–50.

Joerges, C. and Neyer, J. (1997a) 'From intergovernmental bargaining to deliberative political processes. The constitutionalisation of comitology', *European Law Journal*, 3 (3): 273–99.

Joerges, C. and Neyer, J. (1997b) 'Transforming strategic interaction into deliberative problem-solving: European comitology in the foodstuff sector', *Journal of European Public Policy*, 4 (4): 609–25.

Kagan, R. (2003) *Paradise and Power: America and Europe in the New World Order.* London: Atlantic.

Kratochwil, F.V. (1989) *Rules, Norms and Decisions: On the Conditions of Practical and Legal Reasoning in International Relations and Domestic Affairs.* Cambridge: Cambridge University Press.

Lose, L. (2001) 'Communicative action and the world of diplomacy', in K. Fierke and K.E. Jørgensen (eds), *Constructing International Relations*. New York, NY: Sharpe. pp. 179–200.

Manners, I. (2002) 'Normative power Europe: a contradiction in terms?', *Journal of Common Market Studies*, 40 (2): 235–58.

McSweeney, B. (1996) 'Identity and security: Buzan and the Copenhagen school', *Review of International Studies*, 22 (1): 81–93.

McSweeney, B. (1998) 'Durkheim and the Copenhagen school: a response to Buzan and Wæver', *Review of International Studies*, 24 (1): 137–40.

Menéndez, A. (2002) 'Chartering Europe', *Journal of Common Market Studies*, 40 (3): 471–90.

Moravscik, A. (1998) *The Choice for Europe: Social Purpose and State Power from Messina to Maastricht*. London: UCL.

Müller, H. (2001) 'International relations as communicative action', in K. Fierke and K.E. Jørgensen (eds), *Constructing International Relations*. New York, NY: Sharpe. pp. 160–78.

Neumann, I. and Ulriksen, S. (1995) 'Norsk forsvars og sikkerhetspolitikk', in T. Knutsen, G.M. Sørbø and S. Gjerdåker (eds), *Norges Utenrikspolitikk*, Oslo: Cappelen. pp. 80–105.

Neyer, J. (2003) 'Discourse and Order in the EU. A Deliberative Approach to Multi-Level Governance', in *European Governance, Deliberation and the Quest of Democratisation*. Oslo: ARENA – EUI Report, 02/03: 235–65.

Patten, C. (2000) 'Human rights: towards greater complementarity within and between European regional organisations'. Speech by The Rt. Hon. Chris Patten, Council of Europe Conference on 'The Protection of Human Rights in the 21st Century', 3 March, Dublin. Available on http://europa.eu.int/comm/external_relations/news/patten/hr_dublin_03_march2000.htm

Risse, T. (2000) '"Let's argue!": communicative action in world politics', *International Organization*, 54 (1): 1–39.

Risse-Kappen, T. (1996) 'Exploring the nature of the beast: International Relations theory and comparative policy analysis meet the European Union', *Journal of Common Market Studies*, 34 (1): 53–79.

Rosencrance, R. (1998) 'The European Union: a new type of international actor', in J. Zielonka (ed.), *Paradoxes of European Foreign Policy*. The Hague: Kluwer Law International. pp. 15–23.

Sjursen, H. (2002) 'Why expand? The question of legitimacy and justification in the EU's enlargement policy', *Journal of Common Market Studies*, 40 (3): 491–513.

Sjursen, H. (2003) *The United States, Western Europe and the Polish Crisis*. Basingstoke: Palgrave.

Smith, K.E. (2001) 'The EU, human rights and relations with third countries: "foreign policy" with an ethical dimension?', in K.E. Smith and M. Light (eds), *Ethics and Foreign Policy*. Cambridge: Cambridge University Press. pp. 185–203.

Smith, S. (2000) 'The increasing insecurity of security studies: conceptualising security in the last twenty years', in S. Croft and T. Terriff (eds), *Critical Reflections on Security and Change*. Portland: Frank Cass.

Solana J. (2001) 'Some thoughts about the European Union's new approach towards Central and Eastern Europe'. Address at the conference of the

German–Poland Institute and the Germany and Northern Europa Institute, 26 June, Brussels.

West European Union (1992) *Petersberg Declaration*. Council of Ministers.

Whalen, E. (1999) 'The military aspects of European security', in C.C. Hodge (ed.), *Redefining European Security*. London and New York: Garland Publishing. pp. 255–71.

Wæver, O. (1996) 'European Security Identities', *Journal of Common Market Studies*, 34 (1): 103–32.

Wæver, O. (1998) 'Insecurity, security, and asecurity in the West European non-war community', in E. Adler and M. Barnett (eds), *Security Communities*. Cambridge: Cambridge University Press. pp. 69–118.

Wæver, O. (2000) 'The EU as a security actor: reflections from a pessimistic constructivist on post-sovereign security orders', in M. Kelstrup and M.C. Williams (eds), *International Relations Theory and the Politics of European Integration: Power, Security and Community*. London: Routledge. pp. 250–94.

Wæver, O., Buzan, B., Kelstrup, M. and Lemaitre, P. (1993) *Identity, Migration and the New Security Agenda in Europe*. New York, NY: St. Martin's.

Zürn, M. (2000) 'Democratic governance beyond the nation-state: the EU and other international institutions', *European Journal of International Relations*, 6 (2): 183–221.

4 Foreign Economic Policy

Michael Smith

The transformation of Europe since the late 1980s is often – and understandably – defined in terms of security and of 'high politics', reflecting the assumption that what matters in processes of international change are shifts in the balance of politico-military power, the alignments and realignments that may occur as the result of such shifts, and the new constellation of political and military forces that emerges (Laffan et al., 2000: Ch. 3). In the same way, the reconstruction of foreign policies in the 'new Europe' can be seen as a set of responses to the shifting military-political substructure, reflecting the seismic changes in the foundations of national and international action (Smith, 1994; Keohane and Hoffmann, 1993).

The argument in this chapter is couched in rather different terms, starting from the assumption that foreign economic policy – and thus the impact of restructuring in the European and global political economies – is, and ought to be, a central focus of analysis. It takes the position that a key conceptual problem with foreign economic (and much of foreign) policy is its problematic relationship to statehood, a relationship that is given increased significance in the 'new Europe' by the growth and consolidation of the European Union (EU) and by the simultaneous spread of a range of transnational networks and institutional contexts. By unpicking this relationship, we can hope to understand major elements in the dynamics of the 'new Europe' which are left aside by more political-military analysis. The chapter goes on to argue that the empirical implications of these analytical moves are significant not only to our understanding of the 'new Europe', but also to the framing of policy in the post-Cold War era. In a way, this chapter thus follows directly (but at a distance) some of the arguments raised by other analysts in the early 1990s (Tooze, 1994; Junne, 1994), but with the advantage of another 10 years' experience of the post-Cold War order.

The chapter thus represents a sketch of a number of dimensions and axes that are significant to the analysis of foreign economic policy (FEP) in post-Cold War Europe. It is not designed to put forward a definitive argument, but rather to identify the scope and implications of the forces affecting FEP and some of the empirical implications of the broadly changing picture. In doing this, it draws upon a range of approaches to FEP; its analytical perspective is eclectic, but with a leaning towards the form of 'reflective institutionalism' that has been developed by a number of analysts (Keohane,

1989; Smith, 1996). 'Taking institutions seriously' and relating them to the performance of significant international roles and functions generates a series of central insights and subsequent questions for research in the context of the 'new Europe'.

   This chapter proceeds as follows. First, it discusses some of the key axes of change and transformation affecting post-Cold War Europe and the ways in which these might feed into the formation of foreign economic policies. In particular, it explores the argument that in terms of foreign economic policy there is no one 'Europe'; instead, there are at least three 'Europes' expressing different arrays of forces and flows in the European political economy. Second, it discusses the idea of FEP, and adopts the view that it can be identified with the performance of state economic functions in the external domain. These functions are wide-ranging, but the concept of state economic functions crucially makes no assumption about the political and institutional structures through which the functions are pursued. The functions, when combined with the forces affecting the new Europe, give a guide to the possibilities for pursuit of different FEP goals, which can be explored in terms of the classical distinction between 'possession' and 'milieu' goals. Third, the chapter investigates two more concrete manifestations of the problems identified at the conceptual level – manifestations which are central to the overall theme of this volume. It explores the distinction between 'European FEP' and the 'Europeanisation of FEP', and illustrates the ways in which these two aspects can create linkages, tensions and problems of co-ordination. It then goes on, finally, to explore some policy implications of the processes explored by looking at three domains of FEP – institutionalisation and institutional change, negotiation, and the competition/coercion/intervention nexus – and draws some more general conclusions for the study of FEP.

Changing Europe

This part of the chapter aims to identify key axes of change in Europe that have shaped the context for pursuit of FEP during the 21st century, and to relate them to the types of 'new Europes' that have emerged during the past decade. Both awareness of the pervasive nature of change and sensitivity to the fluctuating significance of changes are key to the investigation of foreign policies in general. Where change is radical and at least partly transformatory, this imposes important pressures on the foreign (economic) policy makers, challenging their assumptions and practices at the same time as it creates opportunities for new initiatives. This can be associated with important changes and challenges to the nature of statehood, and thus to one of the key building blocks of foreign policy in general (Smith, 1994).

Axes of change in post-Cold War Europe

When this general perspective is linked to the nature of change in post-Cold War Europe, the key axes seem to be the following. First, the end of the Cold

War was a political-economic event as well as a political-security event, which has created a wide range of new challenges and opportunities for policy makers (Laffan et al., 2000: Ch. 4). At the same time, there has taken place the simultaneous intensification of both globalisation and regionalisation, which has presented FEP makers (whoever they may be) with a further bewildering array of pressures and opportunities, relating to 'territory' and authority, to production and exchange, to security and identity, to institutions and policy instruments, and to the identification of costs and benefits, of 'winners' and 'losers'. In this context, a third factor is significant: the widening and deepening of the European integration project, which can be seen as a subset both of change in Europe and of the tension between regionalisation and globalisation, but which also clearly has a dynamic of its own (Wallace, 2000).

Three new Europes

What kind of Europe has emerged from this welter of coexisting and often contending forces? I have argued elsewhere that it is possible to identify three types of 'Europe', which constitute a set of linked environments or arenas for negotiation and for the formation of policy (Smith, M., 2000). First, there is a Europe of 'boundaries', in which a variety of geopolitical, transactional, institutional and cultural forces create a world of separated spaces, framing inclusions or exclusions. The resulting negotiations are focused on inclusions and exclusions, across boundaries. Competitive bargaining and the creation or maintenance of hierarchies are typical negotiation modes and outcomes. Second, there is a Europe of 'layers', in which political/economic spaces are defined in terms of their scope and scale, and in which issues of competence and linkage are salient. The resulting negotiations are centred on the balance and linkages between layers, and on coalition-building, 'audience management' and adjustment of preferences between a range of agents (primarily governmental authorities operating at different levels in the multi-layered environment). Third, there is a Europe of 'networks', in which the key focus is on spaces of flows, connections and communications, and in which a variety of economic and political agents (both 'public' and 'private') meet on relatively unstructured terms. The resulting negotiations are centred on problem recognition and problem solving, on the formation of understandings and norms and on the maintenance and extension of the networks themselves.

The combination of the forces identified above with these three 'worlds' in the developing European milieu produces a policy-making and negotiation environment in which a variety of agents operates in a variety of modes, with uncertain and interdependent outcomes. In terms of the argument in this chapter, it is important to recognise that this variety of parallel 'worlds' is likely to produce characteristic modes of FEP activity. As can be seen from Figure 4.1, these modes of policy framing and implementation are not mutually exclusive: they occur in a variety of combinations and the analytical

Milieu and concepts	Policy/negotiation forms
Boundaries: define separated spaces or territories, frame inclusions or exclusions.	**Policy/negotiation**: about inclusions/ exclusions, across boundaries. Competitive bargaining and creation/maintenance of hierarchies.
Layers: spaces demonstrating varying scopes/scales of authority and competence, centrality of linkages.	**Policy/negotiation**: about balance and linkages between layers; coalition building, 'audience management' and adjustment of preferences.
Networks: spaces of connections and communications.	**Policy/negotiation**: about problem recognition and solving, formation of understandings and maintenance/extension of networks.

Figure 4.1 *Relationship of milieu/concepts to policy/negotiation forms in the new Europe*
Source: Based on Smith, M., 2000.

intrigue of the conceptualisation lies in the ways in which these combinations are understood and managed by political-economic authorities.

The coexistence of the 'three worlds' will thus be reflected in the practices of FEP, both as developed by national governments and as produced by the EU. But to make such a statement begs the question, whose FEP are we examining, and who is capable of producing FEP in the 'new Europe'? To explore this further demands a more explicit investigation of what we understand by FEP itself.

Conceptualising FEP

For the purposes of this chapter, I take FEP to consist of the performance of state functions in respect of external economic relations, through attempts by the relevant actors to design, manage and control the political-economic environment. Both elements of this definition are significant. In the first place, we need to explore the notion of 'state functions in respect of external economic relations'. Analysis of this problem has some venerable antecedents among those who have tried to explore the relationship between states and markets and states and the forces of capitalist accumulation. On the one hand, the line of argument identified with Susan Strange and others focuses on the idea that 'the competition between states is no longer for territory but for shares in the world market for goods and services' (Strange, 2000: 83). If this is the case, then FEP can in turn be defined as the services provided by political authorities in the furtherance of this competition – as Strange and others again have argued, in complex bargaining and institutional relationships involving states, international organisations, firms and other 'private' agents. This does not rule out the more traditional focus of foreign (economic) policy on the pursuit of political ends through the mobilisation of economic means, but it does argue for the dominance of these new modes of interaction between political authorities, markets and private agents. A second line of argument has been advanced by a number of Marxist analysts, who have focused on the ways in which political and economic authorities have operated to 'make the world safe for capital'. For example, Robin Murray (1971; see also Junne, 1994) put forward a powerful case for the ways in which state authorities can provide 'state economic functions' in respect of the needs and activities of big capital. Broadly in line with the arguments made by Murray and others, I would propose that FEP is to be seen as the pursuit of state functions in the external economic domain. In this context, I would identify state economic functions as the following (loosely based on those originally proposed by Murray):

- *Provision of regulation and safeguarding of property rights*: the ways in which state authorities broadly defined work to maintain or develop stable institutional and legal frameworks based on the identification and defence of ownership, and the negotiation of appropriate international agreements.
- *Promotion of economic welfare*: the ways in which state authorities work to maximise economic welfare for their citizens and their corporate clients, by managing the macro-economic framework both domestically and internationally. Domestically this can be achieved through budgetary and other instruments; internationally it depends far more on negotiation and policy co-ordination.
- *Provision of competitive advantage*: the creation of institutional and policy frameworks that structure economic space and activity in the interests of national or regional economic agents, enabling them to maximise efficiency and to defend themselves against external challenge. Provision of an educational and technological infrastructure aimed at shaping this competitive advantage.
- *Contributing to collective security and autonomy*: provision of public order broadly defined both domestically and externally, both through national or regional agencies and at the global level. Enhancement of the freedom of manoeuvre of national or regional economic agents, and recognition of challenges to this.

As noted above, Murray was making his argument in terms of the ways in which state functions encouraged and defended the concentration of capital, and others have since him identified the role of state authorities in terms of service to free markets and capitalist accumulation. One does not, however, have to be a Marxist to understand the crucial importance of the performance – or non-performance – of these functions in the post-Cold War era. Indeed, for many of the new state actors that emerged onto the European stage during the 1990s, their claims to international efficacy have been based precisely on their capacity to fulfil these functions, in many cases more than on the performance of 'hard security' functions in the political-military part of the spectrum. In the 21st century, it is also clear that these state functions may take very different forms, and that the issues about freedom of movement and autonomy for capital will have a different expression from that implied in the classical Marxist formulation; indeed, that is one of the points made so consistently and effectively by Susan Strange herself. In the context of this chapter, the state economic functions outlined above do provide us with a set of ways in which to evaluate the evolution of FEP in the new Europe, by generating questions about the channels through which and the effectiveness with which they are provided. Crucially, they also provide us with a conceptualisation of FEP which is not simply in terms of national state authorities: the functions can, in principle, be performed by a variety of public – or private – authorities.

The concept of state economic functions also helps us to think about the *goals* and the *targets* towards which FEP may be directed; in other words, about the issues of 'design, management and control' which form the second part of the basic definition used here. Each of the functions identified above implies a set of FEP goals, which are likely to engage the commitment of relevant actors and authorities and thus likely, in turn, to affect the overall climate of the European political economy. Thus, the provision of regulation and safeguarding of property rights implies FEP actions that are designed to enhance the achievement of stable institutional and regulatory frameworks; the promotion of economic welfare implies the attempt to promote the growth and the distribution of resources; the provision of competitive advantage entails the management of relations with competitor nations or regions, often mediated by global institutions; and the pursuit of collective security and autonomy leads fairly directly to the attempt to construct institutions and practices designed to promote collective goods but also to maximise individual autonomy. The potential tensions within and between the four state economic functions should be evident even in this brief discussion. How are we to make sense of them in respect of FEP?

Here we can make use of another venerable conceptualisation, the distinction between 'possession goals' and 'milieu goals' (Wolfers, 1962): the former are dedicated to the maximisation of the agent's welfare and the protection of their economic assets, the latter to the promotion of external conditions in which these possession goals can best be pursued. Clearly, it is impossible for many purposes these days to make the distinction in a cast-iron way: the linkages between possession and milieu goals are as important as the distinctions between them. But in the context of an at least partially transformed Europe since the mid-1980s, there is conceptual purchase to be gained through the initial analytical separation of types of political-economic objectives. Figure 4.2 (p. 81) relates the state economic functions identified earlier to the concepts of 'possession' and 'milieu' goals, and also provides some indicative examples from post-Cold War Europe.

It is readily apparent from Figure 4.2 that there can be conflicts within the range of state economic functions, and also that there can be conflicts

	Possession goals	Milieu goals	Examples
Regulation/rights	Establishment of market and regulatory systems.	Dissemination of market and regulatory systems.	Reform in Central and Eastern Europe.
Economic welfare	Maximisation of growth and employment.	Reducing inequalities and stabilising flows.	Providing market access to the EU for outsiders.
Competitive advantage	Reducing wage and social/regulatory costs.	Ensuring reduction of barriers to free flow of goods and services.	Divergence of competitive contexts within and outside the EU.
Collective security, autonomy	Promoting 'societal security', defending borders and values.	Establishing regimes for migration, etc.	Unplanned flows of economic and other migrants between European countries.

Figure 4.2 *Combination of state economic functions with possession and milieu goals in the pursuit of FEP*

between those functions as expressed in 'possession' and 'milieu' goals, at least in the short to medium term. Whilst over the very long term it might be possible to foresee convergence and the attainment of balance between the several areas involved, it is clear that in the short to medium term FEP has to deal with a number of important potential tensions. It is from these, of course, that the really interesting questions about the goals of FEP in the 'new Europe' will arise. For example, what happens, or is likely to happen, when the 'possession goals' of economic stability and welfare come up against the broader commitment to European stability and welfare, which is itself likely to be linked either tacitly or actively with broader security concerns? What happens, or is likely to happen, when the 'possession goal' of societal security at the national level, expressed in FEP choices, comes up against the 'milieu goal' of ensuring fair treatment of those engaged in migration (planned or unplanned) within the 'new Europe', or between the 'new Europe' and its wider context?

This latter point reminds us that we need to focus not only on goals, but also on the targets of FEP. Precisely who or what is intended to be influenced by the strategies expressed through FEP? This is not something that can be taken as read in the context of post-Cold War Europe. Two distinctions are especially important to the analysis here. First, there is the effect of what might be described as geo-economic distance. Whether we are dealing with a Europe of boundaries, layers or networks, FEP has to be aware of and responsive to the demands of those who are near neighbours, part of the near abroad or part of the broader European/global environment. Given that one characteristic of the 'new Europe' is the shifting mosaic of relationships and institutions, it is clear that for FEP 'target selection' is a key area of difficulty. If an inappropriate target is selected, or if inappropriate means are used in dealing with a target, then the costs, both political and economic, might be substantial.

The second distinction that is crucial to the analysis of FEP in post-Cold War Europe is that between public and private agents. When action is taken through FEP, in pursuit of state economic functions and with due attention to 'possession' and 'milieu' goals, whose behaviour is it intended to modify? The spectrum of potential targets in both the public 'governmental' sphere and the private sphere is, to say the least, bewildering, raising the prospect of unintended effects and outcomes however well the actions are defined and controlled. This is particularly the case if one explores the notions of layers and networks outlined in the previous section of this chapter: what works in terms of public-private interactions at one level may not work at another, whilst the existence of transnational networks composed both of public and of private agents creates the real possibility of conflicts between understandings of policy issues and responses. It also highlights the need for attention to what might be termed 'instrument design' on the part of those conducting FEP. Economic instruments possessed and deployed by governmental authorities may produce the intended outcomes in only a minority of policy contexts, given the rapid change and coexisting trajectories of economic activity to which this chapter has already pointed.

As the result of the argument so far, we now have the beginnings of a conceptual toolkit with which to address the nature of FEP in the new Europe. The main components are:

- Recognition that the impact of a range of environmental forces has thoroughly changed the environment for FEP making and implementation.
- Identification of three 'worlds' (boundaries, layers and networks) for the formation and conduct of FEP and in particular for the conduct of negotiations by FEP agents.
- Identification of a range of state economic functions that constitute the core of FEP when pursued in the external domain.
- Recognition of the distinctions between and the linkages between 'possession' and 'milieu' goals in the pursuit of FEP, and of the significance of these distinctions and linkages in a changing Europe.
- Further recognition of the importance of 'target selection' and 'instrument design' if FEP is intended to be informed not only by strategic considerations, but also of the difficulty of 'target identification' and 'instrument design' in the contemporary European context and the potential for unintended outcomes.

The next section of this chapter will explore two particular directions in which these concepts can be deployed, and the conclusion will attempt to show the ways in which they provide the basis for an empirical research agenda.

Dimensions of European FEP

In line with arguments developed elsewhere in the volume (Jørgensen, Ch. 2), it is important here to make an initial distinction between two aspects of 'European FEP'. First, there is the notion of a 'European FEP' pursued at the collective level through the agency of the EU, and embodying a set of assumptions about the institutions, the resources and the style of operation of the EU. Second, there is the notion of the 'Europeanisation of national FEP', embodying powerful arguments about the ways in which national structures have been restructured and reorientated by the forces operating in the new Europe. In principle, both of these aspects can be analysed in terms of the concepts outlined earlier in the chapter. In their own terms, they embody an important set of distinctions, but they do not imply a separation of 'European FEP' from 'Europeanised FEP'. The important thing is that these two elements coexist in a fluctuating balance in the operations of economic and political agents, and not only that – they also shape the norms according to which both public and private agents structure their activities and their understandings of the political/economic environment.

'European FEP'

Let us first look briefly at 'European FEP'. I have argued elsewhere (Smith, 1998) that if we are to look for a 'European foreign policy' it is to the first pillar of the EU that we should pay immediate attention. It is here that we find the key aspects of 'European FEP'. First, the EU provides a highly-developed institutional framework, resting on grants of competence and embodying material capabilities that can be directed towards state economic functions at the European level. Second, the capacity to act in pursuit of state economic functions is underpinned by a well-developed set of policy instruments (although importantly, those instruments do not yet provide some of the key levers of macro-economic policy action). Third, the EU possesses the ability, through enlargement and other means, to 'capture' national FEPs – both of those inside the EU and of those outside – through the internalisation of major areas of activity and through the provision of incentives for economic agents to shape their actions within the EU context. Fourth, there is a recognition by 'significant others' that the EU (strictly speaking the European Community, or EC) is a capable and valid strategic partner and/or rival. Finally, there is recognition that in a variety of global institutions such as the World Trade Organisation (WTO) the EU/EC speaks on behalf of its member states and that it has acquired institutional legitimacy through the exercise of this capacity – although again it is important to note the many areas in which this capacity does not yet exist in any significant form, or in which it is contested.

This is clearly a powerful *prima facie* case for the recognition of a 'European FEP', although it is clear that its legitimacy and potency are limited in a number of important areas. This FEP is also linked to the emergent 'European foreign policy' both by events (the development of political/economic linkages in a globalising and regionalising world) and by design (the provision for linkage and 'consistency' in successive EU treaties, or the active search for linkage by EU authorities).

The net result of this process is that in many areas of commercial policy, regulatory policy, aid policy and linked areas such as environmental policy, there is a practical European FEP (Smith, M. 1998, 2001; Collinson, 1999; Young, 2000). In terms of the earlier discussion, we have here substantial evidence that the forces operating in the contemporary European environment, the demand for the performance of state economic functions at the European level, and the demands of different negotiating milieux are convergent. To put it crudely, the EU/EC is a valid focus for FEP in the 'three worlds' of the new Europe. It may well be that there are important differences between its capacities and impacts as between these three worlds, and that is a key question for empirical analysis. As noted earlier, a key element in such an analysis must be the different demands of action and modes of policy formation in the different but interconnected 'three worlds'. The EU/EC is also increasingly recognised as a valid interlocutor on FEP by other major actors in the arena, and has gained institutional legitimacy in global bodies. One can go further and also argue that the 'civilian' focus that characterised the EU for much of its early existence has now been influenced by important processes of 'politicisation' which have loaded the FEP of the EU with an increasingly political set of implications and impacts, for example, in the use of economic sanctions and the use of political conditionality in commercial agreements (Smith, K., 1999; Smith, M., 1998).

'Europeanised FEP'

To come to the conclusions just outlined is not to argue that national-level FEP has disappeared in the new Europe. In fact, of course, there has been a substantial net increase in both the demand for and the supply of national FEP since the end of the Cold War. If for no other reason, the creation of 'new' state authorities in the wreckage of the former Soviet bloc has given rise to a new supply of FEP, for which the demand has been magnified by the impact of EU accession negotiations and broader global forces on still-fragile economies. But this last assertion should give us pause. To be sure, the new variety of states in Europe has been accompanied by a new diversity of FEP experiences and by heightened attention to national FEP as a measure of national independence and autonomy. The point here, though, is that although national FEPs have multiplied, they have also been increasingly Europeanised. This is not to play down the impact of independence or 'liberation' on the FEPs of the post-Soviet bloc countries; it is to recognise that both they and more long-established participants in the European economy have had to contend with the forces and factors outlined in the early parts of this chapter (Smith, A., 2000). Thus, the impact of institutional change and institutional structures, the new balance of international economic power, and the relative fragility of new state structures in Central and Eastern Europe have all played their part in developing the 'Europeanised' FEP, which is strongly characteristic of many contemporary European countries and which has been paralleled by the Europeanisation of foreign policies in a more general sense (Manners and Whitman, 2000).

How are we to approach the analysis of this set of changes in national FEPs? It can be argued that there are three key facets to any exploration of the problem. First, there is the process of *policy restructuring*. By this is meant both the internal reshaping of institutions and practices and the external engagement of European countries with the powerful forces of institutional widening and deepening operating within the EU and other bodies (but especially the EU). Market organisation and regulation, legal systems, fiscal regimes, environmental practices … there is a very long list of major policy domains in which all European states have been subject to the combination of internal and external restructuring. And this restructuring also has a normative dimension, in the sense that particular goals and practices have been privileged and 'sold' as part of a valid FEP as well as part of a valid national economic framework. It is not only the influence of the EU that can be seen at play here: the role of other bodies, such as the WTO and the International Monetary Fund (IMF), has both an independent impact and is refracted through the prism of the EU to focus on the FEPs of all European countries. In this context, the EU can validly be seen both as a site for globalisation and as a carrier of globalisation to the parts it had not reached before the 1990s.

Second, there is the process of *policy reorientation*. At its simplest, this can be seen to dramatic effect in the redirection of trade on the part of the Central and Eastern European Countries (CEECs) away from the former Soviet Union and towards the EU/EC (Baldwin, 1994; Faini and Portes, 1995; Smith, A., 2000). There has been a massive shift in the flows of goods, services, capital and (to a more regulated degree) persons within the new Europe, and this has reflected both conscious policy design by political authorities and the activities of a multitude of private agents. In some respects, policy design has struggled to keep up with the pace of events on the ground, and the application of specific policy instruments has often had unpredictable effects, as, for example, in the financial and fiscal domains or in policy-making on issues of asylum and immigration. It must not be forgotten, though, that this process of reorientation has been a two-way process: countries inside the EU/EC have also experienced the demand for new directions and a substantial reorientation, for example, of FDI – some of it the result of conscious policy, other the result of a variety of public and private actions. The debate about the future of regional aid and the Structural Funds in a post-enlargement EU is one of many symptoms of this underlying problem, linking European, national and even subnational FEPs in complex and often unpredictable ways.

Third, as noted before, there has been a significant process of *politicisation* of FEP at the national level, which has chimed at many points with the politicisation of FEP at the European level. The injection of political criteria into FEP actions is a natural consequence of the ways in which the apparently rigid ideological divisions of the Cold War have been eliminated: there is now no simple rule about political acceptability or legitimacy, and also there is the opportunity to frame a range of economic policies with novel political objectives in mind. Very often, as indicated above, there is an interaction between politicisation at the EU level and politicisation at the national level, either in the sense that one reinforces the other or in the sense that one is at odds with the other (for example, in the reactions of different countries to the opening up of trade with CEECs, especially in agriculture and steel, or views on economic sanctions measures).

Finally, it is important to note that there are important linkages between FEP considerations for 'insiders' (that is, EU member states), 'incomers' (those countries on the way into the EU as the result of accession negotiations) and 'outsiders' (those countries that have no immediate prospect of becoming EU members) in the new Europe. Whilst each group has undergone processes of restructuring, reorientation and politicisation in the development of their FEPs, each has experienced it in a very distinctive way. For 'insiders', a key issue has been the preservation of their investment in the assets conferred by EU membership, whilst at the same time realising the maximum benefit from the changing European policy context. For 'incomers', the balance has been different: here, the aim is to gain access to the benefits of EU membership, whilst at the same time preserving as much national autonomy as possible (a key consideration for countries newly independent and in search of national legitimacy). For 'outsiders', the need to adapt to the predominance of the EU and its structures and norms has been matched by the need to maximise national economic performance in the absence of any immediate prospect of membership. Whilst in this context it is not possible to pursue this any further, there are important potential issues of policy viability, consistency and compatibility here; Chapter 11 of this volume, on the EU's Mediterranean policy, focuses especially on the ways in which FEP has been directed towards and received by a significant group of 'outsiders'.

This section of the chapter has examined some of the implications of what might be termed the 'European dimension' of FEP. It has indicated that FEP for all countries in the new Europe has been affected by two key elements: first, the growth of a 'European FEP' centred on the EU/EC, and second, the pervasive process of 'Europeanisation' of FEP for all countries, but with very different impacts on specific countries or groups of countries. It is clearly important to employ both dimensions in assessing the changing nature of FEP in the new Europe, and also to understand these in the context of processes of regionalisation and globalisation more broadly. To put it simply, the process of regionalisation in Europe has created and intensified the 'Europeanisation' of FEP at the same time as it has contributed to the development of a 'European FEP'. In assessing the implications of globalisation for the new Europe, it is important to be aware of the ways in which

'European FEP' can act as a conduit for globalisation, at the same time as providing the potential for more effective management of globalisation processes at the European level through 'political economies of scale'. Not only this, but the 'Europeanisation' of FEP must itself be viewed in the light of broader processes of globalisation and the extent to which 'Europeani-sation' bolsters or undermines the national capacities of countries affected by it (see, for example, Ross, 1998).

Implications and Conclusions

This section of the chapter deals firstly with three sets of implications of the forces and patterns already outlined, with the aim of sharpening a number of important tensions that they have generated, before extracting some more general conclusions from the argument. In terms of implications, first, it is clear from the argument so far that there is a pervasive and differentiated process of *institutionalisation* under way in the European political economy. This process can be observed in the form of the growth of scope and scale of EU policies, and in terms of the growth of cognate structures of fiscal, mone-tary, competition and other policies even in countries unlikely to join the EU in the near future. In relation to FEP, this means that institutions have to cope with the different national and European experiences outlined above, and to accommodate the 'three worlds' of economic transactions and practices identified in the earlier parts of this chapter. As a result, there is a develop-ing institutional mosaic, in which the EU is a predominant, but not the only, focus. Indeed, the extent to which the EU has 'captured' or can 'contain' the worlds of boundaries, layers and networks is a key indicator of the direction of 'European FEP'. The extent to which national institutions retain authority, and the ways in which that authority is adapted to the European milieu, are important indicators of the balance between 'European FEP' and 'Europeanised FEP'. This does not rule out the development of 'globalised FEP' through the operation of global institutions, either through the prism of the EU or inde-pendently of it.

Second, there is an equally pervasive incidence of *negotiation*, which is conducted in several different arenas at the same time, and which expresses the contending forces outlined above. The most obvious example of this is in negotiations between the EU and CEECs, where the shifting types of agen-das and agreements have reflected the interplay of the forces we have dealt with in this chapter, and where the tensions between 'insiders' and 'incom-ers' have been observed in many domains of policy. FEP in the new Europe is conducted predominantly in the negotiated part of the spectrum, and this means there is an important role for the forces of social interaction and social learning that have been identified by many analysts of the European political scene.

Third, this does not mean that FEP has forsaken entirely the modes of *competition, coercion and intervention* that might be seen as more central to conventional state-centric analysis. Indeed, during the 1990s there has been perhaps a greater incidence of coercion and intervention through FEP than in the previous three or four decades (at least in so far as these processes are focused upon and generated by the 'new Europe'). In this context, it is important to retain a sense that the 'three worlds' of FEP in the new Europe do contain the potential for conflicts over and across boundaries as well as problem solving within layers or networks. But there is even so a pervasive sense that competitive FEP has been in decline, moderated by the institutionalisation and negotiation referred to above. A modification to this view is provided by the notion of the 'competition state' as expounded by Phil Cerny and others (Cerny, 2000), which provides for the continuation of inter-state competition by other means, adapted to the world of layers and networks rather than confined by the world of boundaries.

In addition to these broad implications, what can be said in the way of more general conclusions to the argument? This chapter has set out to identify the forces operating in the new Europe to condition FEP, to explore the ways in which FEP has responded to these and other forces, to identify some pervasive patterns in the practice of FEP and to understand in a very preliminary way how these might feed through into major domains of activity in the European political economy. There is much work to be done, but it is possible to pull out of this analysis three sets of questions for FEP in general:

- A set of questions about *conceptual significance*: to what extent has FEP spread and become differentiated in the new Europe, and is this paralleled in other parts of the world? How can the concept of FEP explored here accommodate the coexisting processes of regionalisation and globalisation? What can we say about the shifting balance between 'national' and 'extranational' elements of FEP on the basis of European experience?
- A set of questions about *our understanding of FEP in relation to statehood and state functions*. How does the argument here help us to further the key investigation of international political economy into the relationship between economic processes and political authorities, and between economic agents in both their public and their private manifestations? Does the new Europe provide us with a test-bed for the exploration of new configurations and constellations, and for the evaluation of institutional and ideational forms?
- A set of questions about *policy significance*: to what extent can identification of state functions and the capacity to exercise them on the part of both states and non-state agents help us to understand national strategies and EU policies? How does this then feed through into an understanding of the ways in which FEP is negotiated in the new Europe, under differing conditions and in different domains of activity? How do these insights into the European experience help us to re-conceptualise FEP for the wider world?

The argument here has been designed to sharpen such questions, rather than to provide definitive answers. Indeed, such answers can only really be developed on the basis of a long-term research programme focused on FEP in the new Europe, of a kind that this chapter has pointed to. Such a programme should focus not only on the material dimensions and patterns of FEP, but also on the institutions that underpin it and the ideas around which it centres; by doing so, it can make a profound contribution to the understanding of the new Europes which have emerged and are still emerging in the 'old continent'.

References

Baldwin, R. (1994) *Towards an Integrated Europe*. London: Centre for Economic Policy Research.

Cerny, P. (2000) 'Political globalization and the competition state', in R. Stubbs and G. Underhill (eds), *Political Economy and the Changing Global Order*. Oxford: Oxford University Press. pp. 300–9.

Collinson, S. (1999) '"Issue-systems", "multi-level games" and the analysis of the EU's external commercial and associated policies: a research agenda', *Journal of European Public Policy*, 6 (2): 206–24.

Faini, R. and Portes, R. (eds) (1995) *European Union Trade with Eastern Europe: Adjustment and Opportunities*. London: Centre for Economic Policy Research.

Junne, G. (1994) 'Multinational enterprises as actors', in W. Carlsnaes and S. Smith (eds), *European Foreign Policy: The EC and Changing Perspectives in Europe*. London: Sage. pp. 84–102.

Keohane, R. (1989) 'International institutions: two approaches', in R. Keohane (ed.), *International Institutions and State Power: Essays in International Relations Theory*. Boulder, CO: Westview. pp. 158–79.

Keohane, R. and Hoffmann, S. (1993) *After the Cold War: International Institutions and State Strategies in Europe, 1989–1991*. Cambridge, MA: Harvard University Press.

Laffan, B., O'Donnell, R. and Smith, M. (2000) *Europe's Experimental Union: Rethinking Integration*. London: Routledge.

Manners, I. and Whitman, R. (eds) (2000) *The Foreign Policies of European Union Member States*. Manchester: Manchester University Press.

Murray, R. (1971) 'The internationalization of capital and the nation-state', *New Left Review*, 67 (May–June): 84–109.

Ross, G. (1998) 'European integration and globalization', in R. Axtmann (ed.), *Globalization and Europe: Theoretical and Empirical Investigations*. London: Pinter. pp. 164–83.

Smith, A. (2000) *The Return to Europe: The Reintegration of Eastern Europe into the Global Economy*. London: Macmillan.

Smith, K. (1999) *The Making of European Union Foreign Policy: The Case of Eastern Europe*. London: Macmillan.

Smith, M. (1994) 'Beyond the stable state? Foreign policy challenges and opportunities in the new Europe', in W. Carlsnaes and S. Smith (eds), *European Foreign Policy: The EC and Changing Perspectives in Europe*. London: Sage. pp. 21–44.

Smith, M. (1996) 'The European Union in a changing Europe: establishing the boundaries of order', *Journal of Common Market Studies*, 34 (1): 5–28.

Smith, M. (1998) 'Does the flag follow trade? "Politicisation" and the emergence of a European foreign policy', in J. Peterson and H. Sjursen (eds), *A Common Foreign Policy for Europe? Competing Visions of the CFSP*. London: Routledge. pp. 77–94.

Smith, M. (2000) 'Negotiating New Europes: the roles of the European Union', *Journal of European Public Policy*, 7 (5): 806–22.

Smith, M. (2001) 'The European Union's commercial policy: between coherence and fragmentation?', *Journal of European Public Policy*, 8 (5): 787–802.

Strange, S. (2000) 'World order, non-state actors and the global casino: the retreat of the state?', in R. Stubbs and G. Underhill (eds), *Political Economy and the Changing Global Order* (2nd edn). Toronto: Oxford University Press. pp. 82–90.

Tooze, R. (1994) 'Foreign economic policy in the new Europe: a theoretical audit of a questionable category', in W. Carlsnaes and S. Smith (eds), *European Foreign Policy: The EC and Changing Perspectives in Europe*. London: Sage. pp. 60–83.

Wallace, H. (2000) 'Europeanisation and globalisation: complementary or contradictory trends?', *New Political Economy*, 5 (3): 369–82.

Wolfers, A. (1962) 'The goals of foreign policy', in *Discord and Collaboration: Essays on International Politics*. Baltimore: Johns Hopkins University Press. pp. 67–80.

Young, A. (2000) 'The adaptation of European foreign economic policy', *Journal of Common Market Studies*, 38 (1): 93–116.

5　Diplomacy

Brian Hocking

Despite the fact that diplomacy is regarded as a key dimension of the processes through which world politics are conducted, it represents, as one observer has noted, a surprising lacuna in the study of International Relations (IR) (Reychler, 1979: 2). A variety of reasons can be advanced for this. Sharp has noted the disjuncture between the broad swathe of IR scholarship and the specialist literature on diplomacy (Sharp, 1999: 34), whilst Sofer, amongst others, has pointed to the inherent deficiencies of this literature whose 'conceptual wealth', is limited, divorced from political theory, and descriptive rather than analytical (Sofer, 1988: 196). Analysis of diplomacy in the European arena in its broader and narrower European Union (EU) definitions, reflects these tendencies. Indeed, the changing character of the general diplomatic milieu and the uncertainties that this has generated is reinforced by the EU's multilayered politico-diplomatic environment.

In reviewing these patterns of diplomatic complexity, their relationship to the more general post-Cold War diplomatic milieu and the implications for our understanding of the place of diplomacy in contemporary European foreign policy, the ensuing discussion rests on several assumptions. The first of these is a need to break out of the straitjacket represented by the linked discourses of 'decline' – the well-worn proposition that diplomacy is accompanying the state into oblivion – and 'newness' – the associated notion that what is significant in diplomatic process and practice is the replacement of the old with the new. A second, related, assumption is the need to interpret present trends in the broader context of the historical development of European diplomacy, recognising the consequences of the gradual separation of the foreign and domestic dimensions of public policy which occurred between the 17th and 19th centuries (Hamilton and Langhorne, 1995; Anderson, 1993).

The third assumption is that global, regional and domestic patterns of change, enhanced by the post-Cold War environment, are marked by a growing diplomatic 'ambiguity' clearly manifested in the EU. This can be seen in terms of the uncertainties surrounding a growing EU international capability, the possibility that the Commission delegations might evolve into a European foreign service, and the desire of national governments to retain control in core areas of international policy (Duke, 1997). Such a situation reflects the broader ambiguities inherent in the EU itself. As Laffan et al. have suggested, this reflects its state of 'betweenness' and the 'process of becoming' leading to an end state which may bear little relation to traditional assumptions regarding forms of political order (Laffan et al., 2000: 189).

Precisely the same point can be made about diplomacy: an understanding of its historical development, combined with a relaxation of assumptions about its irrelevance and the dominance of 'new' over 'old' diplomacy, leads to the conclusion that the ideas of 'betweenness' and 'becoming' encapsulate the essence of what confronts us in the EU diplomatic environment. This echoes Der Derian's argument that the continual shaping and reshaping of diplomacy over time sits uncomfortably with the tendency to assume that it has attained its ultimate expression, 'that we have reached – or even that we are approaching – after a long odyssey the best, final form of diplomacy' (Der Derian, 1987: 3).

Against this background, this chapter identifies the ways in which broader global systemic change, interacting with societal forces, has impacted on the conduct of European diplomacy at both the national and EU levels. In doing so, it suggests that we need to reconceptualise diplomacy, particularly in fluid, emerging environments such as those represented by the EU. The identification of diplomacy as a means of securing the state from its international environment is being modified by diplomacy conceived of as a 'boundary-spanning' activity. Here, diplomats are operating not so much within the well-defined 'shell' of the state, but within shifting and reconstituting boundaries as state sovereignty is redefined in the face of globalising and regionalising pressures.

The 'What', 'How', 'Where' and 'Who' of Diplomacy

Underpinning the current debates on the nature, trials and tribulations of diplomacy are a set of interwoven questions which provide a loose framework for the exploration of the changing character of European diplomacy. I shall label these the 'what', 'how', 'where' and 'who' questions. The 'what' questions direct us, first, towards some familiar distinctions. Central to these is that between foreign policy and diplomacy – the former constituting the substance of an actor's international policy, the latter one of the instruments through which this can be effected. My reason for raising this rather obvious point is that diplomacy is often used as a synonym for foreign policy, not least in discussions regarding an emergent EU foreign policy. Thus Jørgensen's (1997) prescription for a research agenda on 'modern European diplomacy' is as much about the nature of foreign policy as it is about diplomacy defined in this more precise way. Similarly, Keukeleire's (2000) study of the EU as an emergent 'diplomatic actor' has as its central concern the ways in which the EU should be analysed as a 'foreign policy actor'. This is more than a semantic point, for it is one thing to argue, for example, that there is a developing EU foreign and security policy in terms of outputs and quite another to posit that this is accompanied by a distinctive style and mode of delivery.

A second set of issues revolves around the essence of diplomacy both as an institution of the international system and as a mode of statecraft. Although it is quite common to regard diplomacy as a feature of the state system, it is equally true, as Cohen (1999) and others have demonstrated, that it has a far longer pedigree, evolving in terms of the methods utilised in different cultures. Sharp has argued that diplomacy should be seen as a resource that is not contingent on its identification with the state system, but as 'responses to a common problem of living separately and wanting to do so, while having to conduct relations with others' (1999: 51). Constantinou argues that this offers the best defence of diplomacy against the decline school: 'a better way of confronting those who herald the end of diplomacy in an era of multiple global actors, mass media and satellite communication is to outflank them theoretically, by suggesting that diplomacy may not simply consist of that interstate, intersovereign, and interambassadorial side that they see as an anachronism' (1996: xv).

This point has a clear resonance in the EU context where the Commission delegations are constrained, as Bruter notes, to adapt to the demands of a 'stateless' diplomacy (1999: 193), but it poses interesting questions as to the relevance of diplomacy to the EU in terms of its internal processes. Whereas their sheer density and boundary-transcending qualities suggest some form of 'post-diplomatic' order, at the same time negotiation, one of the key functions of diplomacy, is central to the way that the EU operates. Smith's image of the EU as a 'negotiated order' underscores the centrality of negotiation and, at the same time, its complex structures and processes (Smith, M., 1996).

Inseparably linked to these issues are questions regarding the 'how' of diplomacy – that is, the methods utilised in its conduct. One way of approaching this is to pursue the common distinction between bilateral and multilateral forms of diplomacy and to suggest that it is the latter, or variants thereof, which are characteristic of EU diplomacy. Thus, in his analysis of an emergent European diplomacy, Keukeleire takes as his comparator traditional state-based diplomacy, which he appears to equate with bilateral diplomacy. As I shall suggest below, not only is this a problematic definition in the sense that it hardly encapsulates the complexities of modern diplomacy, it also sets up assumptions regarding the continued significance of bilateralism in multilateral environments, including the EU. A related problem, of course, is the confusion of 'what' and 'how' questions and to assume that diplomatic processes (for example, bilateralism) are inseparably linked to specific institutional forms (for example, the maintenance of a network of bilateral embassies).

Associated with the what and how issues are the 'where' related questions. One of the key assumptions underpinning Nicolson's writings on diplomacy at a period of tremendous upheaval in Europe is that, there is a clear separation between the formulation of policy and its implementation – the latter being the function of diplomacy (Nicolson, 1939: 12). There is a good case to be made that even in 19th and early 20th century Europe, this distinction was not sustained in practice – hence the continuing debate on the impact of the 19th century communications revolution on the relationship between foreign ministries and missions. But certainly, the growing linkage of policy arenas, as exemplified in the EU, and the multifaceted points of contact between member state governments, has changed hugely the ways in which negotiation is conducted. As in other policy environments, this poses important questions as to the management and sequencing of policy processes and where, precisely, diplomacy occurs. It is made far more complex, however, by the associated erosion of the distinction between foreign and domestic arenas – a familiar point which I do not propose to pursue here. Nevertheless, it is significant in the context of this discussion in as much as another cardinal principle of the 'traditional' diplomatic milieu is challenged; namely the separation of diplomacy and politics. As is often noted, especially by trade diplomats, as much time is spent nowadays in the 'two-level games' linking domestic and international diplomacy as in negotiating in international forums (Evans et al., 1993).

The final piece in the diplomatic jigsaw puzzle is represented by the 'who' questions and these follow logically from what has gone before. State-centred approaches take a very narrow view of this issue and argue, in essence, that diplomacy is conducted by diplomats and that the institutions of bilateral diplomacy are alive and well (Berridge, 1995: Ch. 2). This does not accord with reality or the tenor of the continuing reviews within national foreign services as to what they do and with whom they should engage in doing it. The diffusion that has occurred within an expanding foreign policy community is exemplified in the EU and it is a commonplace observation that 'traditional diplomats' – as distinct from officials from member state sectoral ministries – no longer comprise the greater element in the staffing of the Permanent Representations in Brussels. Beyond this development, however, there is an increasing recognition that the execution of international policy demands the construction of networks of interaction based on the exchange of resources which are no longer the sole preserve of government. To a considerable degree, this acknowledges the challenge presented to the conduct of diplomacy by the growth of civil society and its representatives, particularly non-government organisations (NGOs) (Cooper and Hocking, 2000).

The European Diplomatic Environment

Within the multilayered environment generated by interactions of institutions, member state governments, subnational interests and extra-European actors, we are presented with a number of lines of enquiry regarding the ways in which the general diplomatic puzzles identified above manifest themselves. One of these concerns the patterns of intra-EU negotiation which, as noted earlier, may be regarded as 'beyond' diplomacy with its state-oriented connotations. Thus, for example, Jørgensen (1997) cites one observer's prediction that we are witnessing the end of 'traditional' European diplomacy as intra-European diplomacy is replaced by democracy. This is reinforced by the changing, if still significant, role *vis-à-vis* officials from sectoral ministries, played by national foreign ministries and their diplomatic networks within the EU arena (Hocking and Spence, 2002).

Closely related to this is the debate on the impact of EU membership on member state diplomacy. As Manners and Whitman put it, 'does this act as a constraint or opportunity in the pursuit of international goals?' (2000: 10). Not surprisingly, the conclusion is that this depends on context as determined by the issue and how responsibilities for it are distributed between the national and European levels, the character of the member state, and the extent to which the latter places an issue within what Manners and Whitman categorise as four 'rings of specialness' in terms of its international foreign policy interests (2000: 266–8). Having said that, the general burden of evidence is that the intersection of bilateral and multilateral arenas has transformed the patterns of diplomatic interaction between member states and between them and other international actors, both state and non-state (Soetendorp, 1999: 155; Hill and Wallace, 1996). Taking the instance of the UK, White notes the reconfiguration of British diplomacy as 'British representatives are locked into a complex, well-established, multilateral *and* multileveled process of foreign policy-making' (2001: 132). In terms of diplomatic capabilities, EU membership has added to what Ginsberg has termed the 'weight' and 'reach' of British diplomacy, providing a multilateral framework within which bilateral diplomacy could be anchored. That this might not be a cost-free exercise in terms of the diplomatic leverage over British external policy that such a strategy affords other EU states has also been noted. One of the key tests here for UK diplomatic strategy lies in the demands posed by balancing the demands of EU membership with the recalibration of the 'special relationship' at a moment of transition in American politics.

A further dimension of diplomatic adaptation concerns the impact of EU membership on the structure and operational forms of national diplomatic systems with the possibility that we are witnessing a convergence in diplomatic style and practice. This is noted in the working style of the Committee of Permanent Representatives (COREPER) and the processes of diplomatic socialisation which have been identified as a key aspect of its operation (Blair, 2000). Apart from this, and the legacy of European Political Co-operation (EPC) noted earlier, there are other socialising forces at work amongst the EU member state diplomatic services reinforced by administrative working groups such as the CFSP Committee on Administrative Affairs (COADM) within Directorate General (DG) External Relations. Apart from the latter's focus on administrative issues relating to foreign services, it is also concerned with diplomatic training (Duke, 1997: 6).

This leads us into the area of a 'European' diplomacy viewed as the logical outcome of the evolution from EPC to the Common Foreign and Security Policy (CFSP) and the European Security and Defence Policy (ESDP). Just as this demands that we reconsider the fundamental characteristics of foreign policy and do not simply extrapolate from state-based definitions and criteria, so with diplomacy. Although we have a reasonable amount of evidence regarding the development of European diplomacy in the field, in the shape of the requirements under the Maastricht Treaty – and subsequent developments in the Amsterdam and Nice treaties – for co-operation and consultation between member state missions and in terms of the role of the delegations (Bruter, 1999), this is clearly concerned with diplomatic process rather than broader diplomatic 'style' issues and, often implicitly, rests on the assumption that a European foreign service would possess characteristics not dissimilar to those of national diplomatic systems. At the same time, those ambiguities apparent in the conduct of EU diplomacy noted earlier (including its 'stateless' dimension) are clearly visible in the tensions between, on one side, a growing diplomatic capability in the form of developments such as the High Representative created in the Amsterdam Treaty and a strengthened system of co-ordination in external affairs established at the Nice summit and, on the other, a continued adherence to intergovernmentalism in these sensitive policy areas.

Thus whilst the CFSP can be used as a tool of national foreign policy, at the same time the tools of CFSP are largely constituted from the diplomatic resources of the member states. As Keukeleire notes:

> While declarations of the Council or EU representatives may still be labelled the CFSP's 'own' instruments, most of the other instruments are put at the CFSP's disposal by member states, or are instigated by member states, in particular by the member state that plays a central operational role in CFSP diplomacy as (temporary) chair of the Council of Ministers. (2000: 10)

But he goes on to make a more telling point in the context of defining a European diplomacy. Not only is the image of CFSP often cast in terms of an ideal type of foreign policy, to focus on the second pillar may distort our overall perceptions of an emerging European diplomacy. Rather than solely CFSP-focused, an analysis of EU diplomacy should also embrace intra-EU diplomacy and what he terms EU 'structural' diplomacy. This transcends the different pillars and has as its core aim the development of structural change in those regions of the world with which the EU has differing forms of relationship. Amongst other things, this draws our attention to the fact that what might be regarded as innovative in EU diplomacy may lie outside CFSP and in, for example, the sphere of trade diplomacy with its complex patterns of public and private sector interactions. Focusing on the Commission delegations, Bruter suggests that the constraints and expectations which have developed around the delegations means that they 'have had to find some adaptive and original ways in which to formulate and carry out their activities' (1999: 193).

In relating broader dimensions of change in the structures and processes of diplomacy to the European arena, we are confronted by two interlinked layers of complexity. On the one side is to be found the changing nature of diplomacy as it adapts to shifts in the configuration of both domestic and international environments. A key lesson here is that the idea of 'traditional' diplomacy – equated with state-based foreign policy – as a yardstick against which to measure some new mode of 'European' diplomacy, is problematic in as much as the 'traditional' is itself enmeshed in processes of profound change. The second layer of complexity lies in determining the character of what is 'European' in this context.

Patterns of Diplomatic Change

A dominant theme in diplomatic change which has considerable significance in the EU policy milieu is the compression of time and space. As Keohane and Nye have suggested, however, it is not so much the increase in 'message' velocity which marks out the present era, since the major quantitative leap in the speed of communications occurred in the 19th century (Keohane and Nye, 2000: 113–14). Rather it is 'institutional velocity', the intensity of interactions (what they refer to as the 'thickness' of globalism) and the responses of the actors to this that marks out the present era. The impact of this on the conduct of foreign policy has become a familiar theme. What Ammon has termed 'telediplomacy' is now seen as a key feature of the policy environment affecting the outcomes as well as process of foreign policy (Ammon, 1998; Tehranian, 1999). Consequently, the ability to respond speedily to the ever-quickening flow of events is deemed a key measure of actor capacity and this is reflected in the organisation and operation of diplomacy. Indeed, for Der Derian, speed has become a critical dimension of what he terms 'techno-diplomacy' wherein 'diplomacy becomes governed as much by the velocity of events as by the events themselves' (1987: 208).

Frequently related to the changing relationship between space and time, the concept of 'virtual diplomacy' has become a buzzword within diplomatic circles on a par with globalisation – and is used with commensurate imprecision. At its most general level, as defined by the US Institute of Peace's virtual diplomacy programme, it relates to the application of communications and information technologies (CIT) to diplomacy. More specifically, it has had two impacts on the organisation of diplomacy: first, to enable the rapid establishment of 'virtual embassies' – perhaps no more than a laptop, modem and satellite phone in a hotel room – as several countries did in the course of the Bosnian conflict (Smith, G., 1997: 156). Second, CIT has reconfigured the relationships between foreign ministries and overseas missions, giving the latter a more direct role in the formulation of policy (Eldon, 1994: 22).

In the EU context, this temporal-spatial dimension has been noted by Ekengren and Sundelius (2002) in their analysis of the response of the Swedish diplomatic system to EU membership. This, they suggest, has been marked by the diminution of control over the time-sequencing of the policy processes at national level as these are set increasingly at the European level. They note that within CFSP procedures, the division of national diplomats into working groups means that they are operating on different timetables. As the sequencing of policy formulation and presentation is made more difficult by externally imposed timetables ('... the national present is, if not disappearing, seriously squeezed between narrow time slots of demands for quick action', Ekengren and Sundelius, 2002: 246), the capacity to anticipate outcomes assumes a key feature in both diplomatic process and structure.

At another level, enhanced economic interdependence has helped to redefine the very nature of what is 'inside' and 'outside' the state as the development of a global economy increasingly breaches the uncertain distinctions between domestic and foreign policy arenas. Thus the transformation of the trade agenda from border issues to matters of sensitive domestic political concern, often touching on subnational competencies, carries with it significant implications for the conduct of diplomacy. The growth of the regulatory state is accompanied by modes of regulatory diplomacy as represented in US–EU conflicts over hormone-treated beef and genetically modified foodstuffs (Vogel, 1997). Taken together with the emergence of a global agenda epitomised by issues such as climate change and AIDS, we have witnessed a marked growth in the technical qualities of much contemporary negotiation and an emphasis towards multilateral and mission-oriented diplomacy (Cooper and Hayes, 2000). However, rather than eroding the role of traditional bilateral diplomacy, this has promoted a meshing of bilateral negotiations with those conducted in a growing range of multilateral forums.

Despite the oft-heralded demise of bilateral diplomacy, it is notable that the role of bilateralism within the EU arena secures considerable support. Regelsberger argues that bilateral diplomacy, rather than being rendered redundant, is acquiring enhanced significance because increased majority voting requires governments to engage in coalition-building on issues of key importance to them. Consequently, in terms of diplomatic machinery, bilateral links between member states appear to be gaining in importance as influences over the decision-making processes in Brussels (Paschke, 2000).

Bilateralism as coalition building, however, has changed the role and functions of bilateral representation. Rather than gathering and transmitting large quantities of information which can now be acquired through other channels, the aim is to provide detailed analysis and interpretation of the position that member states are adopting on specific policy issues. Additionally, in the CFSP environment, the much more limited power of the EU in the second pillar means that 'bilateral diplomatic contacts remain essential for creating the required majorities or consensus, for formulating compromises within the Council, and for mapping and reconciling the member states' – sometimes contradictory – interests and sensitivities' (Keukeleire, 2000: 5).

A further point regarding bilateralism relates to the role of national missions in third countries and the requirements of the Treaty on European Union (TEU) for co-operation between these missions and Commission

Delegations. Observers – particularly those concerned with the smaller member states – tend to draw the conclusion that the CFSP has increased the significance of national representation as third states attach more importance to it as part of the EU 'whole'. Once again, the emphasis is not so much on information gathering as *sharing* information with other missions and Commission Delegations. But what is more significant here is not the relative importance of one or other of the two traditional modes of diplomacy, but the way in which they are being interwoven, producing a form of 'bi-multilateral' diplomacy, 'bilateral in its procedures but multilateral in its purposes' (Correia, 2002: 204).

The interpenetration of domestic and international policy arenas, well-developed in the EU, has had the effect of politicising the diplomatic environment. Nowadays, the process of ratifying agreements often involves a continuing dialogue with interested domestic constituencies alongside international negotiation (Evans et al., 1993). This has meant that the demands for co-ordination have expanded from the horizontal plane represented by intra-bureaucratic linkages to the vertical plane of intra-societal relations. Part of this process is reflected in a renewed concern with what has conventionally been regarded as public diplomacy. Engagement with both foreign and domestic publics has long been one sub-theme of the 'new' diplomacy debate, but has been given added significance by the need and ability to influence key policy constituencies through the exercise of 'soft' power reflecting changed policy agendas (Nye, 1990: 188; Leonard and Alakeson, 2000). One manifestation of this is the growing significance of image management in world politics as governments, business and NGOs seek to utilise it both as a power resource and a mode of managing the processes of regionalisation and globalisation (Hocking, 2000). Rather than a form of public diplomacy in which manipulation of foreign publics through the dissemination of what might be deemed as propaganda, what is now required – as a report on the reform of US diplomacy argues – is active engagement with both domestic and foreign publics and their representatives in civil society, based on transparency and information sharing (Center for Strategic and International Studies, 1998: 94–8). In the European arena, the management of image can become a key preoccupation, as Berlin discovered in the context of claims made against German firms by Holocaust victims and their descendants.

Arguably, however, it is in the sphere of commercial diplomacy where the most significant changes are occurring. In the era of the 'competition state', patterns of diplomacy between firms and governments have developed and expanded, encapsulated in Strange's depiction of 'triangular diplomacy' (1992). Governments throughout (and outside) Europe are devoting more and more of their diminishing diplomatic resources to commercial work. Hence the FCO spends 27 per cent of its budget on this area, its largest single item of expenditure. Not only this, but the organisation of commercial diplomacy is under continuing review throughout member state capitals. In the UK instance, a significant development has been the centralisation in 1999 of all commercial promotion activities by creating a single authority,

British Trade International. As Lee has noted, this area is one that is largely ignored in discussions of the changing diplomatic arena, but the implications are significant, not only for national diplomatic systems, but in the EU context also for the evolution of forms of collective European representation (Lee, 2001; Walzenbach, 2001).

Much of the change occurring in the diplomatic environment has been related to adaptation in national bureaucratic structures. Overlaying these, however, is another transformative layer, relating to the implications of deterritorialisation and transnationalism for governmental actors – of obvious significance to Europe and the EU. Here, the focus has often been on the points of discontinuity between differing categories of actor, indicative of zero-sum arguments regarding their respective capacities. As Risse-Kappen and others have noted, the transnationalism literature has too often suggested that the significance of transnational relations lies in their separateness from intergovernmental patterns, with states seen primarily as targets of transnational actor activity as the latter undermine national sovereignty. Rather, what is interesting are the linkages between state- and society-oriented patterns in world politics, and how governmental/transnational coalitions are formed, penetrate one another and are managed (Risse-Kappen, 1995). Moreover, far from being eclipsed by the state, the latter's domestic structures become key explanatory factors in determining the nature of transnational actor behaviour and influence.

This symbiosis between state and non-state actors creates the background for the development of forms of 'catalytic' diplomacy (Hocking, 1999). This rests on the recognition of growing interdependencies between actors flowing from interlinked autonomy and resource dilemmas as they seek to maximise their freedom of action in the pursuit of policy goals whilst devising strategies to compensate for resource deficiencies. Consequently, bargaining relationships are created in which key resources – wealth, knowledge and legitimacy – are traded between actors possessing differing resource bases (Krasner, 1995; Reinecke, 1998). It differs from other designations such as 'track two' or 'unofficial' diplomacy in as much as these are usually employed to indicate supplementary negotiations primarily engaged in by governmental elites. Indeed, these may be associated with catalytic diplomacy but are qualitatively different both in terms of actors and objectives. The multilayered diplomatic processes characteristic of the EU provide an environment in which not only governmental actors operate, but also the representatives of business and civil society.

The implications of this for diplomacy lie outside the narrower confines suggested by some earlier, bureaucratic, phases of adaptation. That is not to say that these are irrelevant, for they have become a key theme in analyses of member state responses to Europeanisation, as reflected in the focus on co-ordination. If anything, the processes of bureaucratic diffusion and consolidation are likely to be enhanced by these developments. However, they are overlaid by a growing emphasis on establishing channels of communication with civil society organisations (CSOs), particularly NGOs. This is most clearly developed in multilateral diplomatic environments (O'Brien et al., 2000). Increasingly, however, the development of NGO linkages has become a recurrent theme in all aspects of diplomacy. To take the UK as an example, the trend towards engaging both business and NGOs has gained momentum in the Foreign and Commonwealth Office (FCO) under the Blair government. In late 1999, a staff member of Amnesty International was seconded as third secretary in the British embassy in Manila (Williamson, 2000). The development of an NGO secondee scheme, reflecting the Labour government's commitment to an 'ethical' foreign policy, complements a well-established system of secondments from business, underscoring the 'commercialisation' of diplomacy. In France, the Heisbourg Report, in criticising the inward-looking character of French diplomacy and its relative insulation from international influences, also pointed to the need to adjust to an international environment in which traditional diplomatic processes are modified by the emergence of informal networks in which non-state actors play a prominent role (Clarke, 2000).

Similarly, dialogues with civil society are becoming increasingly institutionalised within the EU diplomatic environment. This is well established in some areas, particularly development co-operation, where NGOs have been actively involved since the 1970s. More recently, the shaping of international trade policy, stimulated by the impact of the Seattle WTO summit, is now accompanied by a structured Trade–Civil Society Dialogue between the Commission and NGOs (Mackie, 2001).

Images of Diplomacy 'Gatekeeping' and 'Boundary-spanning'

Taken together, these developments indicate a need to re-evaluate traditional assumptions concerning the boundaries of diplomacy and, indeed, the role of diplomacy in mediating boundaries. A powerful image underpinning state-centred analyses of diplomatic processes is that of 'gatekeeping', which rests on a number of linked assumptions regarding the nature of foreign policy and those involved in it. The most fundamental of these is the assumed centrality of the territorial state and the primacy attached to the control of boundaries and the communication flows that cross them. Associated with this are the traditional claims made for the special qualities to be found in foreign policy, inscribed in its 'foreignness', reinforced by its equation with high policy and the pursuit of an identifiable national interest. At the practitioner level, the machinery of diplomacy seeks to establish control whilst recognising the need for co-ordination in the face of a much more diffuse international policy environment. These strategies are most likely to be rooted in the conceptualisation of co-ordination as a hierarchical, top-down process in which the foreign ministry, aided by the diplomatic network over which it presides, assumes the role of dominant central agency.

It is not simply that this image fails to accord with the essence of the developing EU polity, it has tenuous roots in the historical development of European (and non-European) diplomatic systems.

A contrasting image, and one more useful to the interpretation of the European diplomatic environment, is presented by that of 'boundary-spanning' whose essence resides in the changing character and significance of boundaries, both territorial and policy-related. Whereas much of the globalisation and regionalisation literature would accept the notion of boundary porosity, it would go on to suggest that this implies that boundaries have ceased to be significant. Scholte, for example, regards *transboundary* activity as the defining quality of globalisation (1997: 431). From another vantage point, however, border porosity, whilst implying significant change in policy processes, has rendered boundaries more significant. Thus Ansell and Weber (1999), in adopting an 'open systems' perspective on sovereignty derived from organisation theory, suggest that boundaries are fluid and contingent. Rather than viewing organisations as autonomous and strictly defined by their environments, 'they are simultaneously continuous with and demarcated from' these environments (1999: 77). Boundaries, rather than being fixed and permanent, reconstitute themselves in response to shifting patterns of interactions. Far from being irrelevant, therefore, they become sites of intense activity as they are enacted and re-enacted. In such an environment, actors capable of assuming the role of mediators or brokers assume a special significance: 'They aim at modulating, regulating, and sometimes controlling what kinds of resources, signals, information and ideas pass in and pass out of the semi permeable membranes that are the boundaries of the organization' (Ansell and Weber, 1999: 82). In so doing they operate both outside and within the organisation, assuming a diversity of forms in both the governmental and non-governmental arenas. Lobbyists, management consultants, think-tanks, epistemic communities – each may discharge such mediating functions.

This perspective provides an alternative – and, in many policy contexts, more relevant – set of criteria for understanding the role of diplomacy, particularly in complex and densely configured milieus such as the EU. The continuing need to reconstitute sovereignty, combined with a recognition of the advantages conferred by juxtaposing the qualities inherent in sovereignty-endowed and sovereign-free actors, places a premium on structures able to adapt to environments marked by high levels of uncertainty and ambiguity. As Henrikson argues, it is the very qualities implicit in what he terms the *associative* nature of diplomacy that enable it to perform valuable functions in world politics (Henrikson, 1997). This it can do by offering a channel between domestic and international environments in the processes of regime construction, enhancing the transparency of international institutions and, thereby, their legitimacy in the public eye, and assembling and co-ordinating a range of interests in combating global problems. Perhaps most significantly, in a world that is marked by significant levels of cultural conflict, diplomats, through their generic mediative skills, are well placed to 'weave' understanding out of the conflicts over value and institutions that divide communities (Henrikson, 1997: 22–4).

Rosenau takes this theme further when suggesting that we are witnessing the emergence of a world constituted by intermingling 'spheres of authority' (SOAs) in which people may develop affiliations to a variety of entities alongside the state, none of which can lay claim to be the focus of ultimate loyalty: 'people will learn to balance diverse and even conflicting commitments in the absence of a terminal state' (Rosenau, 2000: 12–13). As they do so, Rosenau sees a crucial role for diplomats who, using their experience and skills, should be well placed to assist in the creation and legitimisation of new patterns of social contract between individuals and a plethora of SOAs.

Whereas the gatekeeper image rests on the assumption that its key objectives lie in controlling national boundaries and insulating the state from its environments, the boundary-spanner image defines this in terms of mediating within and across spaces created by points of interface between the state and those increasingly fluid environments. In other words, the logic of boundary control is replaced by a logic determined by an awareness of the limits of control combined with the needs of access to, and presence in, these environments. This, combined with enhanced permeability between domestic and international policy, strengthens the claims of other bureaucratic actors to a voice in international policy and weakens the identity of 'foreign' policy as a category in its own right endowed with distinct qualities which, in turn, demand the maintenance of special policy processes. Bureaucratic bargaining rather than the hierarchical model of co-ordination which, as suggested earlier, is no stranger to the management of the international environment, consequently becomes far more prominent. Co-ordination, as has been amply demonstrated in the case of the EU, becomes a matter of facilitating information flows and sharing 'lead' department status on international issues (Kassim et al., 2000). Equally, as EU-focused lobbying adopts multiple routes of influence, some within and others outside national channels, the co-ordination of national policy becomes at once more critical, yet more elusive (Van Schendelen, 1993: 277).

This is by no means intended to suggest that such a role is easily adopted. In terms of intra-EU diplomacy, part of the problem for member state diplomacy is adapting to a situation in which the demarcation lines between what is not yet a European 'domestic' policy but is neither 'foreign' policy, are increasingly blurred. Rather than a single layer of co-ordinating activity, the EU represents a clear example of the layered co-ordination model within which the foreign policy machinery assumes a role, but not the sole or even dominant role. Lead departments working closely with Commission directorates-general assume a major role here, identifying the implications of Commission policy initiatives for other departments, informing the foreign ministry, and consulting affected domestic interests and their opposite numbers in other member states. And, of course, 'domestic' ministries will establish their own European co-ordinating divisions concerned not with the detail of policy but with the co-ordination of the underlying principles informing that policy. This produces a very decentralised pattern in which the processes of co-ordination become diffused throughout bureaucratic systems.

The overall picture that emerges is one of rapidly shifting boundaries between political arenas as political and bureaucratic actors respond to a more complex environment. 'Gatekeeping', or the attempt to maintain single channels of access between these arenas, is no longer a practicable objective. Rather, what national governments appear to wish to achieve is some measure of coherence in their national positions towards Brussels, and this has both an upward (EU) and – in the case of the decentralised states such as Belgium and Germany – a marked 'downward' dimension towards regional governments increasingly aware of the significance of the European level of policy-making for their own interests.

Diplomacy and Policy Networks

In the light of the trends discussed above, it is not surprising that network imagery has gradually come to be applied to selected areas of diplomacy and negotiation. In particular, the portrayal of EU diplomacy in network terms has become common, gaining expression in concepts such as multi-level governance which challenge intergovernmentalist explanations of EU policy processes. The literature on policy networks, particularly in the EU context, is replete with warnings as to the ambiguity and imprecision that surrounds the term (Jönsson et al., 1998; Pfetsch, 1998), and whether it represents a 'model' or a 'metaphor' (just two of the words which are commonly employed in network lexicology). Moreover, the literature is characterised by a growing typology of network structures such as 'advocacy coalitions' and 'discourse coalitions' as well as 'epistemic communities', a manifestation of the phenomenon more familiar to students of IR (*Public Adminstration*, 1998). But underpinning these various conceptions is the proposition that networks are indispensable in managing increasingly complex policy environments by the promotion of communication and trust. In this sense, a policy network can be defined as 'a set of relatively stable relationships which are of a non-hierarchical and interdependent nature linking a variety of actors, who share common interests with regard to a policy and who exchange resources to pursue these shared interests acknowledging that co-operation is the best way to achieve common goals' (Stone, 1997: 5).

This is the fundamental principle on which Reinecke's concept of global public policy networks rests (Reinecke, 1998, 2000). Starting from the premise that globalisation has highlighted the deficiencies of governments, both acting alone or in concert, in terms of their scope of activity, speed of response to global issues and range of contacts, he identifies the significance of the emergence of networks incorporating both public and private sector actors. It is not, he suggests, that multigovernmental institutions are irrelevant, but that the more diverse membership and non-hierarchical qualities of public policy networks promote collaboration and learning and speed up the acquisition and processing of knowledge. Employing language that has a resonance in the EU context, 'vertical' subsidiarity, in which policy-making is delegated within public sector agencies, has to be supplemented by 'horizontal' subsidiarity through outsourcing to non-state actors. Underpinning the argument is the recognition of the value of division of labour between actors in specific policy settings and the advantages inherent in their respective qualities. If governments are not helpless pawns, neither are they dominant. NGOs, for their part, need openings to diplomatic networks, both bilateral and multilateral, if they are to maximise their influence over internationalised environments such as the EU. This creates a more subtle and nuanced pattern of relationships between state and non-state actors than the conflict stereotype which is frequently suggested. Esty and Geradin, in discussing the most effective form of regulatory system, argue that this is provided by what they term 'co-opetition' – a mix of co-operation and competition both within and across governments and between government and non-governmental actors (Esty and Geradin, 2000).

As Jönsson et al. note, in the EU networks are multidimensional phenomena and assume positions along a continuum of forms which can only be determined by empirical research (Jönsson et al., 1998: 326). Whilst it is beyond the scope of the present discussion to engage in the kind of analysis that would fulfil this requirement, we can identify some of the most obvious variations in the constitution of such networks. A major factor likely to be influential here is the broad character of the diplomatic site. In this context, Coleman and Perl provide a typology of four sites: intergovernmental, multilevel governance, private regimes and what they term 'loose couplings' (1999: 701–7). One of the differentiating features of these sites is the degree of governmental presence, from high in the case of intergovernmental sites to low in the case of private, self-regulatory regimes and loose couplings, where interactions between transnational and governmental actors will tend to be relatively sparse and unstructured. In the context of European and EU diplomacy, examples of each of these forms are clearly visible. As Keukeleire notes, a focus on the CFSP provides a much more traditional, intergovernmentalist diplomatic environment in which the range of actors is limited and in which foreign ministries play a significant role. This stands in contrast to his depiction of pillar-transcending 'structural' diplomacy as defined earlier in this chapter, which is 'centred around quite an extensive agenda of institutionalised dialogue between very diverse actors from the EU and the third states concerned' (Keukeleire, 2000: 25). The constituent networks on which this dimension of EU diplomacy rests embrace not only a proliferation of governmental actors but, as noted earlier, NGOs and other representatives of civil society.

The 'loose couplings' end of the Coleman and Perl network spectrum provides an increasingly rich yet, in traditional diplomatic imagery, unconventional field of activity which European diplomacy is exploring both within and outside the broader and narrower (EU) confines of Europeanness. Often, the form of network resembles that referred to as an 'issue network', based more on a mutual interest in pooling knowledge and ideas rather than a highly developed sense of shared values. Moreover, each is characterised by a varying degree of 'co-opetition' between actors which confers on it significant elements of fragility and uncertainty. It is often noted that such networks, whilst they are differentiated from hierarchical structures in the sense that they are based on vertical organisational principles, are not hierarchy-free. Some actors are likely to be critical nodes in the network, or 'linking-pin organizations' as Jönsson et al. term them: 'Some actors are able to control communication channels between actors that are unable to communicate directly' (1998: 328).

Conclusion

Change is occurring within both diplomatic processes and the diplomatic systems which remain amongst their most significant agents. The long (and continuing) story of intra-bureaucratic adaptation – a dominant theme in the development of European integration – has been overlaid by the need to construct policy networks that transcend the state, reflecting the resource deficiencies experienced by both governmental and non-governmental actors. Within the EU, the resultant patterns of interaction are particularly complex, given its multilayered nature and the possibilities that these provide for member states to pursue their own diplomatic strategies within and alongside an emergent European diplomacy. In turn, this requires us to re-examine the stories that diplomats tell themselves about what they do and how they do it – in other words, the constitution of diplomacy and its practitioners.

The resultant, indeterminate picture is one of ambiguity and contradiction reflecting the uncertainties surrounding the analysis and practice of foreign policy and the interplay of differing dynamics. One conclusion would be to view the emergence of a pan-European diplomacy as the logical and final stage in the development of the European project, reflecting in part the reintegration of the domestic and the foreign whose separation provided the rationale for the development of European diplomacy in the post-Medieval world. Another is to view the development of a nascent EU diplomacy as the 'rescue' of national diplomatic systems (Allen, 1996). Yet another appears to lie in the tensions between these images as the drive towards the construction of a European diplomatic identity faces the growing 'commercialisation' of national diplomacy and the preoccupation with brand and image in the pursuit of enhanced market share in a competitive global economy.

References

Allen, D. (1996) 'Conclusions: the European rescue of national foreign policy?', in C. Hill (ed.), *The Actors in Europe's Foreign Policy*. London: Routledge. pp. 288–304.

Ammon, R. (1998) 'Telediplomacy: collapsing time and space, and a new diplomatic paradigm'. Paper presented at the 39th International Studies Association Convention, March 1998, Minneapolis.

Anderson, M. (1993) *The Rise of Modern Diplomacy 1450–1919*. London: Longman.

Ansell, C. and Weber, S. (1999) 'Organizing international politics: sovereignty and open systems', *International Political Science Review*, 20 (1): 73–94.

Berridge, G. (1995) *Diplomacy: Theory and Practice*. London: Prentice Hall/Harvester Wheatsheaf.

Blair, A. (2000) 'Permanent representations to the European Union', *DSP Discussion Papers*, No. 68. Leicester: Centre for the Study of Diplomacy.

Bruter, M. (1999) 'Diplomacy without a state: the external delegations of the European Commission', *Journal of European Public Policy*, 6 (2): 183–205.

Center for Strategic and International Studies (1998) *Reinventing Diplomacy in the Information Age*. Washington, DC: CSIS.

Clarke, M. (2000) 'Diplomacy, security and the future of European defence: reflections on the Heisbourg Report', *International Affairs*, 76 (4): 725–40.

Cohen, R. (1999) 'Reflections on the new global diplomacy: statecraft 2500 BC to 2000 AD', in J. Melissen (ed.), *Innovation in Diplomatic Practice*. Basingstoke: Macmillan.

Coleman, R. and Perl, A. (1999) 'Internationalized policy environments and policy network analysis', *Political Studies*, 47 (4): 691–709.

Constantinou, C. (1996) *On the Way to Diplomacy*. Borderlines, Vol. 7. Minneapolis, MN: University of Minnesota Press.

Cooper, A. and Hayes, G. (eds) (2000) *Worthwhile Initiatives? Canadian Mission-oriented Diplomacy*. Toronto: Irwin.

Cooper, A. and Hocking, B. (2000) 'Governments, non-governmental organisations and the re-calibration of diplomacy', *Global Society*, 14 (3): 361–76.

Correia, J. (2002) 'Portugal', in B. Hocking and D. Spence (eds), *Foreign Ministries in the European Union: Integrating Diplomats*. Basingstoke: Palgrave. pp. 191–211.

Der Derian, J. (1987) *On Diplomacy: A Genealogy of Western Estrangement*. Oxford: Blackwell.

Duke, S. (1997) 'Diplomacy without a corps: training for EU external representation?', *DSP Discussion Papers, No. 31*. Leicester: Centre for the Study of Diplomacy.

Ekengren, M. and Sundelius, B. (2002) 'Sweden', in B. Hocking and D. Spence (eds), *Foreign Ministries in the European Union: Integrating Diplomats*. Basingstoke: Palgrave. pp. 238–49.

Eldon, S. (1994) *From Quill Pen to Satellite: Foreign Ministries in the Information Age*. London: Royal Institute of International Affairs.

Esty, D. and Geradin, D. (2000) 'Regulatory co-opetition', *Journal of International Economic Law*, 3 (2): 235–55.

Evans, P., Jacobson, H. and Putnam, R. (eds) (1993) *Double-Edged Diplomacy: International Bargaining and Domestic Politics*. Berkeley: University of California Press.

Hamilton, K. and Langhorne, R. (1995) *The Practice of Diplomacy: its Evolution, Theory and Administration*. London: Routledge.

Henrikson, A. (1997) 'Diplomacy for the 21st century: "re-crafting the old guild"', *Wilton Park Occasional Paper 1*.

Hill, C. and Wallace, W. (1996) 'Introduction: actors and actions', in C. Hill (ed.), *The Actors in Europe's Foreign Policy*. London: Routledge. pp. 1–16.

Hocking, B. (1999) 'Catalytic diplomacy: Beyond "newness" and "decline"', in J. Melissen (ed.), *Innovation in Diplomatic Practice*. London: Macmillan. pp. 21–42.

Hocking, B. (2000) 'The diplomacy of image and memory: Swiss bankers and Nazi gold', *DSP Discussion Papers, No. 64*. Leicester: Centre for the Study of Diplomacy.

Hocking, B. and Spence, D. (2002) *Foreign Ministries in the European Union: Integrating Diplomats*. Basingstoke: Palgrave.

Jönsson, C., Bjurulf, B., Ecgstörm, O., Sannerstedt, A. and Störmvik, M. (1998), 'Negotiations in networks in the European Union', *International Negotiation*, 3 (3): 319–44.

Jørgensen, K.E. (1997) 'Modern European diplomacy: a research agenda', *DSP Discussion Papers, No. 31*. Leicester: Centre for the Study of Diplomacy.

Kassim, H., Guy Peters, B. and Wright, V. (2000) *The National Co-ordination of EU Policy: The Domestic Level*. Oxford: Oxford University Press.

Keohane, R.O. and Nye, J.S. Jr. (2000) 'Globalization: what's new? What's not? (And so what?)', *Foreign Policy* 118 (Spring): 104–19.

Keukeleire, S. (2000) 'The European Union as a diplomatic actor', *DSP Discussion Papers, No. 71*. Leicester: Centre for the Study of Diplomacy.

Krasner, S. (1995) 'Power politics, institutions and transnational relations', in T. Risse-Kappen (ed.), *Bringing Transnational Relations Back In: Non-state Actors, Domestic Structures and International Relations*. Cambridge: Cambridge University Press. pp. 257–79.

Laffan, B., O'Donnell, R. and Smith, M. (2000) *Europe's Experimental Union: Rethinking Integration*. London: Routledge.

Lee, D. (2001) 'A new UK commercial diplomacy? UK export promotion in a global economy'. Paper presented at the 42nd International Studies Association Convention, February, Chicago.

Leonard, M. and Alakeson, V. (2000) *Going Public: Diplomacy for the Information Society*. London: Foreign Policy Centre.

Mackie, J. (2001) 'Bringing civil society into foreign and security policy', European Policy Centre, *Challenge Europe: On-Line Journal*. Accessed February. http://www.theepc.be/Challenge_Europe/text/memo.asp?ID=200.

Manners, I. and Whitman, R. (2000) 'Introduction', in I. Manners and R. Whitman (eds), *The Foreign Policies of European Union Member States*. Manchester: Manchester University Press.

Nicolson, H. (1939) *Diplomacy*, London: Thornton Butterworth.

Nye Jr., J. (1990) *Bound to Lead: The Changing Nature of American Power*. New York, NY: Basic Books.

O'Brien, R.A., Goetz, M., Scholte, J.A. and Williams, M. (2000) *Contesting Global Governance: Multilateral Economic Institutions and Global Social Movements*. Cambridge: Cambridge University Press.

Paschke, K. (2000) 'Report of the special inspection of 14 German embassies in the countries of the European Union' (English translation). Berlin: Federal Foreign Office.

Pfetsch, F. (1998) 'Negotiating the European Union: a negotiation-network approach', *International Negotiation*, 3 (3): 293–317.

Public Administration (1998) 'Comparing networks', special issue, 76 (2).

Reinecke, W. (1998) *Global Public Policy: Governing without Government?* Washington, DC: Brookings.

Reinecke, W. (2000) 'The other world wide web: global public policy networks', *Foreign Policy*, 117 (Winter): 44–57.

Reychler, L. (1979) *Patterns of Diplomatic Thinking: a Cross-national Study of Structural and Social-Psychological Determinants*. New York, NY: Praeger.

Risse-Kappen, T. (1995) 'Bringing transnational relations back in: Introduction', in T. Risse-Kappen (ed.), *Bringing Transnational Relations Back In: Non-state Actors, Domestic Structures and International Relations*. Cambridge: Cambridge University Press. pp. 3–36.

Rosenau, J. (2000) 'States, sovereignty and diplomacy in the information age'. *Virtual Diplomacy Series, No. 5*. Washington, DC: United States Institute of Peace.

Scholte, J.A. (1997) 'Global capitalism and the state', *International Affairs*, 73 (3): 453–68.

Sharp, P. (1999) 'For diplomacy: representation and the study of international relations', *International Studies Review*, 1 (1): 33–57.

Smith, G.S. (1997) 'Driving diplomacy into cyberspace', *The World Today*, 53 (June): 156–8.

Smith, G.S. (2000) 'Reinventing diplomacy: a virtual necessity', *United States Institute of Peace, Virtual Diplomacy Series, No. 6*. Washington, DC: United States Institute of Peace.

Smith, M. (1996) 'The EU as an international actor', in J. Richardson (ed.), *European Union: Power and Policy-Making*. London: Routledge. pp. 247–62.

Soetendorp, B. (1999) *Foreign Policy in the European Union: Theory, History and Practice*. London: Longman.

Sofer, S. (1998) 'Old and new diplomacy: a debate revisited', *Review of International Studies*, 14 (3): 195–212.

Stone, D. (1997) 'Networks, second track diplomacy and regional co-operation: the role of Southeast Asian think-tanks'. Paper presented to 38th International Studies Association Convention, Toronto.

Strange, S. (1992) 'States, firms and diplomacy', *International Affairs*, 68 (1): 1–15.

Tehranian, M. (1999) *Global Communications and World Politics: Domination, Development, and Discourse*. Boulder, CO: Rienner.

Van Schendelen, M. (ed.) (1993) *National Public and Private EC Lobbying*. Aldershot: Dartmouth.

Vogel, D. (1997) *Barriers or Benefits: Regulation in Transatlantic Trade*. Washington, DC: Brookings.

Walzenbach, G. (2001) 'Death of a salesman? German foreign economic policy at fifty'. Paper presented at 42nd International Studies Association Convention, February Chicago.

White, B. (2001) *Understanding European Foreign Policy*. Basingstoke: Palgrave.

Williamson, H. (2000) 'Foreign Office may boost secondee scheme', *Financial Times*, 26 June.

6 National Foreign Policy Co-ordination

Magnus Ekengren and Bengt Sundelius

This chapter addresses a classic concern in foreign policy analysis, namely the possibilities of and the obstacles to forging coherent national positions through some form of foreign policy co-ordination by the state. It is widely argued among contemporary commentators that policy coherence is a prerequisite for asserting influence abroad and protecting the state from unwanted foreign influences at home. The essence of traditional statecraft, to protect the state from its enemies abroad, requires the co-ordination of foreign policy. This thesis was formulated in the classic maxim of the 19th-century German strategic thinker, Leopold von Ranke: *Das Primat der Aussenpolitik*. It has been a cornerstone of the constitutional praxis of European governments for several hundred years.

The question that must be asked here is how this tradition of statecraft in pursuit of national interests has been challenged by the voluntary inclusion of European states in the evolving European Union (EU). The notion of diplomacy and its various manifestations has clearly changed within the EU context (see Hocking, Chapter 5 in this volume). Similarly, legal and political requirements for sector-defined interpenetrations among the member states, as codified in the Amsterdam and Nice Treaties, would seem to erode the Rankean tradition of foreign policy co-ordination, including the centrality of bilateral relations with other EU members and with the common institutions. The EU has certainly created an element of external policy fragmentation across many sectors and actors within each state. Nevertheless, we shall find in this chapter and in the subsequent Swedish case study (Ekengren, Chapter 13 in this volume) that national foreign policy co-ordination in support of vital interests is still very much in evidence today. But the context in which national co-ordination operates is being fundamentally transformed by the EU.

The aim of this chapter is to examine how traditional state-oriented European diplomacy is affected by the *multi-level* character of the EU and its particular demands on national co-ordination and interest representation. Jørgensen and Hocking (Chapters 2 and 5 in this volume) show how intra-EU negotiation now extends beyond traditional state-centred intra-European diplomacy. The argument here is that the transformation of diplomacy is also the result of the increasingly marked EU *levels* of governance that have to be connected by national foreign policy co-ordination. In this chapter, we focus on different ideal types of co-ordination measures at the national level that could be used to perform this task. In Chapter 13, Ekengren examines the place of national co-ordination in the multiple level game of European foreign policy (EFP) on the basis of an empirical case study. He shows that the co-ordination of EU member state representation at the EU level is aimed not only at securing the national interest *in* the EU, but also gets its organi- sational dynamics from the tasks it has to perform *for* the Union in the inter- national arena. This is national co-ordination for a multi-layered EFP and can be explained in terms of a notion of *complementary* sovereignty between the national and the EU levels, rather than a *shared* or *divided* sovereignty as often suggested elsewhere.

Interdependence and Foreign Policy

The international and domestic contexts of European foreign relations have changed considerably during the post-war era. Some of the novel conditions are related to the formation and development of the EU, but many are not. Wider international trends have also affected the working conditions in the Union. Membership of the Union merely accentuates these operating conditions.

During the 1970s and 1980s, a considerable body of academic literature was devoted to the analysis of the then emerging trend of complex interde- pendence. US scholars in particular noted this novel feature of international relations (IR). The archetype was US–Canadian patterns of transnational, transgovernmental and intergovernmental relations (Young, 1969; Keohane and Nye, 1974, 1975, 1977). Scholars working on Europe could point to many applications of these ideas in the already intense and multi-faceted intra- European relations (Kaiser, 1971; Morse, 1973; Mally, 1976; Sundelius, 1977, 1980). More recently, the globalisation trend has attracted the attention of leading IR scholars (Zürn, 2002). In many respects, the earlier pattern of complex interdependence is further elaborated in this more recent literature, but expanded beyond geographical pockets of relations among the so-called advanced industrial societies to span across the globe (Morse, 1976; Hanrieder, 1978; Scott, 1982). The impact of finance, media, telecommunica- tions and various non-governmental advocacy organisations have been added to the earlier, more limited, yet still extensive complexity. Intra-EU relations form a fully developed example of this wider pattern affecting the national conduct of foreign policy. The Union, therefore, can be understood as a particular and evolving form of IR as well as being depicted as a European polity in the making (Rosamond, 2000). It is in this context that this chapter focuses on national foreign policy co-ordination as a means of forging coherence in IR and linking levels in an evolving EU constitution.

The European states have penetrated their own societies deeply over the last 50 years. At the same time, they have extended their spheres of involvement more widely across the EU and beyond. Domestic issues in one region of the continent now have direct implications for other corners of Europe with respect, for example, to food safety and other standards. Many countries have experienced similar task expansion processes, leading both to demands for international co-operation and to clashes of interests. As a result, the policy setting for each government is constituted by an entangled web of domestic and external activity, which can still be most appropriately characterised as a systemic structure of complex interdependence. Earlier research has shown that European governments have undergone an internationalisation process that has involved fundamental structural changes (Egeberg, 1980; East, 1981; East and Salomonsen, 1981; Sundelius, 1984; Karvonen and Sundelius, 1987). Much of this structural transformation can be traced to the impact of the evolving EC/EU (Wallace, 1984; Wessels and Rometsch, 1996; Soetendorp and Hanf, 1998; Harmsen, 1999).

Several effects on national foreign policy processes can be associated with these structural changes. National management of external relations is now characterised by a proliferation of actors, issues, channels and procedures. The traditional foreign policy apparatus centred upon the foreign ministry is increasingly unable to control effectively the ever-broadening and intensifying external involvement of the state. To overcome a potential management crisis, several new offices for international affairs have developed in a rather sporadic and *ad hoc* basis. Subsequently, the internationalisation of government structures has been coupled with a decentralisation of foreign policy processes. This, in turn, has raised concerns about the proper co-ordination of external relations and has contributed to jurisdictional conflicts in this area (Morse, 1976; Wallace, 1978; East, 1984; Karvonen and Sundelius, 1987; Underdal, 1987).

The Panacea of Co-ordination

Co-ordination can be classified as one of the 'contested concepts', alongside terms like 'power' and 'security'. It can be viewed as a condition that exists when the parties in question share a common purpose. Alternatively, co-ordination can be regarded as a process involving increasingly shared activity; from information sharing, through task sharing, to joint planning to synchronising an activity or an external position. Some authors emphasise the role of co-ordination as a means of establishing internal political and administrative control of public policy, including foreign relations. Others view it as an instrument to enhance organisational efficiency by determining the division of tasks among the sub-units concerned with an issue or a policy sector.

In abstract terms, co-ordination implies the creation of a common order for a number of separate elements that are distinct, but also linked in some way with respect to their tasks or purposes. It also suggests that the activities of different units are interrelated in a manner conditioned by some overarching value. In the foreign policy realm, the so-called national interest would be such a superior value. From this perspective, the purpose of co-ordination is to ensure that the outputs of the various units are not in fundamental conflict. Others might view this more modestly as an exercise in organisational coexistence rather than policy co-ordination. But the minimal purpose would be to limit competition, divide roles, and share tasks and resources.

Governments undertake a number of co-ordination activities for the ostensible purpose of strengthening their national foreign and security posture in a competitive international setting. These activities also generate effects upon government units and can shift their standing abroad and at home. Thus, they should be evaluated both in terms of their policy coherence objectives and also in terms of their consequential impact on the allocation of resources, status and influence over national policy. This holds true also for attempts to improve policy co-ordination among states, such as those that are members of the constantly evolving EU.

Policy coherence is a major objective of all forms of co-ordination, including attempts at national foreign policy co-ordination. A similar objective underlies the parallel attempt to develop EU-based foreign and security co-ordination. It is an open question whether this process remains an exercise in coexistence among the EU member governments and the several common institutions, or whether a more ambitious effort is underway to forge coherent positions across the broad scope of the EFP agenda. It is also of interest to explore the relationship between the dynamics of co-ordination at the national and at the European level. Do national co-ordination mechanisms facilitate or hinder foreign policy co-ordination across the member states? Is less co-ordination in one sphere of activity necessary to achieve more co-ordination in another? Are highly co-ordinated national foreign policy systems necessary to strike the bargains required to move towards a coherent European foreign and security policy? What differences in procedure and coherence can be discerned between different policy sectors and between routine policy formulation and the making of major EU decisions? Some answers to these questions are suggested here.

Co-ordination processes can be distinguished along several dimensions:

- The *procedural style* can vary from reliance upon sector or issue specialisation to comprehensive control through centralised representation.
- The *decision-making dynamics* can be based upon building consensus among equal parties or upon overt leadership by a political or organisational hegemon.
- *Motivations for unit adherence* to common positions can be based upon respect for the professional expertise of others, or on a gradual socialisation into a culture of shared principles and standards.

Assuming two end positions along each of the three dimensions, we have identified six ideal types of national foreign policy co-ordination.

Co-ordination through specialisation

With this approach, no single ministry or agency has overall responsibility for the co-ordination of foreign policy. Instead, different units perform this function in separate policy sectors. Several specialised co-ordination units coexist within the foreign policy establishment. The foreign ministry has a distinctive authority only in a limited sector, while other ministries or units take lead roles elsewhere. The functionalist theory of integration explains why this form of national co-ordination can serve political objectives beyond the national interest. At the European level, indeed, specialised responsibility for co-ordinating the broad scope of foreign relations may be the most cost-effective way of dealing with the many units and issues involved. By avoiding a tight grip on overall co-ordination, each sector unit may stay closer to the substance of foreign affairs and develop considerable expertise within its area of jurisdiction. Also, one might expect that sector-based co-ordination would facilitate policy coherence at the European level where attempts are made to forge national postures into a common European position.

Co-ordination through representation

This approach recognises that states do not strive for national co-ordination for its own sake, but to face more effectively an adversary, a rival or other foreign stakeholders. They seek a posture which is co-ordinated with respect to the international setting and to various international negotiating fora. From this perspective, it would seem logical to place the responsibility for national co-ordination at the contact point with the identified target. It can be argued that the foreign mission to another state or international organisation has the most comprehensive and informed perspective on the total relationship with this target. This is where all the ties between various functional areas are brought together, allowing for an assessment of their relative importance to the overall relationship. At the European level, the Permanent Representatives can pull together the many diverse links between member states and the policy-making processes of the EU. The Representatives are not merely a 'branch office' of the foreign ministries, but rather an outpost of the entire home government of the member states.

Co-ordination through consensus

With this approach to co-ordination, no single unit is responsible. Instead, this shared objective is achieved by broadly-based committees that include all actors with legitimate stakes in the relevant foreign policy field. If time does not allow for face-to-face meetings, then information sharing, consultation and joint drafting of positions are appropriate procedures. The objective here is to create a consensus on issues before they are placed on the agenda of working committees. Each ministry or unit is then expected to follow the agreed principles or guidelines and to support the implementation of policy based upon them. In principle, this should obviate the need for executive directives and direct overseeing of the post-decisional activities of the various units involved. At the European level, however, national consensus building might be too slow to serve as a foundation for policy-making in rapidly moving EU negotiations. If an intergovernmental EU consensus is to be achieved, this might require more flexibility and speed in forging national positions.

Co-ordination through political leadership

This approach emphasises the central position of the head of government as the co-ordinator of all public policy, including foreign policy. The prime minister or president, together with their cabinet colleagues and executive agencies, can provide a broader perspective on policy than any single ministry or unit. Over the last 25 years or so, centralised mechanisms, such as cabinet offices, in many European governments have expanded their co-ordinating roles, often at the expense of foreign offices.

Co-ordination through professional expertise

A traditional strategy for achieving coherence is to utilise the expertise of foreign ministry staff. Only these professionals, it might be argued, possess the special training and experience necessary to formulate and implement foreign policy. Several areas of competence can be highlighted here. Diplomats are familiar with the protocol of intergovernmental relations and can ensure that negotiations are effectively handled. They have the negotiating skills together with specialist knowledge of the tactics and interests of both adversaries and partners. Through their unique understanding of the dynamics of the international political game, diplomats can protect the national interest across a wide range of policy sectors. The foreign ministry itself has considerable expertise in the details of international law and understands the obligations and the international commitments of the state. In addition, through its control of classified archives, the foreign ministry is the keeper of the 'national memory' with respect to foreign policy.

Co-ordination through socialisation

With this norm-building approach, foreign policy co-ordination is sought through shared notions of what constitutes the national interest. This approach is particularly relevant when the state has a widely supported and well-established foreign policy doctrine. A shared doctrine can be used to evaluate all foreign policy activities for conformity with established norms. The US 'war on terrorism' since 9/11 and its homeland security concept are good examples of recent doctrinal initiatives to enhance national security co-ordination through the socialisation of relevant government agencies at federal, state and local levels.

In this section, we have sketched the general features of six ways of solving the organisational problem of how best to achieve national foreign policy co-ordination. Most, if not all, of the ideal types are used in some form by member states of the EU. The case study developed in Chapter 13 looks at how these types of co-ordination were deployed to forge a coherent Swedish posture during the Swedish presidency of the EU in the first half of 2001. The next section of this chapter looks in more detail at how established national processes of co-ordination have been adapted to operate at the EU level.

National Co-ordination at the EU Level

A heightened concern with co-ordination at the centre of national admini-strations is perhaps the most obvious illustration of common patterns of Europeanisation in EU member states (Soetendorp and Hanf, 1998; Luif, 1998: 125; Harmsen, 1999: 97; Hocking, 1999; Manners and Whitman, 2000: 260). EU concerns and EU deadlines percolate down deeply into national as well as European bureaucracies. But this has both centralising and decen-tralising effects. On the one hand, there is pressure on all national policy-makers concerned with EU affairs to follow centrally determined norms, rules and deadlines. On the other hand, EU time constraints means that there is less time for individual departments, groups and officials to be instructed by higher level authorities which may, in turn, lead to more decentralised decision-making. In order to ease the tensions between these two trends, shifts of institutional powers are taking place within the central governmen-tal structures of member states.

Centralisation

The simultaneous demands for action at the EU level create a demand for a top-down approach to the management of national administrations. There are increasing pressures on national administrations to implement EU decisions within narrow time constraints. As a result, states like the Netherlands, France and Norway have developed increasingly co-ordinated mechanisms at the centre to strengthen and speed up implementation procedures 'downstream' (Harmsen, 1999: 101; Soetendorp and Hanf, 1998: 43–5). Not only modes of co-ordination, but also the extent of co-ordination has changed (Sverdrup, 1998: 160). In many member states, there has been a need for more co-ordinating per-sonnel and their workload has increased (George, 1992; Ekengren and Sundelius, 1998: 139; Sverdrup, 1998: 157). In The Netherlands, for example, 'since both the Co-Co (Co-ordinating Committee for European Integration) and the Cabinet act under the pressure of the deadlines of the coming ministerial Councils in Brussels, another high-level co-ordination committee has been created in the Hague alongside the Co-Co' (Soetendorp and Hanf, 1998: 41).

Centralising trends often include the co-ordination of EU policy within the Prime Minister's own office, leading to what might be called a 'prime ministerialisation' of EU policy-making. In the Netherlands, the prime minister convenes the ministers principally concerned with European policy in the Council for European and International Affairs and there has been a clear concentration of powers in the office of the Prime Minister (Harmsen, 1999: 94–7). The prime minister is ultimately responsible for the co-ordination of European policy and is also responsible to the Dutch parliament for problems of co-ordination. Also the Danish prime minister has been playing an increasing role in shaping EU policy. One of the main reasons for reorganising the prime minister's office has been to create a capacity to control the ministries (von Dosenrode, 1998: 58–9). In Norway, according to Sverdrup, the prime minister's office plays the role of 'a competent commentator providing deadlines and co-ordination of the "national interest"' (1998: 159–60).

Behind this institutional activity lie concerns that the co-ordination of national actions in various EU institutions has been inadequate. Ministries have not been able to formulate clear and timely directives to national representatives in Brussels. Indeed, ministries themselves are considered to be too small to prepare national positions on a daily basis and to act as future-orientated strategic units. The expansion of co-ordinating mechanisms has been justified by governments both in terms of enabling national ministries to work more strategically and to improve the administrative capacity overall to pursue a more proactive and influential posture in particular policy areas (Ladrech, 1994; Soetendorp and Hanf, 1998).

It is often the foreign ministries themselves that have become strong advocates of central co-ordination in order to enhance national influence in the EU. Such a centralising process is necessary if member goverments wish to avoid a disaggregation of the state into sector-defined European networks. The role of EU national co-ordinators in member states sheds further light on the need for active centralised co-ordination in the face of externally imposed timetables for decision making. The co-ordinator is often both the creator and the upholder of coherent national positions which are essential to present an image at least of national homogeneity. In order to manage European policy effectively, the traditonal sequence of govermental activity is now broken up and this includes limiting the autonomy of foreign ministries in the name of co-ordination. There is now little time 'to wait until every different view has been settled' before unified national action. Indeed, there is no purely 'national interval' for forging national action.

This task of managing European policy is reflected in the role of the lead EU departments. Whatever their specific institutional form – whether the department of foreign affairs, the department of the European Union, the EU co-ordination secretariat, or the ministry of finance – they are often the link between the national permanent representation in Brussels and the various 'domestic' ministries. They have the responsibility for ensuring that positions are prepared for all items on the agendas prepared by the EU presidency, and for finalising and transmitting official instructions to the representatives in COREPER and in Council meetings. Moreover, these departments often have the additional responsibility for co-ordinating relations between the ministries and the national parliaments (Luif, 1998; Sverdrup, 1998).

Significantly, new catchphrases are emerging to provide a focus for centralised co-ordination and to counteract any resistance to effective adaptation in an EU context. In Austria, for example, there has been a call for the elaboration of a 'comprehensive strategy' to frame all Austrian action in the EU (Luif, 1998). In Sweden, the aim of central co-ordination should be to form 'common outlooks' that can guide national representatives in complex European policy-making processes (Ekengren and Sundelius, 2002). Such unifying concepts are important because formalised and regularised central co-ordination is very difficult in the complex multi-level EU context. One institutional result is that new government agencies, or 'planning services', responsible for shaping common outlooks across a range of policy sectors are being set up in, for example, Greece (Christakis, 1998: 92), Ireland – the Institute of European Affairs (Laffan and Tannam, 1998: 82), Austria (Luif, 1998) and Sweden – the Swedish Institute of European Policy Studies (Ekengren and Sundelius, 1998: 143). Their purpose is to bring together diverse societal and corporate interests and prepare national directives for long-term strategic priorities.

Decentralisation

A contrasting consequence of high-speed European processes is that national political actors are forced to act more independently of the centre and on mandates defined in advance. Pressures to respond quickly thus create decentralisation and informalisation of administration. As Laffan and Tannam comment in the Irish context, 'An emphasis on the immediate to the neglect of the medium to long term is a feature of this administrative culture. Policy-making in Dublin tends to be reactive rather than active in nature. Position papers and negotiating tactics are worked out at each stage of the policy process. This policy style is reinforced by the Community's decision-making process which is dominated by negotiations and highly segmented' (1998: 79).

The short time spans between EU meetings challenge the logic of appropriate procedures in national administration. In particular, the pace of EU decision making creates problems for the tradition of securing wide support for every decision, both within and outside the administration. There is simply less time for officials to anchor national actions in the EU securely at home, which leads to more autonomy for individuals and a more important role for flexible and informal contacts (Wallace, 1971, 1973; Ekengren and Sundelius, 1998; Luif, 1998: 122). As noted in the previous section, new co-ordinating institutions, such as the Secretariat of State for the EC in the Spanish Ministry of Foreign Affairs, have been created to counteract the decentralising effects of European governance (Morata, 1998: 103). But, at the same time, the permanent delegations in Brussels representing all parts of the government are growing. We may well see in the future co-ordination problems between Brussels-based and home-based national officials.

Member states face a serious strategic management dilemma. To be able effectively to engage in the multiple policy-shaping networks and informal decision fora, experienced and specialised national officials must be free to participate without being unnecessarily hampered by central co-ordination or control mechanisms. But co-ordination at the national centre may actually restrict the ability to maximise national influence at all stages – pre-decision, decision and post-decisional – of vital policy processes. This dilemma raises fundamental questions about the precise purposes of national co-ordination.

Institutionalising a European time line

In an important sense, national co-ordination faces a qualitatively new situation in the EU. Senior officials complain that 'we do not control the timetable any more'. The challenges to existing national procedures not only relate to harmonising the substance of policy, but also to harmonising 'when' questions. Timetables are seen as more important and more constraining because they are now beyond national control. Different ministries and government agencies follow separate timetables for preparing and making EU policy. Consequently, they all need to formulate and schedule positions in relation to these 'external' deadlines. But the Europeanisation of time inside member governments is uneven and this fosters fragmentation of processes and of policy substance. Even within the confines of the Common Foreign and Security Policy (CFSP), the splitting up of national diplomats into working groups means that they work permanently on different timetables or simply different working-group meeting schedules.

The complexity of various timetables, each of which is monitored mainly by the official participating in the particular working group, erodes what might be called a common national foreign policy calendar. Running on different and parallel timetables makes it more difficult to ensure the logical sequence of agreeing a national position internally and then presenting that agreed position to the outside world. In the EU, this national sequence, if not actually disappearing, is seriously squeezed by narrow time slots generated by external demands for speedy action (Ekengren, 2002: Ch. 3).

Due to the number of working groups and the extent of simultaneous meetings, national positions are in a constant formation and re-formation process. For smaller EU member states at least, this process can be described in terms that suggest the national present is, to an increasing extent, being 'crowded out' by a European present. The fact that the common EU present is imposed and enforced by the necessity to participate in the given moment of decision alters the character of traditional ministerial work. EU deadlines are spread deeply into national bureaucracy forming novel time-based norms and rules. The pace of decision making is gaining ground in determining the final policy result, possibly at the cost of factors relating to policy substance. Returning to the argument developed at the beginning of this chapter, this European phenomenon is a manifestation of a wider trend observed by scholars of complex interdependence: space is being replaced by pace as a major determinant of outcomes in international relations (Scott, 1982; Virilio, 1986).

References

Christakis, M. (1998) 'Greece: competing regional priorities', in B. Soetendorp and K. Hanf (eds), *Adapting to European Integration: Small States and the European Union.* London: Longman.

East, M. (1981) 'The organizational impact of interdependence on foreign policy-making: the case of Norway', in C. Kegley and P. McGowan (eds), *The Political Economy of Foreign Policy Behaviour.* Sage International Yearbook of Foreign Policy Studies, Vol. 6. Beverly Hills, CA: Sage. pp. 137–61.

East, M. (1984) 'Coordinating foreign policy: the changing role of the Norwegian foreign ministry', *Cooperation and Conflict,* 19 (2): 121–34.

East, M. and Salomonsen, L. (1981) 'Adapting foreign policy-making to interdependence', *Cooperation and Conflict,* 16 (3): 165–82.

Egeberg, M. (1980) 'The fourth level of government: on the standardization of public policy within international regimes', *Scandinavian Political Studies,* 3 (3): 235–48.

Ekengren, M. (2002) *The Time of European Governance.* Manchester: Manchester University Press.

Ekengren, M. and Sundelius, B. (1998) 'The Swedish state joins the European Union', in B. Soetendorp and K. Hanf (eds), *Adapting to European Integration: Small States and the European Union.* London: Longman.

Ekengren, M. and Sundelius, B. (2002) 'Sweden', in B. Hocking and D. Spence (eds), *Foreign Ministers in the European Union: Integrating Diplomats.* London: Palgrave.

George, S. (ed.) (1992) *Britain and the European Community: The Politics of Semi-Detachment.* Oxford: Clarendon.

Hanrieder, W. (1978) 'Dissolving international politics: reflections on the nation-state', *American Political Science Review,* 72 (4): 1276–87.

Harmsen, R. (1999) 'The Europeanization of national administrations: a comparative study of France and The Netherlands', *Governance: An International Journal of Policy and Administration,* 12 (1): 81–113.

Hocking, B. (ed.) (1999) *Foreign Ministries: Change and Adaptation.* Basingstoke: Macmillan.

Kaiser, K. (1971) 'Transnational politics: towards a theory of multinational politics', *International Organization,* 25 (4): 790–817.

Karvonen, L. and Sundelius, B. (1987) *Internationalization and Foreign Policy Management.* Aldershot: Gower.

Keohane, R. and Nye, J. (1974) 'Transgovernmental relations and international organization', *World Politics,* 27 (1): 39–62.

Keohane, R. and Nye, J. (1975) 'International interdependence and integration', in F. Greenstein and N. Polsby (eds), *Handbook of Political Science,* Vol. 8. Reading: Addison-Wesley.

Keohane, R. and Nye, J. (1977) *Power and Interdependence.* Boston, MA: Little Brown.

Ladrech, R. (1994) 'Europeanisation of domestic politics and institutions: the case of France', *Journal of Common Market Studies,* 32 (1): 69–88.

Laffan, B. and Tannam, E. (1998) 'Ireland: the rewards of pragmatism', in B. Soetendorp and K. Hanf (eds), *Adapting to European Integration: Small States and the European Union.* London: Longman.

Luif, P. (1998) 'Austria: adaptation through anticipation', in B. Soetendorp and K. Hanf (eds), *Adapting to European Integration: Small States in the European Union.* London: Longman.

Mally, G. (1976) *Interdependence.* Lexington, NY: Heath.

Manners, I. and Whitman, R. (eds) (2000) *The Foreign Policies of European Union Member States.* Manchester: Manchester University Press.

Morata, F. (1998) 'Spain: modernization through integration', in B. Soetendorp and K. Hanf (eds), *Adapting to European Integration: Small States in the European Union.* London: Longman.

Morse, E. (1973) *Foreign Policy and Interdependence in Gaullist France.* Princeton, NJ: Princeton University Press.

Morse, E. (1976) *Modernization and the Transformation of International Relations.* New York, NY: Free Press.

Rosamond, B. (2000) *Theories of European Integration.* New York, NY: St Martin's.

Scott, A. (1982) *The Dynamics of Interdependence.* Chapel Hill, NY: University of North Carolina Press.

Soetendorp, B. and Hanf, K. (eds) (1998) *Adapting to European Integration: Small States and the European Union.* London: Longman.

Sundelius, B. (1977) 'Trans-governmental interactions in the Nordic region', *Cooperation and Conflict,* 12 (2): 63–85.

Sundelius, B. (1980) 'Interdependence and foreign policy', *Cooperation and Conflict,* 15 (4): 187–208.

Sundelius, B. (1984) 'Interdependence, internationalization and foreign policy decentralization in Sweden', *Cooperation and Conflict,* 19 (2): 93–120.

Sverdrup, U. (1998) 'Norway: an adaptive non-member', in B. Soetendorp and K. Hanf (eds), *Adapting to European Integration: Small States and the European Union.* London: Longman.

Underdal, A. (1987) 'What's left for the MFA? Foreign policy and the management of external relations in Norway', *Cooperation and Conflict,* 22: 169–92.

Virilio, P. (1986) *Speed and Politics.* New York, NY: Semiotext(e)

von Dosenrode, S. (1998) 'Denmark: the testing of a hesitant membership', in B. Soetendorp and K. Hanf (eds), *Adapting to European Integration: Small States in the European Union.* London: Longman.

Wallace, H. (1971) 'The impact of the European communities on national decision-making', *Government and Opposition,* 6 (4): 520–38.

Wallace, H. (1973) *National Governments and the European Communities.* London: Chatham House.

Wallace, W. (1978) 'Old states and new circumstances: the international predicament of Britain, France and Germany', in W. Wallace and W. Paterson (eds), *Foreign Policy-Making in Western Europe.* Farnborough: Saxon House.

Wallace, W. (1984) *Britain's Bilateral Links with Western Europe.* London: Routledge and Kegan Paul.

Wessels, W. and Rometsch, D. (eds) (1996) *The European Union and Member States: Towards International Fusion?* Manchester: Manchester University Press.

Young, O. (1969) 'Interdependence in world politics', *International Journal*, 24 (4): 726–50.

Zürn, M. (2002) 'From interdependence to globalization', in W. Carlsnaes, T. Risse and B. Simmons (eds), *Handbook of International Relations*. London: Sage.

7 Collective Identity[1]

Ulrich Sedelmeier

There are numerous indications that a focus on identity should yield important insights into the study of European Foreign Policy (EFP). Several studies suggest that the European Union (EU) is a particularly prominent case of collective identity formation. Examples include contributions to the theoretical literature in EU studies (see, for example, Christiansen et al., 2001; Jørgensen, 1997), as well as constructivist analyses in the field of International Relations (IR) theory (Katzenstein, 1996: 518; Risse-Kappen, 1995b: 287; Risse, 2000: 15; Wendt, 1994: 392). Likewise, the discourse of EU practitioners on the Common Foreign and Security Policy (CFSP) is replete with references to 'identity'. For example, Article 2 (ex B) of the Treaty on European Union declares as the goal of CFSP to 'assert its identity on the international scene' and the preamble asserts that the implementation of CFSP will 'reinforce the European identity'. However, the apparent promise of a focus on identity is in stark contrast to the elusiveness of its meaning and the limited progress in our conceptual understanding of its implications for EFP. Despite the growth of research on collective identity formation in the IR literature, scholars have barely started to apply these insights to EFP (see also White, 2001: 175).

Most rationalist, and in particular materialist, approaches would question the usefulness of such an enterprise. By contrast, this chapter argues that the study of EFP can indeed benefit from a more sociological approach to the role of identity, as it allows us to address analytical blind spots and gaps in the existing literature. However, in order to reap those benefits, two important questions need analytical clarification. First, we need to clarify the nature of EU identity, or rather, what particular characteristics of EU identity matter for EFP. Second, we need a better understanding of how such an identity and the norms that constitute it have an impact on EFP.

The next section sketches the main assumptions underpinning a more sociological perspective on the role of identity for EFP. The third section suggests that while many studies of CFSP refer to the EU's 'international identity', they do not share such sociological understanding of identity, but are instead set within a rationalist and materialist framework that exogenises actors' identities and interests.

The fourth section reviews the literature in search for clues as to how a thus understood EU identity can be characterised. It identifies the articulation and validation of norms at the EU level as a particularly important aspect of EU identity formation that has the potential to predispose EFP in particular ways. I argue that one area where such an identity construction has been particularly salient for EFP since the end of the Cold War is the articulation of the EU's role in the promotion and protection of human rights and democracy.

The final three sections suggest how this evolving identity of the EU affects EFP. The fifth section distinguishes three different mechanisms through which norms affect actors' behaviour: a 'logic of appropriateness' (March and Olsen, 1989); a 'logic of arguing' (Risse, 2000); and 'rhetorical action' (Schimmelfennig, 1997). The sixth section argues that in the case of the EU, such processes of communication and the role of norm entrepreneurs are particularly important for the policy impact of the EU's collective identity. This is because norms that characterise EU identity are often diffuse and the behavioural prescriptions that they imply in a given situation are thus open to interpretation and debate. The 'logic of arguing' and 'rhetorical action' thus play a crucial role for the success of policy entrepreneurs who advocate particular foreign policy options with references to the EU's collective identity and, in turn, for the evolution and validation of such an identity. The final section illustrates the potential usefulness of a focus on identity and social norms in the study of EFP with cases that do not seem to fit easily with explanations based purely on bargaining between material utility-maximising actors.

A Sociological Perspective on the Role of Identity in EFP

As opposed to a materialist perspective that underpins most rationalist approaches, the core of a sociological perspective on the role of EU identity in EFP is that it conceives of this identity also in part as social and ideational, and that it attributes to it a causal influence on EFP, independently from material factors.

The key assumptions underpinning this position are usually identified with social constructivist arguments that actors' (collective) identities are not given, but are constructed through (social) interactions (see, for example, Wendt, 1999; Jeppersen et al., 1996).[2] These identities are 'relatively stable, role-specific understandings and expectations about self' (Wendt, 1992: 397). They form the basis for actors' definition of their preferences and provide them with an understanding of the types of behaviour through which these identities are enacted in particular situations.

These basic assumptions are shared with a number of approaches that attribute a causal role to social factors – such as identities, roles and norms – that affect actors' behaviour not only by shaping their strategies, but also their underlying interests. These approaches include (sociological) institutionalist accounts, in which actors conform to institutional roles by following a 'logic of appropriateness' (March and Olsen, 1989) and interaction role theory which suggests that 'norms – and particularly identity – emerge from a process of in-group/out-group differentiation and social role definition' (Kowert and Legro, 1996: 475; see also Walker, 1987 and for applications to the EU, Aggestam, 1999; Lerch, 2001).

In contrast to rationalist approaches that have *a priori* assumptions about actors' underlying interests and thus start from the premise that EFP follows particular (material) goals, such as stability, security or welfare, a sociological approach argues that the very nature of these interests depends crucially on actors' identities and social roles. EFP thus reflects a sense of what EU institutions and national governments consider 'appropriate behaviour' for a certain role that they collectively ascribe to themselves – as 'the EU'. EU policy makers do not simply calculate which strategy is most likely to advance their given interests in a certain situation, but they ask what their particular role in a certain situation is and which obligations that role prescribes in this situation. The formation of preferences – which actors might well pursue strategically – is endogenous to the process of identity and social role formation.

The key questions from this perspective are thus whether the EU has acquired such a collective identity and what the attributes of this identity are, in particular the content of the norms that set behavioural standards for this identity, and how this identity affects EFP.

Analyses of the EU's International Identity in CFSP Studies

The notion of the EU's 'international identity' has become a prominent feature in studies of CFSP.[3] More recently, this notion has also found its way into the analysis of the EU's external economic relations (Damro, 2001). However, these studies usually use the term 'identity' in a quite different way from the more sociological perspective outlined above. Most authors use the notion of the EU's (international) identity interchangeably with the notion of the EU's 'international role' or its 'actorness' in international affairs. The common point in these analyses is the use of these terms as a means to describe the EU's foreign policy behaviour and to assess the performance of CFSP. Thus, the EU's role as an international actor and its international identity are considered a function of the significance of the EU and its member states in international affairs and of the effectiveness of its policy practice. Central questions in these analyses are whether the EU is capable of developing policy instruments that enable it to promote collective foreign policy goals and to assert itself in international politics, as well as how effectively and consistently the EU uses the range of policy instruments at its disposal to these ends (see, for example, Bretherton and Vogler, 1999; Laffan et al., 1999: 167–72; Peterson, 1998: 11–13; Smith, M.H., 2000; Soetendorp, 1994).

A related strand of the CFSP literature aims more explicitly to conceptualise the EU's international identity or its 'actorness'. This literature has identified different roles of the EU in international politics (Hill, 1993) and has generated novel conceptualisations of the EU as a 'civilian power' (Duchêne, 1972) or as an international 'presence' (Allen and Smith, 1990). Whitman and Manners have conceptualised the EU's international identity by considering its '[foreign policy] instruments as identity' (Whitman, 1997) and have thus identified an 'active identity' of the EU through its 'network of relations' (Manners and Whitman, 1998). Still, even these more conceptual studies rarely use the terms 'identity' or 'role' in a 'deeper' sociological sense and do not accord 'identity' a causal impact on EU foreign policy. These studies thus largely share the rationalist assumption that actors are driven by narrow self-interests that are primarily influenced by material factors.

Most analyses of CFSP thus understand the EU's international identity or role as an attribute to which the EU's foreign policy ought to aspire, or a criterion to assess its capacity and performance. Identity and role are dependent variables of the analysis and the main question is, *does* the EU play a role in international affairs? By contrast, from a more sociological understanding of identity, an (international) identity is something that the EU might or might not have, but *if* it has a particular identity or social role, then this is also an independent variable, rather than (just) the dependent variable.

Attributes of EU Identity that Matter for EFP

In order to identify the characteristics of EU identity that matter for EFP, we have to consider that identities and social roles are context-bound. This boundedness means that different aspects of any given identity (or multiple identities) are salient, depending on the policy area in question (see also Risse, 2001: 201). We can distinguish two broadly different (yet complementary) ways to ascertain what aspects of 'EU identity' are salient in the area of foreign policy, according to the level of analysis.

Identities of the constituent units of an international community

The first approach focuses on the domestic level. It considers the identity of an international organisation, such as the EU, as a reflection of the (common traits of the) identities of the states that form this organisation. This approach is characteristic for liberal approaches and is most prominent in the 'democratic peace' argument. From this perspective, we would analyse how the identities and norms that prevail in the EU's member states result in a particular identity of the (international) community that they form. For example, in the case of NATO, Risse-Kappen (1995a) explains the influence of the European member states on US foreign policy with the particular salience of a consultation norm within a democratic community. In the case of the EU, Schimmelfennig (2001) argues that the EU's decision on eastern enlargement is the result of the commitment of a liberal democratic international community to expand to other democratic states. In a similar vein, Lumsdaine (1993) accounts for the establishment of the 'Western' foreign aid regime with the (social) democratic identities of the main donor states.

Norm and identity creation at the EU level

The second approach to identifying the aspects of 'EU identity' that are salient in the area of foreign policy focuses on the EU level as a distinctive location for the creation and articulation of collective identity. It is in this sense that 'Europeanization also consists of *constructing systems of meanings and collective understandings*, including social identities' (Cowles and Risse, 2001: 219, emphasis in original) and that 'the creation of norms at the European level serves as important focal points [sic] around which ... discourses and identities are fashioned' (2001: 221). Within this perspective, we can identity three broadly different research agendas.

The creation of procedural rules   The first research agenda concerns the procedural dimension of CFSP. These procedural norms define appropriate ways of interacting with EU partners in the pursuit of both collective and unilateral foreign policy. Many analysts argue that these norms (especially the norm of consultation) have been internalised by foreign policy makers (see, for example, Forster and Wallace, 1996; Nuttall, 1992; Smith, M.E., 2000).

Identity creation through interaction with the EU's external environment The second research agenda focuses on the EU's external relations as a key area for the definition of an EU identity through the parallel construction of 'others' (Cederman, 2001; Neumann and Welsh, 1991). Michelle Pace (Chapter 14 in this volume) traces such a process of identity construction in the case of the EU's policies towards the Mediterranean. A related area of identity construction at the EU level that affects EFP is the development and articulation of distinctive patterns of affinity (or aloofness) towards particular countries or regions. The articulation of such patterns is particularly salient with regard to the question of enlargement. In the case of eastern enlargement, for example, Sedelmeier (1998, 2000a) argues that the discursive creation of a particular role of the EU towards the Central and Eastern European countries (CEECs), which is characterised by the notion of an EU responsibility, has been an important factor in the EU's decision to enlarge, independently of material incentives (see also Fierke and Wiener, 1999). Sjursen (2002) underlines this point by contrasting the EU's identity construction towards the CEECs with the one towards Turkey.

Articulation and specification of norms at the EU Level   However, neither of the above two types of analyses of EU identity construction tells us much about the substantive content of the foreign policies of the EU and the EU member states towards which EU identity might predispose them. The third strand of research pertains more directly to the *substantive* dimension of EFP by focusing on the creation and evolution of particular norms at the EU level. Norms are 'collective expectations about proper behaviour for a given identity' (Jepperson et al., 1996: 54); their immediate orientation to behaviour thus provides an important link between identity and policy. In the EU, such norms are expressions of which foreign policy goals and foreign policy practices the member states and EU institutions consider legitimate, given their particular collective identities or self-images.

Detailed studies of this dimension are rare. Recent analyses that go into this direction include Manners (2002), who suggests that the EU's 'normative basis' rests on five 'core norms' (peace, liberty, democracy, rule of law, human rights) that are comprised in the EU's *acquis*. Karen Smith (2002) focuses on foreign policy objectives that the EU has explicitly articulated in various declarations. These objectives, in particular the promotion of human rights and democracy, the prevention of violent conflict, and the encouragement of regional co-operation, present 'key elements of its international identity, or the distinctive image that the EU tries to project externally' (2002: 1). These studies provide promising starting points for an understanding of how EU identity might affect EFP. However, they are still not very specific about whether and in which ways these more general normative commitments and identity-related aspects predispose EFP in certain ways. For the purposes of this chapter, I concentrate on one particular aspect of the EU's identity in order to discuss how we can conceptualise the impact of these identity-related norms on EFP.

The EU's identity as promotor of human rights and democracy   Human rights and democracy appear a key area for the creation and articulation of a particular role-specific identity of the EU. Furthermore, it is an area in which the EU's role has evolved considerably since the end of the Cold War. Thus, rather than attempting to give a comprehensive account of the elements of EU identity that matter for foreign policy, this chapter thus focuses only on this specific aspect of its identity.

The EU level has been a particularly salient focal point for the articulation of the importance of human rights and democracy, both internally, as well as in the EU's external relations (see, for example, Matlary, Chapter 8, and Menéndez, Chapter 15 in this volume; Smith, K., 2001). In particular, the EU's policy practice with regard to its eastern enlargement, including discursive practices, is a key source through which the EU has explicitly articulated, made more specific, and codified its role in the promotion and protection of democracy and human rights as a fundamental characteristic that it ascribes to itself (Sedelmeier, 2000b: 193–7). These practices include regular collective assertions of the promotion of democracy as a key rationale for enlargement, the formulation and strict implementation of a specific political accession conditionality, as well as treaty changes motivated by concerns about respect for these principles in the prospective members. Through its policy practice the EU has not only acknowledged that it is a community that is based on, and *adheres* to, these principles, but also that it has formulated a role for itself actively to *promote and defend* them both internally and externally. As the obligations that this role entails for the EU go beyond the specific relationship with the CEECs, the EU's enlargement policy thus contributed to the construction of an EU identity that has policy implications for EFP more broadly.

The Impact of EU Identity on EFP: Three Mechanisms

For the EU's identity as protector and promoter of human rights and democracy to have an impact on EFP, it needs to specify standards of what constitutes 'appropriate behaviour' for particular foreign policy situations. However, this particular element of EU identity is rather diffuse. The behavioural prescriptions that it entails might not clearly prescribe a particular course of action for a given situation, which has implications for the mechanisms through which EU identity affects EFP.

Constructivist accounts predominantly emphasise as the key logic of action a 'logic of appropriateness', according to which actors determine 'what the situation is, what role is being fulfilled, and what the obligations of that role in that situation are' (March and Olsen, 1989: 160). Such a logic of rule-guided behaviour is particularly salient, not only when actors take certain behavioural norms for granted, but crucially also when these norms are fairly specific. Diffuse norms, however, create scope for interpretation and argumentation about what the 'right' course of action might be in a particular situation. Thus, norm-guided behaviour might not only result 'spontaneously' from a 'logic of appropriateness', but instead it might be the result of two other processes that emphasise the importance of communication for the logic of actors' behaviour: a 'logic of arguing' or a process of 'rhetorical action'.

According to Risse, a 'logic of arguing' implies that:

> ... actors try to challenge the validity claims inherent in any causal or normative statement and to seek a communicative consensus about their understanding of a situation as well as justifications for the principles and norms guiding their action. ... [T]he participants in a discourse are open to being persuaded by the better argument and that relationships of power and social hierarchies recede in the background. (2000: 7)

This means for our case that member state representatives seek a reasoned consensus about which particular course of action is justified and appropriate to enact their collective identity as promoters of human rights and democracy in a given situation. Agreement on a particular course of action reflects that all participants are persuaded of the normative validity of the arguments presented for such action.

By contrast, the process of 'rhetorical action', in which actors use normative arguments instrumentally in the pursuit of their self-interests, is consistent with sophisticated, non-materialist rationalist accounts (Schimmelfennig, 1997, 2001). It presupposes 'weakly socialized actors [that] ... belong to a community whose constitutive values and norms they share ... [but] it is not expected that collective identity shapes concrete preferences' (2001: 62). The institutional environment or a community's collective identity empower actors that can justify their selfish goals with references to institutional norms or the collective identity. The legitimacy that their rhetoric bestows on their goals increases their bargaining power. Other actors consent to such initiatives not because they are persuaded by the normative validity of such arguments, but in order to avoid the costs of non-compliance with community norms. Compliance thus does not result from an internalisation of norms, but from a process of 'social influence' in which norm-conform behaviour 'is rewarded with social and psychological markers from a reference group with which the actor believes it shares some level of identification' (Johnston, 2001: 494).

In our case, this means that the EU's collective identity provides an institutional environment for EFP. It increases the bargaining power of actors that can present a certain course of action as the defence of human rights and democracy. Other governments might be reluctant about such action, either because they are not convinced about the normative validity of the arguments presented or because this course of action might compete with their material interests. However, they may decide to back such action in order to avoid the costs to the EU and to themselves of a perceived failure to act in accordance with their professed group identity.

The difficult methodological question is, then, how these claims can be subjected to empirical testing and how these two mechanisms can be distinguished in empirical research. Here my aim is more limited. I primarily aim to make a plausible case that norm and identity formation at the EU level matters for EFP. It might do so through either of the mechanisms outlined above. My main point is that the analysis of EFP should go beyond materialist analyses and consider a causal role of 'identity'. It can be left to empirical analyses to decide whether this causal impact can be explained within a sophisticated rationalist analysis or whether it can only be captured with the tools of constructivism.

It might be objected that if we include concepts of rhetorical action and social influence in an analysis of EU identity, it no longer makes sense to use the concept of 'identity' to start with. To emphasise the importance of identity usually implies a focus on constitutive norms, rather than on regulative norms that might only shape actors' strategies and behaviour, rather than their underlying interests. However, despite the obvious differences between the two mechanisms, a common point is the emphasis on accepted standards of *legitimacy*, based on the collective identity of the political community.

Identity, Norm Creation and Communicative
Practices in EFP

Arguments that relate particular policy options and initiatives in EFP to the EU's collective identity thus enjoy greater legitimacy than arguments referring merely to the expected utility for particular member states. The EU's identity thus limits the realm of feasible policy options (including non-action) and reduces the ground for self-interested objection against particular policy initiatives. In this way, the EU's identity might create the necessary scope for norm entrepreneurs to obtain approval for their policy initiatives. Furthermore, initial disagreements between actors about policy options are not only resolved in a process of material bargaining. Agreements might not only reflect the respective (material) bargaining power of the actors involved, but might also be the result of processes of argumentation, including both persuasion and shaming.

For the concrete case at hand, this means that the stronger the salience of democracy and human rights as constituent principles of the EU, the harder it is to deny that the EU also has to play an active role in the defence and promotion of these norms. This does not imply that it is a *sufficient* condition for the EU to agree on a common, norm-conforming action in specific cases. Nor does it imply that the EU's identity is a *direct cause* if the member states engage in such activities. However, it does create *enabling conditions* and an *argumentative logic* that are conducive to such courses of action. Argumentative consistency bestows legitimacy to calls for action to protect the same principles in other situations in which they are at stake.

Path-dependence of policy and
discursive practices

The diffuse nature of EU identity and the centrality of communicative processes for the impact of EU identity on EFP draws attention to two important aspects of this process. The first is the importance of actual policy *practice*, including discursive practices, such as European Council declarations or Commission documents. These practices might make important aspects of the EU's identity more explicit and more specific. In this way, policy practice might strengthen identity-based arguments and thus affect subsequent foreign policy behaviour. Significantly, this process might be the result of unintended consequences, as well as of deliberate advocacy. For example, a common declaration that emphasises certain norms might be the result of compromises by certain member states or simply reflect their neglect of semantic details. Subsequently, however, these statements of policy goals or justifications for particular actions can be interpreted as explicit expressions of *collective* commitments or shared understandings. In such cases, thus articulated elements of EU 'collective' identity might still have a regulative effect on those actors that do not 'share' this element of identity to the same extent, but find themselves 'rhetorically entrapped' in these collective statements. This argument follows the distinction by Jepperson et al. between 'collective' and 'shared' norms:

> Norms may be 'shared,' or commonly held, across some distribution of actors in a system. Alternatively, however, norms may not be widely held by actors but may nevertheless be collective features of the system – either by being institutionalized ... or by being prominent in public discourse of a system. ... [A] distinction between collectively 'prominent' or institutional-ized norms and commonly 'internalized' ones, with various 'intersubjec-tive' admixtures in between, is crucial for distinguishing between different types of norms and different types of normative effects. (1996: 54–5)

In a similar vein, it can be argued that while general commitments to the norms that constitute the EU's collective identity are also present in the member states, it does make a difference if these norms become explicitly articulated, embedded and specified at the EU level. As Karen Smith argues:

> Once the objectives [to promote certain norms] are adopted at the EU level, the member states become involved in a process in which their initial prefer-ences are reshaped and in which they must make compromises over how these objectives will be achieved. It also makes it very difficult to roll back rhetorical commitments to pursue the objectives. Through this process, the EU's international identity thus gradually acquires more substance. (2002: 16)

The precedents created through such policy and discursive practices provide resources for policy advocates (see also Wiener, 1998). In this way, policy and discursive practices might induce a path-dependence that makes it increasingly difficult to oppose foreign policy options that can be legitimised with adher-ence to EU identity. To be sure, however, these discursive constraints are rather fragile, as inconsistencies in the EU's human rights conditionality policy in cases such as Pakistan or Russia demonstrate (see, for example, Smith, 2001). In turn, repeated instances of inconsistency can undermine earlier precedents.

The importance of policy entrepreneurs

The diffuse nature of the norms characterising the EU's identity makes the role of policy entrepreneurs that advocate particular policy options with ref-erence to such norms crucial for the policy impact of identity. Norms that are not sufficiently specific to prescribe a clear course of action in a particular sit-uation are unlikely to lead to collective norm-conform action by the EU if the situation is also characterised by countervailing norms, uncertainty over whether a certain action (or inaction) is most conducive to producing norm-conforming behaviour in other states, and when certain member states face countervailing material incentives.

Norm entrepreneurs articulate and call attention to norms and identity by making the case that in a particular situation the EU's identity is at stake, by suggesting particular policy options for 'appropriate behaviour', or by warning of potential discrepancies between behaviour and collectively professed norms and identity. Within the norm 'life cycle' (Finnemore and Sikkink, 1998) they might thus either contribute to the emergence of norms (that might already exist at the domestic level) at the EU level, or push it past the 'tipping point' at which a critical mass of states accepts that this norm forms part of EU identity.

Such advocacy is usually attributed to *principled* norm entrepreneurs who are motivated by ideational commitment. However, actors might also advocate norm-conforming behaviour instrumentally, in order to further their material self-interest. The diffuse nature of identity also increases the scope for (but not necessarily the success of) 'rhetorical action': the range of policy options that policy makers might attempt to justify with references to EU identity is larger than if this identity was more specific and hence more narrowly defined. However, if such initiatives are successful, they still result in a strengthening of identity, albeit as an unintended consequence: the success of these arguments validates their salience, and the behaviour that is justified with reference to identity might constitute precedents that facilitate arguing for similar identity-conforming behaviour at a later stage.

Illustrations of the Impact of EU Identity on EFP

This section presents brief illustrations of how a focus on identity can provide important insights into EFP. While each of these instances is difficult to explain purely on the basis of material interests and bargaining, a focus on the EU's identity can provide plausible explanations.

Sanctions of the EU XIV against the Austrian government

The bilateral diplomatic sanctions against the Austrian government in February 2000 concerns member state foreign policies, rather than common EU foreign policy. The strong reaction of the EU XIV to the inclusion of the Freiheitliche Partei Österreichs (FPÖ) into the Austrian government coalition is difficult to explain fully without appreciating the EU's identity as a defender of democracy and human rights (Merlingen et al., 2001). The governments that initiated the sanctions of the EU XIV might well have had instrumental motives. They might have aimed their initiative not so much at Haider, but rather at domestic party politics, in an attempt to discredit far-right parties or those within centre-right parties pondering co-operation with the far right.

However, even from this perspective, it is very difficult to understand the participation of all other member governments in this strong measure without taking into account the EU's role on human rights and democracy. The EU's self-proclaimed role gave a strong legitimacy to the initiative. While it is far from obvious that the EU's identity would have required such a strong reaction, it was difficult to object to once this particular action had been proposed. It was hardly possible for the other member governments to refuse participation, since this could be perceived as a refusal to act according to the EU's identity. It thus made it difficult to voice scepticism against the proposed measures, either on the grounds that their effect might be counterproductive or that such a measure might violate competing norms, such as not to isolate a member state. Thus even in this interpretation, the instrumental use of references to the EU's identity worked only because the EU's role has become so much taken for granted. Furthermore, this case illustrates that instrumental 'norm entrepreneurship', motivated by domestic party political struggles, can contribute to 'norm emergence' at the EU level.

Collective EU endorsement of NATO military intervention in Kosovo

The collective endorsement by all member states of NATO's military intervention in the Kosovo conflict might appear puzzling from a materialist perspective. Some member states are neutral and in many cases public opinion was critical of NATO action. Some policy makers were concerned that the bombing campaign would be counterproductive to achieving the declared goals, while others were concerned about the negative precedents it might set for the credibility of international law and the role of the UN.

One explanation is that the reluctant member states consented to the declaration endorsing the military intervention because this document justified such action with references to norms that are fundamental to the EU's identity. The Berlin European Council stated that:

> ... Europe cannot tolerate a humanitarian catastrophe in its midst. It cannot be permitted that, in the middle of Europe, the predominant population of Kosovo is collectively deprived of its rights and subjected to human rights abuses. We, the countries of the European Union, are under a *moral obligation* to ensure that indiscriminate behaviour and violence ... are not repeated. We have a *duty* to ensure the return to their homes of the hundreds of thousands of refugees and displaced persons. ... We are *responsible* for securing peace and cooperation in the region. This is the way to *guarantee our fundamental European values*, i.e. respect for human rights and the rights of minorities, international law, democratic institutions and the inviolability of borders. (*Bulletin of the EU* 3-1999: 1.40, my emphasis)

Thus it could be argued that once the Council presidency put this particular proposal on the table, it was hard to challenge the argumentative validity of this interpretation of NATO action as the 'appropriate behaviour' in this particular situation, given the particular identity of the EU and its member states.

EU policy for the abolition of the death penalty

The EU's international pursuit of the abolition of the death penalty is difficult to explain on the basis of material incentives (Manners, 2002). There are few rewards from domestic audiences; it creates tensions in relations with countries with capital punishment, not least with regard to extradition. Furthermore, five member states (UK, Belgium, Spain, Italy, Greece) had not yet abolished the death penalty by 1994. How can we then explain that by 1998 not only had all member states abolished the death penalty, but also collectively embarked on a pursuit of the abolition of the death penalty?

Manners explains EU policy with the advocacy of the international human rights movement, the European Parliament, the Commission's Directorate General (DG) for External Relations and a number of member states. The material bargaining power of these actors is certainly not sufficient to induce changes in the more reluctant member states' positions. More promising appears an explanation that focuses on the legitimacy that the EU's identity bestowed on the arguments of these advocates as an important resource.

EU criticism of Russian policy in Chechnya

EU policy towards Russia has long been characterised by tensions among the member states about what position to take on the Chechnya conflict. Some of the big member states, namely the German, French and UK governments, seemed concerned that a too critical position would jeopardise good relations and a strategic partnership with Russia. By contrast, the Nordic member states in particular argued that the EU should take a firm line in explicitly condemning what they considered an excessive use of force against civilians and human rights abuses by the Russian forces. Given this constellation of actors, material bargaining power and the intergovernmental character of CFSP would not lead us to expect that CFSP declarations on Chechnya would be very critical of Russian policy.

However, the CFSP declarations from January 1995 were characterised by very strong normative language. The EU expressed its 'greatest concern' about the fighting in Chechnya; it noted 'serious violations of human rights and international humanitarian law' and deplored 'the large number of victims and the suffering being inflicted on the civilian population' (Council of the European Union, 1995). This language was the result of the strong pressure in particular of the then new member states Sweden and Finland, despite strong initial reservations by a majority of governments.[4] Again, a focus on EU identity would suggest that the latter were either reluctant to oppose such critical language, as it might have raised doubts about their commitment to core norms characterising the EU's identity, or they were persuaded by the normative validity of the arguments used by the proponents of the text. To be sure, this critical approach during the first Chechnya conflict is in contrast to the EU's position during the second Russian military campaign from 1999 to 2000. However, while this contrast illustrates the limitations of identity-based arguments, it also underlines the importance of such arguments in the earlier period.

Conclusions

This chapter suggests that we can gain important insights into EFP from a perspective that acknowledges that the EU's identity matters causally for foreign policy. Materialist approaches and rationalist perspectives that exogenise identity see EFP essentially as the result of competing material interests, namely the member states' different security concerns and their relative vulnerability, as well as of a competition between such security concerns and conflicting economic interests within and across the member states. A focus on identity formation at the EU level allows additional factors to be taken into account, namely the evolving discourse about the EU's role and about constitutive norms at the EU level that defines a collective identity for the policy makers from the member governments and EU institutions. One area where such identity formation at the EU level has become particularly salient for European foreign policy since the end of the Cold War is the area of the protection of human rights and democracy.

The EU's identity creates the scope for policy advocates and norm entrepreneurs to advance, at least incrementally, policy options that can be presented as enactments of this identity, sometimes even in the face of countervailing material interests. The EU's identity limits the range of policy options, including non-action, that are acceptable as appropriate behaviour. It also limits the grounds for opposition against policy initiatives that are justified with references to the EU's identity by inhibiting arguments based primarily on material self-interests. EU identity thus provides enabling conditions for actors who can claim to act in the name of the EU's identity. However, it should be noted that while this enhances the scope to advance policy initiatives aimed at defending democracy and human rights, it might also reduce the grounds for scrutinising potential breaches of countervailing norms that a specific policy option might entail.

As the norms characterising EU identity and the behavioural obligations that they entail are fairly diffuse, I have highlighted two mechanisms that emphasise the importance of communication – a 'logic of arguing' and 'rhetorical action'. I have provided a few empirical illustrations of cases in which a focus on the impact of the EU's identity through either of these two mechanisms might be able to explain aspects of EFP that are difficult to capture otherwise. Clearly, even with more detailed research, it might be difficult to establish enough hard evidence to decide which of these two behavioural logics – the logic of appropriateness and of arguing or the logic of consequences within a normative environment – was operative in the case at hand. But in either case, the EU's identity is an important part of the explanations. Even if in certain cases the advocacy of norm-consistent policy was motivated by the selfish interests of certain governments, it is unlikely that this particular policy would have been adopted collectively by all other member governments without the recent establishment of concerns about human rights and democratic principles as an attribute of EU identity. Thus, while identity-based advocacy might have been used instrumentally, such instrumental use only induces compliant behaviour because EU identity has acquired a certain degree of taken-for-grantedness among the member governments. One theoretical implication of this argument is that rationalist and constructivist explanations of norm dynamics and identity politics should be considered complementary, rather than incompatible (see also, for example, Checkel, 2001; Cowles and Risse, 2001; Finnemore and Sikkink, 1998).

Notes

1   For comments as an earlier draft of this chapter, I would like to thank the editors, especially Helene Sjursen; the participants at a project workshop and at a panel at the ECPR conference in Canterbury, September 2001; as well as Ewan Harrison, Ian Manners and Karen Smith.
2   For a critical account that problematises the link between constructivism and identity, see Zehfuss (2001).
3   For a perceptive overview of different strands of literature on the EU's 'international identity', see Manners and Whitman (1998: 232–8).
4   Interview with official in the Council Secretariat, 15 October 1997.

References

Aggestam, L. (1999) 'Role conceptions and the politics of identity in foreign policy', *ARENA Working Paper* No. 8/99.
Allen, D. and Smith, M. (1990) 'Western Europe's presence in the contemporary international arena', *Review of International Studies*, 16 (1): 19–39.
Bretherton, C. and Vogler, J. (1999) *The European Union as a Global Actor*. London: Routledge.
Bulletin of the EU, 3/1999.
Cederman, L.E. (ed.) (2001) *Constructing Europe's Identity: The External Dimension*. Boulder, CO: Lynne Rienner.
Checkel, J. (2001) 'Why comply? Social learning and European identity change', *International Organization*, 55 (3): 553–88.
Christiansen, T., Jørgensen, K.E. and Wiener, A. (eds) (2001) *The Social Construction of Europe*. London: Sage.
Council of the European Union (1995) Press Statement on Chechnya, 17 January, Document No. 95/018.
Cowles, M.G. and Risse, T. (2001) 'Transforming Europe: Conclusions', in J. Caporaso, M.G. Cowles and T. Risse (eds), *Transforming Europe: Europeanization and Domestic Change*. Ithaca, NY: Cornell University Press. pp. 217–37.
Damro, C. (2001) 'Building an international identity: the EU and extraterritorial competition policy', *Journal of European Public Policy*, 8 (2): 208–26.

Duchêne, F. (1972) 'Europe's role in the world', in R. Mayne (ed.), *Europe Tomorrow: Sixteen Europeans Look Ahead*. London: Fontana.

Fierke, K. and Wiener, A. (1999) 'Constructing institutional interests: EU and NATO enlargement', *Journal of European Public Policy*, 6 (5): 721–42.

Finnemore, M. and Sikkink, K. (1998) 'International norm dynamics and political change', *International Organization*, 52 (4): 887–917.

Forster, A. and Wallace, W. (1996) 'Common foreign and security policy', in H. Wallace and W. Wallace (eds), *Policy-Making in the European Union* (3rd edn). Oxford: Oxford University Press. pp. 411–35.

Hill, C. (1993) 'The capability-expectations gap, or conceptualising Europe's international role', *Journal of Common Market Studies*, 31 (3): 305–28.

Jepperson, R., Wendt, A. and Katzenstein, P. (1996) 'Norms, identity, and culture in national security', in P. Katzenstein (ed.), *The Culture of National Security: Norms and Identity in World Politics*. New York, NY: Columbia University Press. pp. 33–75.

Johnston, A.I. (2001) 'Treating institutions as social environments', *International Studies Quarterly*, 45 (4): 487–515.

Jørgensen, K.E. (ed.) (1997) *Reflective Approaches to European Governance*. Basingstoke: Macmillan.

Katzenstein, P. (ed.) (1996) *The Culture of National Security: Norms and Identity in World Politics*. New York, NY: Columbia University Press.

Kowert, P. and Legro, J. (1996) 'Norms, identity and their limits: a theoretical reprise', in P. Katzenstein (ed.), *The Culture of National Security: Norms and Identity in World Politics*. New York, NY: Columbia University Press. pp. 451–97.

Laffan, B., O'Donnell, R. and Smith, M. (1999) *Europe's Experimental Union: Rethinking Integration*. London: Routledge.

Lerch, M. (2001) 'The important role of roles: a theoretical framework for understanding the external identity of the European Union'. Paper presented at the ECPR International Relations Conference, 8–10 September, Canterbury.

Lumsdaine, D. (1993) *Moral Vision in International Politics: The Foreign Aid Regime 1949–1989*. Princeton, NJ: Princeton University Press.

Manners, I. (2002) 'Normative power Europe: a contradiction in terms?', *Journal of Common Market Studies*, 40 (2): 234–58.

Manners, I. and Whitman, R. (1998) 'Towards identifying the international identity of the European Union: a framework for analysis of the EU's network of relationships', *European Integration*, 21 (2): 231–49.

March, J. and Olsen, J.P. (1989) *Rediscovering Institutions: The Organizational Basis of Politics*. New York, NY: Free Press.

Merlingen, M., Mudde, C. and Sedelmeier, U. (2001) 'The right and the righteous? European norms, domestic politics and the sanctions against Austria', *Journal of Common Market Studies*, 39 (1): 61–79.

Neumann, I. and Welsh, J. (1991) 'The "other" in European identity: an addendum to the literature on international society', *Review of International Studies*, 17 (4): 327–48.

Nuttall, S. (1992) *European Political Cooperation*. Oxford: Clarendon.

Peterson, J. (1998) 'Introduction: the European Union as a global actor', in J. Peterson and H. Sjursen (eds), *A Common Foreign Policy for Europe? Competing Visions of the CFSP*. London: Routledge. pp. 3–17.

Risse, T. (2000) '"Let's argue!" Communicative action in world politics', *International Organization*, 54 (1): 1–39.

Risse, T. (2001) 'A European identity? Europeanization and the evolution of nation-state identities', in J. Caporaso, M.G. Cowles and T. Risse (eds), *Transforming Europe: Europeanization and Domestic Change*. Ithaca, NY: Cornell University Press. pp. 198–216.

Risse-Kappen, T. (1995a) *Cooperation Among Democracies: The European Influence on US Foreign Policy*. Princeton, NJ: Princeton University Press.

Risse-Kappen, T. (ed.) (1995b) *Bringing Transnational Relations Back In: Non-State Actors, Domestic Structures and International Institutions*. Cambridge: Cambridge University Press.

Schimmelfennig, F. (1997) 'Rhetorisches Handeln in der internationalen Politik', *Zeitschrift für Internationale Beziehungen*, 4 (2): 219–54.

Schimmelfennig, F. (2001) 'The community trap: liberal norms, rhetorical action, and the eastern enlargement of the European Union', *International Organization*, 55 (1): 47–80.

Sedelmeier, U. (1998) 'The European Union's association policy towards the countries of Central and Eastern Europe: collective EU identity and policy paradigms in a composite policy'. PhD dissertation, University of Sussex.

Sedelmeier, U. (2000a) 'Eastern enlargement: risk, rationality and role-compliance', in M.G. Cowles and M. Smith (eds), *The State of the European Union. Vol.5, Risk, Reform, Resistance and Revival*. Oxford: Oxford University Press. pp. 164–85.

Sedelmeier, U. (2000b) 'Eastern enlargement and the EU's international role: the interplay between the EU's role and policy', in H. Sjursen (ed.), *Redefining Security? The Role of the European Union in European Security*. ARENA Report No. 7/2000. pp. 185–203.

Sjursen, H. (2002) 'Why expand? The question of legitimacy and justification in the EU's enlargement policy', *Journal of Common Market Studies*, 40 (3): 491–513.

Smith, K. (2001) 'The EU, human rights and relations with third countries: "foreign policy" with an ethical dimension?', in M. Light and K. Smith (eds), *Ethics and Foreign Policy*. Cambridge: Cambridge University Press. pp. 185–203.

Smith, K. (2002) 'Conceptualising the EU's international identity: *sui generis* or following the latest trends?' Paper presented at the ECPR European Union Politics Conference, 26–28 September, Bordeaux.

Smith, M.E. (2000) 'Conforming to Europe: the domestic impact of EU foreign policy co-operation', *Journal of European Public Policy*, 7 (4): 613–31.

Smith, M.H. (2000) 'Negotiating new Europes: the roles of the European Union', *Journal of European Public Policy*, 7 (5): 806–22.

Soetendorp, B. (1994) 'The evolution of the EC/EU as a single foreign policy actor', in W. Carlsnaes and S. Smith (eds), *European Foreign Policy: The EC and Changing Perspectives in Europe*. London: Sage. pp. 103–19.

Walker, S. (ed.) (1987) *Role Theory and Foreign Policy Analysis*. Durham: Duke University Press.

Wendt, A. (1992) 'Anarchy is what states make of it: the social construction of power politics', *International Organization*, 46 (2): 391–425.

Wendt, A. (1994) 'Collective identity formation and the international state', *American Political Science Review*, 88 (2): 384–96.

Wendt, A. (1999) *Social Theory of International Politics*. Cambridge: Cambridge University Press.

White, B. (2001) *Understanding European Foreign Policy*. Basingstoke: Palgrave.

Whitman, R. (1997) 'The international identity of the EU: instruments as identity', in A. Landau and R. Whitman (eds), *Rethinking the European Union: Institutions, Interests and Identities*. Basingstoke: Macmillan. pp. 54–71.

Wiener, A. (1998) *'European' Citizenship Practice – Building Institutions of a Non-State*. Boulder, CO: Westview.

Zehfuss, M. (2001) 'Constructivism and identity: a dangerous liaison', *European Journal of International Relations*, 7 (3): 315–48.

8 Human Rights

Janne Haaland Matlary

The role that human rights play in foreign policy is contested and has not been extensively studied to date. However, it has been argued that human rights play an increasing role whenever there is a public process of policy making and that they constitute a major basis for justification in such transparent public processes (Risse et al., 2000). Moreover, such norms seem to play an increasing role in a world where 'soft power' resources have become more significant (Nye, 1995, 2002; Matlary, 2002). The general thrust of this statement may be contested if one looks at the American emphasis on hard power and coercive diplomacy (Bacevich, 2002). But the 'mix' of moral argument and interest-based discourse is clearly different in the US and Europe. Whereas US foreign policy combines references to national security, a highly moral discourse and coercive diplomacy, European foreign policy (EFP), especially as promoted by the European Union (EU), refers to international legal norms, above all those embedded in the United Nations (UN). Whichever 'model' is regarded as typical of contemporary foreign policy, it can at least be argued that these are two very different models, both in terms of types of power deployed and the justification offered for the use of such power. This chapter focuses on the EU, arguably the most 'legalised' foreign policy actor in the world, and asks how important legalisation is for legitimacy.

Public Diplomacy and Justificatory Politics

In public diplomacy, the mode of discourse is typically tied to rights and cast in terms of moral categories (Leonard, 2002). This can be described as a *justificatory* mode of discourse in contrast to the *bargaining* mode typical of policy making concerning distributive outcomes. Justification here refers to arguments about right in the sense of just decisions according to some standards, for example, legal canons, rather than pretexts for action, such as 'he justified the invasion with humanitarian arguments'.

Though political scientists know a lot about bargaining and have developed complex theories of different types of bargaining, they are only beginning to study policy processes where justification is the main mode of decision making. Chayes and Chayes (1995), for example, note that the legal regimes they study have to be complied with through justification based on interpretation of legal rules and that states often are not the main decision makers in such justificatory processes. Those with superior legal knowledge are the ones who decide what is valid and reasonable and, therefore, decide what are the 'correct' interpretations of compliance and non-compliance in such regimes. Thus, there are canons of interpretation that limit the scope for interpretation and determine what is legitimate. Likewise, in human rights regimes, there are certain standards of interpretation that determine what can be a legitimate interpretation, though the scope is wide.

Goldstein at al. (2001) make the point that world politics is increasingly 'legalised', meaning regulated through hard and soft law, and that when this obtains, the application of the regime enables and empowers actors like lawyers, non-governmental organisations (NGOs) and experts of various kinds. In short, justification as a mode of decision making in a legalised regime implies that there are *correct* ways of applying regimes and *correct* interpretations of regime rules. Such regimes naturally privilege actors who can claim valid qualifications for making such interpretations. Significantly, sheer power does not apply here, although the most powerful states naturally will be able to hire the best lawyers. But the main point about justification is that there are canons of interpretations of rules that cannot be altered by sheer force. If they are, then the regime appears to be illegitimate, and rightly so. Justification has to do with right application according to rules and must be seen by stakeholders as just, right and persuasive. Though in a regime with norms that are not very specific, as in many human rights regimes, there is more scope for interpretation than in very specified regimes.

The differences between bargaining and justificatory modes of decision making are important for political outcomes, and this chapter develops the relationship between general insights about justification in legalised regimes and puzzles about the role of human rights in foreign policy making in Europe. On the one hand, many argue that human rights have little 'real' impact on foreign policy when confronted with competing security and/or economic factors. On the other hand, we have the general argument in the international relations (IR) literature noted earlier about the salience of soft power, which argues that legitimacy also is a key resource in foreign policy. From this perspective, normative legitimacy itself becomes a major resource in a 'post-national' foreign policy.

The argument for soft power seems most appropriate in the EU, where the use of hard power is extremely rare. The EU has, in fact, been dubbed a 'civilian' power (Duchêne, 1972), a designation at the time that implied the lack of military tools. However, the very civilian, soft character of the EU may increasingly come to represent the modern, legitimate type of foreign policy in a transparent world where citizens and NGOs play ever greater roles in policy making.

Human Rights in EFP

In 1999, the EU developed its own Charter of Fundamental Rights (Eriksen, 2002). This marks a watershed in the development towards political union and the Charter will be incorporated in the new EU constitution which, if adopted, will become legally binding with a supranational court for its implementation – the European Court of Justice (ECJ) in Luxembourg. Future legal codification will mean that the Council of Europe (COE) and the EU will have legally binding and enforceable human rights legislation through their own courts which, if we take into account the direct effect (see below) and the individual right of petition, represents the most supranational of all international legislation in this area.

Chris Patten, the EU's External Relations Commissioner, has stated that 'we have a legal framework for human rights in our external policy' and he offers an analysis of the tools of human rights policy that the EU has at its disposal (Patten, 2000; see also below). However, these tools are not very 'streamlined' in actual policy making and the EU does not yet have a common human rights policy. The major volume edited by Alston (1999) is the most comprehensive study to date of human rights in the EU. It is written largely by legal scholars who conclude that the EU is at a preliminary stage of development as a human rights organisation.

The legal basis for human rights tools stems from the inclusion of human rights in the Treaty on European Union (TEU) in 1992 and their elaboration in the 1997 Amsterdam Treaty. Article 6 of the TEU stipulates that 'the Union is founded on the principles of liberty, democracy, respect for human rights and fundamental freedoms, and the rule of law'. Paragraph 2 asserts that 'the Union shall respect fundamental rights, as guaranteed by the ECHR'. The TEU also established 'union citizenship' (Article 8) as a general category and specified some rights for citizens, such as the right to stand for office, to vote in local elections and the right to consular assistance from any EU country. Citizenship, of course, is a constitutional notion; a state or some other political entity confers citizenship on someone. It is not an intergovernmental notion, but rather a concept that defines the union as a contract between ruler and ruled.

The human rights 'toolbox'

The EU deploys a number of policy tools for dealing with human rights as a cross-cutting theme in its foreign policy.

Legal tools   The EU is a community based on law. As discussed earlier, the use of the ECJ to judge on human rights cases is well established as political practice. Weiler (1996) has noted what he calls a 'creeping constitutionalism', which has created legal supremacy for the EU in the form of direct effect. This means that the ECJ has interpreted its mandate in a supranational way by making its judgements apply directly to all states and citizens of the union (Weiler and Friis, 1999).

Conditionality in aid programmes and trade agreements   The EU's development policy aims to 'contribute to the general objective of developing and consolidating democracy and the rule of law, and to that of respecting human rights and fundamental freedoms' (TEU Article 130u). Thus, there is a conditionality clause in all aid programmes except emergency aid (Riedel and Will, 1999).

Suspension of membership and partnerships   Agreements with third states must now include a 'human rights clause'. Since 1995, more than 20 agreements containing human rights clauses have been signed, including the revised Lome convention. To date, no suspensions have been made, and there is a 'clear preference for … a positive approach' (Smith, 2000: 8). Only in grave cases, such as Lukashenko's Belarus, has there been a suspension of a partnership and co-operation agreement.

Shaming in public diplomacy   The EU has one voice at the UN, in the UN Human Rights Commission as well as in the Third Committee which deals with human rights. Next to the US, the EU is arguably the most important actor in the world. Thus, its stance on human rights resolutions is of key importance (Smith, 2002).

Sanctions   The EU has also used hard power in the form of sanctions. Like the US, the EU is large enough to have a real impact with this tool. It has deployed sanctions against, *inter alia*, South Africa in 1985–86; an arms embargo and economic and diplomatic sanctions against China in 1989; diplomatic but not economic sanctions against Nigeria in 1993 and also in 1995 after the execution of Ken Saro-Wiwa.

Case study: human rights and enlargement

As Schimmelfennig (2001) has shown in his analysis of enlargement, all EU member states were agreed on the need to extend the values of democracy, the rule of law and human rights to the newly independent states of Europe. With the exception of long-term prospects for trade, there were no economic reasons why enlargement had to happen. Indeed, for some states, such as Spain, the fear of losing substantially in terms of structural funds was a real concern. Schimmelpfennig describes how this agenda-setting was accomplished by the Commission and key member states in an act of public diplomacy which left the recalcitrant states unable to stop the process.

This is, in fact, an excellent case study of the impact of human rights norms: no state could oppose a values-based discourse with narrow, national interests. It was possible to prolong the process of enlargement and procrastinate over it, but it was not possible to halt it. Here is the difference between two types of political processes and their different logics. In a process of justification, such as the debate over values, rights and what the EU is obliged to do with respect to central and east Europe, it is not legitimate to bargain over narrow national interests. The discourse, the very terms of the debate, is in the justificatory mode. One debates what the duty, the obligation, the just course or action on the part of the EU should be: to enlarge or not?

Sjursen juxtaposes economic, security and value-based explanations for enlargement. She suggests that the values underlying the EU help to explain the decision to enlarge: 'a sense of "kinship-based duty" contributes to an explanation not only of the general decision to enlarge but ... of the differentiated support for enlargement to this group of states in comparison to Turkey' (2002: 508). It is the feeling of belonging to Europe and having a duty towards other Europeans that makes the crucial difference. This takes precedence over general human rights – which should suggest equal treatment to all applicant states regardless of geographical location and cultural legacy – and also over economic and security interests. Sjursen finds that the acceptance of the case for enlargement to the East was much clearer than in the Turkish case, which enables her to distinguish between human rights as a general set of norms and the specific 'EU values' that appear to obligate Europeans. These values are identity-based and include human rights and democracy.

Understanding the Role of Human Rights in EFP

The discussion so far in this chapter has indicated that human rights norms have a growing impact on EFP, particularly towards third countries. This is largely explicable in *instrumental* terms – these states are told to comply; conditionality is applied. Compliance is achieved through pressure, incentives or coercive diplomacy. But it is also apparent from the discussion that norms matter for *non-instrumental* reasons. This is much more difficult to explain because we must then assume that norms are complied with for other reasons, such as rightness, justice or identity. Motivations for political action may thus be rooted in a conviction that something is just and right, and that it should be supported because it is 'European' and conforms to European values and identity. But, as Sedelmeier notes in Chapter 7 of this volume, identity is a very hard concept to theorise about and even to define. What ultimately is a European identity, and how do we bridge the gap between identity and interest? In other words, when does an identity become politically relevant as a preference or an interest, which in turn leads to political action?

Sjursen (2002) suggest there are three types of explanation for political action in the case of enlargement – instrumental, rights-based and value-based, with the latter referring to the specific normative context of a political actor, in this case the EU. She finds that the identity of the EU as a European political project plays a key role in explaining the willingness to expand to the East. Thus, there are more than instrumental interests of an economic and security kind at stake in EU policy making as these interests alone cannot account for the admission of new members.

Value-based interests

Are human rights drivers of foreign policy? Elsewhere (Matlary, 2002), I have proposed three types of interests – security, economic and value-based – as the relevant categories of foreign policy analysis. The poverty of IR theory lies in its assumption that only material – security and/or economic – interests exist. Today, however, norms such as human rights may matter increasingly as new types of actors, such as NGOs and concerned citizens, participate in foreign policy making through their voice in the public debate.

Rationalist explanations in IR have often been confused with economic interests as the motivating force. But rational actions are those based on an individual actor's strategic goals, and rational man, in Elster's formulation (cited in Kahler, 1998: 919–41), may make 'non-Archimedean choices and may be moved by concern for others'. Thus, to be rational does not imply pursuing utility-maximizing economic preferences, but rather it refers to a political strategy to attain a given goal, which can include human rights as well as an economic and/or security tools. To be rational is to be strategic in terms of adopting the most useful means to reach a given goal.

The limitation of modern rational choice theories is underlined by Kratochwil's intellectual history of the concept of national interest. He argues that the concept of *staatsraison*, which followed a logic of public reasoning based on commonly accepted norms, was only replaced at a late stage historically by a privatised assumption of an 'unbridled self-interest'. 'The glorification of unbridled self-interest as the essence of politics remains one of the sad achievements of the period before World War 1' (Kratochwil, 1982: 22). Significantly, he adds that *'the discourse on interests had a discernable logic and the arguments it sustained had to satisfy certain criteria,* which turned out to be those of a weakened form of the public interest discourse' (Kratochwil, 1982: 25, my emphasis).

Combining rationalist strategic models with interest formation on the basis of learning, cultural inculcation and persuasion seems both necessary and feasible for future study of the relationship between interests and values. Moderate constructivist approaches take account of this possibility, yet many other approaches continue to juxtapose rationalism and constructivism. While it may be theoretically productive, this juxtaposition is rather fruitless in empirical terms. Yet much debate at the meta-theoretical level between these two schools of thought remains sterile and and is best characterised, in Jupille and Chekel's (2002: 1–38) phrase, as 'wars of religion', rather than as open-ended scholarly debate.

This chapter follows their argument in calling for empirical testing of both alternative and complementary hypotheses. Noting that 'only in the rarest of cases is there but one plausible account to explain an outcome', Jupille and

Chekel (2002: 17) call for the specification of domain and scope conditions for rationalist and constructivist theories about interests and values. In his study of the impact of human rights, Risse et al. (1999) concludes that initial explanations of human rights compliance are usually instrumental. The longer-term impact, however – explored through a 'spiral model' – may be the result of real conviction through learning and persuasion. The *sequencing* of explanations thus appears to be a salient consideration.

To summarise the argument at this point, it makes analytical sense to focus upon three main types of motivational driving forces for foreign policy action. If we presuppose a strategy of means-ends rationality, these forces become preferences when they are put into a political context of action. There will often be conflicts between preferences, but also 'mixed' preferences where values matter alongside other motivating factors like security. Thus, in the real world, alternative 'either/or' preferences may be rare. Likewise, in the early stages of political processes such as EU enlargement, values may be held instrumentally where human rights conditionality is applied. But values may be held for non-instrumental reasons at a later stage. The complexity of this analytical framework seems warranted if we are to study the role of human rights norms empirically.

The concept of legitimacy

What is the power behind human rights? They may matter simply because we regard them as important, and therefore they motivate our action. They may be more or less imposed on us by coercive diplomacy, so they are powerful for that reason. They may explain political action because we are afraid of being 'shamed' for violating norms that are widely regarded in society around us as being legitimate. Normative legitimacy is increasingly important when a justification for policy is sought in a public process. As the traditional nation-state is integrated in EU networks and policies, justification based upon 'national interests' appears to carry less and less normative legitimacy. We can assume that human rights as a basis for justification is becoming increasingly important. British Prime Minister Blair, for example, justified the war on Iraq in 2003 not only in terms of British security interests, but also as a war for the just cause of democracy and human rights. Deposing the tyrant is a moral argument, quite separate from a traditional security justification.

But how can we understand normative legitimacy and assess its importance in political processes? Legitimacy is a term often invoked in political debates, but seldom defined. Historically, it referred to the rightful ruler of a state: the legitimate king was the first-born male heir to the throne. Likewise, an illegitimate child was a standard term until recent times, denoting a child born outside the juridical contract between its parents, the marriage. But the term has received scant scholarly attention (Hurd, 1999).

Follesdal notes broad, confusing and conflicting uses of the term in the literature and cites at least three meanings: 'Laws and authorities are *legally legitimate* insofar as they are enacted and exercised in accordance with constitutional rules and appropriate procedures. Laws and authorities are *socially legitimate* if the subjects actually abide by them. Finally, they are *normatively legitimate* insofar as they can be justified to the people living under them, and impose a moral duty on them to comply' (2003: 6). We speak about legitimate rule when the rules of democracy have been followed, while we speak about legitimate views when they conform to the dominant norms of society. Thus, while it may be legitimate to discriminate against women in one country, it may be illegitimate in another even when the legislation in both countries is the same. In some cases, there is no relationship between legal and normative legitimacy.

The general assumption here is that legal legitimacy is a necessary but not a sufficient condition for normative legitimacy. To illustrate, a UN Security Council mandate is usually a necessary condition for normative legitimacy with respect to the use of force, but it may not be sufficient for normative legitimacy if the mandate is arrived at through undue pressure and threats. If all the votes in favour are bought or otherwise extorted, the mandate is legal but not legitimate. In the 2003 Iraq case, the legal legitimacy of the action mattered very much and appeared to be a *sine qua non* for normative legitimacy. There are, however, legal disputes about what constitutes a legal mandate in this case (see Thune et al., 2003).

In other interventions, such as Kosovo in 1999, there was no legal mandate but an overwhelming degree of normative legitimacy for the intervention. Normally, though, it does matter whether or not a state is in compliance with international law. The US under George Bush Snr sought the legitimacy of the UN Security Council when attacking Iraq in 1991, although this was not strictly necessary given the Kuwaiti demand for assistance against an aggressor which allowed for the lawful invocation of the self-defence Article 51 of the UN Charter. The reason for seeking a mandate from the UN was the perceived need for legitimacy. Likewise, George W. Bush sought a similar mandate before attacking Afghanistan in 2001 and later sought a mandate to attack Iraq despite the parallel claim that the US had a right to attack on the basis of previous UN resolutions. Thus, to have a legitimate basis for action is evidently very important, even for the world's superpower.

What are the scope conditions for legitimacy based on human rights? Preliminary empirical evidence suggests that only in Western ambits and under conditions of normal politicisation will legitimacy play a key role. This author's study of human rights conditionality in Europe showed that the possiblities of coercion enhanced the impact, making the EU a much more powerful actor than the Organisation for Security and Co-operation in Europe (OSCE) or the COE. But it also showed that 'shaming' rather than coercion worked with states that were in European ambits already, though not with those outside. Those states still required coercion for compliance (Matlary, 2002). Risse at al. make a similar observation: first one learns to 'talk the talk' of human rights, then one learns to 'walk the walk' (Risse et al., 1999). Thus, the reasons for human rights compliance vary in and around the EU. We know that both co-operation and shaming are motivations for government elites that seek memerbship of the EU. But are there instances also of persuasion? If so, how do we study them?

As argued earlier, political scientists appear to have overlooked the possibility that norms of right and justice – human rights norms in this context – may well matter in and of themselves. To be persuaded of values, norms and just causes is clearly much more important than mere instrumental adaptation to such norms because a conviction is lasting and less likely to disappear when the pressure or threat itself disappears. Indeed, we can argue that the relationship between positive law and normative legitimacy is really about the relationship between law and justice, which is what law is supposed to codify. By and large, we expect laws to tell us what is right and wrong, therefore law carries a higher status than 'mere' politics. If something is allowed by law, then we usually assume that in a general sense it must be right. The law must be just; we react against unjust laws. This normative reaction tells us that it is very important that laws are in conformity with a general sense of justice. The legal positivist who denies any relationship between justice and law, or indeed denies that justice is a meaningful concept, should logically do away with law altogether and simply reduce it to politics with a 'time lag' and not expect law to carry any legitimacy as such.

To summarise again at this point: the search for legal legitimacy attains special importance when the issue is discussed in a public-political process where the terms of the debate are already those of justification. The debate about just military intervention will then centre on whether there is a mandate from the UN Security Council and on whether this mandate is arrived at through a just political process. As a general rule, normative legitimacy will result if this is the case. Applied to human rights in the EU, a similar justification is possible if the policy is mandated on existing legal norms which are argued to be just in and of themselves. The fact that human rights are legalised matters, but also the fact that they are justified in a public debate is important. The point here is that the legal and the public aspects of policy making strengthen each other. When the case is human rights, this seems very obvious. We have more respect for a policy based on a legalised regime than one based upon some political deal. The same applies to justificatory processes of policy making: if they succeed, we are persuaded and grant normative legitimacy to a policy. Normative legitimacy also strengthens the foreign policy identity of the EU. A good example of a persuasive EU foreign policy on human rights is the work done to date to abolish the death penalty, where the the EU has been the key European actor (Manners, 2002). Significantly, this policy is based upon a legal regime, Protocol 6 of the European Convention of Human Rights.

An Analytical Framework for the Study of EFP

These general assumptions can provide a basis for further empirical work on how the EU enhances its foreign policy power through the creation of normative legitimacy for a foreign policy based upon a (legalised) human rights regime. The 'outward' foreign policy in this context has already been fairly well researched, with the general conclusion that 'compared to the situation at the start of the 1990s, the place of human rights considerations in the EU's external relations has radically changed … They now form an important part of the EU's international identity' (Smith, 2001: 202). Smith also notes that the norms of international society are changing in the direction of conditional sovereignty: only states that respect and implement human rights are legitimately sovereign (2001: 203). This adds weight to the argument here about the importance of normative legitimacy in the human rights arena for foreign policy. The EU, which lacks the traditional identity of a nation-state with national interests to pursue, may have been regarded as a foreign policy anomaly. Today, however, human rights provide an increasingly legitimate basis for the power projection of a post-national foreign policy.

We now turn to the empirical research about how the EU's foreign policy identity is constructed. We need to study not only foreign policy practices justified in terms of the promotion of human rights – Solana's peace mediation efforts and the EU co-ordination of a common UN policy, for example – but also the ways in which external foreign policy manifestations are 'matched' by internal EU processes of making the Union based on the constitutional human rights of the charter. Is there a process of persuasion that is redefining foreign policy between and amongst member states in the direction of a unified EU human rights policy? The interesting research questions are, first, whether there is an 'inside' process of foreign policy making which is creating a foreign policy identity based on human rights in the charter, treaties and perhaps the constitution, and second, whether this process results in conviction, in short, in a normative legitimacy for European foreign policy. Having argued here that the power of legitimacy is very important in post-national foreign policy, the expectation is that such an EU process would translate into a very powerful EFP.

Instead of juxtaposing interest and identity, as much of the current constructivist literature does, we should look closely at the genesis of agenda-setting in terms of whether there is a justificatory logic proposed. In Chapter 7 of this volume, Sedelmeier concludes that 'we can gain important insights into EFP from a perspective that acknowledges that the EU's identity matters *causally* for foreign policy' (my emphasis) and that this is particularly important in the area of human rights. If we assume that political identity matters in the very basic sense that the EU is a much stronger political actor if it sees itself and is seen by others as a political union promoting human rights, democracy and the rule of law, then these values are given substance and 'life' through being acted upon. When the High Representative of the the Common Foreign and Security Policy (CFSP), Javier Solana, appears in trouble spots around the world in an attempt to negotiate peace, this is a policy practice that tells the world that the EU is an actor that promotes such values. The mandate for this is already there in the treaties, but such mandates can also be found in states' constitutions. Virtually all states and international organisations can find a mandate based upon such values, but the basic identity is only created when the values and norms are 'concretised' in terms of policy practice. This practice has the most effect when it is highly visible, as a way of saying 'this is what the EU is about'.

The formation of an identity is of critical importance to an actor, such as the EU, that is in the process of transformation and needs publicity in order to communicate what the union is to its citizens and to other international publics. The strong element of law underpinning the EU is a great advantage here. In a world where hard power and unilateralism is advocated by the US, the EU can promote itself as a law-based, multilateral polity which should enjoy wide legitimacy. The process of constructing a link between citizen and union through citizenship and human rights is the way of creating democratic legitimacy for a new type of foreign policy from a new type of foreign policy actor. The foreign policy activities which take their point of departure from these rights show the world what the EU is about – its identity. The promotion of the EU as a new type of polity based on particular values must be assumed to be of key importance to EU institutions such as the Commission, the European Parliament and the ECJ. One would therefore expect that the rights language of justification would be the dominant mode of political discussion and agenda-setting on the part of these actors. The Commission in particular as a formal agenda-setter can be expected to frame policy in such terms in order to increase its own and the EU's legitimacy. As discussed earlier, this is what happened with respect to the enlargement issue. Agenda-setting was successful here in so far as a bargaining mode of decision making became the secondary and less legitimate mode.

Three hypotheses about human rights in the EU

Drawing on the general foreign policy literature on why human rights matter and on their scope conditions, three hypotheses are formulated in this final section that need empirical investigation to establish how they might 'work' in the EU. These hypotheses may also be applicable to other international organisations where there are extensive legalised human rights regimes, such as the COE and the UN Security Council. To reiterate, justification is regarded here as the main mode of decision making in the human rights arena. Bargaining is less important though, of course, it may enter into, for example, a closed door deal between the Commission and an applicant state. How much reform of the prison system do we have to make in order to join the EU? If we do more on the penal code, can we postpone prison reform? Clearly, this kind of bargaining takes place, but it is a practical adjustment process rather than a dispute over human rights norms themselves.

It has been argued that human rights are complied with for three reasons or combinations of reasons. They are the same ones that apply domestically when we obey the law: coercion, 'shaming' or persuasion. We pay the tram fare either because the punishment, a heavy fine, is too heavy; or because we are afraid of being caught and seen by people who know us; or because we want to obey a law that we are convinced is right and just. Abbott et al. (2001: 13) propose that 'a key consequence of legalisation for international cooperation lies in its effects on compliance with international obligations'. Compliance is analysed along three dimensions: *delegation, legalisation* and *precision*. These variables are also useful for formulating hypotheses about the role of human rights in EFP.

As we have seen, the EU's human rights regime is embedded in a very powerful organisation with a range of policy tools delegated to it by member states. In terms of delegation, therefore, the regime is strong. Not only are there a number of foreign policy tools available to impose human rights on applicant states and other third countries, but the regime has a supranational court that can define what these rights mean and can impose its rulings directly on member states. The supranational role of the ECJ is well documented and, as Menéndez points out in Chapter 15 of this volume, it is already referring to the human rights charter. If the charter becomes legally binding, the EU in effect has its own human rights court.

Furthermore, the work on human rights conditionality shows that the EU wields considerable power over formerly recalcitrant countries, such as Turkey (Matlary, 2002). Hence a tentative conclusion may be that the EU human rights regime is very powerful in terms of delegation, and that compliance in this context happens for instrumental reasons – coercion and 'shaming'. There is not much justification and persuasion in evidence in this kind of human rights work. We can formulate a first hypothesis thus:

> The EU's human rights regime is powerful in terms of **delegation** and works through coercion and shaming which represent instrumental motivations with respect to third counties and applicant states.

The EU human rights regime is likely to become more legalised in a 'hard' law sense if it becomes a legally binding charter in the new constitution. Such a legal status will add to the power of the EU in human rights and the justificatory process with respect to the interpretation of rules will increasingly involve legal experts. This would make member state influence less salient and more distant.

But we can also expect the process to become more public and transparent as well as more principled, the more legalised the regime becomes. This empowers EU actors, the ECJ in particular, as well as other stakeholders in a general European debate. If there is a public debate which empowers citizens, it also puts the justificatory mode of decision making at the forefront. A second hypothesis is thus:

> The more **legalised** the EU's human rights regime becomes, the more justification as a mode of deliberation predominates. Legal experts, the ECJ and other non-state actors are empowered, and persuasion rather than coercion and shaming becomes the dominant motivation for compliance.

The EU 'scores' high on delegation and legalisation (especially if the charter becomes legally binding), but human rights are often contested in terms of what they should mean in practical politics. There is much room for debate here: is the proposed policy an instance of this or that human right? Since the specification of human rights regimes is relatively low, we can expect major debates on their political implications. If it is correct that legal status is a necessary but not a sufficient condition for normative legitimacy, then the EU is in a good position to acquire the 'power of legitimacy' through an open-ended debate about what constitute appropriate policies according to human rights norms. A third hypothesis is thus:

> The less **specific** the EU human rights regime, the more public debate offers scope for persuasion and justification, creating normative legitimacy for the Union.

Risse argues that 'processes of argumentation, deliberation and persuasion constitute a distinct mode of social interaction to be differentiated ... from strategic bargaining' and adds that 'the more norms are contested ... (the more) the logic of truth seeking and arguing (obtains)' (Risse, 2000: 1, 6). Since the policy implications of human rights are at best unclear because of the very general nature of human rights, we can, nevertheless, expect the EU process of policy making in the justificatory mode to be highly significant in the future, when the issue is not only compliance with minimum standards for applicants and third countries, but also how the EU will ensure human rights for its own citizens. The charter may mark the beginning of a real process of justificatory politics in the EU involving both rulers and ruled within a new type of polity. This process in turn will add substance and power to EFP.

References

Abbott, K., Keohane, R., Moravcsik, A., Slaughter, A-M. and Suidal, D. (2001) 'The concept of legalization', in J.L. Goldstein, M. Kahler, R.O. Keohane and A-M. Slaughter (eds), *Legalization and World Politics*. Cambridge, MA: MIT Press.

Alston, P. with Bustelo, M. and Heenan, J. (1999) *The EU and Human Rights.* Oxford: Oxford University Press.

Bacevich, A. (2002) *American Empire: Causes and Consequences.* Cambridge, MA: Harvard University Press.

Chayes, A. and Chayes, A. (1995) *The New Sovereignty: Compliance with International Regulatory Agreements.* Cambridge, MA: Harvard University Press.

Duchêne, F. (1972) 'Europe's role in world peace', in R. Mayne (ed.), *Europe Tomorrow: Sixteen Europeans Look Ahead.* London: Fontana.

Eriksen, E.O. (2002) *Chartering Europe: The Charter of Fundamental Rights in Context.* Oslo: ARENA, University of Oslo.

Follesdal, A. (2003) 'Competing concepts of legitimacy'. Unpublished paper. Oslo: ARENA, University of Oslo.

Goldstein, J.L., Kahler, M., Keohane, R.O. and Slaughter, A-M. (eds) (2001) *Legalization and World Politics*. Cambridge, MA: MIT Press.

Hurd, I. (1999) 'Legitimacy and authority in international politics', *International Organization*, 53 (2).

Jupille, J., and Chekel, J. (eds) (2002) 'Integrating institutions: theory, method and the study of the EU', Working Paper. Oslo: ARENA, University of Oslo, 7: 1–38.

Kahler, M. (1998) 'Rationality in world politics', *International Organization*, 52 (4): 919–41.

Kratochwil, F. (1982) 'On the notion of "interest" in IR', *International Organization*, 36 (1): 1–30.

Leonard, M. (2002) *Public Diplomacy*. London, The Foreign Policy Centre.

Manners, I. (2002) 'Normative power Europe: a contradiction in terms?' *Journal of Common Market Studies*, 40 (2): 235–58.

Matlary, J.H. (2002) *Intervention for Human Rights in Europe*. Basingstoke/New York: Palgrave.

Nye, J. (1995) *Bound to Lead*. New York, NY: Basic Books.

Nye, J. (2002) *The Paradox of American Power: Why the World's Only Superpower Can't Go It Alone*. Oxford: Oxford University Press.

Patten, C. (2000) 'The protection of human rights in the twenty-first century'. Speech 3 March, Dublin. Conference: Human Rights in the Twenty-First Century.

Riedel, E. and Will, M. (1999) 'Human rights clauses in the external agreements of the EC', in P. Alston, with M. Bustelo and J. Heenan (eds), *The EU and Human Rights*. Oxford: Oxford University Press.

Risse, T., Ropp, S.C. and Sikkink, K. (1999) *The Power of Human Rights: International Norms and Domestic Change*. Cambridge: Cambridge University Press.

Risse, T., Ropp, S.C. and Sikkink, K. (2000) '"Let's argue!" Communicative action in world politics', *International Organization*, 54 (1): 1–39.

Schimmelfennig, F. (2001) 'Norms, rhetorical action and the Eastern enlargement of the EU', *International Organization*, 55 (1): 47–80.

Sjursen, H. (2002) 'Why expand? The question of legitimacy and justification in the EU's enlargement policy', *Journal of Common Market Studies*, 40 (3): 491–513.

Smith, K. (2000) 'The EU, human rights and relations with third countries', in H. Sjursen (ed.), *Redefining Security: The Role of the EU in European Security Structures*. Oslo: ARENA, University of Oslo.

Smith, K. (2001) 'The EU, human rights and relations with third countries: a foreign policy with an ethical dimernsion?' in K. Smith and M. Light (eds), *Ethics and Foreign Policy*. Cambridge: Cambridge University Press. pp. 185–205.

Smith, K. (2002) 'The EU and the promotion of human rights within the EU'. Paper presented to the 2002 ISA Annual Convention, New Orleans.

Thune, H., Eide, E. and Ufstein, G. (2003) 'Krig mot Irak. Foreligger det et FN-Mandat for Bruk av Militaermakt?' NUPI notat nr. 643, Oslo.

Weiler, J. (ed.) (1996) *Constitutionalism in Transformation: European and Theoretical Perspectives*. Oxford: Blackwell.

Weiler, J. and Friis, S. (1999) 'A human rights policy for the European Community and Union: the question of competences', in P. Alston, with M. Buotelo and J. Heenan (eds), *The EU and Human Rights*. Oxford: Oxford University Press.

9 Sovereignty and Intervention

Bertrand Badie

Europe is the birthplace of sovereignty and also very probably of intervention. This, in any case, is what we learn from a review of history. Or rather, history conjoins these two notions, which were developed and refined through opposition to each other. It was in reaction against interference in the affairs of his kingdom from the Pope and the Holy Roman Emperor that the French king Philip the Fair laid claim, as early as the beginning of the 14th century, to the right to be sovereign ruler on his territory. And it was most likely in order to contain the chaos and foreign intervention sparked and facilitated by the Wars of Religion that Jean Bodin, in his *Six Livres de la République*, developed the first theory of sovereignty (Bodin, 1967). Bodin was writing in the context of the Saint Bartholomew massacre, which, while sowing hatred and disorder, also spurred the English to support the French Protestants and the eminently Catholic King of Spain to intervene for the opposite side. To counter intervention, the Republic had to possess and wield absolute, impersonal, ultimate power. Slightly more than two centuries later, the right to sovereignty had developed into the sovereignty right, a notion soon given full theoretical substantiation by Thomas Hobbes, who demonstrated in *Leviathan* the utilitarian, rational foundation for instituted sovereignty (Hobbes, 1651/1991). In other words, the debate is a long-standing one: sovereignty is the power to contain power, to prevent intervention. The European history of sovereignty is mainly the rock of Sisyphus, the never-ending attempt to manage the impossible balance between state powers.

Sovereignty and intervention are thus at the core of Europe's historical experience and perhaps also of its contradictions and tensions. It is clear, in any case, that these two notions cannot be understood one without the other, just as two antonyms mutually define each other and, in order to be meaningful, cannot really stand alone. The concept of sovereignty is in itself ambiguous, since from the moment it was first constructed it has evoked both a demand for emancipation and an ideal system for organising and adjusting power (Badie, 1999). As it emerged, 'sovereignty' took sustenance from a critique of intervention. Intervention may be defined as transgression of the principle of otherness. With this definition in mind, we see how it can be either violent or 'soft,' explicit or implicit, social, cultural, economic or political; and how military intervention is only an extreme variant (Hoffmann, 1984; Bull, 1984; Lyons and Mastanduno, 1995; Moreau-Defarges, 2000; Mayall, 1996; Reed and Kaysen, 1993). For this reason, it becomes more and more difficult to discriminate clearly between international influence and intervention: the former is closely related to soft intervention, particularly to its cultural form. But in a world of globalisation, within which Europe presently finds itself, an organised and recurring influence is challenging sovereignty as drastically as other kinds of interventions, and transgresses the principle of otherness in the same way and to the same degree (Strange, 1988). Several centuries of proclaimed sovereignty, however, have been unable to put an end to intervention. An acknowledgment of just such recurrent imperfections was at the heart of what is known as the Westphalian system, a convenient but highly debatable name for the enduring international order constructed in Europe in the mid-17th century.

The points of uncertainty that emerge from this first overview are many. Jean Bodin had set the bar high: to conceive of ultimate power was to accept the idea that the power of the Republic could be preceded by no other; it meant rejecting the idea of placing any limitations on sovereignty and it meant recognising no distinction between the common good and the sovereign good, which was to be free from any and all international regulation. It also meant opting, as Hobbes did a century later, for a resolutely *national* conception of security, in which each sovereign was to protect his subjects, and thus conceiving *international* security as the result of a precarious balance of powers.

With this construct Europe came to be situated between the ambiguities of fiction and the dangers of radicalism. Conceiving a world order in terms of sovereignty evokes either a sort of coherent imagery that must unceasingly accommodate itself to real situations which contradict it or, on the contrary, the often brutal march towards a type of political construction which, to satisfy the demands of sovereignism, must make ever greater concessions to might, to the charismatic chief, and to unanimity – unanimism – against 'the enemy', as suggested in particular by Carl Schmitt's decisionism and the totalitarian adventure which his thought legitimated (Schmitt, 1985).

The Fortunes and Misfortunes of Sovereignty in Europe

European history has always combined a strong claim to *the right to sovereignty* with constant interference in the exercise of *sovereignty rights*. This is very clear for the absolutist period. As the Westphalian system – a juxtaposition of sovereign territorial states – was being put into place, the wars of succession were succeeding each other: intervention by European monarchs in their neighbours' dynastic successions had become the standard way of proceeding. The progression from royal to national sovereignty did not clear up this ambiguity; it merely displaced it. In conferring ultimate power on the nation, exalting national sovereignty, the French Revolution immediately brought about new forms of intervention, this time in the name of an obligation to help oppressed peoples liberate themselves from the yoke of despotism. French revolutionary messianism may be seen as a distant ancestor of later forms of interference in the other's affairs; namely, all intervention carried out in the name of human rights. And most importantly, underlying the wars sparked by the French Revolution and the myth of the '*Soldats de l'An II*' victoriously battling the counter-revolution wherever it raised its head, we find the assumption that national sovereignty no more mechanically implies the idea of remaining within national borders than it does understanding 'otherness' to be restricted to the domain of 'foreign affairs'.

The 19th century made this point no less eloquently. The Holy Alliance and Metternich's system reflect more than a will to construct or protect a conservative order and a return to the Ancien Régime. They also point to the development of a 'concert of nations' that led each of those nations to intervene in its neighbour's affairs the moment it judged that destabilisation in the other's territory was threatening its own security. It matters little that at the time the reason cited for such intervention did not go beyond the danger of 'liberal subversion'; it was in these terms that Louis XVIII's move to occupy Madrid in 1823 was justified. In fact, the most significant development for our purposes was the decreeing – as early as at the Troppau Conference – of a principle of legitimate intervention, itself clearly linked to another principle: solidarity between allied powers in the interest of a shared cause.

At the same time, in its refusal to follow this doctrine, English diplomacy proposed another interpretation, one ostensibly respectful of the other's national sovereignty in that, among other things, it rejected the idea of interference. Canning's liberal diplomacy, as distinct from Metternich's approach, seemed to reinstate ultimate power as its central construct. Simultaneously, however, it inaugurated a new tradition, to be further developed by Palmerston, in which the idea of interdependence was replaced by that of each state's natural promotion of its own interests. To be sovereign presupposed first and foremost protecting one's vital interests, and it was in the name of those interests that Britain set out on its colonial adventure, meanwhile supporting – in the name of nation and liberty – the Greek and then Serbian insurrections against the Turks.

We see that regardless of the content attributed to the notion of sovereignty, that notion always brought with it – onto both the battlefield and the negotiating table – the reality of intervention. The Wilsonian paradigm that took over with the Peace of Versailles only deepened this confusion. While 20th century Europe claimed to be establishing the right of peoples to self-determination, it in no way freed the principle of sovereignty from the ambiguities undermining it (Danspeckgruber, 1997). The map of the Old Continent drawn in the aftermath of the First World War shows just how difficult it is to define what a 'people' is, to endow that notion with solid, consensual criteria that might serve as a substratum to the principle of sovereignty. The Balkans is a formidable case in point. From as early as 1918 and until today, this region has represented such a complex interpenetration of peoples that constructing them into a territorial political community seems nearly impossible, if not an aporia leading straight to ethnic cleansing. The experience of the Third Reich suggests the same impasses concerning the very idea of the German people. This explosive encounter between an ethnic conception of nation and a Jacobin vision of the state demonstrates just how Europe got taken in and mangled up by the illusions of sovereignism and the dangers of interpreting literally the hypothetical geopolitical order assumed to derive from it. The Yugoslav crisis that closed the 20th century is a perfect confirmation of those dangers (Ramet, 1996; Thomas, 1999).

The End of the Cold War and European Integration

From this perspective, the Cold War made it possible to play on into over-time. Without a doubt, the intense post-War activity of constructing a larger Europe, together with the activist arguments of Mitrany (1943) and his disciples for a world able to transcend the map of states and satisfy human needs directly, worked to destabilise the old constructions. Meanwhile, the harsh bipolar confrontations were fuelling and giving succour to the old dialectic between sovereignty and intervention. It was in the name of sovereignty that each camp categorically refused to countenance any interference from the other in its affairs: the East denounced Western subversion and proclaimed the post-War borders inviolable, while the West lashed out against communist propaganda and went so far as to protect the authoritarian regimes on its periphery in order to fend off Soviet penetration. Meanwhile, implicit interference became the rule: on the one hand, the dissemination of propaganda over the air waves and through newly developing means of communication; on the other, recourse to fellow communist parties and to the other side's pacifists. These insidious threats in turn stimulated and intensified sovereignist tensions between the two camps, while justifying each side's integration policies: in the East, limited sovereignty for the communist countries; on the west, Atlantism, intensified by the consequences of the Marshall Plan. The Cold War clearly confirmed the twofold nature of sovereignty as aporia and indispensable fiction.

The model had to stand up to several stiff challenges. As early as 1945, Europe had to deal with a demand for sovereignty from its own overseas possessions; the effect of this was to make the principle itself both taboo and a new source of bad conscience. Thinking on this issue did not really begin to get free and clear until the 1980s, under the combined effect of advancing globalisation, the realities of European neo-regionalism, and the fall of the Berlin Wall. All three worked to undermine the sovereignty in Europe and reinstate the old sovereignty-intervention pair – now arrayed in new clothing.

Europe was only gradually affected by the shockwave of globalisation: first with the emergence of multinational firms, perceptible over the 1970s; then with the advances of neo-liberalism in response to the oil crisis. The Reagan era was actualised within the Old Continent in the form of Thatcherism. Deregulation, privatisation, the opening of markets, the slow transformation of the GATT into the WTO – these were so many developments that represented and established the principle of state regression, the dismantling of public services, the weakening of the welfare state (Seroussi, 1994). The economic sovereignty of the European states was being defied by and taking a beating from soft forms of intervention, while on the international scene economic and social actors proliferated, actors whose power not only no longer depended on any capacity for sovereignty but, in fact, derived from their very aptitude for circumventing state sovereignty (Rosenau, 1990; Risse-Kappen, 1995). Meanwhile, the move was being made from sovereignty to sovereignism – if we may so designate the new type of political movement, from the extreme right to the extreme left, in which the causes to be fought for, and above all proclaimed, were the reconquest of national sovereignty, anti-globalisation and, in some cases, anti-Americanism.

These new orientations are to be found as early as the 1970s in European neo-regionalism (Gamble and Payne, 1996). The Rome Treaty had officialised rejection of the federalist option and established the principle of intergovernmentalism, fuelled by a kind of co-operation between states in which national sovereignty actually got less bruised than by the Atlantic alliance. With the oil crisis and the increasing effects of globalisation, the situation was reversed: European integration came to seem an intermediate arrangement between states that could no longer go it alone and an as yet merely utopian vision of world regulation. Meanwhile, the European space was being increasingly invested and run by economic, social and professional actors, all playing their own games, either directly among themselves or by passing alliances with the European Commission (EC). These dynamics freed up regional and local actors and made multilevel governance the standard way of conducting affairs. Such governance, of course, ran directly counter to the classic conception of sovereignty in that it deprived the state of its ultimate capacity to lay down the law. The multiple interactions have been further complicated by the rapid intensification of interdependence, tying together not only economies and social systems but also public actions and collective choices: within the European Union (EU), the other's business has increasingly become everybody's business. Mutual intervention is now so common as to have become itself a principle of European governance (Hooghe, 1996; Sbragia, 1992).

The post-bipolar system that settled into place after the fall of the Berlin Wall confirmed and accelerated these developments at the same time as it reoriented them. First, the Cold War's reinterpretation of sovereignty was now obsolete. The Conference for Security and Co-operation in Europe (CSCE), which came into being after the decision at the Helsinki Conference to elevate to highest priority the two principles of state permanency and border inviolability, could now metamorphose into the Organisation for Security and Co-operation in Europe (OSCE), spontaneously more concerned with supervising and ensuring the stable progress of processes now called 'democratic transitions'. Each state's *internal* political developments became a central concern, one that it was acceptable and desirable for the OSCE to survey, though in some cases, namely the developing Yugoslavian crisis, such intervention was hardly effective. The dissolution of the Council for Mutual Economic Assistance (COMECON) and the Warsaw Pact, meanwhile, meant that for the EU and NATO, the issue of their own respective enlargements rose to the top of the agenda. Emerging from nearly half a century of limited sovereignty, the majority of the Soviet-system states, with the Baltic Republics in the lead, immediately reconsidered the question of their own sovereignty, insistently demanding to be integrated into one or the other or both of these organisations. Finally, the end of the East–West split recalls once again the remarkable sinuosities of 'sovereignty': the inevitable decomposition of forced alignments brought back into question the legitimacy of US military hegemony; the European allies began demanding new decision-making roles within NATO at the same time as the clientelist relations Washington had enjoyed across the globe began to loosen a bit, if not come apart (Haas, 1994).

But the last decade of the 20th century must also be counted as a very prosperous one for intervention virtually everywhere in the world. While the Gulf War followed the classic war model, the subsequent interventions in Somalia, Liberia and Haiti instated the idea that interference in the affairs of another state – including military interference – was legitimate when the state in question had collapsed ('collapsed states'; Zartman, 1995). It is true that European contingents played only a modest role in these first undertakings. That changed fairly quickly, however. Europe was gradually called upon to play a leading role in this type of operation, if only in symbolic terms, as in 1994 with France and Belgium's *Opération Turquoise* in the Great Lakes region of Africa, or, a few years later, the British expedition into Sierra Leone and the French unilateral intervention in Ivory Coast (2002). Most importantly, the notion of 'collapsed state' came gradually to concern and be applicable to Europe itself: first to Yugoslavia, then Albania. In both cases, the process of European engagement was slow but decisive. That engagement was at first diplomatic in nature, taking the form of disorganised initiatives on the part of the OSCE and the EU, namely in the unfortunate Inter-European Conferences on Yugoslavia (IECY), begun in 1992. During the war in Bosnia, and within the United Nations Protection Force (UNPROFOR), engagement became humanitarian – but the Europeans' caution in this case has made it possible to impute the tragedy of Srebrenica to them. Engagement became franker and more open with Operation Alba in Albania (1997), aimed at reconstructing the defective state. It became real with EU involvement in the administration of Mostar and the OSCE's overseeing of the Bosnian elections, and just as real, though under US leadership and the NATO flag, during the military operation against Yugoslavia (1999). Finally, with the post-War the European engagement has become determinant: under the aegis of the UN, EU had in charge the reconstruction of Kosovo, while the OSCE had to build democratic institutions.

It can be said that these interwoven events, which marked the last decade of the 20th century, are having a profound, threefold effect on the destiny of Europe:

- The principle of sovereignty is dissolving in the daily construction of a kind of interdependence and co-responsibility no longer restricted by the strategic considerations that dominated the bipolar period.
- Intervention, reborn overseas, has, inevitably, reached the Old Continent.
- Intervention is becoming increasingly multiform, insidious and implicit, and though, of course, it can still take military form, numerous practices of invisible economic, social and cultural interference, both originating in and pertaining to Europe, have become commonplace.

These interactions are the ordinary content of an ever more complex, inter-active, elusive 'soft power' (Nye, 2002).

An Empirical Doctrine of Intervention in Europe

Events have outstripped doctrine. Indeed, doctrine is evolving on the heels of new discoveries and experiences. We may nonetheless affirm that European diplomacy has been redeployed in several discernible directions:

- a more utilitarian and less dogmatic vision of sovereignty;
- a recomposition of the European community in which the EU and its institutions develop outside sovereignty principles; and
- the revenge of power, which may be said to lend support to neo-realist arguments, at least for the time being.

Europe's new utilitarianism may be broken down into three parts. First, Europe, situated between American and Asian strength and growing insta-bility in the South, has rediscovered to a greater degree than many of its partners the virtues of the common good and protecting the common good (Onuf, 1995). Together with Canada, Europe played an undeniably central role in the great international conferences – on ecology (Rio, 1992; Kyoto, 1996; The Hague, 2000); population (Cairo, 1994); social development (Copenhagen, 1995); habitat (Istanbul, 1996); human rights (Vienna, 1993); and women (Beijing, 1995; New York, 2000) – which throughout the 1990s sought to promote the idea of international treatment for major international issues, moving to shield them to some small degree from the arbitrariness of treatment by individual sovereign states. Indeed, the strongest sovereignist resistance to these initiatives has come from the US – on ecology issues, for instance, Europe has taken a direct stand against the US – together with the countries of the southern hemisphere and China. Likewise, Europe was among the promoters of the project to create an international criminal court and has been a main supporter of the relevant text adopted in Rome in July 1998. In sum, Europe's actions have repeatedly reflected the hypothesis that, with the risk of instability on one side and superpower on the other, the most rational policy approach is collective, interventionist management of essential public goods, at the unavoidable cost of limiting individual state sovereignty (Badie, 1999, 2002; Donnelly, 1995). The commitments to a multilateral approach were stressed after 11 September (Resolution 1368 of the Security Council) and about the US intervention in Iraq (Resolution 1441), even though the UK diplomacy decided to opt for a more Atlanticist vision.

Second, this new orientation has been transferred onto the political-military field. The Dayton Accords fully established the hegemony of US diplomacy – while ratifying the process of ethnic cleansing, which continued to be enacted at the very gates of the EU (Gow, 1997). In the light of these failures, polls conducted in early 1999 revealed that, for the first time since 1938, public opinion in the countries of the EU favoured interventionism. Ethnicisation projects, which had been marginalised by the Cold War, were now clearly designated a collective threat that imperiled the security of the Union and justified a policy of intervention. Despite the reluctance of Italy, situated near the field of operations, this policy was fully adopted by the main actors of European diplomacy.

Third, the very idea of intervention restored an active role to Europe, which could become the standard-bearer of a new philosophy of intervention. Europe stood out as the first promoter of the humanitarian intervention doctrine. This new vision came up with the Biafra war (1967) and the creation of the *French Doctors*; but it was mainly realised by the 8 December 1988 UN resolution, which instituted the humanitarian intervention as a duty in case of human disaster. This challenge to sovereignty was mainly conceived by the French lawyer Mario Bettati (Bettati, 1996) and was strongly supported by many human rights non-governmental organisations (NGOs) which flourished during the 1980s and 1990s in Europe.

In this perspective, Europe could at last aspire to the role of regional power, in its zones of influence, namely in Africa, even though it had to overcome the main orientations of its post-colonial policy and had to go beyond the clientelist networks in which, for instance, the French policy was embedded: these main contradictions would explain why Paris was so cautious about promoting new kinds of interventions in Rwanda and took a long time deciding to play a military role in the Ivory Coast crisis that was initiated in December 1999. So, it is first and foremost at home, within the Old Continent itself, that Europe pretends to play this new role, at precisely the moment when the US foreign policy doctrine was vacillating about whether to maintain the policeman role on this continent. Post-bipolar Europe discovered new responsibilities, particularly as one crucial effect of the collapse of the Soviet Union has been to regionalise and even localise new conflicts and issues, and to do away with a structuring international cleavage.

These entirely new orientations have combined with mutations in the development process of the EU itself. Classic conceptions of sovereignty were thoroughly shaken up, first by the Maastricht Accords but most importantly by monetary union. When it touched national currencies, one of the strongest marks of sovereignty, the European process went for the first time beyond the stage of co-operation towards integration. Likewise, the Schengen Accords, by affecting the power of the police, dealt a direct blow to state sovereignty. Lastly, the multiplying and strengthening of transnational actors within the European community itself deprived the states of their exclusive power to control the nature and rhythm of integration processes. These realities taken together have given rise to much thought and discussion on the definition of European identity: how to define a community whose member states are losing their attributes of sovereignty, and that is projected to extend beyond the geopolitical space to which it was confined during the Cold War; a community that, in fact, defies any and all definition in geographical terms and does not meet purely cultural criteria.

The response to these questions has increasingly brought to the fore the criterion of a 'community of values', values which are defined as a shared aspiration to democracy, human rights and the main components of the political philosophy that developed out of the Enlightenment. Such values pretend, of course, to determine the conditions under which Europe may be enlarged and new members admitted. But the community of values claims also to instate the right of member states to survey expressions of national sovereignty within each other. The sanctions decreed against Austria when a governing coalition was formed between the Conservative Party and the Freiheitliche Partei Österreich (FPÖ) have certainly set a legal precedent; though they were not especially effective, the symbolic effect of imposing them was great, and that much greater for being – or appearing to be – a proclamation of one of the aspects of European identity. There can be no doubt that in this context respect for human rights has become a fundamental component in the dialectic between sovereignty and intervention, and this in a way that extends beyond the EU *stricto sensu*, since the European Human Rights Convention is applicable to all states represented on the Council of Europe (COE). This convention has won out over the sovereignty of national legislations: the European Human Rights Court, on the initiative of a single individual, can sanction any one of the signatory states. Judicial intervention is thus gaining in importance, and this may signal the beginning of a wider judicialisation of international space. In any event, suprastate judicial intervention has now affirmed itself over political and socio-economic intervention by the states.

Clearly, these multiple forms of intervention are getting at the very heart of state power, and this in at least three distinct ways. First, they are leading to a sharp *reduction* in state power. States no longer determine norms and, most importantly, it is no longer within state power to ensure that those norms are respected by judicial means. National choice in the domain of public policy has been limited. Transnational actors are acquiring greater strength and co-ordination. The local is becoming increasingly autonomous. All this points to a reduction in states' capacity for action, with *sovereignty decreasing together with power*. Simultaneously, as intervention itself becomes the norm, it is *modulating* and *transforming* the logic of power while *redeploying* it. To use Susan Strange's formulation (Strange, 1988), state interdependence is creating the conditions for a more structural type of power. Power, less and less that of the state, is now instead a subtle effect of the coming together of many actors acting in coalition. Because it belongs to all (and even though it is not shared out equally), the right of each to survey the other creates 'interplays', new manifestations of power that add up and combine within the spaces of regional integration – at least if they are not undermined by internal sovereignist tensions and attempts to take back some control – in such a way that *sovereignty and power act independently of one another*. Finally, intervention also increases the resources of those who are already the most powerful. In interplays, the power to look into the other's doings is never symmetrical: the strong intervenes more in the affairs of the weak than vice versa; in crisis situations, political-military intervention almost inevitably reproduces the old strong–weak dialectic. Ten years of post-bipolar Europe have shown that the strongest are still safe from multilateral intervention. In connection with Chechnya, Russia suffered no more than suspension of its participation in the COE. Likewise, the strong are quicker to intervene than the medium-strong or the weak. The intervention in Kosovo, which mainly involved the UK and France alongside the US, was extended in the form of German and Italian occupation and administration of the different zones – it was in this function that those countries joined the other three belligerents. The power map of the Contact Group thus corresponded directly to that of the European component of the G8. We see very clearly in this case that abandoning sovereignist rigour reinforces the strength of the greater and diminishes that of the smaller.

Europe Grapples with Post-sovereignism

The experience of such multi-faceted intervention, the empirical challenges it poses to the old principle of sovereignty, the new forms of interdependence – all have come together to create a totally new situation, one that political rhetoric has difficulty naming, law has trouble conceiving, and institutions are hard-pressed to oversee or control. This curious mixture is what defines post-sovereignism today. Depending on their traditions and convictions, observers and actors of the phenomenon speak of either chaos, transition, regionalism, either a new world or regional order. Perhaps post-sovereignism comprises all these elements. In the European context, at least, it can be assessed by means of three questions:

- Will the institutions of the EU be able to advance to the post-sovereign phase?

- Can the intervention in Kosovo be considered a model for future policy?
- Can the contours of post-sovereignism in Europe be defined by new, citizenry modes of political action?

The EU's post-sovereignist identity may be assessed in terms of its capacity to move beyond the classic debate between partisans of a Europe that is neither more nor less than the sum of its states and those who wish to see Europe take the form of a unified superstate. Post-sovereignists commonly repudiate both intergovernmentalism (Moravcsik, 1991) and federalism (Croisat and Quermonne, 1996). Post-sovereignism may originate in functionalist principles (Mitrany, 1943), which inverted the classical political grammar by giving priority to the satisfaction of human needs over state self-realisation and fulfilment. The rediscovery of the subsidiarity principle, the propagation of the idea of multilevel governance, and the progress of the very idea of governance over that of state, all clearly support this hypothesis. In this connection, we should also take into account Europe's development in the direction of variable forms of integration. These new flexible ways of integration should be grasped at different levels: varying political geometries according to the issue which is at stake (security with the Schengen zone; currency with the euro zone), diverse actors including states and non-states (pressure groups, lobbies, unions, firms), varying levels of political authority (European institutions, nation-states, subnational regions). This trend increasingly leads to 'sovereignty deregulation', by which decisions are less and less made by a single ultimate power, and more and more as a result of a complex interplay of different kinds of political units. These new forms would seem destined to develop further as Union enlargement brings together states of distinct natures and development histories. Those forms represent institutionally distinct modes of giving up sovereignty within the same institutional space, and they thus switch state sovereignty from the status of a fixed point to that of a variable one, and even to an instrument of negotiation among states (Krasner, 1995).

This twofold development currently affecting the EU weighs directly on the foreign policy of each of the member states. The issue of the relative weight of each state in the functioning of European institutions has been placed at the top of the agenda. And the changes require the states to develop new forms of coalition that will integrate transnational actors. Above all, they are leading them to rethink their policy with regard to the Union in terms of modulated, selective concessions of sovereignty. Instead of seeking to establish alliance systems among the great European capitals, as in the past, such policy aims to define differentiated spaces of integration that will make it possible to abandon sovereignty in a measured, gradual way, and thus to exercise some control over just how readily and frequently recourse is had to interference in the other's affairs.

In this connection, the intervention in Kosovo is doubly emblematic. Following on Operation Alba, it confirms the understanding and reality that European security is the direct result of the internal security of each and every state of the Old Continent, and that concern for security legitimises military intervention. It also demonstrates that such an undertaking cannot be accomplished without a minimally shared conception of what, exactly, security in Europe consists in. The operation conducted in Kosovo put a definitive end to the conception of non-interference formulated in the Helsinki Declaration and reversed the hierarchy, in place until 1999, by which sovereignty came before requirements of collective security and protection of human rights. It was precisely because ethnic cleansing is an assault on both collective security and human rights that it rendered legitimate a policy of military intervention, even though that policy had not been officially approved by the UN and had to be implemented through NATO. In this area the change is quite clear: the humanitarian emphasis of the interventions in Bosnia, passive and conducted in strict accordance with UN principles, yielded, under the weight of this method's failures, to more active intervention, guided this time by the will to put an end to a policy enacted by what was seen as a rogue state.

Nonetheless, the operation in Kosovo seems to have produced contradictory results. Undoubtedly it gave new life to the project of integrating European security policy, which had not got off to a very sure start. And yet it is obvious that the EU states refuse to consider the Kosovo intervention as a precedent to be followed. As early as the St Malo declaration (December 1998), France and the UK reactivated the idea of a common European defence force, and the Franco-German summit at Toulouse (May 1999) confirmed the need for the Union to endow itself with the autonomous means necessary to act in case of crisis; this was the beginning of the Rapid Reaction Force (RRF). The idea first proposed at Amsterdam of transferring the resources of the Union of Western Europe to the new EU defence arrangement was confirmed once at the summit of Cologne, again in Helsinki, and once again in Nice. That the old idea of a European defence has been partially reactualised undoubtedly reflects a readiness to circumvent classic sovereignist theses. For the first time since 1945, multilateral intervention has been carried out on European soil – and not in the name of individual national interests, but rather to make good Europe's shared responsibility to defend its collective values and security. This intervention thus clearly fits into post-bipolar logic, which has, as we have seen, downgraded the principle of sovereignty. The European states, whose armies rediscovered the coalescing effect of fraternity in arms on the field, were also experiencing the needs created by a new kind of military intervention, those connected with the virtually instantaneous organising of the Kosovo Force (KFOR). What was once a theoretical necessity suddenly became a practical one. From now on, the RRF will be in charge of humanitarian actions and peace maintenance; it will also be able to intervene to assist Europeans caught in overseas crises. It cannot go beyond that. In the mind of the European leaders (except the French), everything else would be better secured by the US (and NATO) protection.

Moreover, none of the positions taken by the various governments suggest that the lessons of Kosovo can be extended or applied elsewhere. More modestly, the Kosovo precedent should be taken as a new instrument for dissuading regimes that might like to develop policies similar to Milosevic's. In this respect, the post-crisis management of Kosovo is ambiguous; the temporary administration installed by the UN but mainly applied by the EU is hardly without contradictions. As in Bosnia, it aims to counteract or even cancel the effects of ethnic cleansing, without really managing to do so: both of the policies it sought to implement – bringing the refugees back and reconciling the various communities – have failed. As in Bosnia, it is trying to perform a kind of political engineering feat, but the results are quite mixed and the whole undertaking requires the kind of know-how that Western diplomats and military officers have, with reason, not really acquired. As in Bosnia, European post-crisis management in Kosovo has been conducted first and foremost with the intention of organising and surveying local and national elections aimed at restoring democracy. The ultimate purpose of the intervention thus seems to have been to enable the re-establishment of *national sovereignty*, a sovereignty which would then be authenticated by the Western states as being in line with the right values. But elections have not proven to be a very effective means for coming out the other side of a crisis (Mansfield and Snyder, 1995). They are difficult to organise; give rise to manipulation and intimidation; are frequently boycotted; and the foreign intervention required to implement them inevitably seems to delegitimise them. Above all, the raw, unappeased conflicts and splits that characterise such a situation to begin with seem likely to be confirmed and radicalised by the act of voting; it is the extremist parties that tend to gain strength in such elections. This was certainly the case with the April 1996 elections organised in Bosnia by the OSCE.

These difficulties mean that such intervention usually does not get beyond protecting and valorising *procedural* democracy (Sandel, 1984). When it comes to the twofold objective of protecting democratic culture and re-establishing politics and policies in line with respect for fundamental rights, this kind of intervention is much less active and effective. The speed with which the EU lifted sanctions against Yugoslavia after Vojislav Kostunica was elected, without first making sure that this election really signalled the incriminated state's return to policies that are acceptable with regard to the norms and values which the Kosovo intervention was meant to promote, is, in this respect, quite revealing.

Conclusion

At this level of analysis, post-sovereignism is suffering from a deficit of means – one that probably cannot be imputed to any mere lack of strength, since the US found itself just as much at a loss when confronting similar problems in Somalia, Haiti and Iraq, for example. The difficulties may have to do with the absence of a strategic doctrine – and above all of institutional equipment capable of implementing such a doctrine. The main explanation, however, lies in the ambiguities that are part and parcel of the political mobilisation of citizens. There can be no doubt that a post-sovereign political culture is developing in Europe (Brown, 1995): public opinion concerns itself directly with international conflicts, especially when they involve human rights abuses; it condemns ethnic cleansing and demands intervention policies that, for their part, the chancelleries are reluctant to implement. Unquestionably, true public debate, and even an international public space (Habermas, 2000), are developing around these questions; debate in which NGOs, the media and intellectuals are all active participants. Still, we cannot be sure that this collective demand for intervention actually goes hand in hand with any individual offers of supply that would call into question the 'zero casualties' doctrine. Nor is it clear whether mobilisations calling for the recognition of fundamental rights are not contradicted by increasing calls for recognition of identities, calls that, in various locales, are fuelling enterprises of ethnic cleansing. Above all, it is highly likely that one of the effects of the crisis of the nation-state, aggravated by the rise of post-sovereignism, has been to leave the most generous-hearted political mobilisations without an institutional voice strong enough to make its call receivable to the governing powers. Nevertheless, the present development of this international public space is strong and significant enough for granting it the ability of unmonitoring the main foreign policy decisions in Europe which are decreasingly monopolised by the state.

References

Badie, B. (1999) *Un Monde sans Souveraineté*. Paris: Fayard.

Badie, B. (2002) *La Diplomatie des Droits de l'Homme*. Paris: Fayard.

Bettati, M. (1996) *Le Droit d'Ingérence*. Paris: Odile Jacob.

Bodin, J. (1967) *Six Books of a Commonwealth*. Oxford: Blackwell (first published 1576).

Brown, S. (1995) *New Forces, Old Forces and the Future of World Politics*. New York, NY: Harper Collins.

Bull, H. (ed.) (1984) *Intervention in World Politics*. New York, NY: Oxford University Press.

Croisat, M. and Quermonne, J.L. (1996) *L'Europe et le Fédéralisme*. Paris: Montchretien.

Danspeckgruber, W. (ed.) (1997) *Self-Determination and Self-Administration*. Boulder: Lynne Rienner.

Donnelly, J. (1995) 'State sovereignty and international intervention: the case of human rights', in G. Lyons and M. Mastanduno (eds), *Beyond Westphalia*. Baltimore, MD: The Johns Hopkins University Press.

Gamble, A. and Payne, A. (eds) (1996) *Regionalism and World Order*. London: Macmillan.

Gow, J. (1997) *Triumph of the Lack of Will: International Diplomacy and the Yugoslav War*. New York, NY: Columbia University Press.

Haas, R. (1994) *Intervention*. Washington, DC: Carnegie Endowment.

Habermas, J. (2000) *Après l'Etat-Nation*. Paris: Fayard.

Hobbes, T. (1991) *Leviathan*. Cambridge: Cambridge University Press (first published 1651).

Hoffmann, S. (1984) 'The problem of intervention', in H. Bull (ed.), *Intervention in World Politics*. New York, NY: Oxford University Press.

Hooghe, L. (1996) *Cohesion Policy and European Integration*. Oxford: Oxford University Press.

Krasner, S. (1995) 'Power politics and transnational relations', in T. Risse-Kappen (ed.), *Bringing Transnational Relations Back In*. Cambridge: Cambridge University Press.

Lyons, G. and Mastanduno, M. (eds) (1995) *Beyond Westphalia*. Baltimore, MD: The Johns Hopkins University Press.

Mansfield, E. and Snyder, J. (1995) 'Democratization and the Danger of War', *International Security*, 20 (Summer): 5–38.

Mayall, J. (1996) *The New Interventionism: 1991–1994*. Cambridge: Cambridge University Press.

Mitrany, D. (1943) *A Working Peace System*. London: Royal Institute of International Affairs.

Moravcsik, A. (1991) 'Negotiating the Single European Act: national interests and conventional state craft in the European Community', *International Organization*, 45 (Winter): 19–56.

Moreau-Defarges, P. (2000) *Un Monde d'Ingérences*. Paris: Presses de Sciences PO.

Nye, J. (2002) *The Paradox of American Power*. Oxford: Oxford University Press.

Onuf, N. (1995) 'Intervention for a common good', G. Lyons and M. Mastanduno (eds), *Beyond Westphalia*. Baltimore, MD: The Johns Hopkins University Press.

Ramet, S. (1996) *Balkan Babel*. Boulder, CO: Westview.

Reed, L. and Kaysen, C. (eds) (1993) *Emerging Norms of Justified Intervention*. Cambridge: American Academy of Arts and Sciences.

Risse-Kappen, T. (ed.) (1995) *Bringing Transnational Relations Back In*. Cambridge: Cambridge University Press.

Rosenau, J. (1990) *Turbulence in World Politics*. Princeton, NJ: Princeton University Press.

Sandel, M.J. (1984) 'The procedural democracy and the unencumbered self, *Political Theory*, 12 (1): 81–96.

Sbragia, A. (ed.) (1992) *Europolitics: Institutions and Policymaking in the New European Community*. Washington, DC: The Brookings Institution.

Schmitt, C. (1985) *Political Theology: Four Chapters on the Concept of Sovereignty*. Cambridge, MA: MIT Press.

Seroussi, R. (1994) *Les Nouveaux Gendarmes du Monde*. Paris: Dunod.

Strange, S. (1988) *States and Markets*. London: Pinter.

Thomas, R. (1999) *Serbia under Milosevic: Politics in the 1990s*. London: Hurst.

Zartman, W. (ed.) (1995) *Collapsed States: The Disintegration and Restoration of Legitimate Authority*. Boulder, CO: Lynne Reinner.

Part III
Case Studies

10 Security and Defence: The EU Police Mission in Bosnia-Herzegovina

Annika S. Hansen

On 1 January 2003, the European Union (EU) put its ambitious plans for civilian crisis management into practice by deploying the European Union Police Mission (EUPM). The fact that the first trial of the EU's crisis management mechanisms was a civilian police operation highlights practical and political concerns, as well as reflecting a new emphasis in security thinking on human rather than military security. Efforts to establish a police capability for crisis management are referred to as the Civilian Police Initiative (CPI).

Building on the theoretical discussion of a widened and deepened security concept in Chapter 3, this chapter begins by reviewing the conceptual backdrop for civilian police operations. As will become clear, changes in conceptions of security and sovereignty and the growing importance assigned to human rights have promoted the deployment of civilian police as an integral part of crisis management. The following section sketches developments to date by describing the evolution of the CPI.

The main section of the chapter focuses on the challenges that the EU faces with regard to establishing and implementing the CPI. The success of the Initiative depends on the political will of member states and on identifying the most appropriate institutional home for civilian police issues. Implicitly, the chapter also explores the extent to which the Initiative is an example of how 'shared norms, rules, and principles increasingly regulate relations between states in Europe' (see Sjursen, Chapter 3 of this volume). The analysis here indicates how the Initiative reflects the view of the EU as a 'rights-based community' in two senses. First, the deployment of civilian police is an instrument for jointly promoting shared principles and illustrates a '"collective security" approach to threats arising outside the EU's own borders' (see Sjursen). Second, as a central crisis management mechanism, civilian police operations are a means for protecting Europe – by providing instruments to up-hold the law – and thus counter the potential security risks from for example organised crime or refugee flows.

The Security Concept Behind the Initiative

The growing role of civilian police in peace operations reflects structural changes that have occurred since the end of the Cold War. These changes have created space for the promotion of human rights and humanitarian assistance, but have also challenged the formerly untouchable concept of sovereignty (Suhrke, 1999: 268f). Sovereignty is no longer regarded simply as a sacrosanct right of governments, but as a responsibility of those governments towards their peoples (see Deng, 1996). The inability to provide public security is one of those failures that can lead to an international intervention and the provision of police assistance. The Kosovo crisis in 1999 also had a profound effect on thinking in the EU. The shifting attitude had already been reflected in the 1992 Petersberg tasks that included humanitarian action, but the Kosovo crisis imbued the EU with a renewed sense of urgency to build an effective crisis management capacity.

International police operations and police assistance are instruments that promote human security and are validated by their goal of ensuring respect for human rights and establishing democratic control over local police forces. The establishment of law and order as part of a wider reform of the security sector has several dimensions. First, as human security, it has a normative dimension, in that assistance promotes democratic values and respect for human rights. In that sense, the 'development of "law and order" functions of the state is an intrinsic part of the broader issue of good governance' (Eide et al., 1999: 5f). Second, in recognition of the fact that consolidating the rule of law goes to the heart of a state's sovereignty, assistance also aims at strengthening the state or central authorities. Ironically, the central role of the state and its monopoly on legitimate force resonates the realist view, in which 'the normative justification for focusing on the state as the referent object ... emerges based on the claim that states are the agents that provide citizens with security at the domestic level' (Wyn Jones, 1999: 98).

Similarly, UN Secretary General Kofi Annan underlines how the focus on the role of the state has shifted, in that 'states are now widely understood to be instruments at the service of their peoples' (Annan, 1999). This indicates a general awareness that strengthening the state is counterproductive unless coupled with the normative demands of security sector reform and the rule of law. Security sector reform programmes therefore stress the need for legitimacy and point out that successful reform depends on popular support and participation (Eide at al., 1999: 6, 11).

As the concept's appeal is broad, the actual usefulness of human security is contingent upon its pursuit within a more narrowly defined area, such as law and order. This reflects Baldwin's view that total security is unattainable and that the degree to which there is security is also a matter of costs and the willingness to assign scarce resources to security purposes. He suggests that security is subject to the law of diminishing returns and that '[r]ational policymakers will allocate resources to security only as long as the marginal return is greater for security than for other uses of the resources' (Baldwin, 1997:

13–17, 20, 23). Baldwin's warning is likely to hold true with respect to critical challenges that the EU faces in the implementation of the CPI, especially when it comes to assigning authority and determining just who within the institutional system will foot the bill for civilian crisis management.

This chapter now reviews the EU's practical and political efforts to date, describing the evolution of the CPI before turning to the challenges of implementing the Initiative and looking at how these reflect the current understanding of security among EU member states.

The Evolution of the CPI

With the adoption of the Amsterdam Treaty and the endorsement of the Common Foreign and Security Policy (CFSP), the EU member states committed themselves to building the capacity to undertake the so-called Petersberg tasks, namely humanitarian and peacekeeping operations. But the Treaty, which forms the legal basis for the EU's external crisis management, does not mention the possibility of deploying civilian police, as police operations had not then become prominent and fell in between emergency relief and military crisis management. The crisis in Kosovo, however, clearly reinvigorated institutional developments and brought the distinction between military and civilian crisis management mechanisms into focus. The experiences in Kosovo also resulted in an intricate relationship between the dynamics of the military and the civilian crisis management mechanisms. Developments in the implementation of the CPI were – and are – shaped by progress in the military field (Dwan, 2002: 7–9). At the same time, however, civilian mechanisms are an attractive alternative to member states that are sceptical of an over-emphasis on military interventionism.

The first major step towards an EU involvement in the policing aspect of international operations was taken at the European Council meeting in Helsinki in December 1999 where non-military instruments were highlighted for the first time. Aside from setting the headline goal for the military capacity, the Council also defined civilian policing as a key crisis response tool and decided on an action plan for creating a rapid reaction capability in the field of civilian crisis management. Motivated by a desire to draw on existing resources in member states and in order to move implementation forward, a co-ordination mechanism was established in the Council Secretariat to link the Council, the Commission and member states (*Presidency Reports*, December 1999).

The following European Council meeting at Santa Maria da Feira in June 2000 brought significant progress (*Presidency Conclusions*, June 2000). A 'Committee for Civilian Aspects of Crisis Management' (CivCom) was created, which paralleled the Military Committee under the Political Security Committee (PSC). More importantly for the CPI, member states agreed on the headline goal of 5,000 civilian police personnel by the year 2003, of which 1,000 would be deployable within 30 days. With slow progress on the ground in Kosovo in mid-2000 serving as a backdrop, the main tasks that emerged from Feira were 'to prevent or mitigate internal conflicts, to restore law and order where these have broken down, and to support local police forces in respecting human rights' (James, 2000).

During the French Presidency, frequent meetings of CivCom were held and the link between police and the judicial and penal sectors was established. As a result, the possibility also of establishing a roster for other civilian personnel involved in the security sector, such as public prosecutors and prison staff, entered the discussions at the European Council meeting in Nice in December 2000. As the military consultations were still at centre stage, little energy went into conceptualising what roles EU police forces would take on in a conflict area. As a result, the types of missions that emerged from Feira and Nice were defined very broadly as either strengthening existing indigenous police forces or substituting for local police forces, as United Nations Mission in Kosovo (UNMIK) and United Nations Transitional Administration in East Timor (UNTAET) police were doing in Kosovo and East Timor respectively.

The Swedish Presidency declared policing a priority and took the initiative to hold an unprecedented meeting of member states' Police Commissioners in Brussels in May 2001. The police chiefs developed a Police Action Plan, which was then adopted at the European Council meeting in Göteborg in June 2001. It was also hoped that the police chiefs' conference would be the first step towards regular meetings between senior police officials and that a structure would be established to that end within the term of the Swedish Presidency. Also in May 2001, a Police Unit was created within the Council Secretariat, which would be headed by a police officer and include 6–7 experts, but which, unlike the Military Staff, is not a self-standing body. The Police Unit's vast task is 'to plan and conduct police operations (including integrated planning and co-ordination, situation assessment, preparation of exercises, and preparation of legal frameworks and rules)' (*Presidency Report*, June 2001: Annex 1, para. 22).

The targets laid out in the Police Action Plan remain valid. Priority areas for improvement are: planning, training, command and control, interoperability and the ability to deploy rapidly, through standby units, such as headquarters or integrated police units, and through enhanced military-police co-operation. The development of a rapid reaction capacity in the wider security sector, that is, judicial and penal staff, is underlined as a critical counterpart to the CPI. By early 2003, the efforts had shifted towards developing plans for the implementation of priority areas. Irrespective of its operational relevance, a driving factor behind the Police Action Plan has been to foster consistency amidst rotating Presidencies and to ensure that the EU's efforts in the rule of law field complement the efforts of other international organisations, such as the UN.

During the Belgian Presidency, the implementation of the Initiative made enough progress for the EU to fulfil its ambitious goal of declaring its mechanisms operational. The Conclusions of the European Council meeting in

Laeken on 14 and 15 December 2001 state that 'the Union is now capable of conducting some crisis-management operations' (*Presidency Conclusions*, December 2001). The Police Capabilities Commitment Conference hosted by the Belgian Presidency in Brussels on 19 November 2001 was another key event. Member states – in the form of home affairs ministers – pledged a specific number of police officers to the EU standby capacity and commitments not only met, but with regard to the rapid response component, exceeded the targets set at Feira 16 months earlier.

The following Presidency Conclusions, adopted at the Seville summit in June 2002, confirmed the decision to assume responsibility for the European Union Police Mission (EUPM) and also to look into the possibilities of deploying a military force in Macedonia. In Copenhagen, in December 2002, planning for both operations in Bosnia-Herzegovina and Macedonia had proceeded so well that the Council proclaimed its willingness to take over from Stabilisation Force (SFOR) and to initiate the necessary consultations with the key stakeholders in Bosnia-Herzegovina, including the High Representative and NATO.

The Challenges of Implementing the EU Civilian Police Initiative

When implementing the goals set out in Presidency Conclusions and other EU documents, the CPI meets a number of challenges. First, the willingness to prioritise human over military security is tested in a number of practical issues, such as the allocation of staff and resources by member states. Second, the CPI has struggled to find its home in the complex institutional structure of the EU. How these issues are addressed, ultimately sets the parameters for the prospects of the CPI.

Prioritising human over military security?

The overarching political aim of the CFSP is to improve the EU's ability to act in a co-ordinated fashion and thereby to become a more central and powerful actor in foreign policy. The CPI is a corollary to the military capability, at a time when there are numerous critics that question the feasibility of the military proposals. In the aftermath of 11 September 2001 and the overwhelming US military might demonstrated in the wars in Afghanistan and Iraq, one might add that the EU has acknowledged defeat in the military race and is now more eager to build an alternative capacity. Indeed, it is indicative of this division of labour that the police operation in Afghanistan is in European hands. The urgency that the EU senses with regard to building a crisis management capacity also derives from witnessing the conflicts in the Balkans and from having to deal with very concrete consequences of those conflicts, namely refugee flows and increasingly transnational organised crime.

In addition to the challenges of both co-ordinating policy and co-ordinating policy with action, police operations are a curious beast for most national governments. Police operations are international issues and usually form part of a country's foreign policy. At the same time, police are under the authority of internal bodies, be they ministries of justice or home affairs. The urgency felt by policy makers in foreign offices is not matched in domestic police circles, where deployment abroad remains an afterthought compared to the task of fighting crime at home. A first step towards realising the CPI is, therefore, increasing awareness and understanding of the value of international police work. In order to create a sustainable system for providing police officers for international deployment, national governments will have to make changes to domestic legislation, and not the least to budgets.

UN civilian police operations have suffered from financial and personnel constraints. Most importantly, there has been a shortage of police officers due to the fact that there are no excess police, as the available policemen in any given country are usually tied up in fulfilling domestic needs. Although the EU Civilian Police Initiative is bound to generate a larger number of police officers than are currently available for international deployment, it will not generate 5,000 *additional* officers as the headline goal indicates. In June 2001, the database created at Feira recorded that over 3,750 policemen from EU member states, including police with military status, such as the Italian Carabinieri, were deployed in international peace operations at the time.

The difficulties experienced in recruiting for the operation in Kosovo are a case in point. In the early stages of UNMIK, there was a general reluctance among European governments to participate and the UN struggled to find European contributors to the international police force. It is striking, then, that EU member states have chosen comprehensive and 'muscular' executive policing missions and deliberately have not set geographical limitations for the EU police capacity's area of operation. While this indicates a highly ambitious project, perhaps even with an eye towards the neglected and afflicted African continent, both the example of Kosovo and the political wrangling about what would be the best first test case operation for the EU, remind us that the extent of EU action in a given conflict area remains a political decision.

Proponents of the CPI argue that any increase in the number of deployable staff is an important improvement. While this is true, it also underlines the need to harness the optimism in EU circles about its ability to conduct crisis management and makes the case for developing realistic expectations and practical scenarios for the deployment of civilian police under an EU flag. The decision to restrict the EUPM to monitoring local police rather than enforcing the law in Bosnia-Herzegovina was certainly a wise one in this respect. To date, there is little evidence of governments taking the necessary steps at home to facilitate recruitment and deployment. Deployment abroad and the resulting international experience are not in fact assets, but stumbling blocks in the career path of police officers. Political authorities may be concerned with promoting human rights and human security, but they do little to translate these normative concerns into lucrative options for the policemen charged with putting them into practice. In addition, there has been little or no political debate on key unresolved issues, such as tasks, objectives and areas of police operations on the domestic fronts of EU member states. It appears that there is no absolute normative basis on which these issues could be decided, such as a steadfast belief in the value of each and every individual's personal security: the definition of tasks and goals is influenced by the merits of a given conflict and the member states' interest in its resolution.

The extent to which there is sufficient political will to create propitious conditions for the CPI in member states can be illustrated with the help of two other aspects of international police operations: the need to address problems of low quality staff and the need to recruit and train staff with specialised skills. First, since police deployment became more central to peace operations in the early 1990s, UN civilian police have grappled with problems of low-quality staff. The EU had the advantage of being aware of this particular challenge at the conceptual stage, and the Police Action Plan took it into account by including common standards for selection, training and equipment (*Presidency Report*, June 2001). Similarly, the EUPM emphasised the recruitment of experienced and high-ranking officers. Whether this level of experience can be maintained over an extended period with regular rotations remains to be seen. A system of rosters can provide some relief from this pressure and makes selection criteria more stringent. But it will again depend on whether member states are willing to allocate the necessary resources at home to put in place and apply quality controls.

Second, recent experiences in police operations in the Balkans and in East Timor have revealed the need to develop a better understanding of the specialised skills required in different types of missions. The roster of policemen can facilitate efforts to match available staff with specific positions and tasks that need to be filled in the mission theatre. Again, in the EUPM, planners developed specific job descriptions and tried to match specialised skills with a corresponding position. As mentioned above, member states have exhibited the most resolve where the CPI can be linked to efforts to combat organised crime. It is therefore not surprising that organised crime units are promoted as a critical set of specialised skills in an international civilian police force, and rightfully so. Linking civilian police operations to police co-operation within the Union's borders and to the fight against organised crime points to complex institutional networks within the EU structure, which are discussed in greater detail below. Some of the most scarce personnel resources in civilian police operations, such as forensics experts or narcotics police, are not surprisingly also the most expensive and the most prized domestic resources. While supporting in theory the development of cadres with specialised skills, contributing governments are often reluctant to actually part with these resources.

There is little doubt that the CPI will in fact lead to an increased number of available police officers. The real issue is the difficulty of developing a joint, cohesive approach. Strategic thinking has been sadly lacking from most civilian police deployment and the EU initiative has so far proved no exception. While European governments are genuinely motivated by a concern for human rights and the rule of law in former conflict areas, this objective is not consistently pursued in practice, calling into question the prioritisation of human over military security. The closest thing to defining 'what to do once we get there' have been the conclusions from Feira and Nice, which encompass virtually any possible mission ranging from monitoring to training and police reform to maintaining law and order – so-called executive policing. In the past, virtually all civilian police missions have been hampered by the fact that little serious thought was given to what they hoped to achieve. In practice, this *is* now done in the context of each mission, that is, EUPM and Operation Concordia, and, in the case of the EUPM, the need for a common political framework in planning, financing, exercises and doctrine was heeded.

Introspection and institutional wrangling

The prioritisation of policing as an essential element of civilian crisis management may have been driven by external events, but implementation and operationalisation are dominated by internal politics. At the level of the EU, the power struggle has played itself out in the debate on how to fit the CPI into the organisation's complex institutional structures. Internal wrangling is especially destructive because of the previously mentioned need for a coherent strategy. Dwan has even argued that there has been less focus on adapting the EU to new security challenges and more on adjusting the police capacity to existing institutional structures (Dwan, 2002: 14, 19).

The institutional debate has two main dimensions: the pillar structure and the military–civilian divide. The first dimension of the debate also harbours an underlying contest between intergovernmentalism and supranationalism. Civilian police operations, as part of the EU's crisis management mechanisms, are a part of the CFSP, that is Pillar II. Given that the EU aims at developing a coherent and proactive foreign policy with a wide range of tools at its disposal, Pillar II is a meaningful primary home. However, there is also a link to Pillar I, which deals with longer-term institution building, such as in the Commission's Community Assistance Programmes to Central and Eastern Europe. As the Commission fears being marginalised by the emphasis on external relations – and subsequent growth in the power of the Council – it has welcomed the civilian crisis management aspects, which allow it to build on its own capacity in the Directorate-General for External Affairs (DGE) with the Crisis Prevention and Early Warning Unit and on successful efforts in economic development and technical assistance. Nevertheless, the Commission is not committed strategically to police and security sector reform, in part because it is weary of the sensitive nature of policing issues and in part because it is reluctant to duplicate the activities of Pillar III (Dwan, 2002: 21).

Pillar III itself enters the picture because civilian police operations are also a question of police and justice co-operation. Following the terrorist attacks of 11 September 2001, co-operation on public security and law enforcement gained momentum and Pillar III mechanisms were upgraded. The establishment of the EURO-just programme under the Belgian Presidency and the strengthening of other instruments for police co-operation, including EUROPOL, CEPOL and the Police Chiefs Task Force, are all evidence of this. In addition, EUROPOL and Interpol have extensive experience in police co-operation and have been involved in work with Central and Eastern European countries. More generally, the objectives of successfully deploying civilian police abroad and effectively combating crime within the EU are clearly indivisible and will require extensive co-operation across all pillars.

The pillar debate is more fundamental than the institutional bickering might signify. It involves recognising that police missions are both short-term measures as part of immediate crisis management, mainly Pillar II, *and* long-term development assistance projects, Pillars I and III. It reflects the fact that the Council regards the deployment of police as an instrument of security policy; the Commission considers it a tool for development aid; and ministers of home affairs or justice, which deal with law enforcement co-operation within and the protection of EU borders, view the civilian police capacity as a preventive tool and a continuation of EU-internal police and justice co-operation.

The stated desire to undertake executive policing missions means that the EU civilian police will also engage in reforming and training police forces in conflict areas. The fact that police reform is a long-term proposition has been difficult to translate into practice because it requires unorthodox networks of co-operation, such as between domestic police authorities in contributing countries and the development assistance community. This means that civilian police operations will have to be co-ordinated with EU activity in other rule of law fields, such as support for judicial and penal reform through the Poland and Hungary Assistance for Restructuring the Economy (PHARE) and EURO-just programmes. The popularity of the concept of human security and the broad coalition that it calls for has resulted in a greater openness among all actors to – in principle – take into account the demands of military action, of the rule of law and of development assistance, but the road to institutional co-operation and co-ordination is long and winding in practice.

The second dimension of the debate involves making a decision on the extent of association with the military rapid reaction capability as opposed to the civilian crisis management staff. In the types of missions that the EU is envisaging, especially those in which international police officers replace a local police force, such as in the UN missions in Kosovo and East Timor, the police are dependent upon close co-operation with the military force, including military back-up, logistics support, intelligence co-operation and joint patrols. The argument in favour of a closer link to the military capacity maintains that military–police co-operation, particularly joint planning, would be enhanced if the two were to be affiliated institutionally.

Nevertheless, the critically important fact that police operations are fundamentally of a civilian nature has decided the debate in favour of aligning the civilian police with the civilian crisis management staff in the Council Secretariat, where the Police Unit is located. A fine balance must be struck between the necessary cohesion with the military approach and the need for the police capacity to maintain a separate identity. On the one hand, there is no getting away from the fact that the CPI is intimately related to the development of a military rapid reaction capability. The evolution of the Initiative takes its cue from decisions made in the military sphere, such as on the basic concept of the rapid reaction capabilities, that is, a certain number on standby by 2003, of which a certain share would be able to deploy within 30 days.

Although the CPI at times appears to be overshadowed by military developments, the concurrency of the policing initiative and the development of the RRF offers a unique possibility to institutionalise close co-operation between the military and civilian security actors. This in turn would lead to a better understanding and a practicable distribution of tasks between the military and the police. While placing the police capability among the civilian staff is ultimately most appropriate, there is a danger that two distinct and parallel channels of planning and advice will hamper close military–police co-operation. The operations to date are either civilian police *or* military missions, so that the need for operational co-operation has not been central. This will change should the EU take over from SFOR and become the military counterpart to the EUPM in Bosnia-Herzegovina.

The exercise policy adopted at Göteborg is an important step towards an integrated civil–military approach, which includes *all* instruments of crisis management (*Presidency Report*, June 2001). The first joint exercises took place in 2002 and clearly showed the gaps, the potential *and* the limitations in military–police co-operation. Some meetings on planning for joint exercises and training and mission preparation with military staff have taken place, but contacts are highly tenuous. Overall, the processes have revealed the extent to which it is still the military, rather than the civilian police, that springs to member states' minds, when considering how to service their security interests abroad.

On the other hand, the civilian police benefits from some institutional separation that will help to safeguard the recognition that staging police operations involves unique non-military challenges. This is especially true in light of the numerical imbalance, where military crisis management is handled by the Military Committee (MilCom) and its approximately 150 European Union Military Staff (EUMS), and the Police Unit that manages police operations consists of 6–7 experts.

Prospects for the Civilian Police Initiative

In designing the Civilian Police Initiative, planners and policy makers appear to have taken to heart lessons from past UN operations. The CPI is evolving into a grand scheme on paper, with all the desirable components: standby forces and rosters, joint training and planning, an inventory of specialised skills and critical ties to other elements in the rule of law field. But the challenges that the CPI faces in implementation reveal how difficult it is to translate 'new concepts of security' into workable mechanisms in the EU system. While the incorporation of security issues has in part been hampered by the fact that the EU has found it difficult to break out of its role as a civilian power, the focus on civilian aspects of security and crisis management have also emerged as a comparative advantage. It is true that the implementation of CPI has taken place in the shadow of the development of the more visible military crisis management instruments, but at the same time the Initiative has also been seized upon by some member states as a more civilian – and therefore more acceptable – instrument for the pursuit of security interests.

The institutional process has been a challenge, as the rule of law has so many different elements that touch on the competencies of different bodies. A cynical view would suggest that each body is driven by the desire to maximise its influence at least as much as it is motivated by a genuine concern for the security of individuals and the promotion of human rights. But one might conversely argue that it is the sweeping concept of human security that is difficult to operationalise, as it means all things to all people. While EU member states have indeed shown a steadily increasing concern for human rights and do have a qualitatively different view of state sovereignty, governments are still grappling with how to translate lofty normative ideals into practical policy and effective mechanisms for crisis management.

The challenge is exacerbated by the fact that the delineation of the CPI was event-driven, by earlier Balkan conflicts and more recently by Kosovo and to a lesser extent East Timor, and does not reflect a substantive grasp of the tasks that an EU civilian police force ought to fulfil. The proposal to undertake the full range of possible missions, including executive policing, was coincidental rather than a strategic choice and bears witness to the fact that the EU has not fully understood the scope of civilian police operations. This is especially true when declarations highlighting the need for comprehensive approaches and close co-ordination of various mission components are matched by so little inter-institutional dialogue and co-operation. On the positive side, the potential political fickleness of shifting presidencies has been somewhat reduced and consistency enhanced by the creation of a permanent body to deal with police operations. Still, the lack of communication within EU institutions does not necessarily leave one hopeful for continuity between the intergovernmental decision-making level and the work done in lower tiers of the Council Secretariat.

The CPI and the notion of security that underlies it challenge the distinction between domestic and foreign politics. As a result, one of the main obstacles is the action needed at national levels to implement the proposal, as it affects a host of authorities and costs money. The implementation process places great demands on the political will of member states, but if successful could present a radical step forward in European integration. Responding to Sjursen's question, with the CPI the EU has taken a significant step towards becoming 'a fully effective security actor' (Sjursen, Chapter 3 of this volume). The Initiative has benefited – and will continue to do so – from EU planners' efforts to find practical solutions to formerly unresolved operational issues for the trial police mission in Bosnia-Herzegovina. Having embarked on its first mission, it is virtually impossible politically for the EU to withdraw from it and the organisation is likely to do everything in its power in order not to fail.

In conclusion, despite all the stumbling blocks in implementation, it is difficult to see how intensified European co-operation on police matters can fail to produce added value. This may mean that it generates a small number of additional police officers. It may mean that the Initiative results in better co-ordination in civilian police matters, due to a better conceptual understanding and closer links with both non-members and other international organisations. It may simply mean a more effective deployment of civilian police missions. But given that the promotion of human rights and democracy have become established goals in security policy, that re-establishing the rule of law in a war-torn society is an indispensable part of promoting human rights, and that deploying civilian police is vital to reaching that goal, even minor improvements in efficiency, such as the EU Civilian Police Initiative, will have helped the cause.

References

Annan, Kofi, (1999) 'Two concepts of sovereignty', *The Economist*, 18 September.

Baldwin, D.A. (1997) 'The concept of security', *Review of International Studies*, 23 (1): 5–26.

Deng, F. (1996) *Sovereignty as Responsibility*. Washington, DC: The Brookings Institution.

Dwan, R. (2002) *EU Policing for Peace Operations: What Does It Mean?* European Interdependence Research Unit, St Antony's College: University of Oxford Publication Series, No. 4.

Eide, E.B., Hansen, A.S. and Lia, B. (1999) *Security Sector Reform as a Development Issue*. Room Doc. No. 9 OECD/DAC Task Force, Paris, June.

James, B. (2000) 'EU planning police force for crisis intervention', *International Herald Tribune*, 19 June.

Presidency Conclusions Santa Maria da Feira European Council 19 and 20 June 2000 (2000) (http://europa.eu.int/council/off/conclu/june2000/june2000en.pdf).

Presidency Conclusions Laeken European Council Meeting 14 and 15 December 2001, para 6; Annex II Declaration on the Operational Capability of the Common European Security and Defence Policy (2001) (SN 300/1/01 REV 1). European Council: Brussels, December.

Presidency Reports to the Helsinki European Council on Non-Military Crisis Management of the European Union (1999) Brussels: European Council, December.

Presidency Report to the Goteborg European Council on European Security and Defence Policy (2001) Brussels: European Council, June.

Suhrke, A. (1999) 'Human security and the interests of states', *Security Dialogue,* 30 (3): 265–76.

Wyn Jones, R. (1999) *Security, Strategy and Critical Theory*. London: Lynne Rienner.

11 Foreign Economic Policy: The EU in the Mediterranean

Ricardo Gomez and George Christou

This chapter presents a case study of what Michael Smith terms 'a practical European foreign economic policy'. In examining the development of the European Union's (EU) external Mediterranean policy over four decades, it attempts to apply some of the concepts identified in Smith's chapter (Chapter 4 of this volume). In particular, this chapter focuses on the EU's goals for the Mediterranean region, the institutional machinery and policy instruments for identifying and pursuing those goals and the factors that have determined its ability to deliver on its objectives. Adapting Smith's notion of the three worlds in which foreign economic policy making occurs, the 'boundaries' of EU Mediterranean policy have been renegotiated and modified at regular intervals. The form and content of EU policy have been determined by bargaining and negotiation across different 'layers' – within the EU and between the EU and the partner countries. Implementation of its current Mediterranean policy is reliant on the creation of an extensive range of networks of public and private actors across the Mediterranean 'space'. If this case study encapsulates many of the key features of European foreign economic policy, it also confirms another of Smith's arguments: that policy goals may conflict. The effectiveness of EU Mediterranean policy has continually been limited by the difficulty of reconciling the promotion of European commercial and security interests with rhetorical commitments to encourage sustainable economic development in the region.

This chapter proceeds in the following way. The first section examines the main stages in the development of EU Mediterranean policy. It considers how the EU's objectives were tentatively defined, the policy instruments it subsequently deployed and the problems that arose in the handling of its relationships with Mediterranean non-member countries (MNCs). The second section discusses the origins and negotiation of the Euro-Mediterranean Partnership (EMP), the most recent incarnation of EU Mediterranean policy based on the modification of formal agreements with the MNCs and a multilateral programme for co-operation (the Barcelona process) between the EU and 12 'partner' governments.[1] The third section focuses on the implementation of the EMP. Analysis of some of the problems which have emerged in the implementation process raises several important questions about the performance of European foreign economic policy.

The Development of EU Mediterranean Policy

A brief review of the history of EU Mediterranean policy is necessary to understand the factors that have shaped its contemporary policy in the region. Instruments which were deployed during the 1960s and early 1970s have continued to form the basis of the Union's formal relationships with Mediterranean non-member states. Issues that became 'politicised' during the initial negotiations with the MNCs – particularly import quotas – have tended to remain politicised and play a critical part in determining policy outcomes. For non-member countries the question of access for exports to the Community's lucrative markets – regarded as critical to their economic performance – became their primary concern in dealing with the EU. Though there was no clear definition of common interests and policy objectives in the early days of Mediterranean policy, the Union's handling of the MNCs suggested that the defence of the member states' commercial interests and the protection of the privileged position of European businesses in the MNCs' markets were its overriding concerns. These 'possession and milieu' goals have remained at the core of the subsequent development of the Union's policy in the region.

The keystone of Mediterranean policy was the conclusion of formal agreements between the European Community (EC) and the MNCs. The most advanced agreements were based on Article 238 of the EEC Treaty which provided for 'Associations' with third countries. This form of agreement generally covered much more than trade, with the provisions of Article 238 allowing for the negotiation of 'reciprocal rights and obligations, common action and special procedures'. Greece, Malta and Turkey all concluded Association Agreements during the 1960s. A second form of agreement centred on the negotiation of preferential commercial arrangements for France's former colonies in North Africa. The remainder of the MNCs were offered simple commercial accords which did no more than regulate existing imports and exports. The principal purpose behind the agreements was the maintenance of trade patterns inherited from the colonial period. But in differentiating between the MNCs, the Community attached greater political weight to its relationships with some states than others. The need to bind Greece and Turkey to the 'west' in the Cold War context, for instance, was a higher priority than measures to promote economic development in the North African states.

The emerging institutional framework for European foreign economic policy had a significant impact on the substance of trade and Association Agreements. The Treaty of Rome handed responsibility for the regulation of external trade through the Common Commercial Policy and the conclusion of agreements with third countries to the Community, with the Commission as the sole negotiator on its behalf (Lasok, 1994: 57–66). However, both the Commission's negotiating mandates and the final agreements required the unanimous approval of the member states in the Council of Ministers. The door was therefore left open for the member states to impose their preferences on the specific terms of the accords. Concessions on imports of agricultural goods, a key sector for MNC exporters, proved to be especially controversial and subject to repeated disputes in the Council of Ministers as southern member states sought to block decisions that would increase competition for domestic producers. Such behaviour became a recurrent theme in the Union's negotiations with non-member states.

In the early 1970s, the Community moved to bring greater coherence to its external policies. For Mediterranean policy, this involved replacing the 'patchwork' of agreements with what was described as a framework for the 'overall and balanced handling' of its relationships with the MNCs. A pledge was made to create, over the long term, a Mediterranean free-trade area, a goal to which the EU returned in the 1990s. The geographical boundaries of this self-styled 'Global Mediterranean Policy' (GMP) were expanded as existing agreements were renegotiated and new agreements were concluded with an increasingly lengthy list of outsiders including Cyprus, Egypt, Israel, Jordan, Lebanon and Syria. The introduction of new 'co-operation' agreements, which included provisions on financial, technical and social matters alongside trade, effectively broadened the scope of policy. Pressure from the G77 group of developing countries for a new and more benevolent international economic order, together with demands for fairer treatment for individual MNCs, put the Community's development policy under the spotlight and led to the inclusion of a small amount of financial aid in each of the agreements. Underpinning the GMP was the idea that the Community had both moral responsibilities and a strong strategic interest in promoting economic development in the region.

If the GMP initiative provided a clearer indication of the Community's goals in the region, the negotiating process bears out Smith's argument that the different functions of foreign economic policy may conflict. The restraining effect exercised by national governments was again vividly demonstrated during negotiations on import quotas. In a period of deep recession, the priority was to protect European producers. In response to the demands of domestic interest groups, the Council agreed a number of 'market organisation measures' that amounted to a barrier to imports in the most politically sensitive sectors (OJL198, 1975). Although new tariff and quota concessions were eventually agreed by the Community, the 'politicisation' of the negotiations saw restrictive quantitative limits imposed on several products. Invariably, the products that provoked the most heated discussions were those of the highest value to a number of MNCs in terms of export earnings. By 1979, the aggregate trade deficit of the Mediterranean third countries with the EC stood at nine billion Ecus compared with four billion Ecus in 1973 (Minasi, 1998: 2). Despite the rhetoric, there was little prospect of the GMP acting to reverse the growing prosperity gap between the affluent north and its poorer southern neighbours.

The accession to the EC of Greece, Portugal and Spain during the 1980s altered the boundaries of the Community's external Mediterranean policy and drove home the distinction in treatment between member states (or potential members) and non-members. Given that the application and accession process that eventually brought in Greece, Portugal and Spain began in 1976 – at the same time as the GMP was being negotiated – it was inevitable that the terms of trade offered to the Mediterranean associates were further squeezed. In opening the door to Greece (1981), Portugal and Spain (1986), the Community improved its own competitive position in so-called Mediterranean products at the expense of third countries. Indeed, the Portuguese and Spanish applications initially met with lukewarm responses as Community member governments increasingly focused on the potential impact of the accessions on specific policy sectors. Recession across western Europe had made economic interest groups and governments acutely sensitive to any additional competition.

As the European integration process accelerated during the 1980s with the drive towards the completion of the Single European Market, improving the Community's competitive position in relation to the US and Japan arguably became its key foreign economic policy priority. Along with many developing countries, the MNCs found themselves increasingly marginalised in EU external relations. A powerful indication of the MNCs' growing dissatisfaction with the deal they received from the Community was Morocco's application for membership in July 1987 (Marks, 1989: 14). The failure of external trade with the EC to act as a motor of economic growth and rapidly mounting external debts left the economies of the Mediterranean associates in a parlous condition by the end of the decade. The perceived risk to the Community of social and political fallout from economic crisis in the region began to create a stronger imperative for policy change. These issues were to be addressed in the negotiation of the Euro-Mediterranean Partnership.

The Euro-Mediterranean Partnership

The process that led to the Euro-Mediterranean Partnership emerged out of the EU's own, negative evaluation of its policy in the region and the political opportunity space for external policy change that arose with the end of the Cold War (Cremasco, 1990: 119). In 1989, external relations Commissioner Abel Matutes argued that Europe's security should be seen as inseparable from the prosperity and stability of the wider Mediterranean region (Matutes, 1989). Threats to the quality of the Mediterranean environment, growing food shortages across the region and chronic balance of payments deficits were also identified as key challenges (European Commission, 1989). The connection between 'possession' and 'milieu' goals was unmistakeable in the proposals. Policies to encourage a more secure economic and political environment would enhance the already significant competitive advantage of European capital in the region and bring benefits to 'domestic' exporters and investors.

The EU's recognition of the explicit link between its foreign economic policy and the promotion of security reflected new post-Cold War thinking which called for policies to address the underlying causes of political and economic instability and shifted the emphasis from 'hard' to 'soft' security (Booth, 1991; Buzan et al., 1998; Grasa, 1995). The perception was that weak, internally unstable states were more inclined to resort to violence and challenge the dominant international order. A broader, 'holistic' approach to security, encompassing action on issues such as environmental protection, cultural relations, illegal immigration and cross-border crime, found its way onto the agendas of defence organisations including NATO and the Western European Union (WEU). For the EU, soft security implied a much more significant role for foreign economic policy in the performance of a collective security function. A more benevolent Union would be expected to direct its trade and aid policies towards marked and durable improvements in the economic wellbeing of its southern neighbours.

The bones of the Euro-Mediterranean Partnership started to be fleshed out in 1992 with European Commission proposals for a Euro-Maghreb partnership. The document called for dialogue on 'all matters of common interest' between the EU, Algeria, Morocco and Tunisia (European Commission, 1992: 3). The proposals recommended the creation of a Euro-Maghreb free trade area and a broad agenda of 'co-operation' on issues ranging from environmental protection to support for small- and medium-sized businesses (*Agence Europe*, 1992). A heavy dose of neo-liberalism permeated the EMP initiative, based as it was on the logic that free-trade, increased private investment and macro-economic reform would stimulate socio-economic development, industrial modernisation and macro-economic reform. This approach underpinned the policy developments that followed and inextricably bound up the Euro-Mediterranean initiative with broader processes of regionalisation and globalisation. It would be both a manifestation of a post-Cold War drive for deeper regional economic integration – centred on the EU – and a conduit for the extension of the Western-dominated global economic order.

Two policy instruments – modified Association Agreements (labelled Euro-Mediterranean Agreements) and a new financial aid package – were to be deployed in support of the Union's objectives. The provisions of the revised agreements – initially agreed with Morocco and Tunisia – were based on three lines of action. First, the EU and the individual MNCs would re-examine the terms of trade in their agreements. Second, provisions would be included in each agreement covering rights of establishment, rules on the movement of services and capital, technical co-operation and the possibility of joint research and development projects. Third, the new agreements would include provisions for 'social co-operation', essentially ministerial dialogue on issues such as migration and living and working conditions for Maghrebi citizens in the EU. By 1993, participation by the EU in the 'stop-start' multilateral track of the Middle East peace process had convinced the European Commission that the partnership concept should be extended to Israel and the Mashreq countries. This decision effectively set the geographical boundaries of Mediterranean policy. Twelve 'partner' governments from around the Mediterranean basin would be included, though Libya and the states of the former Yugoslavia were excluded.

Negotiations with Tunisia and Morocco opened in 1994 and gradually took in the other Mediterranean partner countries during the course of the 1990s. Certain commitments were common to the agreements, including the elimination of customs duties on EU exports, a promise to reconsider the difficult question of liberalising trade in agricultural products and some reciprocal extension of preferential trade arrangements. Free trade in the Mediterranean region implied the complete removal of barriers to trade across all sectors, prompting forecasts of massive economic disruption in the partner countries as well as a political backlash from those economic interests in the EU that might face increased competition. Producing agreements that could be regarded as positive by both sides was imperative. Yet, as was the case in previous negotiating rounds, concluding the Euro-Mediterranean Agreements proved to be a painfully slow process, a result of disputes over their terms and laborious ratification procedures in the member states. By the end of 2001, only the agreements with Israel, Morocco, the Palestinian Authority and Tunisia had entered into force.

While much of the EMP drew on the EU's established range of foreign economic policy instruments, the multilateral Barcelona Declaration and Work Programme was a new departure. Signed at a high-profile meeting of Heads of Government, Foreign Ministers and EU Commissioners in November 1995, the Declaration and Work Programme were based on three 'chapters' covering political and security issues, economic and financial co-operation, and social, cultural and human affairs. The centrepiece of the Barcelona process was a pledge to create the world's largest free-trade zone by 2010, a potential market of 800 million people. The measures set out in the Work Programme were designed to complement the Euro-Mediterranean Association Agreements by stimulating regional economic integration, inward investment and infrastructural development, and by setting out guidelines for the management of 'common' resources such as the Mediterranean Sea.

The Declaration's economic and financial chapter laid the foundations for a framework of economic governance to be extended to the region and underscored the neo-liberal thinking behind the EMP. Provisions relating to the extension of existing co-operation in fields such as energy, rural development, technology transfer, technical assistance for business co-operation and investment, were all directed towards readying the partners for the shock of a rapid transition to free trade. A new financial regulation – MEDA (*mesures d'accompagnement*) – provided a modest €3.4 billion from the Community budget (1995–99) for projects linked to economic reform, infrastructural development, production capacity and collaborative investment. Distributed among a large group of partner countries, this level of funding could only scratch the surface of their deep-rooted structural difficulties.

Operationalising the Barcelona process was dependent upon the mobilisation of a wide range of actors ranging from the signatory governments and the EU institutions to the private sector and non-governmental organisations (NGOs). Governments and the European Commission (EC) were placed in overall control of the process through multilateral committees, serviced by the EU institutions, which were established to oversee the process. The political and financial commitment of the EU member governments would be essential if the EMP were to have a transformative impact. Creating a secure, stable Mediterranean region in which trade and investment could flourish demanded greatly improved political relations between governments and a substantial amount of administrative reform on the part of many of the partner countries. However, effective implementation was also reliant upon the construction of specialist networks covering the whole gamut of subjects in the Declaration and Work Programme. The Euro-Mediterranean space, and the achievement of the EU's policy goals within that, had to be filled by transnational activity engaging non-governmental actors across the region. In a sense, networks were to become the agents of European foreign economic policy.

Initially, the prospects for the Barcelona process looked good. The busy schedule of meetings on a wide range of topics that was drawn up in 1996 suggested that the EMP had provided a powerful stimulus for the development of the networks on which the effectiveness of the process depended. However, as the Middle East Peace Process fell apart, it proved impossible to prevent tension between the Arab partners and Israel from infecting the Barcelona initiative. Progress became largely confined to low key, 'functional' co-operation, such as the Euro-Mediterranean transport and information society forums. By 2000, the Union felt compelled to agree a 'Common Strategy' for the Mediterranean, a move intended to restate the organisation's commitment to the region and refocus the attention of the participants. An increase in funding for the MEDA budget (€5.35 billion for the period 2000–2006) was accompanied by changes to the priorities for the programme and new distribution and auditing procedures, an admission that both the take up of funds and results had been disappointing (European Commission, 2002; Karkutli and Bützler, 1999). Without the political power to force high-level engagement between the Israeli and Arab governments, expectations about the EMP had to be dramatically lowered.

Assessing the Euro-Mediterranean Partnership

The overarching aims of the EMP – to make the region more stable and prosperous – attested to the connection between the Union's narrower interest in protecting its privileged position in MNC markets and its broader interest in improving the region's economic performance as a means to promote its long-term security. However, the EU has frequently seemed unwilling to set aside short-term political expediency, manifested particularly in the protection of its agricultural producers, for the supposed long-run benefits of putting the EU–MNC trade relationship on a more equal footing. This problem of conflicting objectives in the EMP has in turn undermined the initiative as a vehicle for the EU's pursuit of possession and milieu goals. This section examines some of the principal goals of the EMP and the problems connected with pursuing and achieving them.

A first set of problems stems from the numerous obstacles to sustained growth in trade in the Mediterranean region, arguably the pivotal objective of the EMP (Aghrout, 2001; Nienhaus, 1999). Several renegotiations of the Association Agreements with the MNCs have failed to substantially prise open the EU's agricultural markets. The partner governments have regularly criticised the EU's position on this issue, pointing to their potential capacity to take advantage of much larger import quotas (Gomez, 2003). Trade among the partner states themselves is insignificant in comparison to their trade with the EU, US and states outside the region. While their openness to foreign trade (measured by exports plus imports/GDP) has improved somewhat since 1992, reaching 58 per cent of GDP in 1999, the region still ranks well behind South-East Asia and the Central and Eastern European Countries (CEECs) (European Commission, 2002). The EMP has so far had little positive impact on the sort of changes in political relations between the partner countries and the cross-regional economic reform that might encourage intra-regional trading activity to take off.

The behaviour of the EU member states in negotiations with the partner countries remains a major influence on Euro-Mediterranean trade relations. The crucial issue of market access in the EMP was once again determined by the 'politicisation' of the key sectors. New concessions on imports from the partner countries during the negotiation of the Euro-Mediterranean agreements were dependent upon member governments permitting the Commission to make the necessary compromises at the table. Egypt's case illustrates the difficulty both the EU and its negotiating partners faced in reaching mutually acceptable deals. Negotiations opened in 1996 but rapidly stalled over the level of market access for imports from Egypt of products such as oranges, potatoes, rice and cut flowers. After six years of protracted talks during which unacceptable offers of concessions were frequently met with unacceptable counter offers, the agreement was only finally initialled by the Commission and the Egyptian government in January 2001. Even then, the agreement allowed for a 12-year 'transition' period for markets to be opened up by both sides and an additional three-year period for the most 'sensitive' products (*European Report*, 2001). The Union's responsibility for defending and promoting European economic interests clearly conflicted with the stated aim of creating a Euro-Mediterranean free-trade area by the 2010 deadline.

A second set of problems centres on the role of investment in the Euro-Mediterranean project. The language of the Barcelona Declaration was unequivocal about the importance of boosting inward foreign direct invest-ment (FDI) in the partner countries, stressing in particular the need to create an administrative and legal climate conducive to investment. Economists argued that it was essential for the developing countries of the region to exploit their potential to attract inward FDI if they were to experience rapid and durable economic growth and, by extension, improved social conditions (Petri, 1997: 11). Administrative reform by the partner countries was ear-marked as an objective of the Barcelona process and several of the sectoral follow-up initiatives, elements of the Euro-Mediterranean Association Agreements and financial resources from the MEDA budget were all directed towards it. Yet progress in this area has been disappointing, a combination of slow responses from the partner governments, the sheer magnitude of the task and the lure of more lucrative markets elsewhere (European Commission, 2002a: 27).

The limitations of EU foreign economic policy are all too apparent here. Other than providing a small number of incentives, the EMP can do little to influence the behaviour of private capital. Pressure from the multilateral financial institutions and the EU, exerted through conditionality provi-sions and 'technical assistance', has thus far failed to galvanise adminis-trative reform in the majority of the partner countries. Moreover, business had limited involvement in the design of the Barcelona process and the response of European companies to the EMP did not represent the essen-tial injection of commercial activity that the architects of the Barcelona process had hoped for. With few exceptions, inward foreign investment in the region has stagnated (European Commission, 2000: 3). It absorbs only 5 per cent of all FDI flows to the developing world, and the proportion of EU FDI going to Mediterranean partners actually fell from 2.2 per cent in 1992 to below 1 per cent in 1999. As George Joffé argues, the area lacks a comparative advantage for foreign investors as compared to Latin America, South Asia or South-East Asia (Joffé, 2000: 34). In a global economy in which the ability of governments to supply welfare and economic goods has become increasingly dependent on transnational capital, European foreign economic policy is proving to have limited utility in bringing its Mediterranean neighbours up to speed.

A third problem relates to the Union's long-standing failure to address the question of international indebtedness. The language of the Barcelona Declaration on this issue was vague, referring only to the 'difficulties' that it created for economic development. A 1990 attempt by the Commission to persuade the member states that the EU should co-ordinate debt policy failed. More than a decade later, only occasional gestures have been made by Western governments and multilateral financial institutions to reschedule debt repayments and offer very limited debt relief. Member states have shown a marked reluctance to stray from the prevailing orthodoxy dominated by the multilateral financial institutions, intergovernmental management of the debt crisis among the biggest creditor states in the G8/G10 and the power of global capital. The Council chose to link any assistance with debt servicing to the implementation of structural adjustment programmes and economic reforms imposed by the Bretton Woods institutions. That is not to claim that EU competence for debt policy would necessarily lead to debt reduction, but its inclusion in the Barcelona process would at least have brought an issue of vital importance into the ambit of the EMP. The substantial debt repayments currently being made by the partner countries hardly bode well for the flagship free-trade initiative.

The capacity of the EU to deliver on the full range of objectives it set for the EMP must be doubted. Although the Euro-Mediterranean project clearly strengthens the competitive advantage of EU businesses in the region, there are few signs that the EMP has significantly enhanced the Union's capacity to exert effective influence over markets and the other agents of change on which the wider success of the initiative depends. These shortcomings in turn raise fundamental questions about the efficacy of European foreign economic policy.

Conclusions

Much of the form and content of the EU's foreign economic policy in the Mediterranean region was determined at an early stage in its development. The twin priorities of defending and promoting 'European' economic interests were reflected in both the arrangements for formal relationships with the MNCs and the negotiating processes that gave the agreements their content. As the dominant partner in those relationships, the EU negotiated from a powerful position and member states were easily able to limit the impact of concessions on 'domestic' producers. As 'outsiders' located towards the base of the external relations pyramid, defined by the setting of 'boundaries' in EU foreign economic policy, Mediterraneans found themselves poorly positioned to secure concessions in negotiations with the Union. These characteristics of the EU's behaviour had a clear impact on the results of its Mediterranean policy. Maintenance of the status quo and short-term political expediency virtually ruled out the possibility of an effective strategic approach towards the region.

The process which culminated in the Euro-Mediterranean Partnership indicated how far the EU had progressed in defining its possession and mileu goals in the region and in designing policies to pursue them. In Michael Smith's terms, the functions of Mediterranean policy appeared to expand during the early 1990s. The principle effects of its earlier policies had been to safeguard EU markets (the promotion of economic welfare) and strengthen its competitive advantage in the region. The EMP initiative began with the recognition of the need for a new and more comprehensive approach to regional security. EU trade and aid policies would be the main channel for measures that would make an important contribution to the security of Europe as a whole. On the face of it, the combination of a more clearly elucidated set of policy objectives, the package of new and revised measures that followed and the identification of 'targets' (the 12 partner countries) added up to a far more strategic approach than had previously been the case.

However, the negotiation and implementation of the EMP illustrate the inherent difficulties of operating a foreign economic policy that serves European interests *and* enables the EU to engage in the type of distinctive and progressive external action that many observers and practitioners expected of the organisation as the Cold War ended. In this respect, the Union has consistently proved more adept at securing possession than mileu goals. Internal constraints continue to stem from the EU's institutional framework, specifically from the decision-making process associated with the conduct of its external negotiations. Politicisation as Smith conceives it may reinforce foreign economic policy at the EU level, but it is also a powerful restraining force on its effectiveness.

The EMP case also demonstrates the growing impact of forces 'outside' the EU on its foreign economic policy. Globalisation, the competitive pressures associated with it and the neo-liberal economic orthodoxy enshrined in a variety of multilateral agreements and institutions have all strengthened the imperative for 'Europe' to assert its presence in the international political economy. At the same time, though, these external factors place strong constraints on EU policy. Obligations imposed by the International Monetary Fund (IMF) and World Trade Organisation (WTO), for instance, are an important feature of the EMP and heavily influence its reform-related objectives. The point here is that has become difficult to determine where European foreign economic policy begins and ends as the EU becomes the conduit for a diverse array of processes that originate beyond its borders and institutions.

Whether or not the EMP is capable of changing the political and economic fortunes of the Mediterranean partners over the long term remains to be seen. Thus far, EU policies have patently failed to promote transformation (Calleya, 1997). An approach whose principal effect is to preserve the status quo is unlikely to meet the challenges posed by a region of vital strategic importance to the future of Europe. In the final analysis, stability, security and prosperity in the Mediterranean may well prove to be beyond the EU's control.

Note

1 The Mediterranean partners include Algeria, Cyprus, Egypt, Israel, Jordan, Lebanon, Malta, Morocco, the Palestinian Authority, Syria, Tunisia and Turkey.

References

Agence Europe (1992) 29 February, p. 7.

Aghrout, A. (2001) 'The Euro-Maghreb free trade area: challenges and opportunities', *The European Union Review*, 5 (3): 15–32.

Booth, K. (1991) 'Introduction. The interregnum: world politics in transition', in K. Booth (ed.), *New Thinking About Strategy and International Security*. London: HarperCollins. pp. 1–23.

Buzan, B., Wæver, O. and de Wilde, J. (1998) *Security: A New Framework for Analysis*. London: Lynne Rienner.

Calleya, S. (1997) *Navigating Regional Dynamics in the Post-Cold War World: Patterns of Relations in the Mediterranean Area*. Aldershot: Dartmouth.

Cremasco, M. (1990) 'The Mediterranean area in perspective', *The International Spectator*, 25 (2): 119–27.

European Commission (1989) *Redirecting the Community's Mediterranean Policy*, SEC (89) 1961 Final, Brussels.

European Commission (1992) *The Future of Relations Between the Community and the Maghreb*, SEC (92) 401, Brussels, 30 April.

European Commission (2000) *Reinvigorating the Barcelona Process*, COM (2000) 497 Final, Brussels.

European Commission (2002) *Communication from the Commission to the Council and the European Parliament: To prepare the meeting of Euro-Mediterranean Foreign Ministers, Valencia, 22–23 April 2002*, SEC (2002) 159 final.

European Report (2001) No. 2564, 31 January, Section V.

Gomez, R. (2003) *Negotiating the Euro-Mediterranean Partnership: Strategic Action in EU Foreign Policy*. Aldershot: Ashgate.

Grasa, R. (1995) 'El Mediterráneo desde una perspectiva globalizadora de la seguridad: Una mirada a la dimensión cooperativa de la conflictividad'. Papers: *Revista de Sociologica*, No. 46, Bellaterra: Universidad Autònoma de Barcelona. pp. 25–42.

Joffé, G. (2000) 'Foreign investment and the rule of law', *Mediterranean Politics, Special Issue on the Barcelona Process: Building a Euro-Mediterranean Regional Community*, 5 (1): 33–52.

Karkutli, N. and Bützler, D. (1999) *MEDA Democracy Evaluation, Final Report: Evaluation of the MEDA Democracy Programme, 1996–1998*. http://www.euromed.net/meda/evaluation/mdp/final-report-meda-96-98-16.htm

Lasok, D. (1994) *Law and Institutions of the European Union*, 6th edn. London: Butterworth and Co.

Marks, J. (1989) 'The concept of Morocco in Europe', in G. Joffé (ed.), *Morocco and Europe*, Occasional Paper 7, London: School of Oriental and African Studies.

Matutes, A. (1989) 'Commissioner Matutes reviews issues for the Community in the Mediterranean'. Speech to Pio Manzu Conference, 17 October. Rimini, Press Release IP/89/776, Rapid Database. http://europa.eu.int/rapid/cgi

Minasi, N. (1998) 'The Euro-Mediterranean free trade area and its impact on the economies involved', *Jean Monnet Working Papers in Comparative and International Politics*, JMWP 16.98, Catania: University of Catania. http://www.fscpo.unict.it/vademec/jmwp16.htm

Nienhaus, V. (1999) 'Promoting development through a Euro-Mediterranean free trade zone?', *European Foreign Affairs Review*, 4 (4): 501–18.

Official Journal of the European Communities, OJL198 (1975) 29 July, p. 7.

Petri, P. (1997) *The Case of Missing Foreign Investment in the Southern Mediterranean*. OECD Technical Papers, No. 128. Paris: OECD.

12 Diplomacy: The Impact of the EU on its Member States

Alasdair Blair

What implication does membership of the European Union (EU) have for the national diplomatic systems of its member states? How valid is the notion of a collective EU diplomacy? These two linked but distinct questions form the focus of this chapter. In examining the impact that the EU has had on its member states, a common approach has been to use the concept of Europeanisation as a means of denoting the way in which national policy-making has adapted to the European context (Blair, 2002). A central feature of this viewpoint is the growth in the number and range of areas of government that are affected by and are involved in European policy. This is a trend that has been particularly apparent in recent years, with the introduction of the Single European Market (SEM) acting not just as a catalyst for closer economic and trading links, but also as the driving force behind further integration in such areas as social policy. Thus, whereas the early years of the Community saw a great deal of activity centred on a relatively narrow group of policy areas, such as agriculture, this has now expanded to cover all aspects of government, including developments at the local, regional and national level.

Such changes have in part been motivated by an acknowledgement by member states of the benefits of establishing collective rather than individual positions. This has directly led to identifiable 'European interests' (Zielonka, 1998) that have, in turn, focused attention on the nature of diplomacy within the EU and the diplomatic role played by the EU (European Parliament, 2000a and 2000b; Bruter, 1999). Focus upon the latter has in recent years been highlighted by Article 20 of the Treaty on European Union requiring external delegations of the EU and member states' diplomatic missions to 'co-operate in ensuring that the common positions and joint actions adopted by the Council are complied with and implemented'. A move towards greater co-operation was confirmed by the decision to commence building in November 2001 a joint embassy compound in Abuja (the new capital of Nigeria). And while the missions of the member states were to maintain national premises within the compound, common facilities such as the visa section would be shared. With this in mind, David Spence has suggested that the principle of EU collective diplomacy 'might be interpreted as the basis for an evolution towards a European Foreign Service' (Spence, 1999: 262).

In examining these changes it is evident that there has occurred an increase in the intensity of interactions among EU member states. This is a development that is reflective of wider global transformations that have resulted in a 'thickening texture of exchanges' (Langhorne and Wallace, 1999: 18). Within the EU, heads of state and government and ministers and officials from government departments, such as foreign affairs and agriculture, have traditionally met at EU negotiating tables and taken part in joint committees and working groups. The scope and number of such meetings have increased in recent years as domestically-focused areas of government have been drawn into the EU policy-making environment, thereby creating a dense network of diplomatic negotiations (Gomez and Peterson, 2001). A particular feature of this change has been that a large proportion of the diplomatic effort now takes place in areas of government that sit outside of the control of the foreign ministry (and for that matter the central apparatus of government (Hocking, 1999b). In short, there has been a 'domestication of European policy' as a result of the erosion of the traditional distinction between domestic and foreign policy (Forster and Blair, 2002: 55).

Linked to this breakdown in the boundaries between the domestic and the international level (which has been a feature of the international relations literature since the 1970s, being termed 'inter-mestic'), there has been a view that the increased level of contacts between nations and advances in methods of communication have lessened the need for governments to maintain as extensive a network of diplomatic representation. Writing in 1978, the British diplomat Nicholas Henderson commented that the then Foreign Secretary (David Owen) considered diplomats abroad to have a limited role: 'Not long ago he said that he did not see any point in having an Ambassador in Paris when all he had to do was to pick up the telephone and speak to the French Foreign Minister' (Henderson, 1994: 243). This position is of particular relevance to the EU, whereby the extensive interconnections between member states and the focus on collective decision-making raises the question for each government of the continued relevance of the presence of embassies and consulate offices in the other member states. This viewpoint is further compounded by the fact that a great majority of EU policy-making is of a regular nature and predominantly involves government ministers and officials dealing directly with their counterparts in other member states. One outcome of this has been to lessen the influence that foreign ministries have over the shaping of each member state's EU foreign policy. A key question that therefore needs to be answered is what role do foreign ministries play within the EU? This is not a particularly new question. Writing in 1975, William Wallace similarly asked whether there could be a continued role for the British Foreign and Commonwealth Office (FCO) in light of the fact that foreign policy was subject to an increasing amount of direct input from domestic government departments (Wallace, 1975: 272).

In addition to this focus on intra-EU diplomacy, this chapter also explores the issues surrounding the development of a collective EU diplomacy. The emergence of the EU as a credible diplomatic partner in its own right raises a number of questions, not least the extent of the validity of the notion of a EU diplomacy. After all, the concept of diplomacy implies the existence of a central governing authority that has traditionally rested in the hands of states. Today, of course, it commonly accepted that diplomacy is not just the prerogative of nation states; a whole range of non-governmental organisations (NGOs), such as Greenpeace and Amnesty International, and international organisations, such as the United Nations (UN), are also engaged in the process of diplomacy. To this end, a shift has occurred in the traditional boundaries and roles of the nation state (Hocking, 1999a: 14–15). Raymond Cohen has observed that 'states remain very important, but observably supranational organizations, traditional corporations, other transnational bodies and non-governmental organizations, have received the medieval right of non-sovereign entities to send and receive envoys, conduct negotiations and conclude agreements' (Cohen, 1999: 2). Thus, while the EU undoubtedly has international presence, is this enough to constitute a collective EU diplomacy? A final question rests on the implications that a collective EU diplomacy has for member states and the implications that it raises for the EU in terms of providing sufficient support and organisational assistance. With this in mind, some commentators have mapped out the procedures that are necessary to prepare for a collective EU diplomacy (Duke, 2002). This has included a call for the creation of a European diplomatic academy (Monar, 2000). But prior to that discussion, the next section examines the context of the relationships that exist within the EU.

The European Context

In our examination of the conduct of diplomacy within the context of the EU, we can point to the fact that there has evolved an interweaving pattern of relationships which involve the member states and the EU institutions, and point to a pattern of interlinked bilateral and multilateral relationships (Spence, 2002). On the one hand, intra-EU diplomacy can be viewed through the actions of member states, both in terms of their direct input to multilateral negotiations within Brussels (such as the Council of Ministers) and at the same time the cultivating of direct bilateral coalitions with other member states and EU institutions. (The Commission's important role in initiating legislation and the European Parliament's ability to veto legislation means that member states have been required to pay just as much attention to the views of the European Parliament as they do to the Commission and other member states.) The presence of such bilateral links in the forging of coalitions within the multilateral framework of the EU has been referred to by one commentator as a process of 'multiple bilateralism' (Kohler-Koch, 2000). On the other hand, the process of European integration has resulted in the fact that there are now few issues of a national concern which are not also of a European concern. Aware of the limitations of their own influence, member states have, in certain areas of policy, been motivated to accept collective representation. As Simon Duke has commented, 'for the member states themselves, there is a growing recognition that the politics of scale outweigh unilateral action in external relations, leading to a collective diplomacy' (Duke, 2002: 849).

One of the most notable examples of this collective action is the Common Commercial Policy and the international trade policies of the EU. In these areas the interests of member states are represented and negotiated by the European Commission. The EU has, for instance, acted as a true partner with the US in establishing institutional frameworks, such as the 1990 Transatlantic Declaration, which was later matched by the December 1995 New Transatlantic Agenda. In this sense, Michael Smith has pointed out that 'the EU has become a credible and legitimate participant in international co-operation' (Smith, 1998: 574). The growing weight and influence of the EU in the international system lends weight to a 'bullish' interpretation of the emergence of a collective EU diplomacy. Yet it is also true that the very advancement of an EU position is dependent on the initial consensus of member states and the presence of distinct and often entrenched national positions can at times create a barrier to the forming of a collective EU stance.

It is therefore evident that relations such as those between the EU and the US are more than just relations between the European Commission and the White House or US State Department. Within each EU member state there are a range of access points that are not just centred on the traditional foreign ministry/executive office axis (Spence, 2002). All EU governments have themselves been 'Europeanised', as the expansion of EU legislation has affected traditionally domestically-focused departments such as the interior ministry.

Just as there is a range of access points where pressure can be applied by EU and non-EU states and pressure groups, the expansion in importance of the EU has witnessed an influx of Brussels-based missions representing the interests of non-EU states, such as the US Mission to the EU.[1] The significance of the EU is further highlighted by the fact that nearly every US state has a representative office in Brussels. What this demonstrates is the sheer range of access points that are available from where pressure can be exerted to influence decision-making procedures. This is further compounded by the fact that the political map of Europe is constantly changing; there is nearly always an election taking place in one of the EU countries, while the impending enlargement of the EU has important implications for diplomatic negotiations within the EU. This in turn impacts on the power structure within the EU, demonstrating the constantly changing nature of the boundaries of European diplomacy. These various developments present a fluid picture of EU diplomatic activity where bilateral and multilateral alliances are constantly changing, depending on the policy being discussed and the particular national foreign policy objectives. More importantly, the changes raise a number of important questions as to the future direction of EU diplomacy and the challenges presented to member states and the EU institutions. Here it is possible to identify two core challenges to European diplomacy.

First is the challenge of 'gatekeeping'. As all domestic policy now has an EU dimension, the task of co-ordinating government policy has become more complex. In the case of the UK, for instance, 'the Scottish Parliament and Welsh Assembly may adopt different national approaches to the implementation of EU legislation within their responsibility, rather than adopting British standards' (Forster and Blair, 2002: 189). This state of affairs is further complicated by the presence of sub-national offices in Brussels, such as those of the German Länder and the Scottish Parliament (Jeffery, 1997, 2000). Member states therefore have to adapt to this changing environment in terms of intra-member state negotiations among relevant parties as well as negotiations within the EU (Hocking, 2002).

Second is the challenge of 'coherence'. Stephanie Anderson has rightly noted that 'collective diplomacy is here to stay' (Anderson, 2001: 480). Yet, at the same time it is evident that not all member states share common interests, a factor that is recognised to be a key feature of a collective EU diplomacy. Britain's strong support for the US in its war against terrorism has conflicted with the views of other member states. Thus, although the constant process of EU meetings ensures that member states are strongly interconnected with each other, the importance of national rather than EU interest remains strong among governments.

With these points as our guide, this chapter first of all takes a closer look at the case of intra-EU diplomacy, paying particular attention to the experience of the UK. A second and related concern is the extent to which there has emerged a collective EU diplomacy, and here our focus is attached to the nature of the EU response since the terrorism attacks of 9/11.

Adapting to Europe: The Case of the UK

As I indicated at the start of this chapter, 'Europeanisation' has become an accepted approach for explaining the impact that EU membership has had on member states. In the UK context, Bulmer and Burch have traced the manner in which the UK administrative system has adapted to the requirements of EU membership (Bulmer and Burch, 1998). A particular feature of much of this literature is an examination of the mechanisms that have emerged for co-ordinating and advancing policy objectives (Blair, 1998; Kassim et al., 2000). Such studies have tended to pay attention to the European Secretariat of the Cabinet Office (which was set up in 1977 to act as an independent body for co-ordinating UK European policy), the FCO and the UK Permanent Representation to the EU. The latter, along with other national permanent representations, has been the focus of a considerable amount of research, not least because of the important role played by Permanent Representatives in EU negotiations (Blair, 2001; Bostock, 2002; Kassim et al., 2001; Lewis, 1998). There is also a growing body of work that has sought to chart the role of the FCO as UK foreign policy has adapted to a post-imperial set of policy objectives (Allen, 1999, 2002).

In contrast to the significant body of literature that has focused on methods of policy co-ordination, less emphasis has been attached to the implications and challenges of adaptation (Forster and Blair, 2002: 171–82). In turning to the nature of adaptation, a significant feature of change has been the emergence of informal policy networks that bypass central co-ordinating structures, such as the European Secretariat. Increasing time pressures on government ministers has meant that much of this work is conducted by officials, with the tendency being for ministers to be presented with pre-negotiated agendas. Thus, the domestication and routine nature of a great deal of EU policy has meant that many discussions involve a limited number of participants and are settled outside time-consuming formal methods of co-ordination (Blair, 1998: 164).

Linked to the emergence of informal policy networks at the domestic level, a further feature has been the growth of bilateral diplomacy on the part of government ministers and officials with their counterparts in national capitals. Bilateral relations play an important part in forming coalitions that are essential for governments to be successful in meeting their objectives within the EU policy-making environment. In the case of the UK, this form of bilateral diplomacy is evidenced by the government making use of embassies in national capitals to sound out member states' negotiating positions prior to every Council meeting through the use of a detailed questionnaire.

It is therefore evident that embassies play an important role in the pre-negotiation phase by providing information on a host country that is necessary to compile speeches, documents, reports and dossiers. But in addition to this information-gathering role, embassies play a crucial part in advancing national negotiating positions to other member states. At the heart of this 'public diplomacy' is the need for embassies to explain national positions to the host country and at the same time to culture support for such policies at both the elite levels of government and parliament and also among the domestic public. This is in turn reflective of the growing involvement of civil society in EU policy (Cooper and Hocking, 2000). And while these tasks are typical of all embassies throughout the world, the regularity and intensity of negotiations within the EU and the politically sensitive nature of many EU policies ensures that there is a special dimension to the embassies of member states within the EU.

The role played by embassies takes on a further dimension for those staff based in the country holding the twice-yearly rotating presidency of the EU. This is a factor that is particularly true at times of intergovernmental conference (IGC) negotiations when embassies keep domestic ministries informed of developments and reinforce national negotiating positions that are officially advanced in Brussels. Thus, in the months, weeks and days prior to the

European Council meeting, embassies based in the host country chairing the negotiations are invariably involved in a great flurry of activity. For instance, at the time of the Maastricht European Council of 10 and 11 December 1991, a number of British Cabinet ministers visited The Hague to try to influence the Dutch government who were responsible for drafting the Treaty text. The British Ambassador to The Netherlands (Sir Michael Jenkins) had the task of trying to broker a deal with the Dutch Prime Minister (Ruud Lubbers) on the then controversial subject of social policy in the wake of a meeting between Lubbers and the UK Prime Minister, John Major.

We can therefore see that while the main preparation for many EU negotiations may be taking place in the multilateral forum in Brussels that centres on the work of the permanent representations, embassies nonetheless play an important role as a means of underscoring national negotiating objectives that are being officially advanced in other forums. Taken together, these points highlight that bilateral diplomacy has not withered away in the European context. Diplomacy within the EU is therefore not solely the preserve of the Brussels-based negotiating table and is instead played out in a range of meetings (often of an *ad hoc* nature). This state of affairs is further confirmed by the tendency of heads of state and government to directly intervene on EU matters.

In the case of the UK, it is evident that the position of the FCO has been challenged in the first instance by the existence of the European Secretariat and secondly by the emergence of informal policy networks. In recent years, the FCO's position has also been challenged by prime ministers who have sought to exercise a more commanding grip on foreign policy through their own personal involvement and by securing alternative sources of advice from the FCO. Under Tony Blair there has been a dramatic increase in staffing levels of the Prime Minister's Office within No. 10 Downing Street, and at the same time a willingness to make use of external policy advice from new bodies such as the Centre for European Reform and the Foreign Policy Centre (Forster and Blair, 2002: 66; Burch and Holliday, 2000). We can therefore see that the activities of heads of state and government have also exercised constraints on the traditional dominance of foreign ministries to seek policy solutions (*Guardian*, 2002, G2: 2–3).

That is not to say that national foreign ministries have been frozen out of EU affairs as a result of the shift towards the domestication of European policy (Forster and Blair, 2002: 173–5). Foreign ministries do, for instance, retain a particularly strong role in IGC negotiations (which have come to dominate the EU landscape in recent years) and in the common foreign and security policy (CFSP), with the latter generally receiving little direct involvement from other government departments. In the case of the UK FCO, this has meant that it has its own *domain privée* (Forster and Blair, 2002: 174). Thus, while foreign ministries continue to play an important role, there has been a reassessment of established negotiating boundaries that have shifted in response to a changed policy-making environment. This is not just the result of changes taking place at the EU level; developments within member states have impacted on the orchestration of government policy. This has been particularly evident in the case of the UK, whereby the devolution of power to Scotland, Northern Ireland and Wales has resulted in the devolved authorities pursuing with greater vigour more independent links with the EU institutions and other member states as part of an effort to establish greater influence within the EU. The net outcome of all this is that there has been a reassessment of the nature of diplomacy within the EU where the ever-growing closeness of bonds between member states might have painted a picture of the 'decline' of diplomacy and a reduction in the importance of the state as a result of convergent trends towards a 'pan-European diplomacy'. With this in mind, the next section examines the nature of collective EU diplomacy.

The Emergence of Collective EU Diplomacy: The Response to 9/11

On 11 September 2001, the US suffered appalling terrorist attacks that resulted in the collapse of the twin towers of the World Trade Centre in New York and structural damage being inflicted on the Pentagon in Washington, DC. For the EU, the events of 11 September prompted a dramatic round of diplomatic action within the EU and at the broader international level. On 14 September the EU adopted a 'joint declaration on terrorist attack in the US' that represented the views of all of the EU institutions as it brought together the Presidents of the European Parliament and the Commission, the High Representative for CFSP and the Heads of State and Government. In the days that followed there were a series of emergency meetings of the Council of Ministers, European Central Bank, European Commission, European Council and European Parliament. A number of initiatives arose out of these meetings. This included the decision by the Transport Council on 14 September to improve air safety and security measures, while the Justice and Homes Affairs Council reached agreement on 20 September on proposals for a European arrest warrant and measures to combat terrorism. When member states met for the extraordinary Brussels European Council of 21 September, they concluded that the attacks represented 'an assault on our open, democratic, tolerant and multicultural societies' (European Council, 2001).

The EU's response accordingly presented an image of a united stance with the US. Mindful of the need to culture as broad as possible a base of support behind the terrorist threat, from 24–29 September the EU Troika (past, present and future Presidencies), along with Chris Patten (External Affairs Commissioner) and Javier Solana (CFSP Representative) visited Egypt, Iran, Saudi Arabia and Syria in an effort to explain the EU's response to the terrorist attacks and to build a broad international coalition against terrorism. A further high-level round of visits took place between 30 October and 2 November, when Belgian Prime Minister Guy Verhofstadt (who represented the Belgian Presidency) and the Commission President Romano Prodi visited the Middle East, India and Pakistan. The EU additionally convened a conference against terrorism on 20 October that included representatives from the European Free Trade Association (EFTA), the candidate countries, the Balkans, the Russian Federation, Moldavia and the Ukraine. Further attempts were made by the EU to bolster the coalition on terrorism at the Euro–Mediterranean partnership of 5 and 6 November and at the meeting of the UN General Assembly in mid-November (Den Boer and Monar, 2002: 15).

At face value, this diplomatic activity signified the emergence of a strong collective position by the EU, a factor that was also reinforced in November 2001 by the EU providing economic and financial support to Pakistan, which was a key country in the anti-Taliban coalition. Despite this image of a collective front, it was noticeable that the EU was not represented in Afghanistan by the European Security and Defence Policy (ESDP); instead, it was member states such as the UK that were most actively involved (Den Boer and Monar, 2002: 16). This development consequently suggested a lack of cohesiveness of the EU position; a factor that was further confirmed when the UK, France and Germany held a mini-summit on 19 October 2001 in the margins of the Ghent European Council. Some two weeks later, Tony Blair invited German Chancellor Gerhard Schroeder and French President Jacques Chirac to an informal dinner in London on 4 November in order to discuss the conflict in Afghanistan. The lack of a wider representative group of member states drew considerable criticism, and resulted in the composition of the meeting being widened to include the Dutch, Italian and Spanish Prime Ministers and the CFSP High Representative, Javier Solana.

These developments raised questions over the degree to which it was possible to establish a collective EU position in the face of strong national positions. Divisions within the EU became increasingly apparent when the Bush administration moved its focus towards the disarmament of Iraq following the collapse of the Taliban regime in late 2001. Within the US administration there was considerable debate as to whether a course of direct action should be taken or whether the support of the UN should be sought. In the end the US took the UN route, with President Bush stating on 12 September 2002 that 'my nation will work with the UN Security Council to meet our common challenge'.[2] This represented a more favourable outcome for the EU and a success for the UK/French 'soft cop, hard cop' routine; the UK's stronger support for the US was contrasted with French insistence that the US should follow the UN route. The pursuit of the multilateral option working through the UN resulted in the Security Council on 8 November 2002 voting unanimously to adopt Resolution 1441 that offered Iraq 'a final opportunity to comply with its disarmament obligations'.[3] In responding to this resolution the EU once again appeared to offer a collective front,[4] although a division would soon emerge when five EU member states (the UK, Denmark, Italy, Portugal and Spain) and three applicant countries (Czech Republic, Hungary and Poland) signed a joint declaration that backed the US in its actions against Iraq.

This division became more entrenched in early 2003 when the UK and US governments concluded that Iraq had not shown the necessary willingness to comply fully with its obligations to disarm. A direct outcome of this was a UK-US-Spanish proposal for a further Security Council resolution that authorised war against Iraq. However, France, backed by Germany, made it clear that it would vote against a new UN resolution authorising war against Iraq because it was not clear that UN weapons inspectors had exhausted all opportunities. France's threat of exercising its veto power (as one of five permanent members of the Security Council) consequently put an end to the UN route and set in motion a timetable for war that commenced on 19 March 2003.

The lack of a common European position on the Iraq war demonstrated the difficulty of establishing a united front in the face of independent national positions. In the period leading up to the Iraq war, policy was shaped and influenced by national governments, with many key figures in the EU institutions being sidelined, such as External Affairs Commissioner Chris Patten and CFSP High Representative Javier Solana. The establishment of firm national positions by the pro-war camp of the UK, Italy and Spain, and the anti-war camp led by France and Germany, have accordingly highlighted the difficulty of establishing a collective European position in the face of entrenched national positions.

Conclusion

A number of questions were set out at the start of this chapter as a means of shedding light on the nature of intra-EU diplomacy and the extent to which there has emerged a collective EU diplomacy. In answering the first of these questions, it is apparent that a great deal of diplomatic activity within the EU now takes place outside of formal methods of co-ordination and is, moreover, separated from the work of the foreign ministry. One implication of this change has been the emergence of a whole range of networks which focus both on the multilateral negotiations that are characteristic of the working groups and meetings taking place in Brussels, and also on bilateral relations with counterparts in other member states. A further noticeable feature of this change is that the vast majority of this work is conducted by officials, as government ministers face tremendous time pressures. To take an example, interior ministries increasingly have to respond to a whole range of issues that now have a 'European' angle, from drugs policy to the fight against terrorism. At the same time, the domestic work of interior ministries has not lessened.

Pressures of time, combined with the fact that a great deal of EU policy-making is of a routine nature, means that officials increasingly play a key role in not just the co-ordination, but also the negotiation of government policy. Within the EU, government ministers are therefore invariably presented with pre-negotiated outcomes. The complexity of modern government and the speed of communications have also increased pressures on workload; governments are faced with having to immediately respond to constantly shifting agendas that are dictated by spin doctors and communications advisers. To cite an example, in February 2003 the UK government put forward a dossier on Iraq that had been compiled by mid-level officials working in Downing Street. The dossier was, however, widely criticised for its absence of high-grade intelligence as it had been quickly compiled though cutting and pasting the work of an American PhD student (*Guardian*, 2003). A more significant implication of the reliance on officials is that it raises concerns over the nature of ministerial supervision of policy. In the case of the UK, a key trend 'is that government ministers have seen the balance of authority (though not responsibility) shift from them to officials' (Forster and Blair, 2002: 176).

Turning to the second question, it is noticeable that while the EU has appeared divided over Iraq, there are a great many other policies upon which the EU is united. Moreover, the defence of EU interests is aided by the Commission which in 2000 had representative delegations in 123 third countries and five international organisations. In terms of size, this meant that it was the fourth largest 'diplomatic service' in the world (Duke, 2002: 858). The collective strength of this body has resulted in a number of proposals with a view to creating a common EU diplomacy (European Parliament, 2000a and 200b). It is, however, unlikely that integrative pressures at the EU level will result in an 'EU' diplomacy that will replace the work of national foreign ministries because of the continuing presence of defined national rather than European interests.

This leaves us with an impression of a process of diplomacy that is reflective of the 'betweenness of the EU' (Laffan, 1998: 236). Any attempt to capture an image of EU diplomacy has to take into account both the steps that have been made to create a more united EU diplomacy that binds all member states together and at the same time the continuing reality of independent national positions. The very process of diplomacy is directly related to a desire to identify common interests and to seek mutual benefits. For EU member states, these are noble objectives, but the reality of national interests continues to exist, which thereby increases the difficulty of establishing a united policy.

Notes

1 The US government offices represented in Brussels are the Department of State, Foreign Agricultural Service, US Trade Representative, Department of Commerce, Office of Public Affairs, US Customs Office, Department of Justice and US Aid, United States Department of Agriculture Marketing and Regulatory Programmes.
2 White House press release, 12 September 2002. http://www.whitehouse.gov.news/releases/2002/09/print/20020912-1.html
3 Paragraph 2, S/RES/1441 (2002).
4 Statement by the Presidency on behalf of the European Union on Security Council Resolution 1441 (Iraq), 14 November 2002, from http://www.eu2002.dk/news/news read.asp?iInformationID=24802

References

Allen, D. (1999) 'The Foreign and Commonwealth Office: "Flexible, responsive and proactive?"', in B. Hocking (ed.), *Foreign Ministries: Change and Adaptation*. Basingstoke: Macmillan. pp. 207–25.

Allen, D. (2002) 'The United Kingdom', in B. Hocking and D. Spence (eds), *Foreign Ministries in the European Union: Integrating Diplomats*. Basingstoke: Palgrave, Macmillan. pp. 250–72.

Anderson, S. (2001) 'The changing nature of diplomacy: the European Union, the CFSP and Korea', *European Foreign Affairs Review*, 6 (4): 465–82.

Blair, A. (1998) 'UK policy co-ordination during the 1990–91 intergovernmental conference', *Diplomacy and Statecraft*, 9 (2): 160–83.

Blair, A. (2001) 'Permanent representations to the European Union', *Diplomacy and Statecraft*, 12 (3): 173–93.

Blair, A. (2002) 'Adapting to Europe', *Journal of European Public Policy*, 9 (5): 841–56.

Bostock, D. (2002) 'Coreper revisited', *Journal of Common Market Studies*, 40 (2): 215–34.

Bruter, M. (1999) 'Diplomacy without a state: the external delegations of the European Commission', *Journal of European Public Policy*, 6 (2): 183–205.

Bulmer, S. and Burch, M. (1998) 'Organizing for Europe: Whitehall, the British State and the European Union', *Public Administration*, 76 (4): 601–28.

Burch, M. and Holliday, I. (2000) 'New Labour and the machinery of government', in D. Coates and P. Lawler (eds), *New Labour in Power*. Manchester: Manchester University Press. pp. 65–79.

Cohen, R. (1999) 'Reflections on the new global diplomacy: statecraft 2500 BC to 2000 AD', in J. Melissen (ed.), *Innovation in Diplomatic Practice*. Basingstoke: Macmillan.

Cooper, A.F. and Hocking, B. (2000) 'Governments, non-governmental organizations and the re-calibration of diplomacy', *Global Society*, 14 (3): 361–76.

Den Boer, M. and Monar, J. (2002) '11 September and the challenge of global terrorism to the EU as a security actor', *Journal of Common Market Studies*, 40 (2): 11–28.

Duke, S. (2002) 'Preparing for European diplomacy?', *Journal of Common Market Studies*, 40 (5): 849–70.

European Council (2001) 'Conclusions and plan of action of the extraordinary meeting on 21 September 2001', Council Document SN 140/01.

European Parliament (2000a) 'Report on a common community diplomacy', Committee on Foreign Affairs, Human Rights, Common Security and Defence Policy, A5-0210/2000, 24 July.

European Parliament (2000b) 'A common community diplomacy', European Parliament resolution on a common community diplomacy, A5-0210/2000.

Forster, A. and Blair, A. (2002) *The Making of Britain's European Foreign Policy*. Harlow: Longman.

Gomez, R. and Peterson, J. (2001) 'The EU's impossibly busy foreign ministers: "No one is in control"', *European Foreign Affairs Review*, 6 (1): 53–74.

Guardian (2002) 'The lost Straw'. 4 January, 2: 2–3.

Guardian (2003) 'Downing St admits blunder on Iraq dossier'. 8 February: 2.

Henderson, N. (1994) *Mandarin: The Diaries of an Ambassador, 1969–1982*. London: Weidenfeld and Nicolson.

Hocking, B. (1999a) 'Introduction: trade politics, environments, agendas and process', in B. Hocking and S. McGuire (eds), *Trade Politics: International, Domestic and Regional Perspectives*. London: Routledge. pp. 14–15.

Hocking, B. (ed.) (1999b) *Foreign Ministries: Change and Adaptation*. Basingstoke: Macmillan.

Hocking, B. (2002) 'Introduction: gatekeepers and boundary-spanners – thinking about foreign ministries in the European Union', in B. Hocking and D. Spence (eds), *Foreign Ministries in the European Union: Integrating Diplomats*. Basingstoke: Palgrave Macmillian. pp. 1–17.

Jeffery, C. (1997) 'Regional information offices in Brussels and multi-level governance in the EU', in C. Jeffery (ed.), *The Regional Dimension of the European Union*. London: Frank Cass. pp. 183–203.

Jeffery, C. (2000) 'Sub-national mobilization and European integration', *Journal of Common Market Studies*, 38 (1): 1–23.

Kassim, H., Menon, A., Peters, B.G. and Wright, V. (2001) *The National Co-ordination of EU Policy: The European Level*. Oxford: Oxford University Press.

Kassim, H., Peters, B.G. and Wright, V. (2000) *The National Co-ordination of EU Policy: The Domestic Level*. Oxford: Oxford University Press.

Kohler-Koch, B. (2000) 'Network governance within and beyond an enlarging EU'. Paper presented at the International Political Science conference, Quebec City, August. Cited in B. Hocking and D. Spence (eds), *Foreign Ministries in the European Union: Integrating Diplomats*. Basingstoke: Palgrave Macmillan. p. 7.

Laffan, B. (1998) 'The European Union: a distinctive model of internationalization', *Journal of European Public Policy*, 5 (2): 235–53.

Langhorne, R. and Wallace, W. (1999) 'Diplomacy towards the twenty-first Century', in B. Hocking (ed.), *Foreign Ministries: Change and Adaptation*. Basingstoke: Macmillan. pp. 16–22.

Lewis, J. (1998) 'Is the hard bargaining image of the Council misleading? The Committee of Permanent Representatives and the Local Elections Directive', *Journal of Common Market Studies*, 36 (4): 479–504.

Monar, J. (2000) 'The case for a diplomatic academy of the European Union', *European Foreign Affairs Review*, 5 (3): 281–6.

Smith, M. (1998) 'Competitive co-operation and EU-US relations: can the EU be a strategic partner for the US in the world political economy?', *Journal of European Public Policy*, 5 (4): 561–77.

Spence, D. (1999) 'Foreign Ministries in national and European context', in B. Hocking (ed.), *Foreign Ministries: Change and Adaptation*. Basingstoke: Macmillan. pp. 247–68.

Spence, D. (2002) 'The evolving role of Foreign Ministries in the conduct of European Union affairs', in B. Hocking and D. Spence (eds), *Foreign Ministries in the European Union: Integrating Diplomats*. Basingstoke: Palgrave Macmillan. pp. 18–36.

Wallace, W. (1975) *The Foreign Policy Process in Britain*. London: Royal Institute of International Affairs.

Zielonka, J. (1998) *Explaining Euro-Paralysis: Why Europe is Unable to Act in International Politics*. Basingstoke: Macmillan.

13 National Foreign Policy Co-ordination: The Swedish EU Presidency

Magnus Ekengren

This chapter examines a case of European Union (EU) member state representation at the Union level in the light of the different ideal types of national co-ordination described in Chapter 6 of this volume. The case is the organisation of the Swedish EU Presidency in the first half of 2001. Traditionally, this representation has been studied as 'foreign policy', guided by 'diplomacy'. This chapter shows that these labels are becoming increasingly awkward in a system where 'national representation' to a large extent functions as a *co-administration* of the Union's own policy together with the EU bureaucracy in Brussels. The argument here is that the linking of EU levels for the everyday internal work of the Union as well as for its performance in the world can be better explained by the dynamics of multi-level governance.

Multi-level perspectives on the EU Presidency have been scarce in the literature. Most studies have focused on the role of the presidency in the 'horizontal' negotiation game between member states or among the EU institutions. These include examinations of the relationship of the presidency to the other EU organs (Hayes-Renshaw and Wallace, 1997), the leadership role and the possibilities of promoting national priorities (Svensson, 2000) and its function as an engine in intergovernmental bargains (Moravcsik, 1998). The role of the presidency in the evolving 'vertical' EU context for the still central intergovernmental negotiations is relatively unexplored. The exception is Kirchner's elucidatory explanation of the growing importance of the presidency as a result of the 'pooling' and mixing of national sovereignty and national resources with Community powers by the European Council, in a system resembling the co-operative federalism of Germany (Kirchner, 1992: 10–14, 114–15). In this chapter, the question of what type of EU constitution or 'federation' we should be looking for is held open. For this purpose the presidency case is understood in terms of *conditions* for the future constitutionalisation of EU multi-level governance. The extent of member state representation has been defined as a decisive condition in the constitution-alisation of levels in the EU (Börzel and Risse, 2000). 'Constitutionalisation' is defined here as the act or process of constituting the formal EU (see Weiler, 1999: viii).

The concept of multi-level governance points to the existence and prolif-eration of networks between newly emerging levels in European policy-making (Risse-Kappen, 1996). Other terms like 'multi-layered' (Wæver, 1994), 'Condominio' (Schmitter, 1996), 'multi-tier' (Kohler-Koch, 1996) and 'multi-locational' (Wallace, 2000) have specified the uniqueness of the new patterns. The objective of these works has been to understand the more enduring modes of governance beyond the state that are emerging as an out-come of the processes of European integration. We can conclude that policy makers are affected by a new network mode of European governance (Kohler-Koch and Eising, 1999) and that multi-level dynamics result in the Europeanisation of the national organisation of political life (Wessels and Rometsch, 1996; Hanf and Soetendorp, 1998; Harmsen, 1999). However, we still know relatively little about *how* the new complex patterns affect policy outcomes (Richardson, 1996; Matlary, 1997; Börzel, 1997; Jönsson et al., 1998) and in what way they condition the process of constituting the legal and administrative EU levels (Armstrong and Bulmer, 1998).

There is, however, a debate about how EU multi-level governance *ought to* be constitutionalised. Scharpf (1999) has called for constitutional reforms strengthening the capacity of 'multi-level problem-solving' in the Union. Börzel and Risse (2000) have asked what principles should be chosen for the formal dividing and sharing of competences between the Union and the member state level in the emerging 'European Federation'. This debate was inspired by the German Foreign Minister's suggestions in 2000 for a future European federation based on 'divided' sovereignty (Fischer, 2000). The normative works have to a large extent been based on comparisons between the Union and existing federal states such as the US, Germany and Australia. The German co-operative model, based on a strong representa-tion of state executives at the federal level, is advocated because it matches the multi-level governance character of the Union, 'where *material* sover-eignty (or action capacities) are shared in networks across and between the various levels' (Börzel and Risse, 2000: 16). Börzel, Risse and others draw the conclusion that the emerging 'European federation' has evolved along the lines of a *shared*, rather than a divided, sovereignty. This is the main reason why they choose the German co-operative model as an analytical point of reference.

In contrast, and in line with sociological-historical approaches elaborated in earlier work (Ekengren, 2002), it is argued here that we should try to avoid as many pre-existing models as possible in our investigation of the EU con-stitutionalisation. Instead, it is important to enrich our empirical data induc-tively in order to discern the conditions or *'constructive potential'* (Wiener, 1997, 1998) of features specific to the European multi-level context. In this way we broaden our possibilities of discovering a new multi-level reality – and defining a new 'European' type of constitution – that might be invisible through the lenses of already given federal conceptions. Preliminary studies of the growing welfare policy co-ordination in the EU show how this multi-level practice must be regulated by new institutional solutions such as the 'open method of co-ordination', involving *complementary* measures and competences at the EU and at the member state level (Ekengren, 2001).

With respect to the Swedish EU Presidency, the following questions are considered to be a reasonable starting point for our inductive approach:

- How was representation at Union level organised by the Swedish administration during the EU Presidency?
- To what extent do established conceptions of divided and shared sovereignty match this EU reality?
- What constitutional 'constructive potential' is crystallising in the empirical investigation?

The Swedish case is an example of the organisation of the 'lower' level representation at the EU level with which every member state has to cope, though member states, of course, differ with regard to the specific organisation for the presidency duties. The general significance of this case is that it shows the engagement of the national level in the everyday running of the Union. It shows the linking of levels of governance that is carried out continuously in the EU, albeit by shifting countries in the chairmanship role. The well-delimited presidency in terms of time and duties is relatively easy to analyse in detail and thus provides a good indicator of the more 'exact' degree to which a national government is represented at the EU level.

Managing Multi-level Governance: New Resource Allocations

The Swedish Presidency could be seen as simply a return to the highly-centralised 'traditional' foreign policy conduct that had characterised Sweden's actions vis-à-vis the Union before membership, and in the early days after the entry in 1995 (Ekengren and Sundelius, 1998; Tallberg, 2001).[1] The foreign policy reflexes in the Swedish administration were strong. A well-performed presidency was defined early on as a unifying national interest of the highest priority. Centralised co-ordination was accepted and trusted as a necessary tool to hold the activities together and to avoid potential difficulties arising from a conflict of presidential and national interests. The strong sense of a common purpose between ministries that developed before and during the presidency resulted in a surprisingly smooth centralisation of co-ordination. Even the most ardent critics, many of them within the Social Democratic Party and in more peripheral parts of the country, buried the hatchet temporarily and decided to make the best of the situation by loyally supporting the government in its endeavours to carry out an efficient presidency. National and regional pride and economic considerations were the underlying driving forces behind this unified national effort to put Sweden on the map in an increasingly competitive wider Europe. A broad range of the co-ordination measures described in Chapter 6 were used by the government in order to establish and at the same time to steer this engagement.

Before looking at those measures, however, data now available from the Swedish Presidency powerfully suggests that managing the presidency is quite different from 'traditional' foreign policy. It is generally acknowledged that, for a small country, the engagement of the national administrative apparatus as a whole is required to manage the EU Presidency (General Secretariat, 1996; Humphreys, 1997). During the Swedish Presidency, from 1 January to 30 June 2001, the 20 different Councils of Ministers held 60 formal meetings in Brussels and Luxembourg.[2] Swedish civil servants chaired over 250 Council working groups in approximately 1,500 meetings. In addition, around 70 meetings were held in Sweden, of which four were 'compulsory' informal ministerial meetings (Gymnich, Agriculture, Justice and Ecofin) and six decided by the Swedish government. Meetings held at different levels in Sweden were located at over 44 different places. The first spring European Council was held in Stockholm on 23 and 24 March, and the traditional concluding European Council meeting took place in Göteborg on 15 and16 June. The meeting in Göteborg was attended by over 4,000 delegates and journalists. Before the presidency, the Government Offices estimated that around 80 per cent of the EU agenda during the presidency had to be taken as given, as a heritage of earlier EU work and plans. The Swedish Parliament (Riksdag) allocated SEK 835 million (approx. €80 million) for the conduct of the presidency as a whole.[3] The budget was to meet the costs of the meetings in Sweden, press, information and cultural activities, training and extra staff, information technology, premises and interpretation at the meetings.

The foreign ministry

The foreign minister led 35 meetings at the foreign minister level, mostly as chairman of meetings between the EU and third countries. Seven meetings of the General Affairs Council (GAC) were held. The agenda of the GAC meetings were divided into 'external relations, including the ESDP' and 'horizontal questions'. In connection with the GAC, third country meetings were held with Uzbekistan, Estonia, Latvia, Lithuania, Mexico, Rumania, countries of the Northern dimension, Russia, Moldova, Cyprus, the candidate states, the countries of the European Economic Space (EES), Chile, Mercosur, Turkey, Slovakia and Ukraine. The minister for foreign trade chaired the internal Market Council and the minister for development and aid led the Development Council. The foreign ministry was responsible for approximately 100 Council and Common Foreign and Security Policy (CFSP) working groups. It also provided presidents for approximately 50 EU Committees (for example, Association Committees).

All in all, approximately 200 Swedish officials functioned as chairmen in Brussels. Most of these had been appointed by July 1999 and given a thorough education in languages, EU processes and negotiation techniques. In addition, foreign ministry officials represented the EU in the capacity of chairmen in a number of international groupings. The embassies played an important role in chairing the EU co-ordination meetings in member state capitals as well as in third countries. The 19 Council working groups that met once a week had a chairman posted at the Swedish Brussels Representation. The chairmen of the 36 groups assembling monthly and less frequently were based in Stockholm.

Most of the extra resources needed for the presidency had to be found from within the existing framework of activity. But it was quickly realised that the setting of new priorities and a reallocation of resources were also needed. Initially, the foreign policy administration wanted 175 'functions' to be added to the ministry's staff for the period from autumn 1999 up until the end of 2001. In the event, 103 extra functions were in fact created, 80 for the home organisation and 23 for the foreign representation. The largest increase was to be found in the '2001–Secretariat', which over the period of the presidency expanded from around eight to 43 posts. Second to this was the Swedish UN delegation in New York (six functions), the representation in Brussels (five) and the foreign ministry's unit for EU affairs (five). The section of the European Correspondent, co-ordinating the GAC, increased by three people. The Permanent Representation in Brussels, Sweden's largest mission abroad, had approximately 120 employees during the presidency. During this period it became even more appropriate than before to describe it as a miniature version of the Government Offices, where all ministries are represented.

Spring 2001: The Swedish 'Co-administration' of the Union

The prime minister has the overall responsibility for Sweden's EU policies. The other government ministers are responsible for their respective issues in the work of the EU. During the Swedish Presidency, the Prime Minister's Office co-ordinated the work of the government on issues related to the EU. The prime minister and the minister for foreign affairs represented the presidency as a whole in its dealings with the rest of the world and represented Sweden at the European Council and other meetings decided on by the prime minister. These two shared most of the representative duties relating to the presidency as a whole.

The Prime Minister's Office was also responsible for the working programme consisting of policy statements and an agenda for each meeting in the Council of Ministers. The direct role and involvement of the state secretary for EU issues during the EU Presidency was extremely important (see Beckman, 2001: 64). In the run up to and during the presidency, there are great demands placed on the prime minister. This has always been the case for EU prime ministers due to their role as President in Office of the European Council and is an expression of the general 'prime ministeriali-sation' of the national work in the Union, as explained in Chapter 6. Since the initiation of the Luxembourg process in 1997, the demands placed on the prime minister have increased even further (Jacobsson et al., 2001). In preparation for the Stockholm European Council, the Swedish Prime Minister Göran Persson visited all EU capitals within 10 days. The tour was repeated before the Göteborg summit in June 2001. Moreover, in order to avoid any surprises at the table, Persson wrote to EU leaders, asking them what issues they wished to have placed on the agenda. The result of the double co-ordination responsibility was that the Swedish Prime Minister, during the EU presidency, was heading two levels of governance simultaneously.

A preliminary inventory of the issues that could be expected on the Union's agenda at the beginning of the presidency was drawn up at an early stage (Statsrådsberedningen, 2001). However, there was a general feeling in the adminstration and among the political opposition parties that the policy priorities for the presidency were set too late. Six to eight areas figured as candidates as late as autumn 1999. The decision on the three so-called 'E's' – enlargement, employment and environment – was taken and launched in spring 2000, less than one year before the start. This delay can be understood in the light of the Swedish government's general difficulty of setting priori-ties in its EU work (Ekengren and Sundelius, 1998).

Within the Prime Minister's Office, a special group called the 'Situation Room' was set up to provide the central overview, daily co-ordination and information about the presidency activities. The main tasks of the Room were to co-ordinate the Councils and COREPER I and II and produce general infor-mation of importance for the presidency that was sent out to all Government Offices officials, including the Swedish embassies. The group was chaired by the state secretary for EU affairs and included, *inter alia*, the state secretaries of the foreign ministry, the ministries of finance and justice and senior civil servants of the foreign ministry (Statsrådsberedningen, 2000).

The Room, as the only institution that had a complete overview, co-ordinated the different Councils. Whenever agreement was impossible between ministries, the matter was submitted to the Room and the state secretary for EU affairs for arbitration. These cases were very rare. The new practice con-siderably strengthened the coherence of the government's action and was not questioned by ministries. The constitution of the Room facilitated the political-administrative interface. The almost daily attendance of the state secretary for EU affairs, in permanent contact with the prime minister, cre-ated a uniquely short distance between the political-strategic level and the day-to-day operationalisation of the presidency. The 'price' of this running of the presidency was a highly centralised and expert-led policy-making structure, giving a privileged position to the foreign ministry. It was European 'foreign policy' conducted by a group of six to eight people.

The new interface was felt throughout the ministries. Officials witnessed a new exposure to the political domain that further narrowed the traditionally close working relationship between the bureaucratic and the political level in the Swedish central administration. The ministers became more dependent on detailed expert knowledge when they were trying to knit together compromise texts satisfying all around the table. Close team building, implying mutual involvement by ministers, state secretaries and officials on a daily basis, was required for an efficient carrying forward of the presidency duties. Not least, the civil servants' political role and weight in Council working groups increased. As chairmen they carried a heavy responsibility for bringing the issues forward to compromises that were acceptable to a Swedish Presidency view *and* to all member states. This was of great help for the minister when chairing the Council a couple of days later. A blurring of the traditional dividing line between national politics and administration, the politician and the bureaucrat, resulted from the chairman's more pronounced responsibility for the *preparation* of EU and Council decisions. In the often technical preparation for the Union, it is no longer possible to find or make a distinction between national preparation and moments of national policy-making, rather it is a question of continuous decision shaping. The national level turns into 'administration' for the higher level decision-making in the EU multi-level game.

Another important task and tool of the Situation Room was the daily issuing by e-mail of the information note called 'Current Presidency Questions' to all the government offices, including the embassies. On certain days it was updated several times. The co-ordination effects of these central information providers can hardly be overestimated. Even though the co-ordination powers of the Room were formalised only to a very limited extent, its informal influence and steering function were great. The information and 'order' relationships were often of a vertical and hierarchical nature, despite the fact that on paper the Swedish Presidency co-ordination was a relatively flat organisation. The result was a system where the need for formal authority and steering was very limited.

Types of National Co-ordination

All of the six types of national co-ordination described in Chapter 6 of this volume could be found in the organisation of the Swedish EU Presidency.

Co-ordination through political leadership

The government's work of domesticising the Union and counteracting the image of a division between Sweden and the rest of the Union into 'us' and 'them' was interrupted by the presidency. All Swedish officials were given a joint task and responsibility; 'we' were mandated to lead and act as the chair of 'them'. In this way, the framing of the presidency for a period of 12–18 months re-invented the EU as a national foreign policy issue. It was to be dealt with on the basis of centrally decided national guidelines. This procedural task would override the three substantive priority issues for the presidency: enlargement, employment and the environment. This contributed to the domestic image of Sweden as primarily a foreign policy actor during its EU presidency. The national orientation was also cast by a sense of competition with the other members over the ability to excell in effectiveness and objectivity in the conduct of the chairmanship.

The strong emphasis on concrete results during the presidency was to some extent formulated as a contrast to the more 'visionary' programmes of several previous presidencies. The Social Democratic Government wanted to prove to internal critics and to external sceptics that they were wrong in portraying Sweden as a reluctant and less than trustworthy European. This experience shows that process management might be of increasing relevance to an evaluation of the performance of each presidency, possibly at the cost of achievements in policy substance.

Co-ordination through representation

In the government's preparations for the presidency, the emphasis was placed on Sweden as an actor vis-à-vis the other EU member states – though with a special responsibility for the collectivity. It was the picture of the prime minister and the foreign minister travelling from Stockholm to their colleagues in the 14 capitals that was painted in the brightest colours – in the Swedish press. The multi-level groundwork made in and through Brussels was not so spectacular and perhaps not fully understood by the media. The role of the foreign policy actor was further emphasised by the top level Swedish contacts with the US, Russia and Canada. Although the prime minister and foreign minister acted in their capacity as representatives of the Union as a whole, in a distinctive way, the meetings evoked the picture of Sweden as an equal among the big powers on the international scene. Thus, both this general image and the government's internal preparation contributed to the image of Sweden as primarily a foreign policy actor during the presidency.

All this contributed to the strong role of the foreign ministry and constituted a powerful ideological basis for the centralised internal co-ordination machinery. More than anything else perhaps, the tasks of high-level representation legitimised centralisation by showing that national co-ordination was not put in place for its own sake, but in relation not only to the European but also to the international setting. It seemed only logical to place the responsibility for co-ordination in the offices of those having to fulfil these presidency duties. This picture was only confirmed by the very low and tacitly supporting profile of the opposition parties in the Parliament. On several occasions, the prime minister declared how grateful he was for being 'backed up at home', as he put it. The Permanent Representation in Brussels played a similar representative role, resulting in a key position in the national co-ordinating structure.

Co-ordination through specialisation

The specialised ministries and the foreign ministry: Each minister and ministry was responsible for its own issues in their EU work during the presidency. Throughout this period, however, the ministries gave special consideration to the demands of the presidency as a whole in their preparation of the Swedish position. Though, from the outset, it was strongly underlined that the country holding the presidency should not promote issues of particular national interest (see Tallberg, 2001).

In practice, there was no need to discuss possible alternative action or stances among the ministries as the overriding task of the national delegate was to support the chairman of the working group. The ministries responsible for the subjects of meetings appointed project managers and other staff in project groups for each meeting. Included in these meeting projects were co-ordinators from the Secretariat for the EU Presidency and representatives from the police authorities, municipalities/county councils, public agencies, non-governmental organisations (NGOs) and other organisations. The inclusion of representatives of the agencies in the new groups was a way of securing a permanent expertise that was often needed in contacts with the EU Commission and in the working out of compromises, where the key to success frequently depended on rather technical issues. In the case of the ministry of justice, the agencies for the first time also participated at some of the briefings of the minister (interview, August 2001). The traditional organisation of Swedish public administration – with small ministries and large independent agencies – had already been affected by the membership of the Union, implying closer ties between the two parts. The presidency meant that the two levels of administration were to some extent merged in order to be able to complement the EU institutions in their carrying out of functional, 'de-politicised', European co-operation.

Never before had the demands on complementarity between the levels of governance been so strong as during the presidency. Before, the specialised ministries could when necessary rely on the political compass when concluding EU negotiations. In the presidency context, in co-operation with the Commission and the Council Secretariat, they had to provide material on a daily basis for functional problem solving – the fuel for the traditional engine of European integration. This multi-level dynamic generated a complementary functional role to the lower level.

The foreign ministry and the prime minister's office: The foreign ministry and the prime minister's office were also 'specialised' in the area of EU decision-making norms and procedures. Their specialisation functioned as the ideological basis and legitimising force for more detailed guidelines and orders sent down through the administration. The foreign ministry worked as a 'process engine' and thereby managed to engage the entire national administration in the running of decision making at the 'higher' level of governance.

The foreign ministry's specialisation, however, was challenged by the strong policy sector specialisation of EU co-operation that came to the surface in the presidency situation. To a large extent, the embassies could act only as a contact point for further 'decentralised' links between specialists in the EU capitals and Stockholm. Thus, they played a very limited role in the resolution of conflicts of interests and in the contribution to policy coherence. In the running of the presidency, the foreign ministry's EU specialisation could not hold back the decentralising forces that are driven by the functional basis of the Union.

The problems of foreign representation can be seen as an inability to adapt to *the demands of the multi-level game*. The multi-level dynamic enhanced the role of the embassies as a branch of the government offices as a whole, rather than exclusively linked to the foreign ministry. In order to be able to drive the 'functional-technical' project of the EU forward, the lower level of governance engaged its entire administration. The multi-level character of the Union gave a qualitatively new role and identity to the Swedish administration in the EU, including the 'foreign' representation in the EU member states. The Swedish representatives shared or rather complemented the EU institutions' role, not only in the exercise of political leadership, but also in their basic way of running the organisation through technical expertise, process and procedure knowledge and the provision of an institutional memory. It was this identity shift in the multi-level system that contributed to the changed role of the embassies. Colleagues in capitals turned to them for similar reasons that they contacted the local Commission office, that is, as parts of an EU administration responsible for the full range of EU questions under deliberations in Brussels. Due to the multi-level system, the Swedish administration for a period of six months was 'moved up', worked in parallel with, and led the administration of the 'higher' level of governance. It is a question of *complementing* rather than sharing the overall responsibilities and sovereignty. In this unique system, the embassies' traditional competence of being able to discuss foreign policy issues was not enough. They were now part of a *cross-level administration* that prepared the decision making of a wide range of EU 'domestic' questions and were expected to possess the same information as other parts, irrespective of geographic location.

Co-ordination through consensus

To a very limited extent only, central directives had to be formalised and enforced. The instructions of the state secretary for EU affairs to the domestic ministries could be formulated more in terms of expectations than commands. The impression of a very flat organisation was upheld with each part of the government machinery contributing what it thought best to the common cause. A light touch by the top-level co-ordinators of national policy was combined with seemingly autonomous ministries that freely pulled in the same direction. The core management group was placed close to the prime minister (and also EU president). This politically central location contributed to legitimising the norms and procedures of the co-ordination effort.

Co-ordination through socialisation and expertise

One of the most important experiences of the presidency was learning how the Brussels machinery functions 'in reality'. The logic of appropriate procedures of the Council Secretariat, the Commission and the European Parliament could never be fully understood without having worked *within* rather than *with* these institutions. The presidency presents a rare opportunity for the 'lower' level of governance to get fully acquainted with the higher level. The fact that this multi-level interaction does not take place until the member state is put in a co-steering position of the whole organisation for a period of six months, is a reminder of the unique character of European governance. The Swedish foreign ministry profited most from this penetration of the EU institutions. In dealing with other ministries, it could to a large extent lean on being the ministry most socialised into the norms and procedures of the EU decision-making process.

Multi-level Linkages: Presiding over the European Present

During the presidency, some new practices were introduced into Swedish administration that changed the *time allocation* and *rhythms* of everyday work within the ministries. For example, the internal rules for reporting from Council working group meetings were changed. One hour after the meeting, the Swedish delegate or chairman had to submit a short report to the Situation Room on the main deliberations. The purpose was to enable the Room to have a speedy overview of the difficulties that could face the minister at Council level and thereby be better able to perform the trouble-shooting role that was one of its main tasks. In close co-operation with the EU co-ordinator at the ministry involved, the Brussels Representation and the Council Secretariat in Brussels, it could then work on a compromise that could suit all member states.

The almost instantaneous transmission of information between levels of governance got its most significant expression in the so called 'flash-system', established for communication between the embassies and the Prime Minister's Office. The embassies were asked to report in the form of very short notes about the domestic situation in their host country. The system was used particularly in the preparation of the European Councils where it allowed the prime minister to follow the domestic scenes on an hour-by-hour basis before arriving in the capitals. As one official at the foreign ministry put it, 'the Prime Minister wanted to know what was in the mind, the main preoccupations, of Mr Aznar at their up-coming morning meeting in Madrid' (interview, Ministry for Foreign Affairs, August 2001).

Member states' active commitment to a common European time for the co-ordination of their meetings and contacts in the *polycentric* system of the EU has been explained in an earlier work. In a polity of several centres, inter-action *between* centres must be co-ordinated within a common uniform time (Ekengren, 2002: Ch. 5). This chapter has shown that co-ordination for syn-chronisation is central not only to interaction *among* the centres but *between the levels* in European governance. The timetables, schedules and meeting agendas of the chairmen also co-ordinate the levels of governance. European hierarchy – in the form of the rotating presidency – for European simultane-ity is needed not only for European polycentrism, but also for multi-level governance. In order to synchronise the two levels, the Swedish Presidency had to change the logic of appropriate procedures within the adminstration. When the Swedish administration became the chairman of the EU's decision taking in the EU political present, a distinct Swedish present was dissolved and 'crowded out' to an even greater extent than before. The further squeez-ing of the national interval between the reporting from EU meetings and the producing of instructions for delegates was basically a consequence of the fact that the Swedish administration functioned as the main engine for European simultaneity. The European timetable was now run by the Swedes. There was no longer a difference between the rhythm and timetables of national procedures and the EU decision-making process.

On the contrary, it was up to the presidency to 'enforce' the European cal-endar on the other member states in order to get them to be 'in time' for EU decisions they in any case had to support. The loss of 'time autonomy' that had been experienced as a result of EU membership was turned to a very large extent into a feeling of controlling the system, not least through the power of the timing of putting issues on the agenda (see Elgström and Tallberg, 2001: 36–7). The setting of EU time created a power position in the Union that was not in proportion to the material resources of the Swedish administration. Much of the Swedish administrative adaptation for presi-dency duties can be explained in the light of this peculiar synchronising of levels of governance.

Complementary Sovereignty for EU Multi-layered Foreign Policy

The Swedish Presidency illustrated a paradox that is probably common to all EU presidencies. On the one hand, the management of the presidency was handled as traditional foreign policy: the national gathering around some clear goals; national prestige at stake; the primacy of national consensus and co-ordination; the privileged position of the foreign ministry and so on. On the other hand, the responsibility for collective EU decisions and adminis-tration; EU time; taking into account the domestic situation in other member states; and the new demands on the Swedish embassies, all underlined the embeddedness of member state administration in the European multi-layered reality. The entire administration of the 'lower' level is engaged to defend national interests vis-à-vis other actors at the 'higher' level, while at the same time being very conscious of common purposes and goals.

The consciousness of this *double* responsibility, made the Swedish presidency actors think in terms of, and thereby mentally to create, a Union of levels. Even though the Swedish government organised more strictly than ever its foreign policy machinery for traditional intra-European diplomacy, it did so in a multi-level context. Today, the frequency and intensity of EU meetings, the domesticised relationship between member states, the strong functional and representative role of the EU presidency, all make national co-ordination 'internal' to the Union. The function of the various types of national co-ordination is to form a coherent and attuned national level in the EU, not only for the purpose of influencing other states, but also for securing responsible and effective Union action. By providing a strong national representation at the EU-level, the national 'foreign policy' actors are unintentionally expressing a decisive condition for the future constitutionalisation of EU multi-level governance.

The mix of foreign policy, marking levels by definitions of 'we' and 'them' in EU negotiations, and the common responsibility for the 'higher' Union level is a unique European feature. The specific multi-level practice of creating levels through national co-ordination is an important element of the constructive potential for a 'European' type of constitution. Another feature specific to the EU is the way the two main levels are interlinked by the lower-level president in office. During the presidency, the Swedish government functioned as an inter-European link between EU levels of governance. The Swedish ministers headed the two levels *simultaneously*. The demands on instantaneous information sharing and full synchronisation of national and European meetings and decision making were only expressions of the need to hold the levels together within a common time framework. The creation and up-holding of a common EU time is one of the most important tasks and instruments for the presidency in the interlinking of levels. The ability to create and manage this time, and thereby hold the *Union* together, is probably one of the keys to a successful presidency.

The running of an EU Presidency is an extreme example of multi-level governance. A conception of *complementary levels* seems to match the form and extent of the member state representation at the EU level. A structure of *complementary sovereignty*, or 'action capacities' as Börzel and Risse call it, is crystallising. This is a system where the lower-level administration, on a rotating basis, not only shares the decision making of the EU institutions, but also functions as their engine by means of a strengthened control of the timetables for decisions. The complementary character of the two levels is strengthened by the chairman's creation of European simultaneity for the synchronisation of action capacities at respective levels. A simultaneous *parallel*, rather than a shared or divided capacity, can also be seen with regard to the responsibility for policy areas. Here, national government in the presidency role is becoming a miniature of the Union's administration as a whole, responsible for all policy sectors involved in EU co-operation. It is less a question of an organised sharing of action capacities between the levels, rather the national level attempts to merge with the Union level by means of exhausting its national assets to the largest possible extent through a broad variety of measures of foreign policy co-ordination that paradoxically helps to constitute the two levels.

This case study points in the direction that the EU multi-layered polity is evolving along the lines of complementary, rather than shared or divided, sovereignty. European foreign policy, as the exercise of complementary sovereignty, certainly takes us beyond intra-European diplomacy in our analysis of the Union. The pattern found here raises fundamental questions about the meaning of concepts of foreign policy, policy co-ordination and the common interest.

Notes

1   This is in contrast to the trend towards a more de-centralised, 'domesticised', policy-making that characterised Swedish EU administration in the late 1990s (Ekengren and Sundelius, 2002).
2   All data concerning the Swedish Presidency are collected from the Swedish Official programme of the Presidency, the Newsletters 'EU info: faktablad' and 'EU-rapport' of the Government Offices and 'UD Aktuellt' of the Swedish Ministry for Foreign Affairs (1997–2001), internal memoranda of the Ministry of Foreign Affairs and the Prime Minister's Office, interviews at the Swedish Government Offices and the website of the Swedish EU Presidency (www.2001.se). See also Regeringskansliet and Utrikesdepartementet entries in References.
3   The total budget of the running costs of the Government Offices (including the Foreign Ministry) in a normal year is approximately SEK 4.2 billion.

References

Armstrong, K. and Bulmer, S. (1998) *The Governance of the Single Market*. Manchester: Manchester University Press.

Beckman, B. (2001) 'Den administrativa utmaningen – svensk effektivitet i EU's tjänst', in J. Tallberg (ed.), *När Europa kom till Sverige – Ordförandeskapet i EU 2001*. Stockholm: SNS. pp. 51–67.

Börzel, T. (1997) 'What's so special about policy networks? – An exploration of the concept and its usefulness in studying European governance', *European Integration online Papers* (EIoP), 1:16. http://eiop.or.at

Börzel, T. and Risse, T. (2000) 'Who is Afraid of a European Federation? How to Constitutionalise a Multi-Level Governance System'. Harvard Jean Monnet Working Paper, No. 7/00.

Ekengren, M. (2001) 'EU och medlemsstaternas regeringar: subsidiaritet, folklig förankring, "tredje vägen" och sysselsättningssamarbetet', in K. Jacobsson, K.M. Johansson and M. Ekengren (eds), *Mot en europeisk välfärdspolitik? – ny politik och nya samarbetsformer i EU*. Stockholm: SNS.

Ekengren, M. (2002) *The Time of European Governance*. Manchester: Manchester University Press.

Ekengren, M. and Sundelius, B. (1998) 'The state joins the European Union', in K. Hanf and B. Soetendorp (eds), *Adapting to European Integration: Small States and the European Union*. Harlow: Addison Wesley Longman.

Ekengren, M. and Sundelius, B. (2002) 'Sweden', in B. Hocking and D. Spence (eds), *Foreign Ministries in the European Union: Integrating Diplomats*. Basingstoke: Palgrave Macmillan.

Elgström and Tallberg (2001) 'Den politiska utmaningen – nationella och europeiska intressen i konflikt?', in J. Tallberg (ed.), *När Europa kom till Sverige – Ordförandeskapet i EU 2001*. Stockholm: SNS. pp. 35–50.

Fischer, J. (2000) 'From confederacy to federation – thoughts on the finality of European integration'. Speech at the Humboldt University, 12 May, Berlin.

General Secretariat: Council of the European Union (1996), *Council Guide – 1 Presidency Handbook*. Luxembourg: Office for Official Publications of the European Communities.

Hanf, K. and Soetendorp, B. (eds) (1998) *Adapting to European Integration – Small States and the European Union*. Harlow: Addison Wesley Longman.

Harmsen, R. (1999) 'The Europeanization of national administrations: A comparative study of France and Netherlands', *Governance: An International Journal of Policy and Administration*, 12 (1): 81–113.

Hayes-Renshaw, F. and Wallace, H. (1997) *The Council of Ministers*. London: Macmillan.

Humphreys, P. (1997) *The Fifth Irish Presidency of the European Union: Some Management Lessons*. CPMR Discussion Paper 2, Institute of Public Administration, Dublin.

Jacobsson, K., Johansson, K.M. and Ekengren, M. (2001) *Mot en europeisk välfärdspolitik? – ny politik och nya samarbetsformer i EU*. Stockholm: SNS.

Jönsson, C., Elgström, O., Strömvik, M. (1998) 'Negotiations in networks in the European Union', *International Negotiation*, 3 (3): 3.

Kirchner, E. (1992) *Decision-Making in the European Community: The Council Presidency and European Integration*. Manchester: Manchester University Press.

Kohler-Koch, B. (1996) 'The strength of weakness: the transformation of governance in the EU', in L. Lewin and S. Gustavsson (eds), *The Future of the Nation-State*. Stockholm: Nerenius and Santérus. pp. 169–210.

Kohler-Koch, B. and Eising, R. (eds) (1999) *The Transformation of Governance in the European Union*. London: Routledge.

Matlary, J.H. (1997) 'Epilogue: new bottles for new wine', in K.E. Jørgensen (ed.), *Reflective Approaches to European Governance*. London: Macmillan.

Moravcsik, A. (1998) *The Choice for Europe: Social Purpose and State Power from Messina to Maastricht*. London: UCL Press.

Regeringskansliet (Government Offices): EU info. Faktablad om EU-samarbetet. 1997–2001.

Regeringskansliet: EU info. *EU-rapport: Nyhetsbrev om EU-samarbetet*. 1997–2001.

Regeringskansliet (2000) Program för Sveriges ordförandeskap i EU's ministerråd 1 januari – 30 june 2001.

Richardson, J. (ed.) (1996) *European Union – Power and Policy-Making*. London: Routledge.

Risse-Kappen, T. (1996) 'The nature of the beast', *Journal of Common Market Studies*, 34 (1): 1.

Scharpf, F.W. (1999) *Governing in Europe, Effective and Democratic?* Oxford: Oxford University Press.

Schmitter, P. (1996) 'Imagining the future of the Euro-polity with the help of new concepts', in G. Marks, F.W. Scharpf, P. Schmitter and W. Streeck (eds), *Governance in the European Union*. London: Sage.

Statsrådsberedningen (2000) 'Lägesrummet i Statsrådsberedningen'. Promemoria 2000-12-14.

Statsrådsberedningen (2001) 'Mötesplanering under ordförandeskapet'. Promemoria 2001-01-15.

Svensson, A.C. (2000) 'In the Service of the European Union – The Role of the Presidency in Negotiating the Amsterdam Treaty 1995–97'. Doctoral Dissertation, Department of Government, Uppsala University.

Tallberg, J. (ed.) (2001) *När Europa kom till Sverige – Ordförandeskapet i EU 2001*. Stockholm: SNS.

Utrikesdepartementet (Ministry for Foreign Affairs) 'UD Aktuellt – Underrättelser från Expeditionschefen och de Administrativa enheterna, 1997–2001'.

Utrikesdepartementet (1999), 'Resursplanering inför Sveriges ordförandeskap i EU's ministerråd första halvåret 2001'. Promemoria 1999-06-07.

Wallace, H. (2000) 'Analysing and explaining policies', in H. Wallace and W. Wallace (eds), *Policy-Making in the European Union* (4th edn). Oxford: Oxford University Press.

Weiler, J.H.H. (1999) *The Constitution of Europe*. Cambridge: Cambridge University Press.

Wessels, W. and Rometsch, D. (eds) (1996) *The European Union and Member States – Towards Institutional Fusion?* Manchester: Manchester University Press.

Wiener, A. (1997) 'Assessing the constructive potential of union citizenship – a socio-historical perspective', *European Integration online Papers* (EIoP), 1:17. http://eiop.

Wiener, A. (1998) *'European' Citizenship Practice – Building Institutions of a Non-State*. Boulder, CO: Westview Press.

Wæver, O. (1994) 'Resisting post-foreign policy analysis', in W. Carlsnaes and S. Smith (eds), *European Foreign Policy – The EC and Changing Perspectives in Europe*. London: Sage.

14 Collective Identity: The Greek Case

Michelle Pace

In Chapter 7 of this volume, Ulrich Sedelmeier makes an implicit reference to a key distinction between the European Union's (EU's) collective identity and the identity of each particular member state of the EU.[1] To complement Sedelmeier, the focus in this chapter will be on the case of a particular member state: Greece. Starting from a weak position in terms of limited resources and limited structural power, one might expect that Greece's integration into the European Community (EC) in 1981 would offer the country an international platform from which to have a voice in international affairs. Moreover, Greece is located in a historically turbulent area in Europe's backyard with close neighbouring nations including Albania, Bulgaria and Turkey. Hence, one might expect Greece to embrace the notion of a collective sovereignty as expressed through the Common Foreign and Security Policy (CFSP).[2] However, Greece did not embrace the EU's notion of collective sovereignty. In fact, many would argue that Greece has often been a difficult partner within the framework of the EU's foreign policy-making process and has persisted in differentiating itself from common European positions on foreign policy.

When Greece became the 10th member of the EC, it came in with an ideological 'baggage' very different from that of the other European member states. The image of Greece within the EU is one of a 'southern' member state. Furthermore, Greece is a relatively small state. Yet, these factors are not enough to understand Greece's role in the EU's foreign policy framework. In this chapter it will be suggested that the identity baggage that Greece carried into the EU is a deeper and more embedded explanatory factor for Greece's position within the EU context, in particular within the latter's foreign policy framework. Greece is often said to have an ambivalent identity that oscillates between a Balkan identity and a blurred European identity (Pace, 2001). This ambivalence is also reflected in Greece's position within the CFSP. Having said this, it is not implied that identity can explain everything about the latter. This chapter points to this particular dimension specifically but does not rule out other factors that can help us understand Greece's position vis-à-vis its EU partners on foreign policy issues.

Identity is understood here as the process of associating oneself closely with other individuals or reference groups to the extent that one comes to adopt their goals and values and to share considerably in their experiences. However, the notion of identity also includes those processes of *disassociation* from other individuals or reference groups, thereby incorporating a rejection of certain groups' goals, values and experiences. In other words, identity is a process of the 'continuous making of the self' through othering. It is therefore a flexible, fluid concept rather than a static, fixed notion. Hence, it follows that national identities, as well as collective identities, have their internal and external others who may be threatening while others may be inspiring.

It may well be argued then that identity is neither an independent nor dependent variable, but rather an *element*, an important one indeed, that influences Greek foreign policy in interaction with other factors. These factors include: ideology (in particular the long-standing Greek ambition of independence from the foreign policy of the US); domestic politics and party-political differences and national policy-making style (most importantly, a tradition of prioritising short-term results and ignoring long-term consequences of specific actions). The national issues/identity pillars that are vital in the case of Greece are Cyprus, Turkey and the Balkans. Moreover, the view that 'the enemy of your enemy is your friend' has been an important feature of Greek foreign policy and is reflected in Greece's position on EU foreign policy (Kavakas, 2001).

The chapter is organised as follows: the first section outlines historical processes of and current changes in state formation and nation building in Greece. In order to understand the key parameters of identity in modern Greece, the historical formation of the Greek nation and the way in which the notions of 'Greekness' and Greek identity emerged are important. The space allowed here does not permit a thorough examination of these issues. Hence, the purpose of this section is to highlight some specific elements relating to the construction of Greek identity, rather than to give a precise chronology of historical events. This will be followed by a second section on the impact of European integration on Greece and of Greece's membership on the EU. This section will highlight the positions of Greece on various instances of EU foreign policy. It will be argued that an identity perspective uncovers Greek ambivalence on the EU's foreign policy and that this in turn is reflected in the image EU partners have of Greece. In the third section it will be suggested that an identity approach can also help us understand the recent change in Greece's position on EU foreign policy.

Historical Processes in the Making of the Greek Nation

The role of history and of collective memory in identity formation, and the discursive repertoires of collective identification, are important considerations to examine in the context of Greece within the EU.

The process towards independence has created a national awareness amongst the Greek people and shaped a nationalist ideology. The historical legacies of this process have formed the Greek national consciousness: the 'nation' as a community of culture and social sentiments preceded the state during the periods of national awakening.

The official history of Greece to date traces a strong tradition in seeing the Greek nation as a continuous line of inheritance from classical antiquity to modern Greece. Since medieval times and in the modern era, the main threat for the Greek people were the 'Latins' – that is, anybody from the West. One can also trace a tradition of the Greek Orthodox Church in opposition to the Western Christian Church. The Greek Church has always felt closer to its Slav neighbours in this respect and to Islam. Islam has not been a threat since it has historically acted as a guarantor of the Greeks' existence – during the period when Islam fought against the Christian Latins (Clogg, 1986).

Therefore, the pro- and anti-Europe positions in Greece can be traced back to this ecclesiastical view.[3] The two main traditions in thinking can be split into one group that emphasises Eastern Orthodoxy and differences and is quite ambivalent (but not entirely negative) on EU membership, and a second group that argues for a European orientation for Greece – in other words, a split identity *within* Greece (Lipowatz, 1994; Fatouros, 1993; Clogg, 1993) – two important sentiments symbolising a crisis in Greek identity especially in the 1980s. This split identity was also reflected after the 1981 elections, when PASOK's (Panellino Socialistiko Kinima) foreign policy approach was one of reluctant but active participation in the EC.[4]

European intellectuals from the time of the Enlightenment and since, have posited Greece as the cradle of European civilisation. Greece was at these times configured as a Western European culture and was associated with modern democracies. The Greek Enlightenment movement accepted this stance and pushed for the Westernisation of their country. This explains the pro-Europe sentiments held by some Greek elite groups up to this day.

The anti-Europe camps can be understood through another aspect of Greek culture that links Greece with the Orient, North Africa, Egypt, Syria and Lebanon. This tradition created cultures of resistance against the West and vernacular (fundamental) groups in Greece.

Political historians cannot omit the war against the Ottoman Empire that started in 1821 and subsequently led to the formation of an independent Greek state by roughly the 1830s (Blinkhorn and Veremis, 1990). The period between 1833 and 1913 was a particularly crucial one in Greek history as it marked a period of independence from Ottoman rule, nation building and irredentism. This period is important for an understanding of how Turkey has been and is still often perceived as a threatening other for Greeks. Since many Greeks still remained under alien rule, this fact had a profound influence on the policies, both domestic and foreign, of the independent state. The educational system of the new state was based on French and German models and institutional structures were moulded in accordance with a conservative European model. This process led to an important European influence on Greek national identity. Still, a lot of emphasis was placed on the study of the classics of ancient Greek literature and on knowledge of a 'purified' form of the language. The Greek Church was declared to be independent but firmly subordinated to the state. The large Greek populations who were still under Ottoman rule had little consciousness of being Greek, in particular the Turkish-speaking Greeks of Anatolia, and the irredentist aspirations of the Greeks had little effect on them. This complex sense of consciousness marks Greek ambivalence, which in turn is mirrored in its position on EU foreign policy.

It was during this period (1833–1913) that the notion of the Greek state and *Greekness* emerged (Blinkhorn and Veremis, 1990). Following the strain on Greek society in the early to mid-1900s due to the radicalisation of the working-class movement and subsequent general strikes, the country also experienced a civil war (1946–49). One could therefore argue that it came as no surprise that when the Continent had recovered from the damage of a Second World War, Europe was very much the focus of the struggle of 1974 for a transition to democratic government. Andreas Papandreou's PASOK came to power on an ideological, anti-imperialist ticket in 1980 and promised the closure of the North Atlantic Treaty Organisation (NATO) bases (thus securing the Greek stand for independence). In 1981, PASOK flagged its pride in EU membership – in this way reiterating how a proud independent people can have their own choice to join a regional aspiring group. With Papandreou's resignation in 1996 (due to old age), Costas Simitis was chosen as PASOK's leader. He called general elections early in September 1996 and PASOK secured a victory over ND (Nea Demokratia). Simitis is far more pro-European than his predecessor and has managed to get the Greek economy in sufficiently good shape to meet the criteria for monetary union.

To sum up, Greece has its nationalist, religious, anti-American and anti-European (anti-Western) elements that hold that Greek interests are in the East (especially spiritually/the Balkan orientation). In this area, Greece stands out as an exception to the shared norms of EU membership based on Catholic or Protestant Christianity.

On the other hand, Greece has had its anti-dictatorship and pro-European movement. Notions of democracy, in particular, link Greece to the EU as its significant and inspiring other of *the* democratic model.

These historical events constitute some of the key parameters of the substance of identity in modern Greece.

What's identity got to do with policy?

Situated between the East and the West, the ambivalence in Greek identity has been reflected throughout the years in Greek foreign policy and relations with other countries (Pace, 2001; Tsoucalas, 1993). Looking to the East, Greece prides itself of its Byzantine traditions as well as its Orthodox heritage. The West, on the other hand, has always served as a political as well as a cultural reference point for Greek aspirations to building democracy. This part of Greek attitude towards the West has found expression in its accession to the EC in January 1981. However, the East as well as the West pose diverse sources of worry or suspicion. On the one hand, the East is equated with Turkey, a long-time rival. On the other hand, the culture of the West is looked upon with distrust and as foreign/strange to the traditions in Greece. Therefore, Greekness is in many ways trapped between an Eastward orientation as well as a Westward direction. This position is mirrored in Greece's interactions with its European partners in foreign policy. Thus, it can contribute to our understanding of why Greece has often chosen to play the part of the 'awkward partner' – even when the gain or effectiveness of such a strategy has not been particularly evident.

The Impact of European Integration on Greece

Greek identity and foreign policy positions are influenced not least by the events before and after the collapse of the 19th-century old regime in 1909, when, following a military *coup d'état*, the country saw its first liberal and modernist government elected under Venizelos (Blinkhorn and Veremis, 1990). Later, when George Papandreou replaced Venizelos, he enjoyed UK support for his anti-communist stance and his determination to prevent a communist assumption of power. In fact, (Western) European capitalist and democratic nation-states served as a forceful model for Greek transformation. Even far back historically, European nations like France and England acted as inspiring significant others for the emerging nation of Greece in the 19th century. However, the EC also acted as a threatening significant other for Greece. By becoming a member, Greece had to accept transferring part of its national sovereignty to the EC institutions. In this process the territorial identity of the Greek nation was challenged. All Greek laws and decisions had to be consistent with European laws and decisions, thereby undermining the exclusiveness of Greek national sovereignty.

Moreover, through its EU membership, Greece also aimed at a more independent relation from the US, a feeling still expressed up to this day. This traditional sense of anti-Americanism in Greek society made it easier for the Greeks to enter into the European fold, but this did not necessarily translate itself into a European orientation. The Greek position of independence in respect of 'threatening others' is one that takes precedence over any other consideration in the perception of the Greek psyche.

Foreign policy

During the first five years of Greek EC membership, 1981–85, Greece consistently abused its institutional powers and caused hostile reactions from its partners in the EC. To obtain a break from the past (as a dictatorship) the then socialist government had to demonstrate ideological differences from the West and reflect a foreign policy stance independent of the sphere of influence of any external power (we are part of the EC/Western identity, but we still have our own Eastern identity). Little thought was given to the likely consequences of an isolated position within the EC framework. This was a deliberately different policy stance that was aimed at a sharp contrast with Greece's European partners: an 'us' and 'them' position. Greece's nationalist behaviour, its confrontational attitude and its pursuit of national gains can be better understood through an identity lens which uncovers Greek attitudes and actions in policy-making contexts.

Understanding Greece's position on EU foreign policy requires looking beneath the surface of policies expressed or enacted and searching for the identity factors that shaped and still shape Greek positions, actions, attitudes and policy stances. During August 1981, Egypt and Israel signed a protocol that led to US responsibility for the organisation of a multinational force and observers (MFO) to monitor the Sinai Peninsula for the withdrawal of Israeli forces as part of the Camp David process. The US was keen to include the EC in the MFO, but agreement could not be reached partly because Greece disagreed as the MFO was not acceptable to the Arabs. The Greek position can be attributed, through an identity lens, to its long-standing amiable relationship with the Arabs. Moreover, a pro-Arab position meant an anti-American stance. Greece thereby blocked a common European action within the European Political Co-operation (EPC) and was not prepared to compromise its pro-Arab position. Beneath Greece's ideological and domestic political reasons for obstructing common European positions lie identity issues that one cannot ignore.

Again in 1982, during the Falklands crisis, Greece took a position in favour of Argentina and condemned the UK's use of force, requesting instead a peaceful settlement of the dispute. Through the Greek identity lens, this conflict was perceived as an expression of the colonial power of the West. Its foreign policy position was thus dominated by ideological concerns. A further example of Greece's unco-operative position on EU foreign policy was when Greece responded negatively to the Council's attempt to agree to a reduction of the Community's imports from the Soviet Union, following the situation in Poland at the beginning of the 1980s, where the EC members feared a Soviet Union response similar to that of Prague in 1968. The Greeks insisted that the Soviet block was simply reacting against the capitalist West from a political position of socialism. In this case, Greece chose not to identify itself with the West's ideology of the market economy. There was no particular benefit for Greece from such attitude: on the contrary, it created a very negative image of Greece in the Community. During its first presidency, in the second half of 1983, Greece once again successfully blocked any common European condemnation of the Soviet Union, just after the Korean Airline (KAL) was shot down.[5] This, of course, created anger amongst its EC partners who wanted to make an official declaration expressing the deep distress of the Ten members for the destruction of the aircraft and the loss of human life. The Soviet Union was not mentioned in the lukewarm EPC declaration that followed (Kavakas, 2001). The fact that Greece had used its power of veto was seen not only as an abuse of the institutional powers of the presidency, but also as a path that Greece used to avoid the development of a common position by the Community. These attitudes positioned Greece at the margins of EC decision making, at the same time as the very same attitudes were celebrated in the domestic arena. This is a good example of how Greek national identity always supersedes any collective identity, such as that of the then EC. The result has been a frequent reference to Greece as the 'awkward partner' within the EU.

The above examples illustrate how a focus on identity is important in enhancing our understanding of Greece's role in EU foreign policy. In several of the cases highlighted here, Greece appears to act more from a particular understanding of what is appropriate given its identity, than for example from a rational and strategic assessment of the material benefits of a particular course of action. Likewise, in the area of common action on international terrorism, the Greek position might be better understood if we take the issue of identity into consideration. For example, during the 1980s, suspect evidence emerged of the existence of 'state sponsored terrorism' and the suspect states were marked as Libya and Syria. Consensus on a common position on international terrorism was not easy since the then Twelve members could harm their relations with the Arab world if they gave in to American pressure. In 1986, Greece refused to agree on the imposition of diplomatic restrictions on Syria. This went down well with the domestic pro-Arab public and ensured that Greek–Syrian neighbourly relations were upheld and not disrupted. Initially Greece had blocked the consensus in the EPC. When the publicity had faded, Greece applied the common agreed measures (Nuttall, 1997).

Greece's special relations with Syria and Libya found their way into a 'black list' of the State Department in the late 1980s, with Athens airport marked as a high-risk target for terrorist activities. From an identity point of view, the Arab states pose no threat to Greece, while Western positions are often treated with suspicion and contempt.

In the beginning of the 1990s, Greece was faced with disputes with all its neighbours. Apart from Turkey, its relations with Croatia fell apart when it declared itself as pro-Serb. This created a negative image for the EU, since Greece was at that time holding the Presidency. During the Gulf War, the new right-wing government was keen to show a different position on EU foreign policy than its previous socialist government. The latter, then in opposition, was quick to attack the government and its alliance with 'American imperialism'.

During the Yugoslav crisis, Greece was the only pro-Serbian member-state in the EU – relating to its Balkan consciousness. This contributed to the failure of a collective European strategy on the crisis.[6] The inability of the then Twelve members to respond to these events led to national responses to the conflict (Regelsberger et al., 1997). Following the eventual development of a joint action in the Balkans in the later months of 1993, Greece took a nationalist stand by imposing its embargo on Macedonia in 1994. In the context of a nationalist regional conflict, this stance by one of its members obviously complicated the EU's position. The embargo (imposed when Greece held the Presidency of the European Council) was extremely damaging for Greece's reputation amongst its EU partners. However, it reflects the strong Greek belief in their right to have control over their own foreign policy. This is what the 'substance' of Greek identity is all about: the fall of the military regime in Greece, the transition to democracy and the underlying anti-imperialist stance reiterate the importance of identity factors.

The significance of Greek identity issues was further illustrated in the more recent challenge posed by the controversy over the name of the Former Yugoslav Republic of Macedonia (FYROM). Around mid-1991, Greece was faced with the prospect of having as its northern border an independent Slav-Macedonian state. The new state was perceived as a threat to Greek national security. In terms of an identity perspective, this threat consisted of the lack of recognition of the existence of a Macedonian minority in Greece by the latter and the lack of recognition of the existence of a separate Macedonian national identity. This would be far too challenging for the cohesiveness of the Greek national identity. Such a Macedonian identity would threaten the sense of Greekness. Greeks believe that the Macedonian name is part of their historical heritage and should therefore not be used to identify another nation. The EC members did not offer immediate diplomatic recognition to the new state, in the hope of understanding the Greek position and to demonstrate solidarity with their partner. During February 1992, Thessaloniki experienced a huge rally reflecting a nationalist hysteria in Greek society. This rally symbolised strong identity claims as in the slogan 'No recognition of the Skopian Republic under the Hellenic name Macedonia'. Eventually, Greece found itself in an awkward position (reflecting its ambivalent identity) when it had to agree to financial aid to Turkey in exchange for Community support on the Macedonian issue.

Greek identity is constructed through the constant threat felt from Turkey, (in particular since the 'occupation' of northern Cyprus in 1974). Hence Greece usually holds very strong positions on any EU policy relating to Turkey, their historical 'enemy'. The substance of Greek identity conditions the perceptions of Greek policy makers and the Greek elite within the context of the EU CFSP. The persistent differentiation of Greek positions from the common European position on foreign policy has led to Greece's isolation from the other EU member states, which in turn hardens nationalist sentiments reflected in Greek national foreign policy-making. Greece's lack of enthusiasm and lack of constructive participation in successful CFSP initiatives within the EU have generated a particular negative reputation for Greece. Because of its identity priorities, the Greek position has often opposed the development of an EU CFSP. During the negotiations for the Single European Act (SEA), Greece finally agreed to sign the Treaty. During this process, Greece requested a guarantee of CFSP involvement in the event of a future dispute with Turkey.

This creates a rather ambivalent scenario for the rest of the EU member states. On the one hand, Greece takes an isolationist position and refuses to participate in any EU foreign policy co-ordinated effort; on the other hand, it seeks to Europeanise certain foreign policy issues: a position which reflects the ambivalence in Greek identity. Greek inwardness does not go down well with the other EU member states, in particular because Greece is already associated with the 'Southern' member states like Spain and Portugal and with the 'small' states like The Netherlands and Belgium, positions not of great strength within the EU framework. If Greece is neither Europeanist nor internationalist, maintaining Greekness comes at some costs: the creation of a negative Greek image amongst the rest of the member states and the loss of influence. This explains the failure of Greece to influence the inclusion of a clause on external borders in the final Treaty of the SEA and again in its demands of accession in the Western European Union (WEU) in Maastricht. Moreover, to its dismay, Turkey was given the status of observer in the WEU and the Greek–Turkish conflict was excluded from the amendment to Article 5 of the Brussels Pact that guaranteed members' territorial integrity. Greece's threat from Turkey was addressed later in Amsterdam, where one of the stated objectives of the CFSP was amended to include the issue of external borders (Kavakas, 2001).

Elements of Change

Upon realisation that EU membership can actually benefit Greece, there have been signs of slight changes in the opposition stance Greece has taken so far with regards to EU foreign policy. This might suggest that there has nevertheless been a process of Europeanisation of Greek national and foreign policies and that interaction within a European framework over time has contributed to strengthen the European or Western dimension to Greece's identity. As a consequence, Greece's image in the eyes of the other member states has also improved and with this, Greece's ability to have a say in EU foreign policy-making. Domestic politics and party political differences have also contributed to this development, as the Simitis government's determination to turn Greece into a committed European member state encouraged a pro-integrationist position on EU foreign policy. From a position of anti-West (anti-enemy) attitudes, Greece has slowly been moving towards becoming an actively engaged foreign policy partner.

In the spring of 1996, Turkey openly expressed its doubts about Greek sovereignty over a group of small Aegean islands, particularly the islets of Imia (for Greece)/Kardak (for Turkey). Greece's disengagement from the islets strengthened its image in Europe at the expense of criticism raised within Greece itself. But with regards to Greece's position on the EU's foreign policy, this proved a new development and provided the opportunity for a constructive role for Greece in building a secure and peaceful region around the Continent. Greece also played a positive role in the summer of 1996 when it mediated in the signing of a peace treaty and exchange of diplomatic missions between Yugoslavia and Croatia. This is where Greece feels more at ease, since the Balkans is a familiar area and 'closer to home'. Because of its strong Balkan identity, this was an issue that Greece could relate to and have an impact on.

After many periods when Greece's influence in Europe was drastically compromised, the recent Iraqi crisis gave the Greek presidency (January to June 2003) a further opportunity to have a say in EU foreign policy. In light of the split in Europe on this crisis and the growing anti-war demonstrations across Europe and the rest of the world, Greece called for a summit in Brussels. In a bold manner, Greece warned that failure to reach a consensus on European policy towards Iraq would plunge the EU into 'deep crisis'. A Greek government official was quoted as saying '[W]e will have a statement on which everyone can agree' (*Guardian*, 2003). It seems that Greece is now more prepared and willing to enter into the European mould and not keeping back from common positions on EU foreign policy. Greece was keen to have all 15 members endorse what they hoped would be a form of words that all members could agree on. This was very important for Greece's position on the EU platform, especially following the famous letter signed by eight European leaders (UK, Spain, Italy, Denmark, Portugal and three of the eight from the 10 candidate EU states – Poland, Hungary and the Czech Republic) in support of the US on military intervention in Iraq, which set up a clear foreign policy split. France and Germany led Greece together with Belgium, Luxembourg and Austria in condemning the 'letter of the eight'.

As the holder of the Union's rotating presidency during the first half of 2003, this pro-American letter gave Greece a challenge and, some might argue, forced Greek embarrassment since it has traditionally opted for an anti-American stance. Apart from those who signed the letter published by Tony Blair, no other current EU leader was asked to sign except the prime minister of The Netherlands, who declined.

The Greek position should not come as a surprise since anti-Americanism is a long-standing identity stance. The letter was a blow for Greece (as holder of the presidency), since it undermined solidarity across the Continent and since the initiative was launched without consultation with Greece.

Upon assuming the EU presidency on 1 January 2003, Greece knew that its turn would be dominated by the Iraqi crisis, but the reality has proven just how tough it was. Due to its historical good relations with the Arab world, George Papandreou, the foreign minister, planned to visit Syria, Jordan, Egypt and Saudi Arabia in an effort to seek regional support for a peaceful solution (before the war broke out). This could be done knowing that Greece has a positive image in this part of the world. It is interesting to note here that Greece did not plan to send a representative to Turkey, its arch rival and the only NATO member with a land border with Iraq.

In its struggle to gain a positive image within the EU's framework, this crisis could not have come at a worse time. At least Greece could comfort itself that for a change it found itself in the 'doves' (anti-American) camp with

France, Germany, Belgium, Luxembourg and Austria. Russia's support for France and Germany also triggered historical sentiments for Greece as a close ally of the former Soviet Union. Also, this time round, it was not Greece that kept the EU's CFSP from being effective.

Conclusion

This chapter has focused on the identity factors, as one set of explanatory factors, among many others, that underline the various controversial actions of Greece within the EU's foreign policy. Situated between the East and the West, the ambivalence in Greek identity is mirrored in Greece's interactions with its EU partners in foreign policy decisions. Looking to the East, Greece prides itself on its Byzantine traditions as well as its Orthodox heritage. The West, on the other hand, has always served as a political as well as a cultural reference point for Greek aspirations to building democracy. Greece's efforts to differentiate itself from common European positions can be better understood against this background.

However, identities are fluid and malleable. They are constantly constructed and reconstructed through communicative processes. Greek policy has slowly changed and moved Greece from its reputation as the awkward EU partner. The recent changes in Greece's position on the EU's foreign policy may arguably reflect a more confident Greece within the EU context. They may also suggest, however, that over time, participation in the CFSP has contributed to strengthening the European and Western dimension of Greece's identity.

Notes

1. The European Community (EC) refers to the European Coal and Steel Community (ECSC) founded in 1951, the European Economic Community (EEC) and the European Atomic Energy Community (Euratom), both founded in 1957, or, in a loose sense to the 'first pillar', once the term European Union (EU) was introduced by the Maastricht Treaty on European Union of 1992. Events prior to the Maastricht Treaty are referred to using the acronym EC, while events following the said Treaty are referred to using the acronym EU (Wallace and Wallace, 2000).
2. The European Political Co-operation (EPC) was established in 1970, while events from 1993 are referred to using the CFSP acronym.
3. There are other factors which may help us understand anti-Western sentiments in Greece. These include the clash between the Duce's Italy and Greece in 1940, the occupation of Greece by Hitler's Germany during World War Two, the perception in Greece of the British as one party of the main culprits of the Civil War (1946–49) in what immediately turned into a Cold War confrontation between the West and the USSR, the US's toleration of the regime of the colonels (1967–74) for which Clinton publicly apologised during his visit to Greece in 1999, and the West being seen in Greece as tolerating the

'occupation' of northern Cyprus ever since 1974. Many thanks to Plamen Tonchev for pointing these out to me.

4. Obviously, there were also domestic political reasons for Greece's sceptical view to the outside world.

5. "In this tragedy, 269 people were killed when the Soviets shot down a Korean Air 747 that strayed over its airspace. The plane was shot down without warning on a flight from New York to Seoul, Korea. The Soviets claimed that the plane was flying on a spy mission. In fact, however, the actions of the Soviets were a horrible accident."

(Source: http://www.multied.com/dates/1982.html)

6. The Great Powers also had clear national priorities in this crisis.

References

Blinkhorn, M. and Veremis, T. (eds) (1990) *Modern Greece: Nationalism and Nationality.* Athens: ELIAMEP.

Clogg, R. (1986) *A Short History of Modern Greece.* Cambridge: Cambridge University Press.

Clogg, R. (1993) *Greece, 1981–89: The Populist Decade.* Basingstoke: Macmillan.

Fatouros, A.A. (1993) 'Political and institutional facets of Greece's integration in the European Community', in H.J. Psomiades and S.B. Thomadakis (eds), *Greece, the New Europe, and the Changing International Order.* New York, NY: Pella. pp. 23–56.

Guardian (2003) 'EU summit set for stalemate', 17 February. Available on http://www.guardian.co.uk/international/story/0,3604,897454,00.html.

Kavakas, D. (2001) *Greece and Spain in European Foreign Policy: The Influence of Southern Member States in Common Foreign and Security Policy.* Aldershot: Ashgate.

Lipowatz, T. (1994) 'Split Greek identity and the issue of nationalism', in N. Demertzis (ed.), *Greek Political Culture Today.* Athens: Odysseas. pp. 115–32.

Nuttall, S. (1997) 'Two decades of EPC performance', in E. Regelsberger, P. de Schoutheete and W. Wessels (eds), *Foreign Policy of the European Union: From EPC to CFSP and Beyond.* Boulder, CO and London: Lynne Rienner. pp. 19–39.

Pace, M. (2001) 'Rethinking the Mediterranean. Reality and re-presentation in the creation of a "region"'. PhD dissertation. University of Portsmouth, UK.

Regelsberger, E., de Schoutheete, P. and Wessels, W. (eds) (1997) *Foreign Policy of the European Union: From EPC to CFSP and Beyond.* Boulder, CO and London: Lynne Rienner.

Tsoucalas, C. (1993) 'Greek national identity in an integrated Europe and changing world order', in H.J. Psomiadis and S.B. Thomadakis (eds), *Greece, the New Europe and the Changing International Order.* New York: Pella. pp. 57–78.

Wallace, H. and Wallace, W. (2000) *Policy-Making in the European Union.* Oxford: Oxford University Press.

15 Human Rights: The European Charter of Fundamental Rights

Agustín José Menéndez*

Human rights concerns did not traditionally shape states' foreign policy. International relations were considered to be the realm where *national interests* were struggled and occasionally fought for. Only after the Second World War, with the emergence of individuals as subjects of international law (Aufricht, 1943) and the proclamation of international treaties dealing with fundamental rights, did it make sense to consider the issue of foreign policy *and* human rights. Relations between European states were until then plagued by wars. Moreover, European states indulged in colonialism and economic exploitation of non-European countries (Hobsbawm, 1989; Wesseling, 2002; Manceron, 2003; Said, 1995; Chomsky, 1991).

In 1945, it was widely perceived that relations between European states should be placed on a new footing (this led to European integration) and that relations with non-European countries could no longer be based on old-style colonialism. *Respect for human rights* was perceived as a potential founding stone of both new departures, whatever the motivation behind such a choice. One of the consequences was that human rights were an essential ingredient of the *identity* of the European Communities since its inception. This was so to the extent that accession to the Communities was conditioned upon respect for human rights *and* that the member states willingly promoted their image as a *'pouvoir civilisateur'* (Duchêne, 1972) in their foreign relations (even if not often for high-minded reasons, critics such as Galtung, 1973, 1975 might say).

At any rate, the rights identity of the European Communities facilitated the later re-characterisation of fundamental rights as a policy objective of the European Union (EU) in its own right. As things stand, fundamental rights have moved from an implicit goal of European integration to one of its allegedly forefront policies. This evolution has come about in a fragmentary and convoluted way. On the one hand, the EC intensified the conditions for membership and rendered explicit the requirement to comply with democratic and fundamental rights standards; moreover, EC legislation was subject to fundamental rights standards as the Court of Justice 'found' an unwritten general principle of fundamental rights protection. On the other hand, the EU has become increasingly confident (despite some eventual difficulties) in the convenience of using its trade, diplomatic and aid policies to what is perceived as promotion of the protection of human rights in third countries (Menéndez, 2002).

Academics have concentrated on two aspects of the role of rights in the external relations of the EU. Some have aimed at testing the sincerity and coherence of the rhetorical statements (King, 1999; Smith, 2001; Clapham, 2001; Youngs, 2002). Others, relying on the well-known academic literature on *conditionality*, have focused on the increasing tribute paid to rights in the drafting of trade agreements with third countries (Smith, 1998; Ward, 1999).

This chapter explores the impact that the Charter of Fundamental Rights of the European Union might have in the foreign policy of the EU. Although not formally incorporated, it is argued in the first part of this chapter that the Charter is legally binding. In the second part of the chapter it is suggested that under such circumstances, the Charter will play a major role in *testing* the democratic credentials of applicant countries, and also of member states. In the third part it is suggested that it might also dissipate the remaining doubts concerning the *competence* of the EU to tie its emerging foreign policy to rights standards. This chapter makes the further claim that such a development is to be seen as 'crowning' the slow process of emergence of rights as *the* fundamental principle of the European legal order, not as a *radical* departure.

A caveat: the rights turn of the EU does not *in itself* ensure that the political and economic action of the EU will actually promote human rights. The proclamation of the Charter of Fundamental Rights does not change the world until it is acted upon as a standard of behaviour. But one should not forget that the endorsement of the Charter implies that the institutions endorsing it raise a claim to comply with the action standards that the Charter establishes. Such a claim can be used *against* the institutions themselves when assessing their own rights record. The proclamation of the Charter is a speech-act, through which the institutions of the EU gave life to such a critical claim.[1] Moreover, and contrary to the vulgar realist understanding, fundamental rights standards should be regarded as critical standards that citizens can use in order to challenge the abuses of power by public institutions when they do not comply with their own commitments (Arendt, 1972). Speech, sometimes, is action, and words bind in a normative sense. The Charter provides European citizens with a clear set of standards that can be used in order to assess critically the actual performance of the EU and its member states. Thus, the key importance of the Charter is to be found in its actual use by human rights activists both within and outside the EU. The 'mere document' becomes a source of power when citizens become aware that it embodies basic principles of practical reason that reinforce – not undermine – the position of those 'at the wrong end of the guns'. At the same time, the articulation of the fundamental rights at the basis of the

EU constrains the ability of the EU institutions to use human rights concerns 'instrumentally' or 'selectively', by means of rendering more difficult an incoherent definition of the fundamental rights implications of concrete factual situations. It is in this specific sense, as an empowering document for critics, that the rise of fundamental rights cannot be reduced to a mere power play or a window-dressing exercise (Mitchell and Schoeffel, 2002: 3–4; Schoultz, 1981: 155).

The Charter as Binding Law

The need for a bill of rights of European citizens can be traced back to the uneasy standing of fundamental rights within EC law (Cassese et al., 1991). While the original six member states included some form of bill of rights in their constitutions, the original Treaties establishing the European Communities did not contain many specific references to fundamental rights.[2] The undesirability of such a state of affairs became crystal clear when the scope of EC law started to go beyond that of the legal order of a customs union. A clear tension emerged between the *supremacy* of EC law and the lack of human rights standards internal to the EC legal system. The European Court of Justice (ECJ) alleviated such friction by means of arguing that the general principle of protection of fundamental rights was one of the basic founding principles of EC law, and thus claiming that the tension was internal to EC law (Cassese et al., 1991). Even if legal scholarship has tended to praise the jurisprudence of the ECJ, the purely *jurisprudential* character of fundamental rights protection was problematic. First, it is far from clear whether the authors of the catalogue of rights of European citizens should be judges. Second, the concrete formula adopted by the ECJ to 'incorporate' fundamental rights in EC law has revealed its shortcomings with the passing of time – to the extent that the protection of whatever right could be subsumed under the 'general principle of rights protection', the result has been the implicit granting of the same constitutional status to *all* rights. The protection of all rights in the same level is not necessarily promoting individual autonomy, and at any rate, is not what takes place in national constitutional traditions. To consider one example: if the right to private property is granted the same status and force as the right to personal freedom, this might result in the impingement of basic social and economic rights. This prompted many attempts at drawing a bill of rights for the EU. A renovated effort towards such an objective was agreed in the Cologne European Council of June 1999 (Council, 1999a). At the Tampere European Council, a specific and representative body was nominated to that effect, and its basic rules of procedure were established (Council, 1999b). Against some odds, the 'body', which had renamed itself 'Convention' (Charter 4105/00: 3), concluded its works in less than one year.

The resulting Charter of Fundamental Rights of the European Union spells out the civic, political and social rights that European citizens are said to acknowledge each other. Inspired by the principle of indivisibility of rights, the Charter proclaims not only civic and political rights, but also 'rights to solidarity', which comprise what is usually referred to as social and economic rights.

The three main institutions of the EU (the European Parliament, the Commission and the Council) *solemnly proclaimed* the Charter of Fundamental Rights of the European Union in December 2000. This action might be interpreted as confining the text to the condition of a mere 'political declaration' without legal bite. However, a proper legal analysis of the Charter makes it clear that it is legally binding. First, any European plaintiff could argue his or her case by reference to the fundamental rights recognised within EU law before the Charter was proclaimed. The Charter should not be an obstacle to the plaintiff's right to keep on arguing his or her case on the said body of law. To put it briefly, the Charter should not undermine already existing rights. Second, the Charter Convention was given a mandate to consolidate the existing EU law of fundamental rights, not to change or amend it. If this is so, the Charter is at the very least the best evidence of the already existing EC fundamental rights. Or to put it differently, the *legal authority* of the Charter would be based not on its formal incorporation into community law, but on its character as *authoritative consolidation* of existing law.

This is reflected in the emerging practice of the Court of First Instance and of the Advocates General of the Court of Justice. The Court of First Instance has already invoked the Charter of Rights as legal authority in two judgments (T-54/99; T-77/01). Moreover, most of the Advocates General of the Court of Justice have referred to the Charter of Rights in their Opinions. By April 2002, we could find the Charter being invoked in not less than twenty opinions.[3] Two of the said opinions are of special interest. In *Unión de Pequeños Agricultores*, the Charter was used as additional evidence to ground the right to access to courts (C-50/00). In *Booker Acquaculture*, Advocate General, Mischo invoked the Charter as additional evidence that the right to private property, according to EC law, did not entail the right to the payment of compensation in case the authorities destroy property to prevent the outbreak of an animal disease. What should be noted in this opinion is that the Advocate General added some major reflections on the democratic qualities of the process through which the Charter was drafted:

> I know that the Charter is not legally binding, but it is worthwhile referring to it given that it constitutes the expression, at the highest level, of a democratically established consensus on what must today be considered as the catalogue of fundamental rights guaranteed by the Community legal order. (Opinion of the AG joined cases C-20/00 and C-64/00)

The emergent practice of referring to the Charter as a legal authority also seems to be followed by the other institutions of the EU, especially the EC and the European Parliament. A non-exhaustive search in Eur-Lex, the legal database of the European Union resulted in more than 200 acts of the institutions in which reference was made to the Charter. As of 1 April 2002, 10 proposed regulations and 20 proposed directives contained references to the Charter. Almost 20 resolutions of the Parliament invoked the Charter, while Members of the European Parliament (MEPs) made reference to the Charter in more than 50 written questions.

The Charter as the Standard of Democracy

It was an implicit but clear rule that the 'Little Europes' of the Coal and Steel and the Economic Communities could admit *only* democratic states that respected human rights. This might have been partially obscured by the fact that Articles 98 TECSC, 237 TEC and 205 TECEA subjected membership to the *European condition* of the applicant country. However, the concept of 'European' was never understood merely in a geographical sense, but in a *normative* sense. The EC Institutions were *European* to the extent that they abode by the ideal of the rule of law and respect of human rights. This was finally clarified by the Birkelbach Report, elaborated by the Assembly in late 1961 (Assemblée Parlementaire, 1962).

The interpretation of Article 237 TEC provided in the Birkelbach Report was implemented in 1962. Franco's Minister of Foreign Affairs Castiella filed the Spanish application for membership on 9 February. The request was merely acknowledged and the EC did not open accession negotiations (Guirao, 1997).

Thus, the identity of *Little Europe* as a *project* of integration was markedly different from that of the *free trade area* of EFTA, which could accept Salazar's Portugal as full member, and the then *socialist* block of the COMECON, where civic and political rights were dismissed as petit-burgeois prejudices. It was also different from NATO, which had Turkey and Portugal as members. Only the Council of Europe shared this *democratic* identity with Little Europe.

The *human rights* requirement has been symbolically marked before or immediately after the conclusion of enlargement processes. The accession of Denmark, Ireland and the UK was followed by the Copenhagen resolution on European identity (Council, 1973). The Southern enlargement to Greece, Spain and Portugal was preceeded by the 1977 inter-institutional declaration on the protection of fundamental rights (Commission; Council and European Parliament, 1977). The negotiation of the European Economic Area and the enlargement to Sweden, Finland and Austria revived the debate over the accession of the EU to the European Convention of Human Rights. The Eastern enlargement was given an original impulse with the establishment of the so-called 'Copenhagen criteria', a set of standards based on Articles 6 and 49 TEU (Council, 1993).

One can speculate that the openly democratic identity of Little Europe stemmed from the traumatic experience of the Second World War or from the harrowing realities of the Cold War. The need to *recycle* national identities too closely associated with the colonial past might also have played a role. Whatever the foundation, what is clear is that the original six member states raised the claim[4] that theirs was a community based on democracy and the rule of law. This self-image seems to have been relevant in the further strengthening of fundamental rights standards within EC law.

Candidate countries

As EC law stands, accession to membership of the EC is subject to the candidate state being democratic and respectful of basic human rights. This rule, in place from the founding of the EC, is now spelled out in Articles 6(1) and 49 TEU. As a matter of law, these articles set strict conditions for admission, not open to be modified by the accession treaty itself. Such an unconditional status is not shared by the four economic freedoms, regarding which transitory arrangements and temporary exceptions can be agreed in the accession treaty itself (Becker, 2001).

It seems pretty safe to argue that the Charter of Rights, whether or nor formally implemented, would become the reference document in order to determine what Articles 6 and 49 TEU require. This does not mean that it would dispense with reference to the other sources of human rights law, but it would play a central role as the best evidence of European law on fundamental rights. This conclusion is supported by present practice. The Commission Strategy Report for 2001 and all the 12 national reports include an open reference to the Charter of Rights. These documents emphasise the EU's commitment to the protection of fundamental rights (Commission, 2001c: 10).

Member states

The catalogue of rights elaborated by the ECJ on the basis of the 'common constitutional traditions' can only be invoked *vis-à-vis* EC secondary legislation and national legislation that implements EC secondary legislation or that claims an exception to the latter. The same applies to the Charter (Charter 4105/00: Article 51). However, this does not mean that member states are not bound by EC fundamental rights. First, the fact that EC standards are derived from the 'common constitutional traditions' implies a substantial resemblance between national and EC standards, even if with marginal differences galore. Second, Article 7 TEU has formalised the obligation of member states to respect EC fundamental rights in order to retain membership in the EU. The said provision states such an obligation and prescribes the suspension of the rights 'deriving from the application of this Treaty to the member state in question' in case of a serious and persistent breach of fundamental rights in a member state. Thus, Article 7 TEU establishes the competence ground for EC institutions to check whether member states are actually protecting fundamental rights *nationally*.

Authoritative commentators argued that such an obligation would require developing 'a methodology and guidelines for dealing' with potential breaches of the obligation (Alston and Weiler, 1999: 40). The Austrian crisis revealed the correctness of such analysis. For our present purposes, it must be noted that the informal 'sanctions' agreed by the remaining 14 member states in 1999 were lifted after a report of three 'wise men' who scrutinised human rights issues in Austria. The 'wise men' made quite extensive use of the Charter of Rights.[5] This is good evidence that the Charter can be seen as providing detailed guidelines on what concerns the application of Article 7 TEU. The European Parliament has started to work in this direction. Stemming from its institutional compromise to regard the Charter as binding (European Parliament, 2000a, 2000b, 2001), the European Parliament has decided to initiate a practice of annual reporting on the protection of fundamental rights in the EU. The reports will follow, article by article, the structure of the Charter (European Parliament, 2001) and will consider developments in the EU institutions and in all member states. At the same time, the Parliament has called upon the Commission and the Council to establish the appropriate institutional arrangements to prevent violations of rights and to handle conflictual situations under Article 7 TEU.

Fundamental Rights as a Frame of Reference for Foreign Policy

The coming of age of fundamental rights within EC law has led to a simultaneous strengthening of the external dimension of rights. This has resulted in the use of European bargaining power in international trade relations to foster respect for fundamental rights abroad. Such a tendency, already present in the late 1970s (Simma et al., 1999: 575), became a pattern in the late 1980s and early 1990s.

This led to the emergence of human rights protection as an essential goal of European development policy. As a consequence, the EC institutions have undertaken positive measures to foster fundamental rights in third countries, such as monitoring elections or assisting non-governmental organisations (NGOs) in the forging of a pluralist society (Simma et al., 1999: 595–614). It also resulted in the 'human rights' clause becoming standard content of all trade agreements established with third countries at the very least since 1995. The clause defines respect for human rights and democracy as 'essential elements' of the bilateral relationship between the EU and the given third country.[6]

However, such policy has been handicapped by the lack of a clear competence base, by the lack of adequate guidelines and criteria on what standards should be respected, and by the lack of an adequate institutional structure to implement it. Until the Treaty of Amsterdam, no Treaty provision established a clear-cut competence of the EU or the EC on human rights.[7] This was not interpreted as an obstacle to the pursuit of human rights objectives within the areas of competence of the EC, as it was explicitly or implicitly argued that such competence should be coextensive with the general competence of the EC (Alston and Weiler, 1999: 23). However, the only legal basis of some of the human rights programmes was their inclusion in the EC budget (Simma et al., 1999: 575).

Opinion 2/94, concerning the accession of the EC to the European Convention on Human Rights,[8] led to a first wave of restrictive interpretations of the EC's competence on human rights matters. Although the reasoning of the Court seems to focus on the question of whether the existing EC institutions can on their own decide accession to the Convention or whether only the direct intervention of member states is necessary, the strict wording of some of its paragraphs has fostered a restrictive interpretation of the general competence of the EC on the matter (Alston and Weiler, 1999: 24–5). Moreover, the judgment on the case *United Kingdom and Ireland v. Commission*,[9] further questioned the legal basis for some of the measures adopted by the EC concerning the fostering of rights protection in external action.

The Charter of rights and the Chartering process might help appeasing concerns about the appropriate legal basis for the EU's emphasis on human rights in its external action. First, the doubts about the competence of the EU to promote human rights through its trade policy and through expenditure, already weakened after the entry into force of the Amsterdam Treaty,[10] should be definitely set aside by the Charter, given its *procedural democratic qualities*. The facts that the decision to establish the Charter was taken by the 'masters of the Treaties' (Council, 1999a: para. 44) and that the Convention was a highly representative institution reinforce the argument that the competence of the EU on fundamental rights matters must be coextensive with its general competence.[11] Hints of this are already to be found in the Communication from the Commission on the EU's role in promoting human rights and democratisation in third countries (Commission, 2001a) and the related Council Conclusions of 25 June 2001 (Council, 2001a).

The 'revamping' of the EU's foreign policy has already been translated into further, more specific guidelines. The Council has produced its 'Guidelines on Human Rights Dialogue' (Council, 2001b). The Commission has presented a Communication on EU Election Assistance and Observation (Commission, 2000) and on conflict prevention (Commission 2001b). As was already indicated, the Cotonou agreement with the African, Caribbean and Pacific (ACP) states of 23 June 2000 has extended the human rights clause to a multilateral setting.[12]

Moreover, the Charter is likely to become the central benchmark in assessing compliance with fundamental rights by third countries. The Commission has already expressed its commitment to such a move (Commission, 2001a). This will have an impact on the drafting of the country and regional Strategy papers.

Finally, as has been indicated, the European Parliament has already argued that the Charter of Rights should be matched by appropriate specific institutional arrangements, such as the nomination of a Commissioner in charge of fundamental rights issues and the companion institutional decisions.

Conclusion

In this chapter, it has been argued that the solemn proclamation of the Charter of Fundamental Rights in December 2000 is not deprived of implications for the development of the EU's foreign policy.

No matter how solemn a proclamation is, it cannot be equated with the formal incorporation of the Charter into primary EC law. However, the Charter is legally binding even if not incorporated, due to the fact that it does not represent a departure from existing EC law, but the consolidation of existing law. The Charter stands as a repository of evidence for legal actors. This has resulted in the growing practice of Advocates General of the Court of Justice invoking the Charter in order to support their arguments. Although the Court of Justice itself has not followed suit (for the time being), the Court of First Instance has called upon the Charter in two judgments. As such practice becomes consolidated, it constitutes a reason *on its own* to claim that the Charter has legal bite.

The particular status of the Charter allows us to understand the increasing use that EC institutions are making of it. The democratic credentials of member states are being checked against the 'Copenhagen criteria', now further spelled out and clarified by the Charter, as the annual reports show. Moreover, Article TEU 7, regarding the situation of fundamental rights in member states, is starting to be *operationalised* in the Annual Report of the European Parliament, which monitors each and every right contained in the Charter. The Parliament has called on the Commission and the Council to establish the appropriate institutional structure to ensure screening of both EC institutions and member states. Finally, the Charter might contribute to dissipate the persistent doubts about the competence of the EU to promote fundamental rights through its foreign and trade policies.

The solemn proclamation of rights does not guarantee their actual compliance. Die-hard 'realistic' critics can safely argue that the Charter is in itself a mere piece of paper. But the proclamation of the Charter can be regarded both as a 'speech-act' through which the institutions of the EU claim to be bound to its content (something of which citizens can remind them) and as a set of action standards that those suffering human rights violations can rely on. Pieces of paper are rather powerful, especially bills of rights, when citizens take them in their own hands. Despite its (numerous) shortcomings, the Charter has a potential to enhance fundamental rights protection in Europe and to place rights as one of the major concerns of Europe in its relations with the rest of the world. This chapter has pointed to some embryonic developments in that direction.

Notes

* This chapter is a contribution to the CIDEL project co-ordinated by ARENA and financed by the Fifth Framework Programme of the European Commissions.

1 Human rights activists agree. See Suu Kyi, 1996 and Bové, 2001.

2 Leaving aside the right to non-discrimination on grounds of nationality (Article TEC 6) and the principle of equal pay for equal work (Article TEC 119).

3 A complete (and updated list) can be found at the Charter Watch webpage. Available at http://www.arena.uio.no/cidel/chtrwatch.html.

4 Raising a claim is not the same as redeeming it. The Algeria War or the Suez episode are good reminders of that.

5 The full text of this untitled report is available at http://www.virtual-institute. de/de/Bericht-EU/report.pdf. See paragraphs 8, 9 and 16 of the report.

6 More than 30 bilateral agreements including a human rights clause had been signed by May 1995. At such date, the Council reconsidered in a Decision the basic modalities of the clause. See Commission (1995). Since then, it has been included in all bilateral agreements, more than 20.

7 Paradoxically, Article J.1 (now 11) of the Treaty of the European Union referred to development and consolidation of democracy and the rule of law, and respect for human rights and fundamental freedoms among the objectives of the Common Foreign and Security Policy.

8 Opinion 2/94, Accession by the Communities to the Convention for the Protection of Human Rights and Fundamental Freedoms, [1996] ECR I-1759.

9 Case C-106/96, [1998] ECR I-2729.

10 Article F.2 TEU (now Article 6 TEU) established a clear basis for fundamental rights protection in Union law. On its basis, Council Regulations (EC) 975 and 976/1999 established the basic new legal framework for the promotion of human rights and democratisation through the Union's policy. See OJ L 120, of 8.5.1999, p.1ff. Moreover, the Council and the Commission adopted a Joint Statement on the European Community's development policy on 10 November 2000. See http://europa.eu.int/ comm/development/lex/en/ council20001110_en.htm. In addition, Article 13 TEC was amended. See also Council Directive 2000/43/EC, of 29 June 2000, implementing the principle of equal treatment irrespective of racial and ethnic origin, OJ L 180, of 19 July 2000, p. 13 and Council Directive 2000/78/EC, of 27 November 2000, establishing a general framework for combating discrimination on the grounds of religion and belief, disability, age or sexual orientation as regards employment and occupation, OJ L 303, of 2 December 2000, p. 16 have further specified Article TEC 13. This further spells out not only internal but external commitments of the institutions of the Union. See also the Declaration on the occasion of the 50th Anniversary of the Universal Declaration of Human Rights, of 10 December 1998. Available at http://ue.eu.int/Newsroom/ loadDoc.asp?max=21& bid=73&did=56499&grp=1541&lang=1.

11 The new Article TEC 181a provides a legal ground to extend the objective of promoting the respect of human rights and fundamental freedoms to all forms of co-operation with third countries, beyond pure development policy, as indicated in Article TEC 177.

12 See especially Article 9, section 2. See also Article 96 for dispute resolution. The text of the Agreement is available at http://europa.eu.int/comm/development/cotonou/pdf/agr01_en.pdf. A quick assessment can be found in Hilpold, 2002.

References

Advocate General, Opinion in joined cases C-20/00 and C-64/00 (2001) *Booker Aquaculture Ltd trading as Marine Harvest McConnell and Hydro Seafood GSP Ltd vs The Scottish Ministers*. Opinion delivered on 20 September 2001, not yet reported. Available at http://www.curia.eu.int/jurisp/ cgi-bin/gettext.pl?lang=en&num=79989079C19000020&doc=T&ouvert=T&seance=CONCL&where=(). AG Opinion in Par. 126 of the Opinion.

Advocate General, Opinion in case C-50/00 (2002) *Unión de Pequeños Agricultores v. Council of the European Union*. Opinion delivered on 21 March 2002, not yet reported. Available at http://www.curia.eu.int/jurisp/cgi-bin/gettext.pl? lang=en&num=79979678C19000050&doc=T&ouvert=T&seance=CONCL&where= (). AG Opinion in par. 39 of the Opinion.

Alston, P. and Weiler, J.H.H. (1999) 'An "ever closer union" in need of a human rights policy: the European Union and human rights', in P. Alston (ed.), *The EU and Human Rights*. Oxford: Oxford University Press.

Arendt, H. (1972) *Crises of the Republic*. New York, NY: Harcourt Brace Jovanovich.

Assemblée Parlamentaire Européenne (1962) 'Rapport de la Commission politique de l'Assemblée Parlamentaire Européenne sur les aspects politiques et institutionnels'. Document 122, Janvier 1962. *Archives of the European Communities*, 07.515:32;X3.075.15.

Aufricht, H. (1943) 'Personality in international law', *American Political Science Review*, 37 (April): 217–43.

Becker, U. (2001) 'EU-enlargements and limits to amendments of the EC treaty'. Jean Monnet Working Paper, 15/01, available at http://www.jeanmonnetprogram.org.

Bové, J. (2001) 'A farmers' international?', *New Left Review*, 12: 89–101.

Cassesse, A., Clapham, A. and Weiler, J.H.H. (1991) *Human Rights and the European Community: The Substantive Law*. Baden-Baden: Nomos.

Charter 4105/00 (2000) *Charter of the Fundamental Rights of the European Union*.

Chomsky, N. (1991) *501: The Conquest Continues*. Boston, MA: South End.

Clapham, A. (2001) 'On complementarity: human rights in the European legal orders', *Human Rights Law Journal*, 21 (8): 313–24.

Commission; Council and European Parliament (1977) 'Joint Declaration on the protection of fundamental rights', OJ C 103, of 27 April.

Commission (1995) 'The inclusion of respect for democratic principles and human rights in agreements between the Community and third states', COM (95) 216 final.

Commission (2000) 'Communication from the Commission on EU election assistance and observation', of 11 April.

Commission (2001a) 'Communication from the Commission to the Council and the European Parliament on "The European Union's role in promoting human rights and democratisation in third countries"', COM (2001) 252 final, 8 May.

Commission (2001b) 'Communication from the Commission on conflict prevention', of 11 April.

Commission (2001c) 'Making a success out of enlargement', available at http://europa.eu.int/comm/enlargement/report2001/strategy_en.pdf.

Council (1973) 'Document on European identity, adopted by the Ministers of Foreign Affairs of the member states of the European Communities', Bulletin EC 12–1973.

Council (1993) 'Presidency conclusions of the Copenhagen European Council', 21–22 June.

Council (1999a) 'Presidency conclusions of the Cologne European Council, 3–4 June 1999, European Council decision on the drawing up of a Charter of Fundamental Rights of the European Union'.

Council (1999b) 'Presidency conclusions of the Tampere European Council, 15 and 16 October 1999'.

Council (2001a) 'Council conclusions on the European Union's role in promoting human rights and democratisation in third countries', of 25 June.

Council (2001b) 'Council guidelines on human rights dialogue', of 13 December, available at http://europa.eu.int/comm/external_relations/human_rights/doc/ghd12_01.htm.

Duchêne, F. (1972) 'Europe in world peace', in R. Mayne (ed.), Europe Tomorrow: Sixteen Europeans Look Ahead. London: Fontana. pp. 32–49.

European Parliament (2000a) 'Resolution on the establishment of a Charter of Fundamental Rights', OJ C 54, of 25 February.

European Parliament (2000b) 'Resolution on the drafting of a European Charter of Fundamental Rights', OJ C 377, of 29 December.

European Parliament (2001) 'Report analysing the situation as regards fundamental rights in the European Union', Report A5-0223/2001.

Galtung, J. (1973) The European Community: A Superpower in the Making. London: George Allen.

Galtung, J. (1975) 'The Lomé Convention and neo-capitalism', Prio Papers, 20.

Guirao, F. (1997) 'Association or trade agreement? Spain and the EEC, 1947–64', Journal of European Integration History, 3 (1): 103–20.

Hilpold, P. (2002) 'EU development cooperation at a crossroads: The Contonou Agreement of 23 June 2000 and the principle of good governance', European Foreign Affairs Review, pp. 53–72.

Hobsbawm, E.J. (1989) The Age of Empire. London: Cardinal.

King, T. (1999) 'Human rights in European foreign policy: success or failure for post-modern democracy', European Journal of International Law, 10 (2): 313–37.

Manceron, G. (2003) Marianne et les Colonies: Une Introduction à l'Histoire Coloniale de la France. Paris:La Découverte.

Menéndez, A.J. (2002) 'Chartering Europe', Journal of Common Market Studies, 40 (3): 471–90.

Mitchell, P.R. and Schoeffel, J. (2002) Noam Chomsky: Understanding Power. New York, NY: The New Press.

Said, E. (1995) *Orientalism*. Harmondsworth: Penguin.

Schoultz, L. (1981) 'US foreign policy and human rights violations in Latin America: a comparative analysis of foreign aid distributions', *Comparative Politics*, 13 (2): 149–70.

Simma, B., Aschenbrenner, B. and Schulte, C. (1999) 'Human rights considerations in the development of co-operation activities of the EC', in P. Alston (ed.), *The EU and Human Rights*. Oxford: Oxford University Press. pp. 571–626.

Smith, K.E. (1998) 'The use of political conditionality in the EU's relations with third countries: how effective?', *European Foreign Affairs Review*, 2 (2): 253–74.

Smith, K.E. (2001) 'The EU, human rights and relations with third countries: "foreign policy" with an ethical dimension?' in K.E. Smith and M. Light (eds), *Ethics and Foreign Policy*. Cambridge: Cambridge University Press. pp. 185–203.

Suu Kyi, A.S. (1996) 'Towards a culture of peace and development', in H. Kung (ed.), *Yes to a Global Ethic*. New York, NY: Continuum. pp. 222–36.

T-54/99, *max.mobil Telecommunications Service GmbH v. Commission*, Judgment of 2 May 2001, not yet reported. [2002] ECR II-313.

T-77/01, *Territorio Histórico de Álava – Diputación Foral de Álava, Territorio Histórico de Bizkaia – Diputación Foral de Bizkaia, Territorio Histórico de Gipuzkoa – Diputación Foral de Gipuzkoa y Juntas Generales de Gipuzkoa, Comunidad autónoma del País Vasco – Gobierno Vasco contre Commission des Communautés européennes*, Judgment of 11 January 2002. [2002] ECR II-81.

Ward, A. (1999) 'Frameworks for cooperation between the European Union and third states: a variable matrix for uniform human rights standards?', *European Foreign Affairs Review*, 3 (4): 505–36.

Wesseling, H.L. (2002) *Le partage de l'Afrique*. Paris: Gallimard.

Youngs, R. (2002) *The European Union and the Promotion of Democracy*. Oxford: Oxford University Press.

16 Sovereignty and Intervention: EU's Interventionism in its 'Near Abroad'

Frédéric Charillon

Can the foreign policy actions of the European Union (EU) be taken seriously as a case study of intervention? The 1990s, one might argue, have provided many opportunities to witness Europe's absence, or its unreadiness in dealing with international crises, from Bosnia or the African Lakes to the last Iraqi crisis. At best, the recent international events were viewed by the Europeans as warning signals and incentives to improve their political cohesion and military reaction capacities.[1] Still, three considerations point to a different assessment.

First, as Bertrand Badie writes in his contribution to this volume, the concept of intervention cannot be reduced to its military facet only. Hence, the European ability to carry out such actions must be assessed in a manner which includes all of these.[2] Second, what is to count as European foreign policy is more complicated than often assumed, since it encompasses not only the Common Foreign and Security Policy (CFSP), but also the foreign policies of EU member states as well as other overlapping external relations of the Union (White, 1999; White, 2001; see also Chapter 1 of this volume). Third, although Europe as an international actor is still in the process of being fully constituted, its attempts to move from vacillating and reactive foreign policies to more consistent and proactive policies is impressive, if not always successful (Holland, 1997; Durand and Vasconcelos, 1998; Sjursen and Smith, 2001). In Amsterdam, Saint-Malo, Cologne, Helsinki or Nice, new tools for action have been established.[3] The new assertiveness of the EU goes far beyond the CFSP, and includes a range of economic, social as well as political approaches. In lieu of the former protection-bound Western Europe that existed during the Cold War, the EU has become a projection-oriented actor, with increasing foreign policy responsibilities and an expanding involvement in international crises. Although neither detectable everywhere nor always successful, such a projection-oriented posture can be clearly observed in the EU's geographical neighbourhood.[4]

In this chapter it will be argued that the EU has become an interventionist actor, capable of acting in a 'hegemonic' fashion in what it conceives to be its sphere of influence. Although far from being an effective military actor, Europe is nevertheless re-inventing and utilising the concept of intervention in its direct political environment. The shaping – or re-shaping – of its 'Near Abroad' through various tools and modalities shows an ability to make up for its lack of 'hard power', and to overshadow what Christopher Hill rightly deemed an 'expectations-capabilities' gap (Hill, 1993). Whatever its limits, the EU has *political* objectives in its Near Abroad, and is in the process of developing various tools to pursue them effectively. This entails a serious reappraisal of the concept of intervention, but also offers new perspectives on sovereignty.

The Political Objectives of Intervention: Shaping the Near Abroad

Critics have pointed not only to the lack of a clear EU scheme in the pursuit of any strategy, seeing in its stead only the existence of a smallest common denominator standing for a European *grand dessein*, but also to a lack of proper means for successfully being able to pursue policies of intervention. Still, the significance of the EU's relations with its three peripheries – the East, the South-East and the South – has increased since the end of the Cold War. And the study of EU's achievements in the 1990s shows a remarkable continuity in European goals, in addition to resorting to multifaceted forms of intervention in order to reach them.

Defining the 'Near Abroad'

The concept of 'Near Abroad' was first coined in the analysis of the former Soviet Union's foreign policy (Skak, 1996; Hopf, 1999), referring to the foreign policy priorities located in its immediate geographical neighbourhood, which were deemed to be vital to its continued security. In the case of the Soviet Union, this concept also implied that the involved areas were considered to lie within its sphere of influence, and hence possessing only limited sovereignty in key sectors such as foreign policy, defence, visa policy and trade.[5] Can this concept be of any use in the analysis of the EU's external relations?

The nature of the principles and values promoted by EU member states of course excludes all meaningful comparisons with the former Soviet regime. Nevertheless, the concept of the Near Abroad may be fruitful here for several reasons. First, the EU has given top priority to developments in its direct geographical neighbourhood.[6] Second, security – broadly defined – is indeed at the core of the member states' concerns. Third, the EU has succeeded in its attempt to wield a strong influence in these areas, having linked the future and wellbeing of these areas close to that of the EU.

Three regions can be viewed in terms of such a perspective, although to various degrees. The foremost of these is undoubtedly Central and Eastern

Europe. The region is composed of Poland, the Czech Republic and Slovakia, Hungary, Bulgaria, Romania, Slovenia, Estonia, Latvia and Lithuania. What is at stake here is nothing less than the integration of the Central and Eastern European Countries (CEECs) into the EU, as a result of the 'new *Ostpolitik*' implemented since the collapse of communism in Eastern Europe.[7]

The Balkans – or South-East Europe – can be viewed as the second component of the Near Abroad. As much 'European' as the first, it is nevertheless composed of states emerging from the ruins of former Yugoslavia and is hence still marked by the Balkan wars of the 1990s. Located in the close neighbourhood of the EU, and unlike Slovenia already placed within the first group, Croatia, Bosnia, Macedonia, but also Serbia, Albania, and possibly Montenegro and Kosovo in the future, are states in need of being rebuilt (Ramet, 1999).

The Mediterranean area constitutes the last component of the Near Abroad. Since the beginning of the Barcelona process that institutionalised a 'Euro-Mediterranean partnership' in 1995, it refers to the geographical area stretching from North Africa (Maghreb) to the Near East (Mashreq), including the states on the southern and eastern coasts of the Mediterranean sea (Libya remains excluded for political reasons). The group is composed of 12 actors that can be divided into three categories:

1   The three Mediterranean applicants to membership, namely the Mediterranean islands of Cyprus and Malta, plus the special case of Turkey.
2   North Africa (Morocco, Algeria, Tunisia), whose trade dependence on the EU is substantial, and whose historical ties with France remain strong.
3   Egypt, Jordan, Israel and the Palestinian Authority, plus Lebanon and Syria, who were all involved in the Middle East peace process before its collapse.

Region-Shaping and Security-Building

In the three areas forming its Near Abroad, the EU has been trying hard to build 'imagined communities'[8] with the ulterior motive of creating a larger European regional security order. A process has been initiated whereby the internal situation and evolution of each element of the Near Abroad matters to the EU. Economic crisis in Poland, political mayhem in Algeria, the resurgence of war in the Balkans, all play havoc with EU goals. Hence, real or imagined security communities are being set up, where the evocation – and invocation – of the past plays a significant role: the CEECs, and to a lesser extent the Balkans, are invited to 'rejoin' a Europe they once belonged to, while the Southern and Eastern Mediterranean countries are called upon to retrieve the spirit of the *Mare Nostrum* once shared with Europe. This region-building process requires the pursuit of objectives that involve various forms of intervention.

A first objective, especially applied to the CEECs, Malta and Cyprus, is to make the Near Abroad simply *resemble* Europe from an integrative perspective. This entails setting into motion socialisation and identity-shaping processes based on the principles of pluralist democracy, multiparty systems, elections and civil society – plus the rights of minorities, especially important in Eastern Europe (Rummel, 1997). This also implies the application of European norms and rules to various sectors, institutions and administrations, which have all become the objects of a wide range of transition programmes.

The economic and commercial opening of the Near Abroad to the EU is a second priority, and corresponds to a well-defined common interest among the member states. Here again, these processes can be analysed in terms of economic – but also political – intervention. Central and Eastern Europe has been subject to gradual schemes designed to accompany the liberalisation and democratisation process. The intensification of European Community (EC) – later EU – trade with the CEECs, as well as improving market access, have been facilitated by successive agreements (for instance, interim agreements in the early 1990s). In a different fashion, the Southern and Eastern Mediterranean countries are invited by the Barcelona process to follow along the same path (Joffe, 2001).

As suggested above, security-building also remains a key concern underlying region-shaping. As noted by Karen Smith, '[e]nlargement was agreed to because it should help spread stability and security in Europe' (Smith, 1999). This requires coping with both internal and external sources of instability, and hence the use of intervention in order to counteract such processes. Internal sources of insecurity in Central and Eastern Europe can stem from economic turmoil, nationalist resurgence (for instance, in Romania and Slovakia in the mid-1990s), as well as from ethnic tensions. External threats can be found in Russia's reaction to the EU or to NATO's enlargement, interstate tensions over minorities (for instance, between Hungary and Romania) or in national territorial claims. Security-building in the Balkans requires the rebuilding of peaceful civil societies through aid programmes (in partnership with the Organisation for Security and Co-operation in Europe (OSCE), but also with private actors), while it takes more subtle forms in the Mediterranean – promoting a dialogue over migrations, culture and democracy, as well as initiating military co-operation in various forms.

The Tools for Intervention *à l'Européenne*: Change-making, Change-appraising and Conditionality

In so far as it is primarily a 'civilian power' (Duchêne, 1972; Whitman, 1998), the EU relies essentially on non-military tools to shape its Near Abroad. Its instruments are essentially of an economic kind, but also incorporate various political dimensions. Changing the societies of the Near Abroad, evaluating the depth and pace of change in them, being ready to control its implementation and possibly to sanction any breach or slowdown in these processes, requires the availability and use of various effective and appropriate policy toolkits.

Change-making: Turning the Near Abroad into a Convenient Partner

'Rejoining' Europe and being granted membership are the foreign policy priorities of many of the states in the Near Abroad. Such a policy goal requires fundamental and *accompanied* reforms, as well as *controlled* restructuring. In Central and Eastern Europe, this has taken the form of various aid programmes, association or accession schemes, or conflict prevention policies. In the Balkans, war and its sequels left the EU with a narrower room for manoeuvre, but enabled it to find a political space – or niche – as peace monitors. In the Mediterranean, two avenues of action have been pursued: finding similar diplomatic niches in the Middle East peace process not filled by the US (Charillon, 1998); and a more constraining and global framework for co-operation, provided by the Barcelona process.

Loans, aid programmes, trade concessions and financial backing were intended to reshape the former communist backyard of Europe, to help the recipients adopt the *acquis communautaire*, and thus to transform the social and political fabric of the Central and Eastern European states. Among the programmes that were initiated, PHARE,[9] with its huge resources in terms of grant financing, stands for the main framework within which most of the EU's initiatives to assist the reform process in Eastern Europe are developed.[10] As a whole, the effort has been impressively consistent. In 1997, the Commission assumed that the budgetary ceiling to pay for enlargement would remain at 1.27 per cent of the Union's GNP from 1999 on. Granting non-state actors substantial support (assistance has been given to various NGOs) also aims at developing civil societies.

Conflict prevention[11] also contributes to the reshaping of Central and Eastern Europe (Rummel, 1997; Jopp, 1996). The Pact on Stability in Europe (initiated by French Prime Minister Edouard Balladur in April 1993) remains a prominent example. Based on the idea that all border disputes should be resolved before accession, the Pact required the associates to refer their disputes to the International Court of Justice and resulted in 100 agreements. On this occasion, the image of the EU as a problem solver was considerably enhanced.

In the Mediterranean, schemes to change the local societies were necessarily less ambitious. In the Near-East, the Israeli–Arab peace process first raised high hopes that Europe could have a say in a new regional deal through co-operation programmes and financial support. But the stalemate in the Oslo negotiations, the outburst of the second Intifada and more recently the attitude of Ariel Sharon, have left Europe with a narrow space for manoeuvre. In a context marked by a US leverage second to none and by the Israeli reluctance to let the Europeans play a role, the EU has managed to retain a double card: a 'micro-social-oriented' foreign policy, and 'niche-finding' diplomacy (Charillon, 1998). This is a low-profile combination consisting of paying for concrete improvements in local daily life (infrastructures, hospitals, roads and so on),[12] and for the building of political and civil society[13] in so far as this does not interfere with the US handling of the political situation. But the reshaping of the Mediterranean essentially lies in the more global initiative launched in 1995 under the name of the Barcelona process. Located at the geographical margins of the EU and linked to it by strong economic ties, North Africa and the Middle East were offered the creation of a common space for co-operation, aiming at establishing, by 2010, the liberalisation of trade, as well as a vaguer set of security, political, social and cultural co-operative relationships.[14] Here again, what is at stake is the economic opening and possibly a larger reshaping of the region, through its modernisation and restructuration, by encouraging growth and foreign investments.

Change Appraising: The Tools of Control

Not only is change promoted, but its implementation is also controlled by the EU. This holds especially true for Central and Eastern Europe. The CEECs are annually reviewed to evaluate progress in their liberal and democratic transition,[15] and the 'screening' procedure enables the EU to wield a continuous control over the Near Abroad's evolution in very diverse sectors, and to place itself in the position of a political, economic and even moral authority in this context.[16] A number of political forums provide for permanent frameworks to initiate common projects and to accelerate the political socialisation of the CEECs: the structured relationship implemented in the early 1990s,[17] the pre-accession strategy[18] and the accession process.[19] Agenda 2000 (since 1997 and subsequent discussions held in Berlin in March 1999) and the Reinforced Pre-Membership Strategy (since March 1998) have provided for a more detailed roadmap for enlargement.

A comparable constraining framework does not exist to the same extent in the Balkans or the Mediterranean. Still, the provision of aid programmes and financial facilities have had similar effects, since their implementation remains linked to the accomplishment of reforms, to the acceptance of EU-defined 'good governance', and hence to substantial transformation in general within these two regions.

Change Enforcing: The Politics of Conditionality

'Conditionality entails the linking, by a state or international organisation, of perceived benefits to another state (such as aid or trade concessions), to the fulfilment of economic and/or political conditions.' This definition, proposed by Karen Smith (Smith, 1999: 198; see also Sorensen, 1993), can be used to sum up the attitude of the EU towards its Near Abroad. Its policies of encouragement, trade concessions and aid are conditional on making progress towards democracy and human rights, as well as on the establishment of a liberal economic system. It is the threat of interruption of these and other economic benefits that, in the absence of military force, constitutes the main deterrent or punitive instrument available to the EU (Bretherton and Vogler, 1999). Since the end of the Cold War, the capacity of Europe to use 'carrots' in lieu of foreign policy has remained at the core of its approach. The agreements struck with each of the involved countries are intended to reflect the state of their political and economic reforms.

Conditionality has gradually developed as a norm and a method to shape the Near Abroad. In Central and Eastern Europe, its use has been explicit and evolutionary. In December 1992, the Edinburgh European Council redefined the conditions for potential Eastern European recipients to be granted support, with *membership* rather than *assistance* in view. The candidate states were asked to integrate the *acquis communautaire* by establishing stable institutions guaranteeing democracy, the rule of law, human rights and respect for minorities; possessing a functioning market economy; endorsing the objectives of political, economic and monetary union; and being able to cope with competitive pressure and market forces. Any delay in reforms and bad economic performance or a poor political and human rights record could result in the suspension of aid or – more significantly – in the rescheduling of the timetable or even in diminishing the prospect of achieving membership.

Such a direct form of conditionality is not as manifest in the Balkans, nor *a fortiori* in the Mediterranean region, where the involved countries are not included in membership discussions with the EU (except for Malta, Cyprus, and, in a more complicated way, Turkey). In spite of strong economic and political relations, EU pressures are here neither of a legal nor institutionally binding nature (Wessel, 1999). Still, the fact that, in principle, European 'rewards' or facilities can be cut off by the EU (should it so wish) may nevertheless be effective as a strong incentive even in the case of non-applicant countries.

Europe thus has the means to impose a certain amount of change in its Near Abroad through conditionality and 'carrot and stick' policies, based on its ability to provide support, to implement reforms and to create new norms. This constitutes intervention, at the same time as it raises the question of sovereignty.

From 'Muddling-through' to 'Meddling-in'?

The term 'muddling through' (Lindblom, 1959) has often been applied to describe the European objective to build a CFSP for its slow decision-making system and its incapacity to act decisively. In view of this, it is surprising that CFSP as a political objective has proven so durable (Sjursen and Smith, 2001).

Still, the kinds of interventionism discussed above involves far more than just 'muddling through'. How should we assess this development? Is there a hidden 'hegemonic' agenda or a 'logic underpinning EU enlargement' (Sjursen and Smith, 2001)? What theoretical insights can be drawn from the double standpoint of foreign policy interventionism and sovereignty?

Although not always plainly visible as a convincing international actor on the world stage, the EU has proved capable of being a point of reference and a pole of attraction to its Near Abroad. In Eastern Europe, it was possible for the EU to become a leading actor in a region where its founder member states were previously excluded for political reasons. But this has not been feasible in the Mediterranean, where the absence of integrationist/ application movements has rendered European leverage weaker. In the Near East, the case proves probably too complex for Europe to handle alone: in a Near Abroad which is more 'abroad' than 'near', the member states have been divided as to how far they should support the Palestinians and avoid criticising Israel, how far they can take the risk to compete with the US in the region, and how far they must reconsider the association agreement with the local trouble makers. Europe's attitude in the Balkans and even in Central and Eastern Europe has revealed the same weakness: a poor crisis management capacity. This raises a much more embarrassing question, central to the debate over the EU's credibility: how far is European conditionality really binding? Is Europe just a fair-weather friend, with a micro-social-oriented foreign policy but no capacity to handle tricky political situations?

Building Common Value or Defending Supervisory Rights?

Conditions for accession have often been considered to be the most effective lever for exercising EU influence, as in Central and Eastern Europe (Jopp, 1996). When used as a form of intervention, this policy is claimed to be utilised for good reasons. This building of a common space is regularly referred to in the European rhetoric. But decision-makers and observers from third countries instead speak of an asymmetrical partnership, referring to the following arguments:

- The European agreements create a 'hub-and-spoke bilateralism' that marginalises the spokes' economies and increases the dependence on the EU of its external partners.
- The process is 'accession driven' rather than 'demand driven' (Bretherton and Vogler, 1999), which means that the EU has the possibility to impose concessions on their external partners, whereas the reverse does not hold.
- Assessing the nature and quality of change in the Near Abroad societies also raises a number of issues that are unilaterally settled by the EU with little or no interaction with the applicant states.

- It is also highly debatable whether conditionality is efficient as a political tool: the most acute problems are hardly dealt with by this policy, and the difficult decisions are postponed.[20]
- The EU's initiatives reflect its own experiences, with a stress on dialogue and co-operation as found and developed in Western Europe.[21] But how far is the EU ready to deal with dissimilar logics?

Criticism and frustration have in sum been voiced by third countries in the name of sovereignty. The values that are promoted and deemed 'common' are in fact one-sidedly defined by the EU itself. Their implementation provides the EU with a right to supervise the political, economic and even social evolutions of its neighbours.

'Of What is it an Instance'? (Rosenau, 1980)[22]

In sum, what does the EU's attitude towards its Near Abroad teach us from a more theoretical point of view, as far as intervention and sovereignty are concerned? Is it just old hegemonic wine in new European bottles? Or is there any ground-breaking European approach and behaviour worthy of further analysis in a new research agenda (see also Jorgensen, 1997)?

It is first necessary to return to the concept of common foreign policy in order to assess what it brought to the practice of intervention. At least two related questions must be raised in this context: does the European building of a common foreign policy entail a new and accepted form of collective interventionism?; and does EU interventionism constitute a true European 'foreign policy system' (Clarke and White, 1989; Smith, 1989; Carlsnaes and Smith, 1994)? The first question raises the issue of to what extent EU member states have succeeded in turning several divergent national approaches into a common approach to intervention (Manners and Whitman, 2001). Whatever its limits and shortcomings, this policy constitutes a unique collective response to external pressures and demands, as well as exhibiting new forms of collective foreign policy anticipation and implementation. But is this sufficient for us to speak of an EU foreign policy system? As already mentioned, a micro-social-oriented foreign policy has been developed, based on technical and economic as well as institutional competences. This enables the EU to shape its Near Abroad beyond the traditional 'trade plus' formula, with wide-ranging provisions, technical assistance, but also political dialogue and cultural co-operation. This also opens new perspectives, since the combination of political engineering and monitoring, as well as financial resources to pay for it, increasingly appears to be the key mechanisms of conflict prevention and peacemaking. This is not yet a fully developed or consistent foreign policy system; but it arguably at least reflects the beginning of a new interventionist *savoir faire*, and a promising rethinking of foreign policy making on the part of the EU.

Other lessons can be drawn, this time for the analysis of sovereignty. First, a double disbanding of sovereignty can be observed, both within the Near Abroad and within the EU itself. As previously indicated, the EU's interventionism in its Near Abroad has led to harsh criticism, for it puts sovereignty into question in the involved states. States – be they in Central and Eastern Europe, in the Balkans or in the Mediterranean – are viewed by the EU as something to be rebuilt, by external actors, and even by private ones if necessary.[23] New types of authorities emerge (special envoys in the Balkans and in the Middle East, the European Bank for Reconstruction and Development and so on), producing new types of intervention and limitations to national sovereignty. But what is at stake is also the sovereignty of the EU member states themselves, through their conception of foreign policy. The building of common schemes to shape their common Near Abroad requires a post-national definition of security, and hence the definition and adoption of common priorities, a common discourse and common positions, actions and strategies. New EU tools (such as the Policy Planning and Early Warning Unit) also tend to establish a common analysis of the international situation. The mere existence of such schemes involves dynamic changes in the style and nature of national foreign policies, as well as diminishing their room for independent manoeuvre.

In summary, rather than any existing and well-defined CFSP producing clear-cut intervention schemes, what can be witnessed today is the pragmatic emergence of new European methods of intervention in the making, in the process forging a dynamic European common foreign policy. Interventionism à l'européenne is a strange object indeed: without a well-defined doctrine or an accurate roadmap, a standardisation and transformation of non-military intervention has taken place on the European continent which has made interventionism a common occurrence. Although awkward at dealing with 'hard security' challenges, the EU has proved skilful at pursuing common interests, at shaping new political surroundings, and at practising soft power. Two centuries after the French Revolution and its 'Soldat de l'An II', Europe, whatever its difficulties in issuing common positions, is meeting 'messianic intervention' again.

Notes

1   Although Europe took the lead in some crisis situations (in northern Iraq, ex-Yugoslavia, and during the post-interventionist phase of the Somalia crisis), its recent interventions have been marked by an inconsistency between stated principles and actual action, by humanitarian and financial aid, by local and intellectual rather than global and political contributions (Jorgensen, 1997).
2   Intervention 'can be either violent or soft, explicit or implicit, social, cultural, economic, or political; … military intervention is only an extreme variant' (Bertrand Badie, Chapter 9 of this volume).
3   A Standing Political and Security Committee (PSC), a Military Committee (MC), and Military Staff (MS), as well as a Policy Planning and Early Warning Unit of the EU.

4 On differences between 'protection-oriented', 'projection-oriented' and 'compromise-oriented' foreign policies, see Charillon (2001).

5 See the Brezhnev 'limited sovereignty' doctrine, concerning the former Soviet 'satellites' in Central and Easter Europe.

6 The Lisbon European Council in June 1992 identified an 'urgent Foreign policy co-operation' based on 'geographical proximity, overwhelming interests in the political and economic stability of a region or state, and existence of a potential threat to the EU's security interests'.

7 The EU opened enlargement negotiations with six countries in October 1998 and broadened the field to 12 in 1999. Turkey is presently not negotiating.

8 See Anderson (1991).

9 Poland and Hungary Assistance for Restructuring of the Economy.

10 The PHARE programme was launched in 1989 for Poland and Hungary but has been extended to 13 Central and Eastern European countries (Albania, Bosnia-Herzegovina, Bulgaria, the Czech Republic, Estonia, Former Yugoslav Republic of Macedonia, Hungary, Latvia, Lithuania, Poland, Romania, Slovakia and Slovenia).

11 In the sense of preventing disputes from arising and deteriorating into armed conflict.

12 The Gaza airport and harbour being among the most symbolic achievements ... until their tearing down by Israeli air strikes in December 2001.

13 Such as paying for the organisation and supervision of the elections, equipping the Palestinian police and paying its salaries (Soetendorp, 1999).

14 Three chapters were designed at Barcelona: political and security, economic and financial, and social-cultural-human affairs.

15 Since the Helsinki summit in December 1999.

16 On 31 themes, from the most technical to the most political ones, the performances of the applicants and their integration of the *acquis communautaire* are evaluated in multilateral and bilateral discussions, then regularly published in reports.

17 This was supposed 'to help integrate the associates into the process of consensus-building in the EU and acquainting them with EU procedures and dossiers' (Smith, 1999: 127).

18 The pre-accession strategy was endorsed by the Essen European Council in December 1994 and fostered initiatives in several key areas: creating the legal environment for integration; improving trade opportunities; promoting co-operations in several sectors (energy, transport, environment); assistance for reform through financial aid (PHARE) and loans and so on.

19 The Luxembourg European Council (12–13 December 1997) agreed to the Commission's proposal for a new pre-accession framework, calling it an 'accession process', involving all 10 East European countries on an equal footing.

20 For instance, the Pact on Stability in Europe, initiated in 1993, was 'not concerned with countries in open conflict'.

21 Encouragements are given to regional co-operation at the margins of the EU: the creation of the Central European Free Trade Agreement (CEFTA), signed on 21 December 1992 in Krakow, has been encouraged by the EU and especially propped up by Italy.

22 'To think theoretically one must be predisposed to ask about every event, every situation, or every observed phenomenon: "of what is it an instance"?' See Rosenau (1980: 19–31).

23 Rebuilding civil society is also achieved through encouragement given to NGOs, banks, associations, and so on.

References

Anderson, B. (1991) *Imagined Communities: Reflections on the Origin and Spread of Nationalism*. London: Verso.

Bretherton, C. and Vogler, J. (1999) *The European Union as a Global Actor*. London: Routledge.

Carlsnaes, W. and Smith S. (eds) (1994) *European Foreign Policy*. London: Sage.

Charillon, F. (1998) 'La politique étrangère de l'Union Européenne au Moyen-Orient', in M. Clarke, 'The foreign policy system. A framework for analysis', in M. Clarke and B. White (eds), *Understanding Foreign Policy: The Foreign Policy System Approach*. London: Edward Elgar.

Charillon, F. (2001) '*Fin ou Renouveau des Politiques Étrangères?*', in F. Charillon (ed.), *Les Politiques Étrangères: Ruptures et Continuités*. Paris: La Documentation Française.

Clarke, M. and White, B. (eds) (1989) *Understanding Foreign Policy: The Foreign Policy System Approach*. London: Edward Elgar.

Duchêne, F. (1972) 'Europe's role in world peace', in R. Mayne (ed.), *Europe Tomorrow*. London: Fontana.

Durand, M-F. and Vasconcelos, A. (eds) (1998) *La PESC. Ouvrir l'Europe au monde*. Paris: Presses de Sciences Po.

Hill, C. (1993) 'The capability–expectations gap, or conceptualizing Europe's international role', *Journal of Common Market Studies*, 31 (3): 315–28.

Holland, M. (ed.) (1997) *Common Foreign and Security Policy: The Record and Reforms*. London: Pinter.

Hopf, T. (ed.) (1999) *Understandings of Russian Foreign Policy*. Philadelphia, PA: Pennsylvania State University Press.

Joffe, G. (2001) 'Moyen-Orient et Afrique du Nord: une paix introuvable, une stabilité menacée', in F. Charillon (ed.), *Les Politiques Étrangères: Ruptures et Continuités*. Paris: La Documentation Française.

Jopp, M. (1996) 'The strategic implications of European integration', Adelphi Papers No. 290. London: Brassey's.

Jorgensen, K.E. (1997) *European Approaches to Crisis Management*. The Hague: Kluwer Law.

Lindblom, C. (1959) 'The science of muddling through', *Public Administration Review*, 19: 79–99.

Manners, I. and Whitman, R.G. (eds) (2001) *The Foreign Policy of the EU Member States*. Manchester: Manchester University Press.

Ramet, S. (1999) *Balkan Babel: The Disintegration of Yugoslavia from the Death of Tito to the War for Kosovo* (3rd edn). Boulder, CO: Westview.

Rosenau, J.N. (1980) *The Scientific Study of Foreign Policy*. London: Pinter.

Rummel, R. (1997) 'The CFSP's conflict prevention policy', in M. Holland (ed.), *Common Foreign and Security Policy: The Record and Reforms*. London: Pinter.

Sjursen, H. and Smith, K.E. (2001) 'Justifying EU foreign policy: the logics underpinning EU enlargement', *ARENA Papers*, No. 1.

Skak, M. (1996) *From Empire to Anarchy: Post-communist Foreign Policy and International Relations*. London: Hurst.

Smith, K.E. (1999) *The Making of EU Foreign Policy: The Case of Eastern Europe*. Basingstoke: Macmillan.

Smith, M. (1989) 'Comparing foreign policy systems. Problems, processes and performance', in M. Clarke and B. White (eds), *Understanding Foreign Policy: The Foreign Policy System Approach*. London: Edward Elgar.

Soetendorp, B. (1999) *Foreign Policy in the European Union*. New York, NY: Longman.

Sorensen, G. (1993) *Political Conditionality*. London: Frank Cass.

Wessel, R.A. (1999) *The European Union's Foreign and Security Policy: A Legal Institutional Perspective*. The Hague: Kluwer Law International.

White, B. (1999) 'The European challenge to foreign policy analysis', *European Journal of International Relations*, 5 (1): 37–66.

White, B. (2001) *Understanding European Foreign Policy*. Basingstoke: Palgrave.

Whitman, R.G. (1998) *From Civilian Power to Superpower? The International Identity of the European Union*. London: Macmillan.

Index

Please note that references to figures and other non-textual material are in italic print